Barry White is a columnist, leader-writer and feature journalist with the *Belfast Telegraph*, and contributes political comment to numerous publications, including the *Irish Independent, New York Times* and *Newsweek*. He has won awards as Northern Ireland Feature Writer of the Year in 1980 and Columnist of the Year in 1982. In 1979 he was commended as a columnist in the British Press Awards. He has known John Hume since 1964, when he was political correspondent for the *Telegraph*. He is married to a languages teacher and they have three children.

JOHN HUME

STATESMAN OF THE TROUBLES

BARRY WHITE

THE
BLACKSTAFF
PRESS

For Joy, Andrew,
Alison and Cathy

First published in 1984
by The Blackstaff Press Limited
3 Galway Park, Dundonald, Belfast BT16 0AN
Reprinted January 1985, September 1985

© *Barry White, 1984*
All rights reserved

Printed in Northern Ireland by
The Universities Press Limited

British Library Cataloguing in Publication Data
White, Barry
John Hume: a biography.
1. Hume, John   2. Politicians – Northern
Ireland – Biography
I. Title
941.60824'092'4   DA965.H8

ISBN 0 85640 327 X (hardback)
0 85640 317 2 (paperback)

CONTENTS

Foreword		vi
Prologue	Loophole	1
1	Derry boy	5
2	Training for the priesthood	17
3	Self help	27
4	Speaking out	40
5	Politics and fish	52
6	Civil Rights	61
7	Bogside at war	74
8	Free Derry	89
9	A new party	94
10	Bloody Sunday	109
11	Talking to the IRA	125
12	The Sunningdale experiment	140
13	Loyalists say 'No'	162
14	Into the deep freeze	174
15	Kennedy connections	183
16	A healing force?	197
17	Party leader	206
18	Hunger-strikes	218
19	Seeking a New Ireland	235
20	Inside the Forum	253
21	Future options	272
Index		285

FOREWORD

Anyone writing about politics in Northern Ireland, or indeed Ireland, knows what a central role John Hume has played since 1968. He made Derry the cornerstone of the successful civil rights movement, and out of it founded the first coherent nationalist party for fifty years, the Social Democratic and Labour Party. He was the chief architect of the 1973 Sunningdale agreement on power-sharing devolved government for Northern Ireland, broken by the loyalist strike of May 1974, and since then has kept constitutional nationalism alive – in the face of IRA destruction – with a series of policy initiatives in Europe and America, culminating in the New Ireland Forum of 1983–4.

But despite his high political profile as a party leader and member of both the Westminster and European Parliaments, he remains an enigma, even to his close associates. Little is known about his impoverished childhood – so that Bernadette Devlin was able to describe him in her 1969 autobiography as 'one of the wealthier Catholics of Derry' – or about his training at Maynooth seminary, before his emergence in the mid-1960s as a campaigner for justice on behalf of his own community. By his own estimation, his seminal work in the Credit Union organisation, providing the basis of self-respect from which political development has flowed, remains his most worthwhile achievement. Today there are houses standing in Derry, and jobs occupied, because of his years of unpaid community work, even before he led a single civil rights march.

This book was born out of a desire to discover the special qualities that took a boy from an ordinary out-of-work Bogside family and made him the symbol of a generation of ambitious but politically frustrated Northern Catholics, thrusting him into the corridors of power not only in Belfast, Dublin and London, but in Europe and America, too. By telling his story, one is telling the story not only of the Troubles, but of the causes which brought them about. Much of the book is based on interviews with Hume, but I have also interviewed many politicians, journalists and civil servants who have encountered him. To all of them, who will remain anonymous, and to the ordinary people of Derry, who easily opened up their hearts about a favourite son, I tender my deepest thanks.

The difficulties of following and assessing the ups and downs of a working politician in constant motion can be appreciated, and my task has not been helped by the fact that most of the SDLP's early records were stolen in 1975 and that Hume has never kept a diary. He has provided as much of the background as he can remember, in a life that has spanned at least half a dozen careers already, but all the interpretation is mine, not his. Posterity will judge his contribution to a solution of the Irish question, but it may not improve on the words of Seamus Heaney, the poet and friend from school days, who wrote in 1969: 'His understanding of the community is his understanding of himself. His ambition to set Derry's house in order is altruistic and whole because it is obviously an extension of an inner achievement of tolerance and concern. To call him a spokesman for the minority is only one way of putting it. He is the best consciousness of a submerged population group, the questing compass needle of another hidden Ireland. Speaking a lucid language of sociology and politics with untrammeled conscience, he comprehends the bitterness and negation of Derry without being possessed by it. By a generous effort of imagination, he has let any bad blood he may have harboured and thereby earned the right and the skill to diagnose bad blood in the community.' It was a rare tribute, and even rarer is the fact that an Irish politician in whom such hope has been invested should still be in business, fifteen years on.

Barry White
Belfast, October 1984

PROLOGUE

Loophole

John Hume was limping from a bruise on his leg as he made his way homewards up Westland Street in Derry's Bogside. He had had an exhausting afternoon, in his role of trouble-shooter, stepping in between the British Army and the angry Bogsiders, trying to cool civilian tempers and persuade the soldiers to retreat. Near the Bogside Inn he had been standing with his back to an army personnel carrier when suddenly the driver panicked, threw it into reverse and knocked him to the ground. Just as he was disappearing under the wheels, someone dragged him clear, and he was carried into a nearby house to collect his senses. It had been his closest brush with death in the three years since the beginning of the civil rights movement in 1968, and now he felt it was time to return home to take stock of the situation.

From early morning on 18 August 1971 the army had descended in strength on the Bogside, in a follow-up to the introduction of internment nine days before. House-to-house searches were taking place, in an apparent attempt to impose army control on an area that was always on the verge of revolt; and Hume recognised the danger. As he reached the top of Westland Street, just below his house in West End Park, he saw a crowd strung across Lone Moor Road, creating a human barrier against an army unit that was approaching from the left. There was only one thing to do, as he had done so often over the past few years, and that was to sit down on the road and persuade the crowd to join him, singing as an alternative to stone-throwing. The tactic worked, the tension eased, and he approached the army commander, introducing himself as the local MP in the Northern Ireland Parliament at Stormont. 'If you will withdraw, I will get the crowd to go home quietly,' he said, leaving the soldier to weigh up the possibilities.

With a sympathetic shrug of the shoulders, the Englishman radioed headquarters and got permission to retreat, accepting that there was no alternative to a pitched battle. The armoured trucks were turned

1

around, and the victorious crowd was getting to its feet when a hundred yards away, from the opposite direction, another army unit came into view. It stopped at the sight of the civilians and, alone, Hume went to parley with its commander, and explain the situation. But this time the British officer was adamant: 'You're not running this place. I am, and I'm going through.' Hume could see that his whole reputation as a peacemaker was on trial, and that he would never be trusted again if he let the soldiers pass. 'If you're going through,' he said, with all the authority he could muster, 'you're going to have to drive over me.' He walked to within ten yards of the leading truck and sat down squarely on the road, facing it. At this, the crowd behind him surged forward and sat down beside him. The soldiers' response was to fire rubber bullets from close range, bouncing them off the street in a vain effort to intimidate the crowd. Next the water cannon was called up, and as the jet streamed out, dyed purple for easier identification of the victims, Hume knew it was time for a dramatic gesture.

Getting up from the sitting position, he slowly walked towards the water cannon, with his hands above his head in a gesture of peace and determination. As he explained to friends later, it was a spiritual experience for him. He did not plan it, but he knew instinctively what to do. The soldiers were unmoved, however, and the purple water drenched him from head to foot, knocking him down repeatedly with its force before he stumbled to his feet and marched slowly forward. Eventually he came within range of the snatch squad and was grabbed and thrown against a wall while the rest of the crowd was chased down side streets. Hugh Logue, a party colleague, was caught and pulled by the hair up Westland Street, while Hume, who had broken free, protested. Soon five of the ringleaders, Hume included, were arrested and stood against a wall, facing inward, their clothes and skin stained with dye. Even by Derry standards, it had been an eventful afternoon, and as the culprits were transported off to the city's Waterside for questioning, to the cheers of the crowd, Hume had a feeling that a turning point had been reached.

In Ebrington Barracks Hume explained how he had come to an agreement with an officer, before another had overruled him, but to no avail. The five were formally charged, under a 1970 regulation of the 1922 Northern Ireland Special Powers Act, with failing to disperse when ordered by a soldier, and they were then released, to be carried shoulder-high into the Bogside. Predictably, rioting had broken out after the arrests, and women had staged a protest march through the city centre. The heavy hand of the army had been felt: immediately nationalist representatives withdrew in protest from public bodies, and the troops' action was to have even more momentous consequences.

At the hearing on 8 September, the Derry five were convicted and fined £20 each, but their barrister Charlie Hill – an old friend of Hume's, who had represented the defendants after the original Derry civil rights march three years earlier – pointed out several grounds for appeal, one of them questioning the army's right to proceed on the basis of a Northern Ireland Act of Parliament, when British law, as expressed in the Government of Ireland Act 1920, expressly excluded Stormont from legislating for the armed forces. Clearly there was a chance of making a major constitutional point, for Hill had raised the issue in another case of arrest by the army and had noticed that the judge had carefully avoided a ruling. Hill warned Hume that if the appeal on this one ground failed – and there were about ten others which would be easier to argue – he would go to jail. 'This is the one I want,' said Hume, unerringly choosing the ground with the heaviest political implications. It was also agreed with Hill – who sensed that the appeal would go down in the history books – that Hume's name should appear first, making the case Regina (Hume and others) versus Londonderry Justices.

Five months went by – and Bloody Sunday intervened, with its toll of thirteen Derry civilians shot dead by British paratroopers – before, on 23 February 1972, three judges of the Northern Ireland Court of Appeal accepted that the army's actions since its arrival on Ulster streets two-and-a-half years previously had been unlawful. Hume had won his acquittal, and an Achilles heel of Stormont rule had been pierced. On the day of the judgment, High Court officials had warned the British Government, in a telephone call, that an appeal was being allowed which would create a legislative problem. The wheels were set in motion at Westminster, and the Northern Ireland Act 1972 was prepared and rushed through both Houses of Parliament in a day-and-night sitting, both to legalise the army's future operations and to prevent an avalanche of damages claims by ensuring that the law was retrospective. It was an unprecedented piece of legislation, which was a watershed for a British Government deeply concerned about its moral responsibility for the mayhem committed by its army in Derry four weeks before, when the soldiers were technically answering to Stormont, as well as Westminster.

Reginald Maudling, the Home Secretary, gave the broadest hints of what was to follow when he assured MPs that the passing of the Bill would not affect the debate about law and order responsibility, which 'can only be discussed in the broad context of a total settlement for Northern Ireland'. In the Lords, the Chancellor, Lord Hailsham, went further, in a late-night speech which was largely unreported: 'I think probably events will overtake this Bill, which is less important than some people have thought.'

The scene was set for the Government's ultimatum to the Stormont Prime Minister, Brian Faulkner, which was delivered at Downing Street just four weeks later. Not only did the British demand Westminster control of all security matters, including the police, but also the running of the courts and prisons. Stormont's cupboard was to be stripped bare, and Faulkner's government had little alternative but to resign in protest on 24 March, bringing fifty-one years of exclusively Unionist rule to an ignominious end and introducing direct rule from London. Hume's defiance on the streets of Derry had had its reward, and his goal of reconciliation in Northern Ireland, followed by reconciliation in Ireland, looked as if it might yet be achievable.

Eleven years later, Hume was sitting in the British House of Commons, as the Member for Foyle, when the Ulster-born Liberal MP for Yeovil, Paddy Ashdown, introduced himself. 'The last time I saw you was in Derry when I was an army officer,' he said. 'You were the only person with any sense, and I kept telling the army to listen to you.' He had been an observer during the events at Lone Moor Road, and had tried to avoid the confrontation; if he and Hume had been listened to, the history of Northern Ireland might have been very different.

1
Derry boy

Derry's housing shortage is of long duration, and it was in his grandparents' small terrace home in 20 Lower Nassau Street that John was born on January 18 1937. Sam Hume and Annie Doherty had married the year before – Sam at forty-six, his bride fourteen years younger – and like many another Derry couple had to live in one room of the family home, then on the northern outskirts of the city, between Rosemount and the Glen. With the baby's arrival they moved briefly to the Brandywell district, to the home of Neil Gillespie, an old Derry republican friend of Sam's, at Southend Park on the other side of the Bogside, below the walls of St Columb's College. Not until John was four, and had two brothers and two sisters, did the Humes find a place of their own, another small rented house, 10 Glenbrook Terrace, with two rooms upstairs and two down, no bathroom and an outside toilet in the yard. But it was a homely, neighbourly district, with steep cobbled streets sloping towards the green hills of Donegal and hardly another house in between.

By the time he married, Sam Hume had lived a fuller life than most of his contemporaries and was widely respected for his wit and wisdom. The Humes were from the border counties of Scotland, a great-grandfather of John's having emigrated to the Co. Donegal village of Burt, just seven miles from Derry, in the mid-1800s. He worked as a stonemason on the Donegal railways, leaving his mark on the bridges and stationmasters' houses still standing today. He was a Presbyterian, a rarity for the area, and inevitably married a Catholic, leaving his religion but retaining his genes for succeeding generations. In the Humes of today, there are some of the Scottish traits of taciturnity, single-mindedness and a lack of emotion which distinguish them from their contemporaries. All four of John's grandparents were country folk from the Inishowen peninsula in Donegal; his mother's mother, of the Barr family of Fahan, grew up a short distance from Burt, below the ancient round fort of the

High Kings of Ulster, the Grianan of Aileach. Not far away is Lough Swilly, from where in 1607 Ireland's leading chieftains sailed into European exile in the 'Flight of the Earls', ending resistance to the English.

The Hume family moved to the city of Derry, the source of any prosperity in the area, when the staple industry of shirt-making was establishing itself in the late nineteenth century, and Sam was the youngest of the brood, born in 1890. Times were hard and he left school at twelve to live with his older sister in Glasgow and find work in the shipyards in Greenock. He joined up when war broke out in 1914 and served in the Royal Irish Rifles in the trenches in France, having one lucky escape when a shell fragment bounced off his brass buckle to kill the man beside him. After the war, he decided not to return to Scotland, but to join the army of the new Irish Free State, founded in 1922. A picture shows him amid a group of Irish soldiers at Fermoy, Co. Cork, and family legend has it that he ended up a sergeant major, though he talked little about his military career.

The ties with his native city were strong, however, and he returned to find his two brothers comfortably established, one with a poultry business, known as 'Johnny the fowl man', and the other an employee of the Londonderry and Lough Swilly Railway. Sam, the brightest of the three, became a clerk in the Ministry of Food, probably on the strength of his military record, and was responsible for distributing ration books at the beginning of World War II. Donegal, where there was food in plenty and unrationed clothes, was just three miles away, but the border was the border, in official eyes. Soon there were other job openings in the Derry shipyard, where a branch of Belfast's Harland & Wolff serviced the Atlantic fleet of British and American warships, and Sam Hume took up the skills he left in Glasgow, as a riveter. It was a hard life, for someone better suited to the pen, but it paid more and there were now nine mouths to feed.

By the time Jim, the last child, was born in June 1945, the two-bedroomed house was splitting at the seams. Sam and the four boys – John, Harry, Patsy and Jim – slept in one room, two to a bed and Annie and the three girls – Annie, Sally (a twin of Patsy) and Agnes – in the other. But the end of the war eventually meant an end of the ship-repairing work and Sam's attempts to get his old job back failed, probably as much on account of his age – he was now nearly sixty – as his religion. Derry was living up to its reputation as a city

6

where Protestants were decidedly more equal than Catholics when public service jobs, whether in local or provincial government, were at stake. In any case, Sam Hume never worked again, but used his natural gifts in letter-writing and book-keeping for the service of his fellow citizens, Catholic and Protestant.

He could have been embittered, as many others were, turning their hands and minds to actual or imaginary subversion, but that was not his nature. He became an unpaid social worker, advising a largely illiterate people how to write job applications, make complaints and fill in the mountain of forms accumulated by the welfare state. His copper-plate writing was renowned and his head for figures envied. Many a perplexed local businessman or shopkeeper would call at Glenbrook Terrace with his books under his arm, for Sam to decipher. Next day the job would be done and the only reward would be a packet of cigarettes.

This was the background, of social concern and service, that John Hume grew up with. There was grinding poverty too, as the Humes strove, like many another family, to keep their heads above water on a miserable unemployment allowance. Annie Hume would spend her nights with a pile of unfinished shirts from a local factory, her smoothing-iron heated by hot coals, earning a few shillings a week as a patent turner. By day she would scour the town for bargains for her growing family, making regular calls on the local pork butcher for leftovers. The Hume family diet, in those days, largely consisted of pig's trotters, knees, skirts or anything that could not be sold over the counter.

The injustice of the Northern Ireland system was self-evident but Westminster took little interest, leaving the Unionist Government free to carve out its own empires, using council employment and housing allocation to ensure that the balance of power remained unchangeable. Sam Hume was just as aware of this as any working-class Derry man, and yet perhaps because of his wartime experience, it did not make him a republican, or even a strong nationalist. His politics were unmistakably Labour, untainted by sectarianism and motivated by a desire to help others as powerless as himself. They were to play a large part in forming the outlook of his eldest son, who from his earliest years knew what it was to take responsibility for others' affairs. There was a self-help message mixed in with Sam Hume's freely-offered advice and although he would compose a job application for a caller in his neat handwriting, he would insist on it

7

being copied out. For his children, he would rule lines in their exercise books and encourage them to take an ordered approach to their work.

Meanwhile John was growing into an unusually mature child for his years, quiet and responsible, as befitted the eldest son, and a natural leader. At primary school, St Eugene's Boys, off the nearby Creggan Road, his reports were never less than glowing. At eight he was chosen as an altar boy at St Eugene's Cathedral, a huge nineteenth century Gothic edifice overlooking the Bogside and obviously intended to dominate the lives of its inhabitants. There were four Masses daily, every hour from 7 to 10 am, with the penalty of an early start for the first two and the prize of missing school classes for 9 am or 10 am. When Bishop Neil Farren was served, it meant an 8.30 Mass, and one of John's earliest nightmares was a breakfast at the bishop's house. Breakfast at home was a bun and a mug of tea, so the ten-year-old's nervousness grew as he was invited to share the bishop's table and his bacon and eggs. He literally could not speak with fright and the old man, understanding what was wrong, did not force the issue and let him escape to school. Despite his apparent seriousness, John was not above mischief, as a carved 'J.H.' on the bishop's altar rail proves.

Every penny counted in the Hume household, with an income of £1.50 a week, and as soon as 'wee Johnny' was big enough to carry a wad of newspapers, aged eight, he began an evening round for four shillings (20p) a week. For the next seven or eight years he tramped the streets of the Glen and Rosemount areas six nights a week, getting to know all the families and learning about life. Some, who could afford it less than others, would have a threepenny piece waiting for him on a Friday night and there would be tips at Christmas time, all of which would go straight into his mother's purse. His brothers loved to accompany him, whatever the weather, and one particularly wet night he was stopped by a woman with a sixpence tip, and scolded for subjecting his small brother to such conditions. John knew that it would have been more cruel to leave Patsy behind than to allow him to get soaked, and he quietly filed the experience away, remembering not to try to live other people's lives for them, or make too many assumptions on behalf of others.

His first encounter with a politician dates back to his newsboy days. The Rev. James Macmanaway was the Ian Paisley of his day, an awe-inspiring Protestant cleric with a thundering delivery of invective against Catholics, and every night the tiny Hume had to make his way up the long, dark drive of 'Redroof', fearing the worst. When the politician died, falling downstairs and stabbing his throat with his pipe, the prospect of a ghost appearing made the ordeal more frightening still. Unusually, the newsboy not only delivered the newspapers, but read them too, especially for news of what was happening in Derry. One day when he overheard an ill-informed conversation about a news item, he was able to give the full story, because he had read it in the *Derry Journal*. The adults were surprised and one of them secretly noted that such a boy would go far. But Hume himself was equally astonished, for until then he thought that everyone read the papers as thoroughly as he.

He was known as a quiet, studious child, competent rather than brilliant, but he also mixed well with his peers and joined them in every sport imaginable. No one in the small narrow streets had money for elaborate games, but there was a stream at the bottom of Glenbrook Terrace which could be dammed in the summertime, making a swimming hole, and there were woods for games of cowboys and Indians. Even the football they played with had to be improvised out of an old sock, stuffed with rags by Mrs Hume. John was a useful right half, with a good turn of speed and a sense of generalship that made him the popular choice as captain of the St Eugene's team in the parish under-twelve football league, run by Father Desmond Mullan. Two years in succession his Glen Stars team won the Father Brown shield, fought out on the bare pitches of nearby Rock Park, with a hedge providing the only changing facilities. According to Father Mullan, John never had to grow up. 'He was always older than his years – serious but not humourless, and self-assured without being cocky. The boys looked up to him as a natural leader and, although he mixed well with the others who were from the same background, he was not quite one of them. He was extraordinary.'

He was already a shrewd judge of human nature, telling the diffident Father Mullan, after a particularly rowdy scene: 'There's no use telling these boys to be quiet or behave themselves. They ask only one thing, "Will he hit us?" If the answer is you won't, they don't have to take you seriously.' A contemporary remembers John being too cool, calm and collected on the field, with a footballing brain that ran well ahead of his legs: 'He never got excited or angry during a game. It used to annoy me intensely.' Football also brought him his first brush with the law, at twelve, when he was prosecuted and fined 20p for playing in the street.

The Glen, as his district was known, because it bordered on the Glen Road, was 'mixed' in Derry terms – though in John's particular street there were more Catholics than Protestants. Religion was still a dividing line, because the Catholics went to St Eugene's Boys and the Protestants to a state school, but after hours they played together and ran in and out of each other's houses for most of the year. The summertime was the exception, when the Orange and then the Green drums beat out their tribal rhythms during the traditional marching season and schoolboy backs would be pressed against walls, with threats of a beating up.

Christmas was always a happy time, with presents from the uncles and aunts and an orange or an apple stuffed in each child's stocking. The summer holiday consisted of a yearly day out by bus to Buncrana, a quiet little one-street seaside resort fourteen miles away across the Co. Donegal border. There might be an ice cream or a bar of chocolate as a special treat, but those were the only luxuries. It was not that the Humes were especially poor; most of those they lived among had nothing more.

The newspapers were an education in local politics – there was no radio until John was twelve – and were avidly read from front page to back, with detailed accounts, in the Catholic-orientated *Derry Journal*, of rows in the gerrymandered corporation. There the 35 per cent minority of Unionists held sway over the Nationalists because Catholics were in the majority only in one huge Nationalist ward, while Protestants topped the poll in two smaller wards. Derry had always been hotly contested by the native Irish and the Protestants who were settled there in the early seventeenth century, and it was only by careful manipulation, after Catholics were allowed the vote in 1829, that the balance remained unchanged. Since Derry – given the title Londonderry in 1613, after the London companies which financed its development – had been fought over in 1689 by rival claimants for the English throne, resulting in victory for the Protestant King William III, it had a special significance for unionists.

The diminutive Johnny, who was a year younger than the others in his class and did not sprout to average height until fifteen or sixteen, sat an examination one cold January morning thinking it was just another class test. He did not know, until he was told he had passed, that it was probably the most important examination of his whole life – the first of the notorious 'eleven-plus' tests, designed to

10

separate primary school children at eleven into sheep and goats, according to intelligence. The top 25 per cent were awarded scholarships to grammar school and a possible university career, while the rest were destined for a non-academic future, leaving school at fourteen. This form of selection was written into the British 1944 Education Act and the Unionist Government at Stormont had no choice but to follow suit three years later, even though the more far-sighted of its members might have predicted that the change heralded the beginning of the end of Northern Ireland as they knew it. If the Catholic middle class were to grow, through an influx of bright working-class boys and girls to the universities, then it was unlikely to accept the second-best status accorded to it. A new generation of teachers, solicitors and doctors would be demanding its place in the sun and equal opportunities in the competition for jobs in local and central government, where Protestants traditionally had first choice. Where discrimination was not deliberate, it was brought about by the defeatist attitude of Catholics, not bothering to apply, or by the historical reluctance of nationalists to involve themselves in the institutions of a disputed six-county state, whose legitimacy they had never accepted.

Soon the eleven-plus would be condemned by liberal educationalists as an examination which favoured middle-class children from literate families, but for John Hume it opened up a world of scholarship undreamed of by any of his forebearers. The usual fees for St Columb's, the local Catholic boys' grammar school, were £7 a year, and before the state stepped in it would have been impossible for the Humes to raise such a sum, with seven children aged between two and ten. If John had been born a year earlier, he would have been destined to follow his father's footsteps, a clever child forced into a job below his capabilities or exiled for life. Sam Hume, in fact, was a symbol of Derry's lost opportunities: a man commonly regarded as more brilliant than his son, who spent most of his life on the breadline, unrecognised, unrewarded and surprisingly unresentful. But he knew, if John didn't, the significance of the eleven-plus success and quietly encouraged his son to stay at his books, for acquiring qualifications was the only way to get ahead. John needed little prompting, even though he felt something of an outsider, as the first of the new generation of scholarship boys in the solidly middle-class environment of St Columb's. He was also a day boy among the majority of boarders, many from a rural background which was foreign to him.

In those days, St Columb's, like St Eugene's Cathedral, was one of the few imposing Catholic institutions in the city. The site of the school had Protestant connections, for it had belonged to the eccentric eighteenth-century Bishop of Derry, the Earl of Bristol, an early tourist who had many Continental hotels named after him, but who is remembered in Ireland chiefly for his extravagant life style and now ruined residences. Where he would go walking, on a hill overlooking the scenic valley of the Foyle, there are now the massive school buildings, with the chapel on the site of the Earl Bishop's casino or summer house.

The Protestants might have been wary of selling the site to the Catholic Church, but symbolically it entailed little sacrifice, as it lay just outside the famous city walls and was occupied by the defeated forces of the Catholic James II during the Siege of Derry in 1689. The Catholics had failed then to breach the walls to conquer the Protestant garrison, and there had been no sign, since the college's foundation in 1879, that their centuries-old struggle for political recognition would ever succeed. In any case, St Columb's was a minor seminary, preparing many of its best students for the priest-hood, where they could hardly challenge Protestant commercial supremacy. Like the Protestant Cathedral, a few hundred yards away inside the city walls, the college was named after St Columb (also known as Columcille or Columba) who brought Christianity to the area in the sixth century and founded the monastery at Iona, off the Scottish coast. With its trim lawns and shady trees, St Columb's had a gracious air unassociated with Irish Catholic institutions. But this concealed a stern educational regime, designed to prepare the best and brightest of the Catholic middle classes and farming community for the professions or the Church – the only sure passport to success.

Until 1948 the college had stood aloof, physically and psycho-logically, from the squalid streets of the Bogside but with the arrival of the first eleven-plus students it was forced to come to terms with the social deprivation all around it, since that was the background of many of its scholarship boys. The pupils had their adjustments to make, too, to the old-fashioned teaching methods, the copious homework and the stern discipline meted out by the 'professors', as all the teachers were known. One was legendary for his arbitrary punishments – 'It's raining today, so I'll give you a smack. If it's sunny tomorrow you'll get another.' Or again, 'I see Seamus at the back of the class not paying attention, but I'm too tired to walk down there, so I'll punish you instead and you can take it up with him after class.'

John began in a special class for under-age pupils, but instead of repeating the year – in which he was taught nearly all subjects by one teacher, Jack 'Rusty' Gallagher – he continued up the school, a year younger than the rest. Gallagher was later to write about his star pupils, Seamus Heaney, the celebrated poet, and Hume. He recalled giving Heaney, who was two years behind Hume, 100 out of 100 in an English exam, which some said was an impossible mark in the subject. Hume he described as the best all-rounder he had ever taught – good at every subject and particularly mathematics. Heaney, a farmer's son from Magherafelt, was idolised by teachers and contemporaries alike for his literacy and his unassuming and genial nature. There was never a doubt that he would be head boy and then a writer of international distinction. If there was a quality the two schoolboys were to share, in later years, it was their complete lack of affectation or sense of their own importance. Heaney avoided involvement in politics, though he was a participant in Hume's civil rights marches of 1968.

The intensive study routine suited Hume well, although some of his Bogside contemporaries found that overcrowding in the home interfered badly with their school work. Hume's solution was to wait until the rest of the family had finished their homework – seated at the kitchen table, with Hume senior watching for untidiness – before getting out his books after 10 pm. Then he would work late into the night, establishing patterns which meant that he has always functioned best, as an adult politician, in the evenings. His grades were always excellent, but probably because of his three-hour paper round, six nights a week, and restricted study time, the strain began to show. From being top of his class in his early years, he slipped to fourth or fifth.

At the same time he kept up his interest in sport, tackling everything with enthusiasm and dedication, earning a reputation as a solid centre half at soccer and an occasional full forward at Gaelic football, an uncommon game in Derry. His summer game was cricket which, surprisingly, had mixed participation in Derry and district, despite the fact that it was introduced by the British. John was a subtle left-arm bowler, with marks still on his index finger, which spun the ball, to show for a short but successful career. He played first with a Waterside team in the intermediate league and then had three years with the mostly Protestant City of Derry side in the senior league, before public duties intervened. His cricketing memories included one of his first experiences of sectarian attitudes, which had a profound effect. After a match, he was returning home by bus when he overheard one of his fellow players say to another 'He's a great bowler, Sam. [In Derry a well-known father's name is applied to his lesser-known son.] Isn't it a pity he's one of them?' John froze and pretended not to hear, but the wound went deep. His father hadn't prepared him for a world where a person's merits were determined, at birth, by which church he went to.

School was a means of escape from the enclosed world of the ghetto and it was also an avenue for advancement that would otherwise be impossible. John had the two choices open to all clever Catholics of his day, a career in the professions, such as teaching or the law, or the church. As an altar boy, familiar with the ritual and conscious of the respect that the clergy won from the faithful, he naturally turned towards the church. No pressure was applied by the clerics on the staff at St Columb's, although John would have been a natural choice, and he made the decision himself. His mother, a devout Catholic, was delighted, as in those days every large Catholic family would hope to produce a priest or nun – even if the chances of doing so in a poor Bogside family would have been minimal, until the eleven-plus revolution.

Socially, there was an enormous gap between the sons of prosperous farmers or teachers and the working-class lad from the Bogside, who would have his lunch, every day, with his granny in a tiny terrace house just behind what is now known as Free Derry corner. But he slowly gained in confidence through his school work and was known as one of the most accommodating day boys, who would save a crust or two for the perpetually-starving boarders. Thankfully there was no uniform for St Columb's in those days, as that would have been an intolerable burden for his parents, but there were school books to be paid for. The grammar school scholarship included a books allowance but one time Hume drew out more books than could be covered and a bill arrived at home for £3. His mother assured him that she would pay it off somehow, at a later date, but the fear of being a debtor worried John so much that eventually Mrs Hume had to see the headmaster about it. The school

President, Father Anthony McFeely who was later made Bishop of Raphoe, took John aside and told him not to worry his head about the money. A middle-class child would not have given the bill a second thought, but for John, who was desperately anxious to conform, it was a matter of life and death. He slowly blossomed out, as he threw himself into the life of the school and excelled at exams and games, but something of the quiet, diffident first-year boy remained. He was never to become an easy-going back-slapping character, preferring to make his mark with ideas and conversational skills rather than false bonhomie.

The ethos of the school was unmistakably Catholic and Irish, as befitted its foundation and the predominance of priests on the staff. '*Quaerite primum regnum Dei*' was its motto – 'Seek first the kingdom of God' – as a reminder of the place accorded to religion and the encouragement given to vocation, or entry to the priesthood. Twice a year there were 'retreats' – days given over to religious contemplation and prayer by all the pupils – and one of these was connected with John's first and last experience of being bullied. The President lost his strap, used for corporal punishment, and when he asked for help in finding it, John volunteered that his had been the last class out of the room. At that time the strap had been lying on the teacher's desk. No one confessed to taking it, so the prefects were called in and proceeded to accuse Hume, giving him a sound beating. His face was red and swollen at the next class and, when Rusty Gallagher asked what was the matter, Hume told him, without any public-school reticence. It was than a matter for the Dean, and the prefects spun a yarn about Hume being mischievous during retreats and not obeying the rules of silence. It was untrue, and Hume was absolved. Much later, the real culprit was discovered. He had stolen the strap and thrown it over Craigavon Bridge into the River Foyle.

While Catholic teaching was emphasised, in and out of the classrooms, Irish nationalism was not. Politics was rarely talked about in the 1940s and 1950s, because the positions adopted by the Unionists and Nationalists had solidified and Irish history was taught, as in state schools, merely as an adjunct to British history. (The common view, among Protestants, was that Catholic schools – which had 65 per cent of their building costs, later to rise to 80 per cent, plus teachers' salaries and maintenance, paid for by the state – were dens of republicanism. State schools were totally Government-funded but 50 per cent of their management committee members were Protestant clergy.) Still, there were history teachers in St Columb's, as elsewhere, who left no doubt about their sympathies in the historic struggle between the British and the Irish. One of them would order his classes to go through their British textbooks scoring out references to 'our Queen' and deleting anything which admitted British rule in Ireland. Such behaviour was simply regarded as eccentric, however, and Hume did not acquire his sense of nationalism at school, any more than he did at home. Religion was still the biggest factor in his life, inspired by his long association with sympathic clerics, in and out of school. By the time he was thinking about university, he never considered for a moment going to Queen's University in Belfast, but set his sights on Maynooth, the Catholic seminary, as a preparation for the priesthood. His father, who was not as religious as his mother until his latter years, simply asked him, 'Are you sure you know what you're doing?' 'Yes', said Johnny, without hesitation.

All that stood in his way were two examinations – the state A levels, in which he won one of only ten university scholarships in Derry city, and the Bishop's Examination, to decide which direction his career as a priest would take. The academically bright went to Maynooth for three years of undergraduate study, for a basic secular degree, followed by four years of theological studies. They were destined for higher things, mostly in Ireland, while the others would go to rural colleges to prepare for a career in the foreign missions, without a primary degree. In the case of John Hume, by this time a dark-haired handsome seventeen-year-old, there was never any doubt about his ultimate destination, the British foundation of St Patrick's College, Maynooth.

2
Training for the priesthood

Just as Hume had been one of the first of the non-paying, working-class pupils at St Columb's, he arrived at Maynooth at a time of transition, in the last years when the old guard of the Catholic Church was in sole control. There were no lay students and the strictest of seminary rules applied, but a fresh wind was beginning to blow – in the history faculty for instance – which would lead to the gradual introduction of lay students in the 1960s, and to Maynooth's acceptance as a full college of the National University of Ireland.

Maynooth had been founded by William Pitt's government in 1795 as a means of compensating Catholics for the failure to introduce emancipation in Ireland, and as a counter to dangerous revolutionary influences during the wars with France. The Penal Laws against Roman Catholicism, introduced after William III's defeat of James II in Ireland in 1691, effectively meant that all Catholic priests and bishops – against whom a blind eye was turned, despite the law – were trained in Spain, France and Belgium, where the deeply conservative church authorities were contending with radical ideas thrown up by the French Revolution.

St Patrick's College, Maynooth, fifteen miles west of Dublin, was to be the British solution to a potentially dangerous Irish problem, but it was far from successful. Although the aim was to ensure that the most revolutionary ideas from the Continent were excluded, by concentrating the priesthood in a conservative environment and providing a focus for the organisation of the church, St Patrick's soon became a hotbed for constitutional nationalism. Physical-force nationalism, on the other hand, was always condemned from the pulpit, and one bishop in the 1860s was moved to say that for the Fenians, 'Hell is not hot enough and eternity not long enough'.

In the late nineteenth century the church became even more closely identified with the nationalist cause when a new Catholic religious fervour blended with a revival of Gaelic nationalism under the Gaelic Athletic Association, whose first president was Bishop Croke. Nearly all bishops and clergy supported the new Home Rule movement for Ireland, despite some reservations about the British Liberal Party's opposition to the power of the Catholic Church. After the War of Independence against Britain, partition and the setting up of the Irish Free State in 1922 gave Maynooth – now synonymous with the Catholic Church in Ireland – the chance to play a formative role in a clericalist state. Violent republicanism, as represented by the 'irregulars', who opposed the partition solution in the 1922–24 Civil War, was condemned and the bishops co-operated with different governments to write Catholic Church policy into legislation on divorce, contraception and censorship. Finally, in the 1937 Constitution, they acquired an acknowledgement that the church had 'a special position'.

Against this background, the most reactionary elements in the church, with their admiration of Franco and Mussolini, were in the ascendant, and any wind of change in the years after World War II was feeble. Nevertheless the convulsions of the war and the influence of the welfare state policies of the British Labour Government were eventually to have their effect and John Hume was in the vanguard of the new breed of clerical scholars. Previously they had been dominated by sons of policemen, teachers and farmers who traditionally valued having 'a bull in the field and a son in Maynooth'.

For the boy from the Bogside, who had no experience of boarding school and had never left his home in a close-knit Northern city, Maynooth was a supreme test of both his dedication to the priesthood and his determination to achieve academic success. The first was found wanting, eventually, but somehow he survived to get a good degree and avoid being ground down or ostracised by the system. The regime, a hangover from the nineteenth-century monasteries, could hardly have been more Spartan, or less in tune with Hume's natural gifts. The Maynooth day began at 6 am, in silence, and one washed, shaved and made one's bed before hurrying to be in place for morning prayer and meditation from 6.30 to 7 am. Morning Mass was at 7 am, breakfast at 7.45 and not until it was over, at 8 am, could the students speak, for the first time. After clearing one's room, there was a chance for an hour's walk until morning study. Lectures were from 9.30 to noon and lunch would be a single slice of bread and a cup of tea. There were two lectures in the afternoon, and 'dinner' was at 3 pm, again in silence. Recreation was

18

from 3.45 to 5 pm, and then it was back to silent study until evening prayer in the chapel at 7 pm. After supper there were about forty minutes of free time before the second study period and night prayer.

Into this enclosed world, hardly any outside light was allowed to shine. Newspapers, magazines and non-religious periodicals were prohibited and even regional newspapers and cuttings of sports fixtures had to be smuggled in. Radio was banned – as well as TV when it arrived – and in the library the only window on the contemporary world was the Catholic periodical, the *Tablet*. Alcohol was taboo, as was smoking in one's room and, for some reason, probably to do with self-indulgence, there had been a ban on chocolate, the ultimate luxury.

But this was all in the future for Hume as he joined with 102 others in the class of 1954 – representing a peak in the 'vocation boom' of post-war years – to hear the results of the annual 'draw' for seniority. All the names went into a barrel and the order in which they were drawn out decided the order of seniority not only in the college, and the diocese, but for as long as one remained in the church. John came out third, meaning that he was the senior man in the Derry diocese for his year, determining his place in class, in the refectory, in the dormitory and in chapel. As students with seniority drop out, the others are promoted up the rankings and the senior man of his year, according to his Maynooth standing, is usually first in line for the next parish which falls vacant. He may have to wait forty years, but his fate can be decided by the order in which his name comes out of the barrel in Maynooth.

The authorities would make sure the first one, two or three in any year were responsible citizens but otherwise denied any seeding in the process. Hume, who may have been spotted as a high flier, fell into his role with ease, although it meant that one of his 'immediates', who sat beside him everywhere, was a Cork man, separating him from a Northerner, Bertie Watson, who was much more akin to him. At this stage, Hume had a very pronounced Derry accent, which reduced vowel sounds to an 'uh', and Watson was forced into the role of interpreter between the two seating partners, who might have been speaking foreign languages for all they could understand of each other. Some noticed that the less sympathetic Hume was to the person he was addressing the thicker his accent would become.

Contacts with other colleges, through sports or debates, were not encouraged. All activity had to be generated from within, with a heavy emphasis on inter-diocesan rivalry, particularly on the sports field. The team was the diocese, Derry versus Down and Connor, or Cork, or Cloyne and this extended even to social activity. The students were expected to mix primarily with those from their own diocese, and their own year, and to form any attachment outside this group was to invite criticism. From entry at seventeen or eighteen, the system provided senior students to monitor the younger ones, to make them toe the line, if not to spy on them. The unforgiveable sin was 'singularity', or standing out from the crowd in any way, for good or ill. Exceptional talent at sport, music or debating was as culpable as exceptional ineptitude. Students were expected to merge with the pack, demonstrating their humility and, above all, obedience to authority.

The intention was to inculcate an unquestioning loyalty to the powers that be, whoever they were, as a prelude to a life of service to the diocese and to the church. One's parish priest could be a pedant or a bully but one had to obey him to the letter for the system to work. Individuality in such a situation would be a hindrance, so Maynooth did its best to discipline it, almost to the point of extermination, with results that were not always humane or successful. There was a lot of mental suffering concealed in the statistic which showed that up to a third of the entrants at Maynooth failed to stay the course. Out of eight entrants from Derry in Hume's year, only four were ordained and three are still priests.

To encourage a community spirit, each diocese was allocated a section of a wall, to which the students would retreat after meals. There they would acquire a sense of group solidarity, it was hoped, but the result was to reduce the effect of mixing with others from very different backgrounds and acquiring a better sense of Irish identity. The sons of the small farmer from Kerry and the teacher's family from Belfast might have found they had more than they imagined in common but they seldom got the chance. To have a special friend, even in one's own diocese, was not approved of, but to have a close relationship with someone from another diocese and, worse still, of a different age group, was decidedly frowned upon.

The rule at Maynooth was that all students did a three-year primary degree, before four years of divinity studies, and Hume was in the select honours school, majoring in French and History, with Philosophy and Logic as subsidiaries. It was a tough grind, cramming a normal four-year course into three years, and the pressure was added to by the authoritarian attitude of the lecturers, known as professors. Few would exchange a word with the students from start to finish of the course and they would expect to deliver their lectures in total silence, accepting questions only in writing. Luckily Hume had two of the exceptions to the rule, the fanatical French professor, Hubert Schild, from Lorraine, and Tom Fee, later Cardinal Tomás Ó Fiaich, who took him for history. Before Ó Fiaich arrived in 1953, history was confined to ecclesiastical history, but gradually the arts and science side was broadened. Schild was a true enthusiast and eccentric, insisting on lecturing only in French and conveying in every way possible his reverence for the language and its people. At the end of the first year the students were packed off to college in France for an intensive summer course, and in St Malo Hume began to acquire his enduring affinity for the French way of life. The Derry boys had a reputation for their aptitude in French, in contrast to the products of other minor seminaries which concentrated on Latin and Greek.

Meanwhile Tom Ó Fiaich, a graduate of the class of 1940 and lately returned from Louvain University, was helping to break down some of the barriers between teachers and students with his open-door approach. While his fellow lecturers kept their distance in accordance with tradition, Ó Fiaich combined a sense of enthusiasm for his subject with a warmth of personality which was almost unique. Unlike the others, he made a point of talking to his students as he walked around the college and even inviting them to his room for a cup of tea and a chat. Sport was his obsession, creating a common bond with the students, and he would be as excited as any of his charges before a big match. His subject was modern history, which in Louvain and the Continent generally meant anything from the Reformation and the Renaissance onwards, so he had to revise rapidly on the nineteenth and twentieth centuries. Nevertheless, Hume appreciated and learned from his analytical approach to the subject, finishing the first year with first-class honours in History and French and a second in English. As always, Hume was able to combine his outside interests with his studies without much apparent effort, so that for all his good grades he never acquired the reputation of a 'swot'. But the academic life did seem to suit him, for when the conversation lapsed, or a game lacked sparkle, he would retreat to read, as likely as not, a book on Irish history.

As a first-year student, or 'chub' – the second-years were 'logs' and the third years 'ba's' – John threw himself into the life of the college, perhaps to compensate for the doubts he was already having about his vocation. He was still a retiring, self-conscious boy in his own eyes and he soon began to feel he was not at home in the clerical atmosphere. It was difficult to describe and he never talked it out properly, either with staff or students, but he knew instinctively that this life was not for him. He was still trying to work out what he wanted in life, but if the church was to be bound up with so much bureaucracy and so many rules, he wondered if he could be a part of it.

Although no rebel, Hume would take a liberal attitude to the more restrictive rules, habitually reaching his place in chapel just a minute before 6.30 prayers. Silences were seldom strictly observed, except by the pious, and on one occasion a future Bishop of Achonry, Tom Flynn, was wedged, in his role as monitor, near Hume and his friend Bertie Watson. The practice was for six or seven of the third-year students to stay with the juniors, commonly sitting beside the number one in the class and trying to give a lead. Flynn would not speak because of the rule of silence, so every time he wanted milk, butter or bread, he had to nudge Watson, who would ask Hume to pass it up. Finally Hume, exasperated by the stream of requests, lifted the butter slices in a lump and threw it to his friend, who caught it and put it on the monitor's plate. Scowling, John said 'Ask him now would I ate it for him!'

Frustration with the system and the intensity of the heavy workload would at times become unbearable but Hume and his roommate had an answer. They would roll up socks in a ball and spend half an hour kicking penalty goals at each other against their door. John had a notoriously sweet tooth which would afflict him at times of self-denial. His habit before Lent was to save up pocket money to buy a dozen or more cream-filled chocolate eggs, and on Easter Sunday to scoff them all, one by one.

Money was not a problem at Maynooth, mainly because there was virtually nothing to spend it on, except sweets. The ankle-length black soutane, which everyone wore, covered up a multitude of differences in economic circumstances and Hume's colleagues were amazed later to learn that his family had been so poor. His habits were so frugal in fact, that, between the Northern Ireland scholarship and the Bishop's Examination allowance, he was able to save modestly and he sent everything he could home.

22

As well as playing football – though not in the worst weather conditions, friends noticed – Hume was an avid follower of the fortunes of the Derry City team. After one particular crucial tie, which was lost, he went into virtual mourning for three days. From his own personal partisan reaction, be believed from an early stage that sporting contests were a valuable safety valve for subconscious emotions, and were withdrawn to everyone's cost. Sectarian bitterness increased in intensity following the withdrawal of the Catholic team, Belfast Celtic, from the Irish League in 1944 after clashes between Protestant spectators and players. Derry City, too, was forced to bow out soon after the Troubles started, removing a useful tribal symbol and destroying friendly contact with rivals.

Logic was only a small part of Hume's course but it appealed to the mathematician in him and left its mark on his thinking. When confronted by a seemingly insoluble problem he would apply a logic which detractors would say was 'Jesuitical'. The legacy of Professor Dermot O'Donoghue's lectures was to be felt far and wide in the years to come, even if they did not always relate to Northern politics.

Meanwhile, John put heart and soul into work and games, playing for Derry – they were usually the team to beat – at soccer and Gaelic football, which came a poor second with him. He even tried basketball, tennis and that most English of games, croquet. But it was in the debating chamber that he made his mark, as a member of the three-man Derry junior team, in the weekly debates on such non-political subjects as 'A woman's place is in the home'. He was his own greatest critic and thought himself tongue-tied and ineffective, but contemporaries noted his often emotional delivery and the homework he put into his speeches, whatever the weight of the subject. His first contribution caused him nightmares. Due to speak for fifteen minutes, he dried up after five – probably for the only time in his life – but thereafter he gained a reputation as an argumentative and highly effective performer with a needle-sharp Derry wit. The typical Irishman will conceal his real feelings behind a smokescreen of words, but Derry Catholics have always expressed themselves bluntly, briefly and with a deflationary sense of humour that spares no one.

John soon revealed himself as one of the most perceptive of commentators in a reticent and far-from-articulate student body, mostly from rural Ireland. They admired his turn of phrase and daring, so much so the word would go round, about any topic of interest – 'Did you hear what Johnny Hume said about it?' Humbug was his prime target and he left no doubt in private about his opinion of some of the staff whose lectures were not up to scratch. One day he was beside himself when he was describing to a friend how a new student, an Englishman, tried to impress the French class with his knowledge of languages. 'I asked him what languages he knew and he said he could speak Swuss! Could you believe it?' The friend had to think hard, translating from Derry into the English 'Swiss', then laughing a little unsurely, until he realised there was no such language.

John had developed his father's gift for story-telling and regaled his colleagues with many tales about Derry and its characters, complete with mimicked gestures and voices. He was steeped in his native city and his obvious love for it came as a surprise to some of his listeners who had seen it as a city of mean streets and equally mean inhabitants, torn by sectarian hatreds. The rural Southerners, in particular, had no conception of the housing and social conditions in a city like Derry and to one of them Hume's description was an insight into the Papal encyclical, *Rerum Novarum*, on urban poverty, more valuable than anything he learned in class. There were also some eye-opening facts and figures produced about the Derry gerrymander, more than ten years before it became an issue in British politics. Hume's father often figured in his accounts of Derry life and John would help out himself, during holidays, with unofficial advice-centre work.

Light relief at Maynooth was rare but whatever form it took – a visit by the Irish Radio Orchestra, or the college play – Hume was there. The students who dressed up in drag for plays usually got all the laughs, but Hume brought the house down in the lead role of the janitor in the popular farce of the day, 'The Mummy and the Mumps'. His individualism was respected in a college of conformity and his advice was eagerly sought by rural colleagues who lacked his all-round experience. If a game or contest of any kind was proposed, in which Derry would be taking part, nothing would happen without his approval. 'We'll have to see what Doctor Hume thinks,' one of them would say when the question was put. 'You never can tell what his reaction will be.'

St Patrick's, Maynooth, was a cold, dark, unremarkable, Victorian institution, with two quadrangles, one classical and the other Gothic, and cloisters on three sides. Visits by parents were rare – in Hume's case they came only once, when a lift was available – and some students would actually discourage them, such were the facilities. Rooms were of the usual Spartan university type, either single or double, made for work and sleep. Clearly, the whole institution and its long list of prohibitions, read out annually, were designed for another age, before the emancipation of youth and the demise of automatic deference to tradition. The new generation of students, many of them recruited on merit from the working classes, were questioning the value of such a regimented life style but no-one, and certainly not Hume, was going to appeal for change before the authorities themselves conceded the need. Hume was no revolutionary, even though he recognised what had to be done. As a contemporary said, 'He quickly learned to distinguish the doers of this world from the thinkers, which included him. He would produce the ideas and depute them to someone more energetic than himself to carry out.'

So his brushes with authority were few and not comparable with those of near contemporaries who earned themselves trial by the discipline committee for more heinous offences. The penalty for misdemeanours was a 'cat', short for *'caveat'* (beware) and, when two or three were accumulated, expulsion was obligatory. One well-known Northern priest, Denis Faul, was tried and convicted for ordering textbooks direct from Blackwells, in Oxford, without letting his tutor see what he was buying. Two others, around the same time, were expelled for playing billiards when they were supposed to be at prayers.

But John did run foul of the authorities in his last year, for the crime of having a visiting student in his room – the rule was a hangover from boarding school practice and presumably a defence against homosexuality. His own room-mate was leaving and when a friend came to call, John invited him in. They were talking when the Dean looked in, saw the visitor, and went out again. The following Monday, to his complete surprise, John was summoned to appear before the disciplinary committee, including Professor William Conway, a future Primate, where Hume explained in uncompromising terms what he had done and why he thought he had nothing to answer for. But rules were rules and he had to pay the penalty – a reprimand and failure to be awarded 'tonsure', like the others, at the end of his year. Tonsure, which involved a ritual shaving of a small part of the scalp, was the first of the holy orders, announced on 'Black Fridays', which culminated in ordination after seven years at Maynooth.

Not surprisingly, he was sickened by the way he had been treated for performing what he regarded as an act of Christian charity and his doubts about his vocation, which were already considerable, were further increased. If this is what is done in the name of Christianity, he thought, what is it all about? His mind was already well on the way to being made up, as he and the other students picked over the eternal subject – would they stay the course, or, (in Maynooth terminology) 'cut'?

Some students were surprised, even shocked, by his defection, but others had seen it coming. He had social concern and was devout, without being too 'holy'; but he had no gift for small talk, preferring more serious discussion, and his Northern directness made it difficult for him to hide his true feelings in tedious company. His talents were obvious, said a knowing colleague, but they were not designed for the priesthood. In the end, several factors combined in his decision – his lack of vocation, the rigidity of the system, the need to supplement the meagre family income and a painful inflamation of the stomach, which hospitalised him for a month and prevented him from sitting his honours exams in September. It was a college tradition that a stay in hospital, among pretty nurses, was often the prelude to dropping out, but this had nothing to do with Hume's case. He had already been in hospital in his first year, with knee trouble, from too much bending at prayer, and by the end of his degree course was simply restless.

When he told the authorities of his decision to leave, their reaction was one of concern – probably tinged with regret over their reprimand – for the loss of such an able student, of bishop material. A professor was deputed to drive him into Dublin for a meal at the five-star Gresham Hotel, in an attempt to change his mind, but to no avail. Like many of his contemporaries, he found the reality of the priesthood too different from the vision, which in Hume's case was wrapped up with service to one's fellow men and security of tenure.

His father, sitting in his usual chair in Glenbrook Terrace, cried but was sympathetic when he heard that John was to leave Maynooth: 'It takes a good man to enter the priesthood – and an even better one to leave it'.

3
Self help

There were few openings for a twenty-year-old Maynooth student who had missed his final B.A. examinations through illness and would be counted as lost to the priesthood – although he could return, as some did, after a year's interruption. Teaching was an obvious way out and it was with some luck that he obtained a temporary full-time job in the Christian Brothers' Technical School, teaching French and Irish, without formal qualifications of any kind. Another Maynooth drop-out before him, Brian Friel – later to become an internationally-celebrated playwright – had found the same temporary haven in which to gather his thoughts about the future.

Hume found it difficult to explain, even to himself, but the certainty he had about his vocation had gradually been extinguished in the suffocating atmosphere of pre-Vatican II Maynooth and he knew he would be a misfit. As well as this, there were pressures on the eldest boy, with a father aged sixty-seven, to make a contribution to the family income. Times were increasingly hard for the Humes, now that the family was growing up, and the first real income for ten years came from John's first pay packet.

His mother was still doing the rounds of the shops, never accepting the first price that was quoted for anything and with her good-natured banter – '£10 did you say? I'll give you £8' – generally getting her way. Sam Hume was already an old-age pensioner, with the youngest of his family only twelve, but he was still sought out by the unlettered for advice. He was one of the senior members of what was known as the 'university of the streets', where the district's unemployed men would meet to discuss world affairs, and demonstrate a surprising erudition. Together the Humes were known as good neighbours, who would do anyone a good turn if they could. As Sam used to say, 'If you can't say anything good about a person, at least don't say anything bad.' It was a generous attitude to adversaries which he passed onto his son. His wife's philosophy was more religiously based. 'Sure God's good,' she would say. 'Trust in God and it'll come out right.'

Later in life, she had a daily routine which helped to fill the gap created by the death from kidney failure of her beloved husband at seventy-seven, and made her one of Derry's best known characters. She would make a tour of her favourite shops – her 'stations of the cross', as she called them – and in some of them would be given a chair for her bulky frame from which she would chat to everyone in sight. On the way home by bus she would always have a bun for the driver and would be let off between stops at 'Annie's corner'. Her family were as proud of Johnny as she was, and every day a sister in the Bogside would look up towards his house, sprinkle holy water and say a prayer for him, wherever he might be. Every day Annie Hume insisted on all nine saying the family Rosary together and even when the sons were of working age there would be prayers after the evening meal. The essential optimism in John's nature, which eventually overcomes his blacker moods, is not difficult to trace. It was a typical Derry home, where the girls in the family waited hand and foot on the boys, even cleaning their shoes, and it left the eldest son hopelessly unfit for domestic chores in later life.

Back in Derry and involved, through his father, in all the social problems of that divided city, John began to think about solutions which would lift the community up by its own bootstraps. If the Unionist corporation had nothing to offer, the people would have to help themselves. But to do so, they needed organisation and a sense of their own worth, which had been badly battered over the years. Hopelessness and apathy were part of the Derry way of life and most of those who rebelled simply got out – as seventeen out of twenty of John's contemporaries in his street had done.

Meanwhile there were teaching skills to be acquired, as well as a degree, and reports of his progress were enough to get him a firm offer of a post in the first secondary intermediate school in the Derry diocese, St Colman's, Strabane, when it opened in 1958. He had hoped to take with him a first class honours degree but the break in his studies had taken its toll and he had to settle for a good second. In Strabane the teaching staff were confronted with a new kind of student body – boys who had failed the eleven-plus intelligence test, which had started Hume on his academic career, and who were destined for manual or semi-skilled jobs or unemployment. It was a challenge to bring out the best in the 'rejects' of an unjust system and

Hume approached it with his unusually direct and self-taught educational methods.

From day one, he taught pupils who had no experience of the language through the medium of French – after the example of his Maynooth professor – and the results were impressive. Out of seventeen boys entered for the under-fifteen Junior Certificate examination, which was considered to be beyond non-academic pupils, thirteen finished with distinctions, over 70 per cent. Word spread further afield of his success in putting language fluency before grammar and a Ministry inspector asked for his scripts, for use in teaching French in Edinburgh University.

At the same time he organised the publication of an internal school magazine in French – which won a commendation from the French consul in Belfast – and a local history magazine, illustrated with archaeological finds. Older teachers noticed his capacity for hard work, which seemed to inspire his pupils, and his pastoral interest in the boys and their welfare. After school he ran an oral French class, enlisting the headmaster to play the piano and sing French songs.

Against this background and daily commuting from his over-crowded home in Derry, he began to prepare his M.A. thesis on 'Social and Economic Aspects of the Growth of Derry, 1825–50', bouncing ideas off the other three teachers with whom he travelled by car. His sources were the local newspapers of the day and his researches turned up much original material, helping to explain how the city had suddenly mushroomed, providing the genesis for many of the problems that still plague it. His history professor at Maynooth, Tom Ó Fiaich, who was tutoring his first post-graduate student, had high hopes of a first, but the verdict of two visiting professors was a second. Students still use the thesis as a source document and Dr Ó Fiaich sought Hume's permission, readily given, to supply it to Leon Uris, the novelist, in his preparation for his best-seller on Ireland, *Trinity*.

For Hume himself, the thesis provided a solid base of knowledge on which to build his own ideas for a better future, largely dependent on self help. Others were thinking along similar lines, as all other avenues appeared to be blocked, and Paddy Doherty – later more commonly known as 'Paddy Bogside' – was one of the most active. He had met with blank indifference when he applied for a rented house from the Unionist-dominated corporation. 'Only two children?'

said the official, looking over his spectacles, 'Come back in nine years and I'll take your name.' But instead Doherty bought a cheap plot of land in Westland Road and built his own house in his spare time, with his own hands. He realised, with wry satisfaction, that it was the attitude of the official which had goaded him into helping himself, and while he was pondering on the implications of this for his fellow Bogsiders a tall young man introduced himself. 'I'm John Hume,' he said, and proceeded to launch into a discussion of the total inability of the Catholic population to improve the appalling conditions in which they lived. Both were agreed that leadership was needed and out of this 1958 encounter – and many more – a group of concerned people got together to devise ways and means of helping people to help themselves. Finance was obviously a major problem for such a deprived community and the answer that emerged had been born in Germany in 1848 – as a consequence of the same famine that decimated Ireland – before being refined in America and Canada this century into the Credit Union organisation.

The birth of the idea in Derry is disputed but Hume and Doherty both saw the value of a community banking system to encourage saving and foster wise investment. Advice was sought from many quarters. An American Air Force officer serving at a base near Prestwick in Scotland was contacted as a result of articles he had written and a copy of the Credit Union constitution was obtained. Around the same time Father Anthony Mulvey had acquired information on the organisation, including an article in the *Reader's Digest*, and his lecture to the Knights of Columbanus, a Catholic society which was deeply involved in the early stages of the movement, was followed by another in May 1960 to a more general audience.

After a little more pushing and nearly a year's research by Hume into the workings of the organisation, a group of seventy got together in 1960 to found a Derry branch – the first of its kind in the North, although since 1958 sixty branches had been formed in the South. The legal advice was that forming a Credit Union would be breaking a series of laws on banking, charities and moneylending but Paddy Doherty's answer was typically blunt: 'Is there anything in the law which says that people can't come together and pool their savings to help each other?' The lawyers fell silent and for ten years the Credit Union operated in Northern Ireland without any covering legislation – before Hume himself, by then a Stormont MP, helped steer it through. John, at twenty-three, was easily the youngest person involved in the formation, but his obvious commitment to the ideals and his eloquence won him the key post as treasurer. After inviting various groups along to an explanatory meeting in Rossville Hall, the five founders invested a total of £7.50. From these small beginnings grew three city branches – Pennyburn, Bogside and Waterside – with share capital passing the £1 million mark in 1973 and £4 million eleven years later, by which time there were ninety-four Northern branches.

On the face of it, the Credit Union movement was about money management and how to help people to cope, but the founders, including Doherty, Michael Canavan, a local bookmaker-business-man, and Hume, had a wider vision. One of the fundamental principles was that every Credit Union branch should be grounded in a community of some description where people felt responsible to each other, in a city, town or village, or in a large firm.

That was the insurance against bad debts which could quickly bring the edifice down, but it also had a positive unifying influence. People who found they could manage their financial affairs collect-ively developed a self confidence that encouraged them to tackle other problems together. In Derry, where there had been an acceptance of second-class citizenship, that was the beginning of a political movement, or at least a self-help movement that could move the politicians. This thought was not foremost in the mind of Hume, who was still as apolitical as his father, but it grew as he took on the role of Credit Union missionary, travelling the length and breadth of Ireland to spread the word. Incidentally, he learned to drive with typical disregard for convention, or his own safety. A nun needed a lift to Donegal, and Hume volunteered to take her, although he had never driven. He sat behind the wheel, learned where the gears were, and drove off jerkily. By the time he returned, he could drive.

The Credit Union system worked like a co-operative bank, with members paying into a central pool, which entitled them to both low-interest loans and low interest on their deposits. While bank rates fluctuated, Credit Union terms remained the same – 1 per cent per month interest on loans on the descending balance, or a net 6 per cent, which was distributed as a dividend to members. If a member died, his debts were cleared or his savings doubled and distributed to the family. Thus it provided a form of insurance, as well as loan finance, and helped to stimulate a sense of thrift in a community which traditionally lived from hand to mouth.

31

Hume knew from his own family's experience how much reliance there was on credit, sometimes exacted at exorbitant rates. The best example was the club system, by which the keeper of the household money – in John's family, Mrs Hume – would pay into a savings fund, to a collector who called every Saturday. When she wanted clothes she would get a club ticket with the instruction, 'Please supply goods to the value of £10', and use it in place of cash. It was effective, but to Hume there was more pride and dignity in paying in banknotes, rather than pieces of paper, and this was what the Credit Union offered. It also provided a discipline for those who would borrow their way through life scarcely knowing what they owed to whom.

It was a condition in the early years that new members had to attend an introductory lecture, to get the community aspect across, as well as the personal benefit. Self help was the keynote and many a village hall heard John's favourite theme, which is still largely unchanged: 'Any country without its people is only a piece of earth, only a jungle. The real worth in the world is actually people. Take the people out of it and you have nothing.' It was a philosophy which he later applied to politics, in a way that challenged the conventional nationalist approach to a united Ireland. But in the early days of the Credit Union movement it was used only to convince people that they had many of the solutions to their problems in their own hands, if they would pool their talents. It was as if he had found the cause he had been looking for when he entered Maynooth, and persuading canny country folk to invest in an untested scheme absorbed all his energy and ability. He wore out two Morris Minors in his travels and drove himself to the limits of physical endurance, but the experience, for his political life to come, was invaluable.

The development of the Credit Union movement in Ireland has been closely associated with the Catholic Church, as the common bond in rural communities, but Hume and the others were insistent that it should be broadly based in both communities, and that Protestant office-bearers be appointed where possible. In Derry this was feasible but in his travels Hume discovered, to his regret, that Protestants did not respond positively to the message. He addressed one women's meeting in Mountpottinger Hall, in the heart of Protestant east Belfast, with a Union Jack draped across the table, but although he was warmly received, nothing came of it.

It was his first real sight of the gulf between the communities. Here, he had thought, was an idea that could benefit everybody, but clearly the women regarded it as a Catholic idea and therefore not for them. He concluded that the general failure of Protestants to adopt the Credit Union system reflected the difference in the community structure – Catholics were more community-orientated, in parish structures, with a sense of local identity and a tradition of voluntary effort, while Protestants tended to be more individualistic and loyal to their separate churches. In any case, it was a revolution in money management which the Protestants did not join. Although thrift was an important part of the make-up of the Protestant community, it was innately suspicious of an apparently Catholic-based organisation which depended so much on mutual trust. The trust was lacking, so the banks got the savings of the Protestant working classes, even if they did not lend so freely.

Even in Derry, where initially the Pennyburn and Waterside Credit Unions were very mixed, the idealism was eventually overtaken by events and population shifts. In the South, large concerns like Aer Lingus and the Electricity Supply Board had their own branches and it was Hume's regret that Harland & Wolff's Belfast shipyard, which would have been an ideal base, did not take it up. If it had, the socialist ethos which it encouraged might have caught on, countering sectarianism.

Before he immersed himself in community affairs, the former Maynooth student, now in his temporary teaching job, had met at a dance his first and only girlfriend, whom he was to marry in 1960, after a nine-month engagement. Pat Hone, the youngest child (by eleven years) in a family of six, was the daughter of a clever handyman and house repairer from the Waterside, on the opposite bank of the Foyle to the Bogside. Her father had been involved with the old IRA in 1916, winning several medals, but, like Sam Hume, he identified more with British Labour than with any Irish party. In later years he could never understand the Provisional IRA's campaign. He was secretly proud when Pat passed her eleven-plus, like John, and became the only child of the family to go to grammar school and then to St Mary's teacher training college in Belfast. Romance blossomed under the auspices of the Derry Dancing Club, which Hume had helped to form with some friends in the Legion of Mary, of which he was the local vice-president. He and his ancient car became frequent visitors to the flat Pat shared with fellow students on Belfast's Springfield Road.

Clearly Hume had to marry a Derry girl, and from every point of view it was a perfect match. Clever, perceptive, diplomatic, self-sufficient, good-humoured and unflappable, she was to bring up a family of five in turbulent conditions, smoothing feathers that John, with his occasionally blunt manner, had ruffled, and generally making life as agreeable as possible for a man who had so little time to spare for domestic details. From the start, she admired John's great sense of responsibility, especially to his family. Even when they were saving to get married he continued to give the bulk of his meagre teacher's pay cheque to his mother, conscious of the fact that he was the only child to get a formal education.

Whatever criticism there might be of John, whose opinions are too strong to please everyone all the time, there is none at all of Pat. She has let him become the personality he is, just by being at his side, taking care of the family and leaving him to concentrate on the intense involvement of the moment, free from most everyday concerns. Only those nearest her know the sacrifices she has made in her own life, bringing up the children almost single-handedly and later abandoning her teaching career to become her husband's indispensable office manager. She has never regarded herself as highly political, but her instinctive feel for people makes her a natural social worker and smoother of problems for Derry's dispossessed. From their first meeting, Pat recognised John's potential in the life of the community, and did nothing to stand in his way. She had no idea of how his career would develop, as she married a schoolteacher in St Colman's, but she soon learned to regard his absences philosophically. 'It was like being married to a travelling salesman,' she would say. But her serene exterior concealed worries as the family grew up with an absentee father. Some of the adolescent children missed his mellowing influence, at difficult times of their lives, and resented their home being in the limelight. But Pat battled through, with the daily help of 'Nana' Doherty, a friend of John's mother, and the storm clouds passed, as the family learned to live with the pressures. Through all the ups and downs of politics, Pat strove to make life as normal as it could be for the family of the North's leading nationalist politician, making a point of leaving for school with the children every morning, until she was forced to transfer to her role as manager of the constituency office in 1979. From there, she acts as Hume's eyes and ears in Derry, sensing the changing moods of the people and keeping him constantly in touch, wherever his parliamentary duties take him. When John Hume told an American journalist, 'Pat is my anchor. I could not survive in politics without her' – before confessing that it sounded 'too corny' – all Derry would have known exactly what he meant.

Married life began in a terrace house in the Waterside – the only brief time in his life John has left the Bogside – where friends found they had to lower their heads to enter, so small was the doorway. Soon they moved to Beechwood Avenue, not far from his old haunts, where they stayed until the Troubles began and they installed themselves in nearby West End Park, in a three-storey terrace house with a commanding view of the Bogside.

Meanwhile, there were public-speaking skills to be polished, and the Columcille Debating Society was Hume's finishing school. Derry has produced almost as many powerful public speakers as singers, because of its long oral tradition, and many of them cut their teeth in this once all-male, all-Catholic society which vigorously debated all the subjects of the day. The formal rules of debate were obeyed but, while many took the opportunity to exercise their oratory rather than polish up their principles, John Hume was noted for his devastatingly serious approach. Whatever the subject, he would not only prepare his own arguments but would have anticipated those of his opponents and have answers for them – much to the frustration of those who took things less seriously.

One of his chief sparring partners was Eamonn McCann, another eleven-plus St Columb's boy from a similar Bogside background, but very different in temperament. While Hume represented the new generation of nationalist intellectuals, McCann was the eloquent, impatient voice of the republican left, eager to tear down the whole rotten Stormont system. Caught in the middle were the Nationalist city councillors, and one of the most prominent, James Doherty, felt obliged to resign from the society in protest against a motion disapproving of 'the antics of Nationalist members of the City Council,' critical of their ineffectual protests. In its small way, the debating society helped to raise the level of nationalist-minded political debate in a city that had for too long suffered the stultifying effects of irreconcilable division. Traditionalists were forced to reconsider their attitude of non-co-operation with Unionists, as the new Catholic middle class began to question the old values – not only in Derry – and the old simple answers failed to suffice.

But before this conflict came to a head, Hume himself was

beginning to spread his wings, looking for promotion in teaching, or education generally, that would offer the rewards for which his newly-acquired master's degree qualified him. St Columb's, his old school, beckoned and no sooner had he accepted a post to teach French and history than Magee College – at that time a constituent part of the Presbyterian College, preparing students for the ministry – offered a librarian's job.

Because he felt committed to St Columb's – even though only priests could aspire to the two top posts, and promotion of lay teachers was on length of service – the librarianship went begging, so a possible career in university administration or teaching was by-passed. But less than a year after joining the staff at St Columb's, another tempting job was advertised – that of administrative assistant in the Londonderry City Education Board – and he duly applied. Few Catholics would have given it a moment's thought in view of the Unionist majority on the education committee but Hume, ever the optimist, had no doubts that he would get fair play and a recognition of his talents, even at the age of twenty-five.

He was wrong on both counts, for when the committee had to decide between Hume and a Coleraine teacher with lesser qualifications, the vote divided twelve-nine against the St Columb's man, on the usual party lines. Under the local government system of the day – still perpetuated though in different proportions – some members of the committee were ministers of religion, representing Protestant schools which had been taken over by the state, or Catholic schools which received Government grants, and even they were undeviating. The Rev. Victor Griffin, later Dean of St Patrick's Cathedral in Dublin, seconded the appointment of Hume's rival and he had five Protestant ministers in support, against two Catholic clerics, representing 70 per cent of the city's population.

It was a situation that seldom had to be faced, because of the unspoken agreement that top administrative jobs in local government were automatically reserved for Protestants. But Hume had thrown down the gauntlet and the Nationalist councillors were quick to pick it up the following day, at the full council meeting in Derry's Guildhall. James Doherty described the vote as 'a disgraceful episode' and went on to sing Hume's praises in glowing terms: 'We were fortunate in having among our citizens a young man who proved himself to have one of the most brilliant minds in the city at the moment; a native of the city with a brilliant academic record. . .

His interview was one of the best performances I have ever seen, and persons with wide educational experience present were in a position to say that it was one of which the city could be proud.' The proceedings of the committee, he said, had been a travesty of justice, and Catholic members had a feeling of revulsion. (They also felt, inwardly, that although Hume had been the better candidate, he had talked too much, and ranged too widely.) Angry words were exchanged, as the Hume episode unleashed years of resentment. 'We, the vast majority of the citizens of Derry – our city – have come to the end of our tether,' was another warning. But Doherty, later to become a long-standing chairman of the Western Education Board, covering a much bigger area, delivered the most telling blow of all, which struck at the whole local government system, administered by the Unionist Government: 'In this city where there are 36,000 Catholics, only two clergymen of the Catholic religion are appointed to the education committee whereas, for the other denominations, involving 16,000 people, five ministers of religion have been appointed. Something will have to be done about this business, not only of gerrymandering the city but of picking committees.'

His plea fell on deaf ears for another six years, but the confrontation brought Hume face to face with the political reality in Northern Ireland which he had done his best, like his father before him, to ignore in his belief that reason would triumph. As disillusion set in, he knew that to change the system which produced such bigotry he would have to get involved in politics himself. Ironically, the education post would have given him 'an office of profit' under the Crown and prevented him from standing for election. As a teacher he was still debarred, but he could have resigned to enter politics with far less to lose than he would have had as an education board administrator.

Nothing was changing in Derry, but there were faint stirrings of a new era at Stormont, with the retirement in 1963 of the long-serving Unionist Prime Minister, Lord Brookeborough, and his replacement by Captain Terence O'Neill – an aristocrat, like his predecessor, but also a realist. O'Neill genuinely wanted to make Northern Ireland a model, modern province and knew that to do so, he needed the co-operation not only of Catholics, but of the Irish Republic. Britain's help was needed too, to finance his plans and he calculated rightly that it would be more sympathetic to a 'fair-play' Northern Ireland, rather than one that was wide open to charges of discrimination.

But first the foundations had to be laid and a series of reports were commissioned to point the way ahead for transport, education, regional planning and the economy. It was the era of new towns, new universities and new roads to replace the railways, so it was hardly surprising that Derry found itself increasingly isolated in the upper left-hand corner of the map, as most of the development was sited east of the River Bann, around new or existing growth centres. In quick succession, there were decisions on a new city, just twenty-five miles from Belfast, new motorways in the Belfast area, closure of one of the two Belfast-Derry rail links and severing of Derry's shipping link with Glasgow. The maiden city's honour was at stake, and both communities united to defend it against the unsympathetic powers that be in Belfast. The last straw was the rumoured spurning of the north west as a base for Ulster's second university and when the rival Protestant town of Coleraine, thirty miles east, was asked to redraft its submission, signifying that success was imminent, all Derry erupted in righteous indignation. The University for Derry Campaign was lost before it began but for Hume, its chairman, the rare opportunity of uniting both communities was too good to miss. A mixed committee of Protestants and Catholics was chosen, and a public meeting, called in Derry's historic Guildhall, drew a full house. Here was one issue on which all could agree, the Catholics because they traditionally looked to education as their way out of the ghetto and the Protestants because it represented the best chance of preserving Magee College and of finding student tenants for their property. It was an emotional occasion in the crowded public hall, with Unionists and Nationalists taking their places together on the platform for the first time anyone could remember and Nationalist Party leader Eddie McAteer sharing a leading role with the arch-Unionist Gerald Glover. But it was not until Hume, a very junior master at St Columb's, made the final speech, after the reporters had dashed for the phones, that the meeting really came alight.

His theme was the need to unite the two communities, not just for the duration of the university campaign, but for the good of the city in the longer term. Derry stood for both traditions, he said. There was the Protestant siege tradition, followed by the sacrifice in two world wars; and the native Irish tradition of St Columcille. For one tradition, it was the place where the battle had been fought and, for the other, the place where the battle was being fought. The university issue could provide a marriage of both traditions and both points of view. It was a unifying speech which perfectly caught the mood of the meeting and brought the crowd to its feet in recognition of this new ideal, so powerfully expressed by someone who was unmistakably a Derry man and yet could not be slotted into any of the existing pigeon-holes. For once, there was no reference to the aspiration of Irish unity, and the hearts of Protestants and Catholics alike could swell with civic pride. As a last throw, Hume organised a mass motorcade to Stormont, led by a limousine containing Derry's foremost Unionist and Nationalist politicians, Mayor Albert Anderson and Eddie McAteer. As chairman of the campaign, Hume was invited to join them, but declined, in order to leave the religious balance even.

But the die had already been cast, it turned out, in favour of Coleraine, and the campaign ended on an angry note. While many of the city's Protestants backed the siting of the university in Derry, some of their political leaders had secretly advised against it, on the grounds that any growth of Derry would inevitably threaten their slender majority. The 'faceless men', as they were called, preferred to leave Derry a stagnant backwater rather than see it develop out of their control. Almost for the first time, Unionist power politics was exposed to the public gaze on a major issue and the birth of the civil rights movement can be traced to those stormy days of February 1965.

Even before the university was considered, the Unionist corporation had embarked on a farsighted campaign of self-preservation, in face of growing nationalist numbers. As far back as the 1940s and 1950s a deliberate policy could be detected to site as many public buildings and services as possible on the east bank of the Foyle, where there was a Protestant majority, rather than the west bank, where the city centre lay. Both hospitals were placed on the east, leaving the only public buildings on the city side the police station, the unemployment office and the courthouse. To the most politically-minded citizens in Northern Ireland, this spoke volumes and should have explained to others, who had no direct experience of discrimination, why the wounds in Derry went so deep.

4
Speaking out

An arts festival, to combine the considerable musical and dramatic talents of the city, was planned for the spring of 1964 and, at short notice, Hume was asked by the BBC to script a TV film for showing the same week. Already his Credit Union work was thrusting him increasingly into the limelight, and the invitation followed immediately after his first TV appearance in a local discussion programme, *Target Derry*. One of the participants, giving a Protestant view, was the Rev. Brian Hannon and it was no coincidence that Hume asked him to do the commentary from the script, to build in an ecumenical flavour.

He agreed, though not before a careful study to make sure that a curate of the Church of Ireland Cathedral would not be embarrassed by the content. *A City Solitary* had a sadness, as well as a lyrical quality that caught the essence of Derry down the centuries, whether coping with emigration – 'Today the flood continues, and for the same basic reason, dissatisfaction with their lot at home and with their almost total lack of opportunity – or unemployment – an idleness drawing the strength from the city, shrouding it in hopelessness. . . the effect on the city is immeasurable'. The ending, however, was more hopeful, as the cameras swung away from the slums, towards the river, and the commentary called for the unity of 'the great streams of Derry's population. . . The independence and seriousness of the Derry Protestant, allied to the discipline and resourcefulness of the Catholic, will build the bridge for Derry's future. The symbol of the bridge could be the future full acceptance of the term "Londonderry", for in it are summed up the two great traditions of the city.' Hume saw the name as a link word in more senses than one, for both 'London', meaning 'fort of the ships' and 'derry' – 'oak grove' in Irish – had Celtic origins. Already he was nailing his colours to non-tribal politics, based on mutual respect, a concept years ahead of its time. He had a dream, long before any party had put it in words, that unionists and nationalists could combine for short-term economic objectives, leaving aside the contentious issue of the constitution.

Some saw the film as a rather bland account of the growth of Derry, strangely lacking in explicit political content or commentary on the exploitation of one class by another, while others found it a moving experience. One declared nationalist, who saw it in the Guildhall, told a journalist he stood for the British anthem 'God Save the Queen' for the first time in his life and another said he had broken a lifetime habit by writing 'Londonderry', instead of his usual 'Derry' at the top of a letter. Certainly it had an impact that belied its amateurish production. The cameraman was a teacher friend of Hume's, Terence McDonald, using his own £30 camera, and the black-and-white film was completed inside a month for a total cost of £50. They made two other films together, with Hume in the role of producer, director, script-writer and narrator – *The Open Door*, about the role of Gransha psychiatric hospital, Derry, and *Two Hours From London*, an attempt to promote tourism and industrial investment in the north west.

Hume's career was at a turning point, and he might well have chosen a life in the media if the right job had come along. Already he had made his debut, writing and performing in *64 Group*, BBC Northern Ireland's answer to David Frost's satirical TV programme, *That Was The Week That Was*. It was a brave attempt, never repeated, to subject the Stormont scene to the caricaturing it so richly deserved, and it provided a contact for Hume with a Belfast couple in a mixed marriage. Nonie McClure, a singer in the TV show and a friend of Pat's, had married a Belfast doctor, Garth McClure, from a loyalist background, and so impressed were they with Hume's new non-sectarian approach to politics that he became godfather to their first child. (Later they were to drift away from him politically, as the SDLP took up a more nationalist stance, and they felt Hume's early idealism had been crushed by the system.)

Two years after making his Derry film, Hume went as far as to submit an application in 1966 for a BBC schools broadcasting job in Belfast, which would have cut him off from his Derry roots and changed the direction of his life. He was told apologetically after his interview that the post had already been filled, but that he would be offered the first vacancy. When he had the choice, a year later, he turned it down, but his fascination for radio and TV as educational and political media dates from those days.

The BBC film also brought him to the notice of *Irish Times* writer Michael Viney, who began his newspaper's long-running affair with the Northern Ireland question in the spring of 1964 with a perceptive series of articles on a 'Journey North'. In them he investigated the new thaw in Protestant-Catholic relations, as a result of Captain O'Neill's premiership, and probed the conciliatory mood of some Nationalist politicians. In Derry he found that, although the Arts Council's insistence on playing the National Anthem at orchestral concerts lost it Catholic support, subjects like discrimination were being discussed openly by Protestants and Catholics, and the Londonderry Light Opera Society had finally become 'integrated', to tap the best musical talent in the city.

Viney also focused on Paddy Gormley, a supremely pragmatic Nationalist MP at Stormont, who would 'rather see the small farmer stay put under the Union Jack than emigrate with a Tricolour on his back'. It was still an unusual sentiment for a Nationalist – though it followed moves by leading Catholic intellectuals, like educationalist J.J. Campbell, solicitor Brian McGuigan and charity administrator G.B. Newe, to urge their co-religionists to play their full part in the disputed state – and it was very much in sympathy with the newly-formed National Unity group's attempts to promote a much more professional and organised nationalist party. Gormley, too, was a 'participator' and Viney quoted his story that after he had stood for the loyal toast at a dinner, a condescending Unionist told him he had won a bet from Brian Faulkner, who thought he would not rise. 'Tell Mr Faulkner,' said Gormley, 'that I do have manners.' (Later, Viney noted that when he and Gormley were in a bar in the Creggan estate – which then had forty-eight Protestant families as well as 1,800 Catholic – two Catholics walked in, one with a blazer of the Royal Army Medical Corps, and the other a former British soldier. A few years later, they would have been risking an IRA death sentence.)

It was Viney's praise for Hume's film and his influence in getting Irish TV (RTE) to show it, that won an important commission for the young schoolteacher. The *Irish Times* asked him, on the strength of Viney's investigations indicating a sea change in Catholic political attitudes, to write an article – which had to be split and run on two consecutive days – on 'The Northern Catholic'. It was probably the most thoughtful and analytical study of the changing needs and obligations of the Catholic population in the 1960s which had yet been committed to print and, coming from such a rising star in the

Derry Catholic community, with impeccable working-class credentials, it had an influence far and wide.

The articles in the *Irish Times* in May 1964 provided the first evidence of Hume's knack of articulating the feelings of ordinary Catholics before they had even been recognised by the politicians, and proposing unique solutions based on reason and fair play. If he was critical of the Unionists for their neglect, he also castigated the Nationalists for sulking in their tents and failing to give positive leadership.

He wrote from the point of view of younger Catholics, for whom the crux of the Northern question was the continued existence of the great social problems of housing, unemployment and emigration. 'It is the struggle for priority in their minds between such problems and the ideal of a united Ireland with which they have been bred that has produced the frustration and the large number of political wanderers that Michael Viney met on his tour. It may be that the present generation of younger Catholics in the North are more materialistic than their fathers, but there is little doubt that their thinking is principally geared towards the solution of social and economic problems. This has led to a deep questioning of traditional nationalist attitudes.'

After admitting that the Unionist Government was mainly responsible for the situation, Hume launched into a blistering attack on the Nationalist Party, which bore a share of the blame. 'Weak opposition leads to corrupt government. Nationalists in opposition have been in no way constructive. They have – quite rightly – been loud in their demands for rights, but they have remained silent and inactive about their duties. In 40 years of opposition they have not produced one constructive contribution on either the social or economic plane to the development of Northern Ireland. . . leadership has been the comfortable leadership of flags and slogans. Easy no doubt, but irresponsible. There has been no attempt to be positive, to encourage the Catholic community to develop the resources which they have in plenty, to make a positive contribution in terms of community service. . . Unemployment and emigration, chiefly of Catholics, remain heavy, much of it no doubt due to the skilful placing of industry by the Northern Government. But the only constructive suggestion from the nationalist side would appear to be that a removal of discrimination will be the panacea for all our ills. It is this lack of positive contribution and the apparent lack of interest in the general welfare of Northern Ireland that has led many Protestants to believe that the Northern Catholic is politically irresponsible and therefore unfit to rule.'

Bigotry and a fixation about religious divisions were the first things to strike a visitor to the North, he wrote, and the nationalist line of the past forty years had contributed to this. 'Catholics of all shades of political thought are expected to band together under the unconstructive banner of nationalism. This dangerous equation of nationalism and Catholicism has amply contributed to the postponement of the emergence of normal politics in the area and has made the task of the Unionist ascendancy simpler. Worse, it has poisoned the Catholic social climate to the extent that it has become extremely difficult for the Catholic to express publicly any point of view which does not coincide with the narrow nationalist line. Disagreement with, or criticism of, the nationalist approach – or lack of it – inevitably brings down upon one's head a torrent of abuse. "Obsequious", "Crawling", "Castle Catholic", "West Briton", are samples of the terms used.'

The result, he declared, had been that many Catholics were unwilling to speak their minds for fear of recrimination. The nationalist Press were the chief perpetrators – 'witness the bitterness of their attacks on people like Messrs Campbell, McGuigan and Newe'. Apart from the censorship on the unionist side, it was clear how little freedom of thought or expression existed in Northern Ireland, and how tremendous were the obstacles in the way of the emergence of a third force in politics, between unionism and nationalism. Such a concept, suggesting a moderate, non-tribal party, was years ahead of its time, and was not realised until the formation of the Alliance Party in 1970, by which time Hume was committed to the establishment of a social democratic party.

'One of the greatest contributions, therefore, that the Catholic in Northern Ireland can make to a liberalising of the political atmosphere would be the removal of the equation between nationalist and Catholic. Apart from being factual, it ought also to be made fashionable that the Catholic Church does not impose upon its members any one form of political belief. There is nothing inconsistent with such acceptance and a belief that a 32-county republic is best for Ireland. In fact, if we are to pursue a policy of non-recognition, the only logical policy is that of Sinn Fein. If one wishes to create a united Ireland by constitutional means, then one must accept the constitutional position.' This was a major break with the past, which he thought would remove 'a great stumbling block to the development of normal politics'. Catholics could then throw themselves fully into the solution of Northern problems without fear of recrimination.

'Such an attitude, too, admits the realistic fact that a united Ireland, if it is to come, and if violence rightly is to be discounted, must come about by evolution, i.e. by the will of the Northern majority. It is clear that this is the only way in which a truly united Ireland, with the Northern Protestant integrated, can be achieved. Who can conceive a prosperous North, attached to either London or Dublin, without the Northern Protestants? If the whole Northern community gets seriously to work on its problems; the Unionist bogeys about Catholics and a Republic will, through better understanding, disappear. It will, of course, take a long time.'

The importance of Hume's contribution was that it was the first time that the principle of unity by consent had been articulated so strongly. The standard nationalist argument for fifty years had been that the obstacle to unity was Britain, which had only to abolish the border to wipe out unionist objections. Here was someone from a nationalist background saying that territorial unity was not at issue – Ireland was united but its people were divided by more than a line on the map. Logically, they had to be brought together before political unity was worth having. Turning to party politics, he commented that the need for 'a complete revitalisation' of the Nationalist Party had long been felt. The head-without-a-body type of party which existed was bound to lead to political immaturity among Catholics. 'The necessity for a fully organised democratic party which can freely attract and draw upon the talents of the nationally-minded community is obvious. It is to be hoped that the new Nationalist Political Front will create such an organisation. . .'

The need for action on a non-political front was probably greater, he wrote. Most people felt that little could really be achieved politically in the existing stalemate. But there existed a greater wealth of talent than ever before, with a growing desire to get together and tackle community problems. Such community activity could do nothing but create mutual respect, build up the country and water down the deep prejudice which was at the root of discrimination.

'Few people in Northern Ireland seriously deny the existence of

45

blatant discrimination. It is at its point of origin, prejudice, that discrimination should be tackled. Many Protestants firmly believe that the Catholic is a social inferior. There also exists among them a real fear of Rome rule. Without discussing the obvious irrationality of this prejudice, the very fact that it exists and produces discrimination on a widespread scale places a duty on all Catholics to do all in their power to remove it and so to remove the disabilities under which their fellow Catholics suffer as a result. . . People who discriminate through prejudice believe that they are justified. Catholics can contribute to a lessening of prejudice by playing a fuller part in public life, as some of our religious leaders have been urging. Undoubtedly in the beginning they will be neither wanted nor welcome in many spheres of public life in Northern Ireland. But public life means more than service on statutory or local government committees. It means the encouragement and participation in community enterprises designed to develop the resources of the community and done in conjunction with all those in the community who are willing to co-operate.'

He ended with a warning to the Unionist Party of their obligations, if they were serious about their concern for the future of Northern Ireland. 'To date none of their leaders has shown any response to repeated statements of Catholic willingness to get together. Unionists must realise that if they turn their backs on the present goodwill there can only be a considerable hardening of Catholic opinion, only this time it will be supplemented by liberal Protestants who have lost faith with Glengall Street.

'If they are to accept the olive branch there are certain points which they must clarify. Firstly that discrimination, whether religious or political, is unjust and must be removed and the blatant plan in operation in the North must cease. As proof of this, public invitations should be issued to Catholics to accept membership of statutory bodies where they are unrepresented or under-represented already. Secondly they must accept that nationalism in Ireland is an acceptable political belief and that nationally-minded people are entitled to put forward their views constitutionally without prejudice to the right to any position which they might seek. Thirdly they should realise that the vast majority of Catholics in Northern Ireland are responsible people, anxious for an improvement in community relations and for the future of the Northern Ireland in which they live and rear their children. It is only perhaps when many of the above suggestions are in operation throughout the Northern community that religion will begin to make its exit from politics and that socially it will no longer be necessary to forewarn about the presence of those who "dig with the other foot". In the waiting, the fear is that frustration may force one to leave the North. It is little wonder that many do.'

Not surprisingly, the articles caused a considerable stir in the nationalist community, some dismissing his arguments as a 'sell-out', in the way he had forecast, while others readily accepted the need for greater participation, to give them the right to demand fair play. Basically, it was an optimistic Christian message, calling for a rendering unto Caesar, in the expectation that there would be a generous response from the Unionists. But he was quite aware of the penalties of failure. If peace gestures were made and rebuffed, the situation would be worse than before, showing that moderate opposition to Unionism was doomed. Hume was giving Stormont the benefit of the doubt, in the hope that it could see the danger, and would move.

After Captain O'Neill's historic meeting with the Irish Taoiseach, Sean Lemass, at Stormont the following January, 1965, progress along the lines Hume was urging seemed possible. But although the Nationalist Party was goaded into accepting the official role of Her Majesty's Opposition and the violent republican movement was at its lowest ebb, the extremists soon reasserted themselves. Captain O'Neill had promised salaries for the Opposition leadership – then, like all MPs, on £1,400 a year – but found hardliners in his Government unyielding, and nothing happened. Neither could the newly-organised alternative to the Nationalists – the National Democratic Party – deliver votes. The expectations that had been founded on the hope of gradual movement and reasoned response were unfulfilled, and the extra-parliamentary agitation that began in Belfast in 1966, with the fiftieth anniversary celebrations of Dublin's Easter Rising, grew year by year.

Hume could see what was happening, if others could not, and one of his first public speaking engagements was a lecture in October 1965 to Queen's University's New Ireland Society, a refuge for concerned Catholic undergraduates, disillusioned with old-style nationalist politics. 'The West's Asleep' was his critique of a planning report by Sir Robert Matthew, and he accused the Government of a new 'plantation of Ulster', mirroring the first one in the early seventeeth century, with a depopulation of the west and development of a 'second city' in Protestant north Armagh, named after Lord Craigavon, the first Ulster premier and coiner of the infamous description of Stormont: 'a Protestant Parliament for a Protestant people'.

Although politics was looming ever larger in Hume's life, he still fought shy of direct involvement and his main preoccupation was the practical concerns of his fellow citizens. The Credit Union had partly relieved the crushing burden of hire-purchase debt, but the problems created by the perennial housing shortage remained. Living conditions in the worst parts of the Bogside, where several of Hume's relations still lived, were nineteenth-century standard, recalling the not-so-distant days when tuberculosis was a scourge. When Hume's parents were young it had killed half the young people who had died and, because of the risk, kissing and touching had been taboo. Despite, or perhaps because of the overcrowding and the male unemployment which made women the breadwinners, Derry continued to top the Northern European league for births – compounding the problem. In 1964 the birthrate was 31.8 per 1,000 of the population (above that of Italy), with four out of five children born to Catholics. The 1961 census showed a population increase of 21.2 per 1,000, nearly twice the Northern Ireland average.

Any local authority would have had difficulty meeting the housing demand, largely from the Catholic community, but Derry's Unionist corporation hardly even tried. It knew that its electoral majority had to be preserved and that meant containing the nationalist population in one ward of the city; meanwhile the surrounding rural council – also Unionist – refused to jeopardise its majority by allowing a boundary extension. The only solution was to build upwards, in multistorey flats, and the first and only experiment, the Rossville Flats, ironically turned out to be the headquarters of the August 1969 rioters, who helped eventually to bring Stormont down. There was one other attempt at a high-rise development, but the Nationalist members of the corporation, who felt obliged to support it in order to provide some housing for their people, ran up against the formidable Paddy Doherty, who had built his house directly opposite the site in Westland Street. Appealing craftily to the Protestants to respect the hard work and dedication he had put into it, he won his case, averting another disaster.

While the loss of a university or a railway line caused psychological damage, the lack of public rented housing for Catholics was a major physical disability, contributing to ill health and emigration. Something had to be done, leaders of the community decided, and since the corporation insisted that any development be confined to the South ward, with its 10,000-plus Catholic majority, leaving untouched the North and Waterside wards with Protestant majorities of 1,000 and 2,000, the people would have to do it themselves. Protests in Stormont had no effect, as even 'liberals' like Captain O'Neill regarded Derry as a symbol to be preserved at all costs, so self help was the only answer. The Credit Union had provided a new sense of confidence and it was a logical development to branch out into a self-help housing association, to fill the gap which the corporation had left. The Government-financed Housing Trust had built the windswept Creggan estate, a grey, concrete-block monument to 1950s planning, filling in where the corporation had opted out, but it was not geared to the small-scale development and conversion work that was also necessary. That was a job for a local housing association – a concept lately imported from Britain – and Father Anthony Mulvey, who was the driving force, made sure to get John Hume as chairman from its outset in 1965.

Mulvey, who was also behind the Credit Union development, had completed much of the groundwork and there was a useful meeting with Father Eamonn Casey – later Bishop Casey of Galway – who had started a housing association in London. There were also consultations with the McCluskeys of Dungannon, a doctor and his wife who had been making a name for themselves in the early 1960s, drawing up the first factual data on local-government discrimination in jobs and houses. Their highly professional pamphlets marked the first shots in the civil rights campaign, alerting Labour MPs at Westminster to injustices and challenging the bland assertions by Prime Minister Sir Alec Douglas Home that Northern Ireland citizens could pursue their charges of discrimination through the courts. (A Catholic Queen's Counsel offered his services free but proved unsuccessful.) When building houses was mentioned, doubts were expressed about the sixty-year commitment to pay back the loans, but Con McCluskey's advice was 'Build them! They won't tear them down.'

The first task was to identify the need, and two nights a week Hume and the others would listen to those who had housing problems pouring out their tales of woe. As a result of their research, of a kind that had never been done before, they discovered three types of problem, requiring three solutions, and laid the basis for all future approaches to the subject. Firstly, there was the person who could never own his own home and needed publicly-owned rented accommodation. Secondly, there was the person who could well buy his own home, but had no idea how to go about putting down a deposit and getting a mortgage. Typical was a breadserver, with £500 in savings, who simply thought that people like him could not own houses. Thirdly, there was the young couple who could be saving up for a house before there were children, but paying an exorbitant rent for a flat and becoming the social problems of the future. For them a novel halfway-house scheme was devised, by which the housing association would borrow from a building society, buy a big house, convert it into flats and charge double the economic rent. At the end of two years, the couple got back half the rent they had paid as a deposit on a new house, and arranged a loan from the building society. It was a small enough beginning, by a seven-member association, but in the first year it housed 100 families.

As a recognised housing association, the organisation had virtually the same rights as a council in terms of government grants and borrowing powers, so it relished doing what the corporation should have been doing but wasn't. In a sample scheme, it built twenty-seven houses on a green-field site on Buncrana Road and named the development 'Farren Park', after the Roman Catholic bishop, to emphasise its independence. In that same year, 1967, Derry Corporation created an unenviable record, in a city with 10 per cent registered homeless, by failing to build a single house itself.

Fired by the Farren Park success, the housing association decided, in Hume's words, 'to go for the big one'. The BSR record-player turntable factory had tragically closed, with the loss of 2,000 jobs, and its owner, Dr Daniel McDonald had fifty acres in Duncreggan Road which he was willing to sell, provided planning permission was granted. An elaborate plan was drawn up for a 700-house estate complete with ornamental lake, but it was turned down on planning grounds, because the site was zoned for industrial use. Even the Nationalist members of the corporation were hostile, seeing a better alternative in a long-term area plan and a 'new town' development at Shantallow, north of the city.

The association appealed the ruling, and Hume was its spokesman at a two-day hearing in Derry Guildhall. But although he was able to produce nearly 150 pages of documentation of Derry's housing crisis from two years of interviewing by the association, the appeal was rejected – and the industrial site remains undeveloped. It was a serious psychological blow for Hume, who had firmly believed that if one went rigorously by the book, and presented all the facts and figures, justice rather than politics would triumph. That was in the spring of 1968, and it was to provide much of the motivation for the protests that were to follow on the streets.

5
Politics and fish

The dissatisfaction with conventional Nationalist politics which Hume had expressed in his *Irish Times* article was not confined to Derry, and he soon found he had pushed at an open door. An IRA campaign of violence from 1959 to 1962 gradually petered out for lack of Catholic support, and the alternative negativism of Eddie McAteer's Nationalist Party offered little hope of progress. Middle-class Catholics had begun as far back as the late 1950s to press for a more positive approach, and a National Unity movement – formed in 1959 to urge reform on the Nationalist Party – was the forerunner of individual attempts to engage Unionists in dialogue. The most significant of these attempts was the Dungannon-based Campaign for Social Justice, started in 1963 by Dr Con McCluskey and his social-worker wife, as a means of highlighting the discrimination which Nationalist politicians constantly harped upon, but never found time to document.

Against considerable Catholic opposition – from Nationalists fearing a threat, and from Republicans disdaining any dealings with the British establishment – the McCluskeys and their nominal committee of professional people amassed a catalogue of damning evidence on housing allocation and employment patterns in rural Ulster, which they proceeded to shower on Westminster MPs. In Dungannon, for instance, Mrs McCluskey found two estates of ninety-five and ninety-eight houses where all the families were Protestant and another of 187 houses where there were 184 Catholics. Allocations were carved out according to religion, rather than need, and when Mrs McCluskey arranged for thirty-three families to squat in new houses, their case was so strong no attempt was made to move them. Local government votes went only to householders, in which group Catholics were under-represented, so there was every incentive for Unionist councils to maintain their grip on allocations.

Despite having to finance their pamphleteering out of their own pockets, the McCluskeys were showing the dividends that could be obtained, mostly among sympathetic Labour MPs at Westminster, by a professional campaign based on facts, rather than aspirations, and Hume's articles were perfectly timed. Eddie McAteer's jibes about preferring no job, rather than a job with the British, rang hollow, after the failure of the latest campaign of violence, and in the light of the new era ushered in by Terence O'Neill's premiership, rapidly followed by Harold Wilson's accession at Westminster. But the Unionists were oblivious to any threat and happily used their twelve votes at Westminster to accentuate the Labour Prime Minister's difficulties with his overall majority of four in the 1964 parliament. It was to prove a costly misjudgment, for by voting on issues that did not apply to Northern Ireland, they called attention to the convention that Westminster could not debate matters reserved to Stormont.

Frustration with this state of affairs – a hangover from the 1920 partition – and the inspiration of the CSJ pamphlets led to the formation in late 1964 of the Campaign for Democracy in Ulster, a pressure group of Labour backbenchers who kept up a constant barrage on Ulster issues, up to and during the civil rights campaign of 1968 and 1969. They got no encouragement, even from their own government, but their British airing of Catholic grievances, especially after the arrival at Westminster of Gerry Fitt, elected Republican Labour MP for West Belfast in 1966, was crucial. They gave Hume his first public platform in Britain at Fulham town hall in July 1965 when he accused the Stormont government of developing the east of the province to cause migration from the west and scatter the minority in order to bolster Unionist strength.

A few months after the McCluskeys launched their campaign, a National Political Front was formed after a meeting in Maghery, Co. Armagh, to co-ordinate reform of the Nationalist Party, which had only now reached the stage where it was ready to hold an annual conference. But reform was impossible, since the Nationalists were trapped by their contradictory mandate – calling for a united Ireland while demanding fair play in Northern Ireland's political institutions – and the result was the formation of the National Democratic Party, an attempt to provide a democratic and co-operative alternative. It should have been a natural home for Hume, but a decision had been made by the NDP not to organise in constituencies held by Nationalists, and when Captain O'Neill called his surprise election in March 1965 – hard on the heels of his historic meeting with the

Taoiseach, Sean Lemass – an ad hoc caucus of Derry businessmen and Credit Union activists approached Hume to stand against McAteer.

It was a bold move, for not only was McAteer a respected, avuncular and well-liked Nationalist politician, with a thriving accountancy business in the city, but he had the backing of the local Catholic establishment, including city councillors, businessmen and churchmen. The church connection was important, for the usual process for selecting candidates in nationalist constituencies was that the local clergy called a convention, with every Catholic organisation qualifying for two delegates. The system of keeping the register of Catholic voters up to date – to help gather all possible votes – depended on a collection in the Catholic churches. In Derry, the Catholic Registration Office employed two people to plot where every Protestant and Catholic lived in the city, in red and green ink, while in country areas one volunteer would have this responsibility. Paddy Doherty and others knew that the Nationalist Party's grip on the city and on Catholic politics generally had to be broken, if there was to be any hope of challenging Unionist ascendancy, and Hume was the obvious candidate of the reformers. A meeting was called in Doherty's house, starting at 7 pm, and for nine hours the issues were fought out, with Hume on the defensive. To contest the seat, he would have had to quit his teaching post – teachers were still debarred at Stormont – and all the hidden insecurity of the Bogside boy rose to the surface. He had to be much more certain of winning before risking his future in politics, and for a twenty-eight-year-old novice to take on an established party leader was too big a gamble. It was a trait that was to reappear, throughout his career, to the frustration of those who looked to him for radical leadership.

At 3 am one of his backers, Dr Jim Cosgrove – a future chairman of the SDLP – left in disgust. 'John,' he said, 'I thought you had guts. You're not the man I thought you were.' He and Michael Canavan, both associates in the Credit Union, had constantly urged Hume to enter political life, but met with dogged resistance. Hume could not see himself in any of the existing parties, and stood aloof, though ever since he has regarded both Derry men as his political mentors, to be consulted over major decisions. Paddy Doherty would have run himself against McAteer, but would not have stood a chance; everyone knew it was Hume or nothing.

Inside the Nationalist Party itself, McAteer was beginning to tire of the thankless task of leading a political movement which in forty-five years had succeeded in getting one item of legislation passed – the Wild Birds Act of 1931. Hume had his backers among Nationalists, although he was not a member, and at home, his father gave him no encouragement. 'Not this time,' he advised from his chair in the kitchen. 'It's only sectarian. You'll never get anywhere with that.'

Hume did not opt out of the election completely, for he threw his weight behind one of the few Protestant liberals in Derry, business-man Claude Wilton – later to become an SDLP senator at Stormont – who was contesting the solidly Unionist City constituency against a barrister, Teddy Jones, a future judge. Wilton was unsuccessful, but it was a first taste of electioneering, and of personation. Vote-stealing was, and is, all part of the Ulster election game, with each of the sectarian candidates supplementing their valid poll with votes claimed in the name of those (including the dead and emigrants) who had not already voted. Everyone did it, so the advantage was effectively cancelled out. The most honourable thing for a candidate who wanted to stay untainted was to leave such matters to those who knew them best, and look the other way.

It was the last election in which the Nationalist Party was un-challenged – except by Labour – for the leadership of the Catholic people, and even those who backed the socialist candidates had qualms of conscience. One of the workers for Stephen McGonagle, who took on McAteer in Foyle, confessed later than when he went to the polling station he reneged. 'I couldn't vote against the flag,' he said. The Nationalists had thirteen MPs elected in Northern Ireland as a whole, on the strength of the more hopeful climate encouraged by the North–South summit meetings. Change was on the way, although the NDP had only one mediocre candidate elected, and Hume was tempted to involve himself to find out how serious the Nationalist Party was about reform. Representing traditional, con-servative Catholics, it was a mirror image of the Unionist Party and, apart from its base in Derry, was mainly a grouping of small farmers and businessmen. Hume attended a few party meetings, without fully committing himself to membership, and eventually decided that it was incapable of the reform of organisation and policy which he thought was essential. He left, and the mantle which McAteer might well have decided to put on his shoulders remained where it was. The party continued to languish, despite efforts by the brightest and youngest MP, Austin Currie, of Dungannon, to improve its image. Captain O'Neill made encouraging noises, but nothing more, and the Nationalists were becoming vulnerable to pressure from the NDP – which compensated for poor Stormont results with a better performance at council level – and from various brands of socialism.

The first party, in fact, to invite Hume to fight a seat was the NDP, flexing its muscles in the 1966 Westminster election. It was almost a tradition in Catholic politics that Nationalists fought the Stormont seats, leaving the Republicans to contest Westminster elections on an abstentionist ticket. That gentleman's agreement was out of tune with the new thinking, and after a long and amicable meeting in a north Belfast flat between Hume and some leading NDP men, including John Duffy, a New Ireland Society activist at Queen's University, Hume was asked to contest Mid-Ulster. There was little difference between their political ideals, aimed at justice within Northern Ireland rather than instant Irish unity, but the NDP men were not greatly surprised by his refusal. Hume was going for an important role in a mass movement and the NDP, overloaded as it was by teachers and intellectuals, did not have the makings of a winning combination.

At St Columb's Hume was doing his best to combine his teaching with his various extramural activities, with more and more difficulty. At night, he might be speaking at a Credit Union meeting in Galway, just getting back in time for a few hours' sleep before classes began. Phone calls on business were causing some ill-concealed annoyance and he was refused time off. But he was still obtaining results from his classes by his old method of getting the pupils to research the work by themselves, rather than listening to him, and callers became used to finding St Columb's boys at his home consulting him about projects. (At this stage he was beginning to feel the strain of his punishing schedule and attended a neurologist for weakness in his hands, diagnosed as the result of too many hours at his books, leaning on his elbows.)

The Credit Union was helping with Derry's financial problems and the Housing Association had begun to tackle the dreadful living conditions, but there was still the perpetual scourge of unemployment, which had been made infinitely worse by the closure of the BSR record turntable factory. It had provided the jobs for men that were so badly needed in a city renowned for the way its women went out to work, mostly in shirt factories, while its men stayed at home and looked after ever-growing families. In face of this devastating shutdown, and Stormont's continuing neglect, Hume and Canavan felt they had to do something to prove that the self-help principle could provide jobs too. They came up with two approaches, the first of which was to set up their own Derry development organisation – long before any town in Northern Ireland had hit on the idea – independent of government. Hume drew up a prospectus, setting out the advantages of Derry, and business directories were pored through to find companies with Irish names, both in America and Britain, that might be persuaded to come and take a look.

It was an ambitious plan, the forerunner of many such local-government ventures in years to come, but the results were hardly promising. Out of thirty or forty companies contacted, only two actually turned up in Derry, including a tyre company which said it had been told nothing of Derry by the Government but had been advised to go to a place called Craigavon. Goodyear did set up their plant in the new Co. Armagh city, providing the nucleus for its development. But the factory never became profitable, in fifteen years of trading, and finally closed in 1983, with only 800 of its 2,500 jobs left.

The second idea of Hume and Canavan was to set up a business of their own, without anyone's assistance. Funds from the Credit Union would have helped, but as its money could be invested only in bank deposits or savings certificates, not risk businesses, Canavan had to raise the finance himself. In the search for a new product, Canavan discovered that the River Foyle, which flowed through Derry, was one of the biggest salmon fisheries in Europe, with fish being boxed in ice and exported to the Continent. He knew there was a highly-priced delicacy, smoked salmon, which neither he nor Hume had ever tasted. They thought the smoking could not be such a complicated process and started to research the subject in libraries and encyclopaedias. It turned out to be an ideal industry for their purposes, based on locally-bought fish, adding a high value and needing little enough capital outlay. They even had a factory available, since Canavan had already taken out a twenty-one year lease on an old bakery near the city centre, on the grounds that he was sure to think of some use for it. All they had to do was pull the ovens out and replace them with the machines for smoking. They then bought two salmon to experiment upon. But after gutting them inexpertly, they had no means of smoking them – so they ate them.

John had to give St Columb's three months' notice, to quit his job in April and just before he took up his new post as managing director of Atlantic Harvest Ltd there was a Credit Union conference in America to attend. Thereafter the new world of salmon absorbed his energies and he had to learn everything about the business, from buying to smoking and marketing. At the start, neither the owner nor the managing director even knew what a whole smoked salmon looked like, and when they told buyers that the tradition was handed down from father to son, they carefully omitted to mention that the father was not theirs.

But the skills soon came and Hume developed strong contacts with fishermen throughout the north west, which have stood him in good stead. They now had a local buyer, who was creating local employment and was out to increase the market. Even the Unionist MP for Derry at Westminster, Robin Chichester-Clark – a cousin of O'Neill – played his part, picking up a hint at a banquet where there was smoked salmon on the menu that the ships' chandlers to Cunard would be interested in an Irish supplier. As soon as Canavan was told, Hume set off hot foot, with sides of smoked salmon in his luggage. After hitching a lorry ride to Southampton he clinched a contract for the lucrative cruise ship market which virtually guaranteed the future of the Derry operation. The staff of two doubled inside a year, a van was acquired and soon they were producing half a ton of salmon a week.

For Hume, who had decided not to remain in a job longer than four years, it provided an opportunity to make the transition between teaching and politics. When business was slack, observers noticed that the manager would tramp the streets, sounding out opinion like a politician-to-be. His desire to communicate has been an enduring trait, whether it is with loyalists or republicans and he has a respect for others' opinions – even those of enemies – which is rare.

The business carried on after his departure to full-time politics in 1969 but eventually Canavan asked a Derry man, who had been supplying Jewish food shops in London, to take it over. It has since moved to new premises in Pennyburn and still provides an object lesson in self help. The partnership between the sharp, business-minded bookmaker – who had been trained in a bank – and the politically-ambitious intellectual was unlikely but crucial to Hume's career. Canavan had spotted his leadership potential in the Credit Union and recognised that if there was anyone capable of lifting

58

Derry's Catholics out of the slough of political despond it was Hume. He offered his backing, at a time when it was most needed, and although they were to disagree on tactics at a later stage – with Canavan reverting to a more traditional nationalist position – they were a powerful political combination in the run-up to the civil rights period.

Meanwhile Hume was coming to be recognised as a major force in nationalist politics, although he still had no party attachments and rarely made political statements. When the Northern Ireland Civil Rights Association was set up in February 1967 he was asked to join, but again he declined. Their initial goals were very much in line with his own – to defend basic freedom, to protect the rights of the individual, to highlight all possible abuses of power and to inform the public of their lawful rights. But although he attended an early meeting in Belfast, he held back. He sensed, unlike others, that the association was not as responsible as it seemed. Although its first fourteen-member council contained members of seven political parties – including a Unionist, as well as Con McCluskey – it had its origins in the Wolfe Tone Society, a left-wing republican front organisation. By the late 1960s most of its cross-community support had vanished, and McCluskey resigned in 1969 in protest against an extremist takeover.

But Hume was fully aware, through his Credit Union and Housing Association contacts, of the head of steam building up in the Catholic community, as the Unionist government resisted all protests against discrimination in local government and continued to isolate the mainly Catholic west of the province. Austin Currie started the ball rolling and attracted vital British media attention with his occupation in April 1968 of a house in Caledon, Co. Armagh, which was allocated to a single secretary of a Unionist solicitor, rather than to a homeless Catholic family. He was evicted, of course, and the Protestant installed, but the age of the public demonstration aimed at pressurising governments had been launched in Northern Ireland, after its successes in America and Europe. In Derry the normally staid Northern Ireland Labour Party was dominated by left-wing activists, led by lately-expelled Queen's University undergraduate Eamonn McCann, and its reaction to the housing scandal was to stage a sit-down on Craigavon Bridge, when the Ulster Governor came to open a new section. From there, it was a short step to the first civil rights march in August from Coalisland to

Dungannon – the ancestral home of Unionist housing discrimination – and student involvement, copied from France and Germany, was noticed for the first time. The marriage between the old political hands like Gerry Fitt, who could hardly believe that his message was at last getting through, and the young radicals was almost complete. But it needed a confrontation between the political underdogs and the authorities, in Derry, to seal it. October 5 was the date.

6
Civil Rights

Early in 1968, the Northern Ireland Civil Rights Association (NICRA) held a press conference in London, giving notice that this was to be a year of action. No one paid much attention, although there was an increasing awareness of a smell emanating from the northern part of Ireland, with Gerry Fitt stirring the pot and newspapers and television wakening to the mediaeval phenomenon of the Rev. Ian Paisley. The *Sunday Times* was the first in the field, with a feature on 'John Bull's Political Slum' and memories were jolted in the BBC of Alan Whicker's critical features for *Tonight* in 1959, aborted after protests from the Stormont Government. Only one of these reports was shown, giving too much prominence to sectarian graffiti and seedy betting shops for the Unionists' liking.

The build-up to the civil rights explosion in Derry on October 5 began months before, with a calculated campaign by a group of frustrated young socialists, led by the firebrand Eamonn McCann. While Hume always played according to the constitutional rules, McCann knew no such inhibitions. Just as the Derry Housing Association appeal was lost, traumatically affecting Hume, McCann was in the process of forming his own Derry Housing Action Committee, with the object of highlighting the problem of the homeless by creating havoc, as publicly as possible.

Committee members began by invading the public gallery during the monthly meetings of the Corporation at the Guildhall, reducing them to chaos. When the protesters moved outside, blocking a main road with the mobile home of a family of four to call attention to their housing need, they finally got the result they wanted – a home for the family and summonses for obstruction. It was straight confrontation, aimed first at embarrassing the authorities and then forcing them to over-react, alienating public opinion. Critics on the Catholic side who had regarded the committee as 'communists' gradually swung behind them, and their publicity-seeking antics appealed to the Derry sense of humour, as well as to the city's simmering discontent. By this time, Austin Currie had staged his sit-in at Caledon, and the whole civil rights scene had been infected by the TV images in 1968 of direct action, whether in France, Germany or America. NICRA followed up with its own six-mile 'freedom march' from Coalisland to Dungannon on 24 August – protesting mainly about housing allocations, not political issues – and suddenly there was the makings of a mass movement.

There was no NICRA branch in Derry, largely because of a reluctance by Catholic leaders to compete with the politicians in what they regarded as left-wing political agitation. As far back as the mid-1960s an attempt had been made, after a meeting called in Derry by the National Council for Civil Liberties, to set up an organisation to work for a change in the constitution, but Hume and others felt this was a job for politicians, not a conglomerate group. Eventually NICRA took over and although two members travelled to Derry to ask Hume and James Doherty to form an independent organisation, they met with a cool response. The Derry men had heard warnings, from within NICRA itself, of its extreme left-wing bias and they decided to have nothing to do with it. Thus McCann had the field to himself, and was able to choose for the first NICRA march in Derry a route of the maximum provocation – through the Protestant walls, into the 'forbidden' city centre – unknown to the Belfast group. He also made sure, through pre-march publicity, that the demonstration was to have a decidedly socialist flavour, to emphasise the challenge to the nationalist, as well as the unionist establishment. Respectable Catholics looked askance at a coat-trailing exercise and it was not until the Protestant Apprentice Boys gave notice of a counter-demonstration, prompting the anticipated Government ban on all marches, that McCann's protest gathered support. Even so, it only went ahead against the opposition of the NICRA leadership, when the local organisers said they would not be deterred, and in the end only 400, instead of the expected 5,000, turned up.

Hume was in a difficult position, as someone who largely sympathised with the protest, yet was wary of associating himself and the non-sectarian Credit Union organisation, of which he was all-Ireland president, with a potentially explosive march. Michael Canavan, his partner, had long predicted that 1968 would be a critical year in Derry's history and earlier had persuaded Hume not to undertake a long Credit Union trip to Australia, via the United States, in case the lid blew off when he was away. But the Government ban, by the hated Home Affairs Minister Bill Craig, united all shades of nationalism and socialism behind the march and Hume was among the crowd, an ordinary citizen, as it gathered in Duke Street for the march across Craigavon Bridge to the city centre.

Although he had earlier expressed opposition, because of the divisive nature of the demonstration, he supported the right to march, and resented the oppressive presence of so many police, brought in to enforce the ban. In accordance with strict NICRA rules, no Irish Tricolours were flown to identify it as a nationalist parade, but that was clearly how the authorities viewed it, regardless of the motley political representation at its head. (With an eye to the publicity value, Gerry Fitt had brought over MPs from the Labour Party conference, which was in session, to sense the political reawakening.) A line of police blocked the way forward, and after five minutes of speeches, which Lord Cameron's subsequent inquiry said gave 'encouragement to the use of violence to break the police barrier', the police moved in to disperse the crowd. But when Hume tried to escape, like the rest, he found himself trapped by another line of police to the rear.

The next few minutes changed the course of Irish history, with police batoning people from all sides, first 'without justification or excuse', according to Cameron, and then in response to stones being thrown and placards launched in their direction by a Belfast socialist group. All hell was let loose and Hume saw hate, which he was never to forget, in the policemen's faces. He found an escape route up steps at the foot of Duke Street, but others were not so lucky. One of these was Paddy Douglas, a Tyrone businessman, who stopped to plead with a baton-wielding policeman, only to be poked savagely in the stomach. Nearby, a scowling police inspector broke into a run, to strike down a fleeing marcher, then turned to adjust his cap.

These were two fleeting images, captured by an RTE cameraman, the late Gay O'Brien, who alone stayed with the action – oblivious of the dangers – and was rewarded by a few hundred feet of film which speeded the demise of devolved government for Northern Ireland. Along with shots of Gerry Fitt's head wound, from a police baton, and water cannon on the streets of a British city, these pictures went round the world to testify to the suppression of free speech, in what was thought to be a liberal democracy. The Humes were late for a concert that night in the Guildhall, because John had arrived home soaked by water jets; and Pat sensed that their lives had changed. As John put it later, a bonfire of resentment had been built for years, and the batons were the spark.

In the aftermath, the atmosphere in Derry was electric and found its expression in the first of the Bogside riots into the early morning. The police were praised by Craig, the march leaders charged with law-breaking, and by Tuesday plans were laid for a repeat of the march the following Saturday. This time, many more people, who had been outraged by what had happened, wanted to be involved, and Hume was one of 150 invited to a public meeting in the City Hotel on Wednesday, which effectively wrested control from the original organisers.

McCann could see the way the wind was blowing and, after restating his socialist principles, refused a place in the sixteen-strong committee that was elected. It was, he said, 'middle-class, middle-aged and middle of the road', even though Michael Canavan insisted on the name 'Citizens' Action Committee' to place the emphasis on demonstrations rather than talk. Hume recognised the advantage of a broad-based, cross-community committee like his own University for Derry organisation and he readily accepted the vice-chairmanship, with a Protestant, shirt factory manager Ivan Cooper, as chairman. Unusually, Cooper had a history with the Unionist Party before joining Labour and his instinctive soapbox oratory was a perfect balance for the calming influence of Hume. Canavan was secretary, with James Doherty as treasurer and a Protestant store-owner, Campbell Austin, as press officer. The mixture was as varied as Hume wanted it.

The first business was to cancel the Saturday march, while feelings were running too high. Then, with his schoolteacher's gift for preparation and inspiration, Hume devised a plan of action over the next six weeks that would gradually take the people with him, educating them in the difficult discipline of non-violence and thus exerting an irresistible moral pressure on the authorities. Everything else had failed, against Unionist intransigence, but Hume saw that here was a new weapon, which had reaped amazing dividends wherever it had been used, from Gandhi's India to Martin Luther King's American South. It was highly dangerous, too, to take thousands onto the streets, and from the start Hume insisted on giving the highest priority to the organisation of a stewards' system under a Bogside doctor, Raymond McClean. Hume knew the responsibility he had shouldered, as guiding spirit to the movement, and those near him could see, before every major march, the toll it took. He looked pale and drawn, and literally shivered with fright.

The first demonstration was a sit-down in Guildhall Square, on a wet Saturday, 19 October 1968, as a means of testing the crowd-control system and getting the normally volatile crowds used to the idea of turning the other cheek, whatever the provocation. It was unnatural as well as illegal – forcing the Protestant press officer to resign – but it built self-confidence and sent 5,000 away with a warm glow of communal solidarity. It had been an emotional occasion, the end of an era of submission, and the uplifting American civil rights anthem, 'We Shall Overcome', was heard for the first time, led by Hume. (One of McCann's group had tried it during the summer, but no one then knew the words.) Two weeks later, the stakes were raised a little higher, with the fifteen members of the committee tracing the route of the banned 5 October march, along Duke Street, across Craigavon Bridge, and through the city centre to Guildhall Square. By this stage, the unionist community was thoroughly alarmed, as well as confused, by this unique form of protest and, although rumours of armed intervention came to nothing, the police were sufficiently wary to halt the parade briefly outside the city walls. Afterwards, stones began flying over the rooftops, from Protestant houses, but retaliation was negligible and the committee had proved their right to march through what had been regarded as a Protestant stronghold.

Spirits were rising in the previously downtrodden community, as it realised its own strength and there was room for good humour, as well as earnest endeavour. When a police Land Rover stalled awkwardly in Shipquay Street, which falls precipitously towards the Foyle, crowds gathered round to give it a push. In Guildhall Square, Eamonn McCann jauntily introduced James Doherty, the local butcher: 'He'll not chop or change or mince his words!'

Six days later, the first cracks in the unionist edifice showed, as the Corporation quickly set up a three-man committee – two Unionists and a Nationalist – to allocate houses, in place of the absolute right of the Unionist Mayor. But it was far too late to buy off the biggest demonstration yet, planned for 16 November, which would be a re-enactment of the 5 October march, establishing the right of an organised parade of anti-unionists, as well as unionists, to march through Ulster's second city.

By now the world's media had homed in on this new trouble spot, after exhausting the Soviet invasion of Czechoslovakia in September, and Hume was developing his ability to communicate simply and forcefully, in both English and French, much to the delight of foreign reporters. While unionists regarded journalists as a hostile intrusion on their well-ordered province, the civil rights activists welcomed them with open arms, telling a black-and-white story of colonial oppression to which the majority of nationalities could easily relate. There was even a politician-cleric figure in Ian Paisley, re-enacting centuries-old religious wars, and Hume made a suitably personable white knight, with no sword but the righteousness of the civil rights cause. To Hume it was all part of his simple strategy, based on the proposition that if one asked for justice in Northern Ireland it could not be delivered, because of the sectarian nature of the state, which depended on majority domination of the minority.

The situation was tense enough, but a ban on all non-traditional parades, imposed just three days before the demonstration, confirmed that there would be a maximum turnout by media and public. Deeply concerned at the prospect of violence, the liberal Church of Ireland Bishop of Derry, Charles Tyndall, wrote to Hume, declaring his support for what was being done and asking to see him. When they met, Tyndall said he would like to do anything he could to be of assistance, and offered to throw open St Columb's Cathedral for an all-night vigil, so that Protestants and Catholics could meet and pray together. He was hesitant to act alone, in case the Catholic bishop would be offended, so Hume immediately went to see Dr Farren. In return, the Catholic cathedral was also opened throughout the night, and Hume made a point of attending both, after setting the scene with a TV appearance in Belfast. Ecumenism was still a very tender plant in Derry, despite Vatican II, and only a few years previously Catholics had had to get permission even to attend weddings in Protestant churches. They were not allowed to listen to a Protestant preacher taking a service, even in a private home, and at Protestant funerals had to stand outside the door. Among Protestants there was an equal reluctance to cross the divide. Tyndall's gesture was greatly appreciated, at a time when people were at their most vulnerable, and St Columb's had seldom had such a large congregation. Later the bishop was to show how untypical he was of his flock, with a farewell letter to Hume – by then unloved by most Protestants – about his admiration for him and his hopes for the future.

Tyndall would not have been aware of the full significance of his support, but Hume saw it as vital to the whole success of the movement he was now effectively leading. He believed that so long as it could be proved to be non-sectarian, and representative of all who desired 'civil rights and social justice' it had an unanswerable case, which would transform the Northern Ireland state. But it was essential to keep the best in both communities involved, for as soon as it became one-sided or nationalist, the old tribal loyalties would re-emerge. It also had to be scrupulously non-violent, and seen as threatening no one but those who were defending privilege. If necessary, it had to be prepared to be batonned off the streets, without retaliation, to show the world the depths of feeling that were involved. That way, he insisted to some doubting colleagues, using all the power of his priestly past, the whole world would be on their side – just as it supported Martin Luther King. He did not consciously ape the American civil rights tactics, but had seen them on TV. In a city where symbols are a part of everyone's identity, there were to be no flags of any kind carried, and Raymond McClean's wife came up with an acceptable emblem, a white oak leaf, standing for the Irish *doire* – the oak grove after which the city was named – against a black background.

Even the adoption of this emblem was to emphasise that, although the Derry marches were supported by the Belfast-based Civil Rights Association and the rapidly-growing students' movement at Queen's University, the left-wing People's Democracy, they were totally controlled by Derry people. Hume wanted a mass movement for reform, knowing that in Derry, where he was in control, there were all the makings of it. Civil rights groups were springing up in most of the main towns in the North, particularly where there was a sizeable Catholic minority, but only in Derry were there the numbers and the organisation to achieve results. From his knowledge of NICRA, in his travels to civil rights meetings, he could see that republican and far-left influences would soon distort the simple demands of citizens, as distinct from politicians. There was no time to lose if Stormont – and, more important, Westminster – were to be convinced of the need for change.

The day of the march dawned bright and sunny, but there was grim foreboding in the hearts of the organisers as they saw the crowds mass for the start of what was an illegal demonstration, which the police might choose to confront as openly as on

5 October. This was the big test, for the CAC, for Derry, for the Government and primarily for the army of stewards, with white arm bands, who had to try to control up to 20,000 demonstrators, including potentially dangerous left-wing elements. Again the police blocked the route, but they did so at the city end of the bridge, giving the front ranks a chance to lead the throng onto the bridge before halting for the inevitable negotiations.

For a few minutes there was the possibility of a major disaster, with the crowd bottled up on the bridge and only a thin black line of police to stop them. But Hume's contingency plan was quickly put into operation, with the results he had hoped. Alone, the members of the CAC executive made a token breach of the waist-height steel barriers, Michael Canavan having to be helped over by an embarrassed policeman, and the word was passed back that the crowds were to filter through to the town centre, not in a parade, but along footpaths and side roads. It worked like clockwork and despite a few missiles from the Protestant quarter, a bloodless victory was achieved.

The success of the march went like wine to the heads, and feet, of the working population and the following Monday and Tuesday were marked by carefree, impromptu parades in the city centre by factory workers, shop assistants and nurses, just to defy the Stormont ban. Hume was constantly on call, trying to head off police over-reaction, and eventually had to appeal for a moratorium on marching. Meanwhile the lines between London and Belfast were buzzing, as pressure mounted for some response to the events in Derry, and on Friday 22 November, six days after the march, Captain O'Neill delivered a five-point reform package, tacitiy admitting that the civil rights case was proved. Derry Corporation was to be replaced by an appointed development commission; a fair system of house allocation was to be recommended to local councils; machinery for investigating citizens' grievances, through an Ombudsman, was to be created; universal adult franchise (giving the vote to non-ratepayers) would be considered in local government reform; and sections of the draconian Special Powers Act which conflicted with Britain's international obligations would be repealed. (The Act dated back to the foundation of the state and permitted arbitrary arrest and detention.) O'Neill avoided explaining his turnaround, but later he was more explicit. In his autobiography he said, 'the civil rights movement brought about reforms which would otherwise have taken years to wring from a reluctant Government'. While the civil rights demands had been for one man, one vote in local elections, an end to discrimination in housing and jobs, the repeal of the Special Powers Act and the disbanding of the exclusively Protestant Ulster Special Constabulary (the B Special auxiliary police force), the Government's package came close enough – and contained the added bonus of abolition of Derry Corporation – to receive a guarded welcome.

The abolition of Derry Corporation was a momentous enough event for O'Neill to invite all the councillors to Stormont to break the news as gently as possible. The Unionists, not unnaturally, took it badly, but the Nationalists greeted it as a victory for civil rights. Quipped James Doherty to Captain O'Neill, referring to a long-serving Nationalist councillor, 'there's just one thing that would make us very happy – a knighthood for Joe Hegarty'. Then it was down to Stormont Hotel together, where the Nationalists celebrated with bottle upon bottle of wine and the teetotal Unionists drank their bitter orange juice. In just forty-eight days since the first Derry march, the Catholic community had obtained more political gains than it had in forty-seven years. The next sixteen years, because of their accompaniment of violence, were to produce virtually nothing more of substance.

A march in Armagh on 30 November went ahead as planned and only the police presence prevented a clash with a Paisley counter-demonstration – hinting at the loyalist backlash to come. Craig again accused NICRA of being masterminded by IRA men and Trotskyites and, in the mounting clamour for the troublesome Minister's dismissal and Paisley's arrest, Captain O'Neill produced his ace card, going on TV to warn that Westminster was ready to 'act over our heads'. It was an appeal to the moderates in both communities to help him, for fear of an extremist takeover, and the response was so favourable – despite his limp delivery – that two days later he felt strong enough to sack Craig.

The achievements of the civil rights movement had cost not a single life, nor even a serious injury. The stress, however, caused the non-smoking, non-drinking Hume to break the habits of a lifetime, although he scarcely smoked the cigarettes he constantly lit up, and his intake of Irish whiskey seemed to clarify his thinking processes.

But even as NICRA and the CAC declared a truce, to give the

Government time to show its good faith, and Dublin's *Sunday Independent* was choosing Captain O'Neill as its 'man of the year', the ex-student activists in the People's Democracy were planning another confrontation with unionism. To them, there was no real difference between the sectarianism of O'Neill and that of his right-wing colleagues, and they aimed to expose his weaknesses by an eighty-mile march from Belfast to Derry – based on the Selma to Birmingham, Alabama, model – which was bound to provoke extremist opposition. After three days of near misses, on 4 January 1969 the Protestant ultras caught up with the marchers at Burntollet, an ideal ambush point near Derry, and the police guard looked on as stones and clubs rained down on the defenceless students. The clash which Hume had so much feared in Derry had taken place at last, and a weekend of rioting and police retaliation in the city was to follow. On the previous evening, a Paisley rally in the Guildhall had ended in serious rioting, and an offer by the Citizens' Action Committee to steward the PD march into Derry had been rejected. Consciously or unconsciously, the protagonists were squaring up for the fight which had until then been avoided.

The police, who had for so long been accepted in the Bogside, were now branded as enemies of the people. Vigilante patrols were organised, carrying clubs, and barricades were thrown across three or four of the main entrances to the Bogside. A painter, with a sense of the dramatic, wrote 'You are now entering Free Derry' on the gable end of a house near to where Hume's maternal grandmother lived, and a radio transmitter appeared, broadcasting as 'Radio Free Derry, the Voice of Liberation'. The police kept their distance for five days, and eventually Hume, Cooper and Canavan – fearful of a violent attempt to clear the barricades – managed to persuade the Bogsiders to remove them. But the seeds of revolution and secession had been sown, which were never to die.

More violence flared on 11 January, in the border town of Newry, where a badly-organised NICRA march was taken over by teams of rioters, burning police vehicles and pushing them into a canal. Hume, whose loud-hailer was snatched from him as he was speaking, was appalled by the total lack of crowd control, unlike Derry, and could see that the days of the peaceful mass marches were at an end. The tactic had helped to galvanise a demoralised community, but unless the energy that was released could be channelled into political activity, there could only be more disruption and bloodshed, which the extremists were intent on creating. A Westminster vacancy occurred in Armagh, with the death of a Unionist, but Hume turned down another NDP request to run. His excuse was that there would be a Stormont election soon and he would reserve himself for that. Labour also tried to recruit him, but was deterred by his nationalism.

By now, Captain O'Neill was well and truly on the run from his own hardliners, despite evident moderate support, and when he ordered an independent assessment of the troubles by a Scottish Judge, Lord Cameron, two Ministers, Brian Faulkner and Billy Morgan, promptly resigned, criticising his handling of the crisis. A week later, twelve Stormont backbenchers plotted his overthrow and to thwart them he called a snap February election, just as Hume had forecast, hoping to appeal over their heads to the moderate majority.

Until this point, the civil rights movement had steered clear of party politicians – although the pioneering Austin Currie was a notable exception – in order to broaden its appeal. But the election faced its leaders with a difficult choice – to cash in on their popularity or maintain their purity, as external guardians of the citizens' rights. Most decided the chance was too good to miss and threw their hats in the ring along with the O'Neillites and the anti-O'Neillites, helping to blur the stark presentation of the issues which the Premier had hoped would work in his favour. For Hume, there were some initial doubts, but he wanted to use what remained of the non-sectarian civil rights spirit to test Captain O'Neill's reforming zeal before the Prime Minister was a spent force. If civil rights were left to the traditional Nationalist MPs, they would be lost, and an opportunity for changing the nature of the state, to include Catholics as equal partners, would be thrown away. He had no choice but to stand, and even though he was subsequently to credit Paddy O'Hanlon for persuading him to run, on the grounds that he had a moral duty, not even the Newry man believed it.

Hume had already turned down a request to stand as a unity candidate in a forthcoming Westminster by-election for Mid-Ulster, leaving the way open for Bernadette Devlin, then a psychology student in Belfast, to launch her political career. If he had concentrated on Westminster, the history of the next few years might have been very different; as it was, the fiery student activist, whose ability to articulate Catholic frustrations was something new on the nationalist political scene, soon alienated her one-time supporters with her left-wing bias, after promising so much. As the years went by, and she narrowly escaped death in a loyalist murder attempt in 1981, she veered increasingly towards republican extremism. In 1969 Hume's sights were set on Stormont, however. Announcing he would stand as an independent, he issued a manifesto saying he stood for a just society in which people of all religions would work together and in which religion would not be used as a political weapon.

McAteer's familiar, folksy approach to politics was no match for Hume's ruthless professionalism, and their programmes were equally contrasting. While McAteer patiently waited for the inevitability of Irish unity, Hume sought a mandate based on bread and butter issues, and civil rights principles. Even his colours and emblems were borrowed from the CAC, and he and Paddy Doherty made an effective platform team. Hume would appeal to the voters' idealism, while Doherty would eagerly seize on McAteer's blunders – as when he fatally argued that 'half a loaf is better than no bread', in relation to reforms. McCann was the third man, having helped to create the situation which Hume was exploiting, but his extreme socialism was against him. He polled 1,993 votes, to Hume's 8,920 and McAteer's 5,267.

Hume had arrived, but even in his hour of victory, he was learning how politics divides. The split with the old Nationalists was a long time healing, and Paddy Doherty bade a surprise farewell, instead of staying to help create Hume's social democratic party. He knew a change had been necessary and he was glad to have been a part of it, but he found Hume's one-track ambition difficult to live with. He would not be the last to break with him.

The election results proved a deceptive victory for O'Neill over his Unionist opponents, which was turned, in nine weeks, into defeat. The sweeping successes he asked for were denied him and although his party picked up thirty-nine out of the fifty-two seats, twelve of them went to his old enemies. He himself, after a twenty-year career of unopposed returns, finished only 1,414 votes ahead of Ian Paisley, also fighting his first election. With three civil rights candidates elected, and People's Democracy taking 24,000 votes in eight constituencies, he was too weakened and demoralised to carry on for long.

A series of loyalist bomb attacks on water and electricity targets, mistakenly thought to be the work of the IRA, helped to usher him out on 28 April, though not before he had helped to nominate a cousin, Major James Chichester-Clark, as his successor. (In a confused situation, Chichester-Clark had resigned over O'Neill's insistence on one man, one vote in local government elections, yet was the 'liberal' candidate for PM, winning by a single vote over Brian Faulkner.) Ironically, the first moderate Unionist Prime Minister was beaten because he had tried to hold on to Derry's west bank, his Achilles heel. If he had let it go Nationalist, democratically, or had let Derry have its university, he might never have had to deal with John Hume, whose control of a mass movement had destroyed Unionist power in Derry and ultimately was to succeed in bringing down Stormont.

7

Bogside at war

In his 1969 election manifesto, Hume had left no doubt about his intention to transform the face of politics in Northern Ireland along totally new, non-sectarian lines, without taking sides on the central constitutional question. He stood, he said, for a just society in which people of all religions could work together and in which religion would not be used as a political weapon. It was a wildly ambitious, optimistic platform, in a country where there had only ever been one political issue on which electors were asked to cast their votes – for or against the existence of the state. But much of the original, unifying civil rights spirit still persisted despite the divisive efforts of leftist extremists, and Hume could claim to have won an overwhelming mandate – with some Protestant assistance – for his four-point plan. This was to form a new political movement based on social democratic principles, an open executive, and complete involvement of people in decisions; to provide strong energetic opposition to conservatives, 'pursuing radical social and economic politics'; to root out 'the fundamental evil in our society' – sectarianism; and to provide a movement committed to the ideal that the future of Northern Ireland should be decided by its people 'and that there should be no change in the constitution except by the consent of its people'. As he explained in his regular *Sunday Press* column, his overall strategy was contained in the 'three Rs', reform, reconciliation and reunification. Reforms which made people equal helped to bring them together and unite them.

The insistence on consent, without coercion of unionists, was now enshrined in the policy of the leading civil rights politician, and was fully supported by his two elected colleagues, Ivan Cooper and Paddy O'Hanlon, who fought the Stormont election on similar tickets. All that remained was to try to forge a new party grouping from all the various strands of anti-unionist feeling represented among the thirteen opposition MPs, and it was this which occupied Hume's attention, on and off, for the next eighteen months.

Meanwhile his own independent organisation rapidly became a model for others to follow, with numerous public meetings to mull over policy and an advice centre to handle constituency problems. In Britain, this was standard practice, but in Northern Ireland, where votes split automatically green or orange, without any effort required, it was almost unprecedented.

The talks began almost immediately after the election, but events were moving too quickly to allow them to bear fruit. Besides the three civil rights MPs, who were on the crest of a wave, there were three others who were in a similar mould – Gerry Fitt, Paddy Devlin and Austin Currie. All were in their own parties – respectively Republican Labour, Northern Ireland Labour and Nationalist – but had taken an individual, supportive role in the civil rights movement and were obvious candidates for a new grouping. Later, Hume was to regret not proceeding to launch his own party, with Cooper and O'Hanlon, in order to provide a strong lead to the others, but for the moment, there were more important items on the agenda. O'Neill was sinking fast, and the vultures in Unionism and the more extreme factions of the civil rights movement were determined to keep up the pressure.

Hume showed himself willing, in his maiden Stormont speech in March, to give O'Neill the benefit of the doubt about his reforming zeal, but added that he hoped the new Unionist MPs would make it possible to have sentiments transformed into action. 'The failure of Unionists to listen to those opposite over the years when they complained about various grievances,' he said, 'has been one of the causes of people losing faith in parliamentary democracy.' Focusing on his speciality, housing, he said the underlying evil was the way that houses were used as a political instrument at local-government level – because they meant votes. The only solution was to transfer housing from the local council politicians to a central housing authority, building and allocating houses on a provincewide basis – a recommendation which was later carried out to the letter.

A march for 19 April was organised by North Derry Civil Rights Association over the old controversial route from Burntollet to Derry, and Hume was well aware of the dangers. Having appealed to the police in Derry for restraint, he was driven out to Burntollet to see the situation for himself, and narrowly escaped a mob of cudgel-wielding loyalists when he vainly asked police to arrest them. Back in Derry rival crowds were massing – unaware that the march had been called off – and when stones were thrown into Guildhall Square the police response was to baton-charge the attacked, rather than the attackers. That was the spark which was needed and rioting again flared in William Street, leading to the Bogside, with stone-throwing and arson.

At one point some teenagers found their escape route cut off and dashed through the open door of a terrace house to safety over a back wall. They were gone, but the police proceeded to kick down the door and baton those inside unconscious, splashing blood over the walls and ceiling. They were not to know it, but they had picked one of the most innocent and well-loved bystanders in the Bogside, Samuel Devenney, and when he died in July, after two heart attacks, he became the first Catholic martyr of the troubles.

The Sunday following the assault, about 500 police gathered on the edge of the Bogside and, fearing the worst, Hume decided that the only salvation of the young and old was to evacuate them from the area. There were dramatic scenes as old women were carried from their homes and ferried, with the children, up to the heights of the Creggan, well out of harm's way. It was a major operation, winning a breathing space for negotiation and involving the whole community in a positive alternative to violence. Meanwhile Hume had persuaded a group of civic and church leaders to join him in asking the Minister of Home Affairs, fellow Derry man Robert Porter, by phone, to withdraw the police from the Bogside by 5 pm. After that, Hume warned, he could not be responsible for the consequences. Porter agreed, with what Lord Cameron later called 'great political courage', but the dispersal of the crowds was more difficult.

In the Creggan the Bogsiders had gathered, angry at having to retreat from their homes and unhappy with calls to return quietly, because of the danger of police using their guns. After listening impatiently to speeches, they headed down Eastway to the Bogside, ready to defend themselves, with a man carrying an axe in the lead. Father Mulvey was at the foot of Fahan Street, an anxious spectator, when he saw two police cars, on a token patrol of the Bogside, head unwittingly for the mob. Luckily, they realised their mistake in time, and turned back to Butcher's Gate, but at this stage events were rapidly moving out of control. Ahead of the mob was John Hume, trying to hold the crowds back, but being swept along towards the city walls, where the police were waiting. It was like the storming of the Bastille, thought Mulvey, as he and six others stood their ground and blocked the narrow twenty-five-foot entrance of Butcher's Gate, just as he had done before, during the 1952 riots. He wondered if a priest would still be respected, or would be trampled down, and he said a silent prayer as the march halted. A few stones were thrown, but there was no attempt to force a passage, and eventually Hume arrived on the scene.

Climbing on Mulvey's broad shoulders, the new MP delivered what was long regarded as the best speech of his career, sharing the crowd's anger, but appealing to its better nature and common sense as only a born-and-bred Bogsider could. There were other ways of getting justice, he argued, and they could rely on him to see that they were pursued. It was a *tour de force*, later described by Lord Cameron's inquiry as 'an amazing achievement', but not everyone agreed that Hume's evacuation policy had been strictly necessary. While confrontation in the Bogside was avoided, some thought it had risked an even greater conflagration by assembling an uncontrollable mob. Hume saved the day, in the end, but he needed Mulvey to make his Horatio stand.

Cameron's praise for Hume was unstinted: 'It may be invidious to name a single individual, but Mr Hume's work in Londonderry since October has been so outstanding that it seems appropriate to name him'. Commending the influence of the Citizen's Action Committee in favour of non-violent protests, he said 'much, if not most, of the credit must go to Mr John Hume who from the beginning has taken the lead and shown himself to be both responsible and capable'.

The cool restraint of civil rights days had given way to angry retaliation, as footloose teenagers, in particular, reacted to old-fashioned police repression and an emerging Protestant backlash. At first the rioting was confined to baiting the police, and challenging them to enter the lion's den of the Bogside, but Hume knew of the wider dangers that were involved. When asked, during a meeting at Free Derry Corner in April, why he objected to 'wee boys' throwing stones, he gave a prophetic reply: 'Because you don't know what effect it will have – whether it will be a broken window, twenty broken windows, or a thousand dead. When you can't control a weapon, you don't use it.' He felt the same anger, as police attempted to re-establish their dominance by strong-arm methods, but he was determined to channel it in non-violent ways. Others, however, believed the seeds of real revolution had been sown and cared nothing for the political process Hume was embarked upon.

Chichester-Clark's first act as premier was to declare an amnesty, clearing everyone, including Hume, committed for trial since 5 October on riot-related charges, but welcome for this measure was not universal. Paisley was released, having refused not to repeat his occupation of the centre of Armagh to frustrate a civil rights march, and the police were absolved of criminal charges arising out of their violence against Bogsiders in January and April. Worse, the findings of an internal police inquiry into the incidents of 4 January and the Devenney case were not to be published, nor was the report which Hume had done so much to publicise. Nevertheless, Chichester-Clark was successful in getting party approval by twenty-eight to twenty-two for one man, one vote in local elections, a complete reversal of his previous stance.

At Stormont the opposition MPs combined to impede progress of the Public Order Bill, a legacy of O'Neill, which was designed to show his hardliners that even if concessions were being offered to the civil righters, the Government could still make life more difficult for demonstrators. The increased penalties for law-breakers, however, only helped to unite the opposition around a common cause, and an organised sit-down in the Commons chamber in March heralded a long series of all-night sessions which laid the foundations of a parliamentary alliance. The sit-in, accompanied by a singing of 'We shall overcome' earned a week-long suspension of those taking part. Hume considered applying for unemployment benefit, to draw attention to Derry's high jobless rate – in 1967 it was 20 per cent, compared to 6 per cent in the rest of Northern Ireland and 2.6 in Britain – but decided better of it when he heard his salary would not be cut. Money was never a major consideration for Hume, but he had given up two jobs with good prospects to settle for a salary of £1,450 plus £300 expenses, while Pat had to surrender the teaching job she loved to act as Hume's unpaid assistant.

On the streets of Derry, tensions were rising to their summer climax, with the Protestant demonstrations of 12 July – commemorating the victory in 1690 of Protestant King William III over the Catholic James II – and 12 August, celebrating the relief of the city from a 105-day siege mounted by the same James II in 1689. Normally these demonstrations were quietly resented by the Catholic population, but after a year of near-revolution, it was impossible that they should pass off peacefully. The July demonstrations gave a hint of what was to come, with widespread rioting in Derry and the nearby Catholic town of Dungiven, and on 2 August there was further looting and vandalism in Belfast after reports that a Junior Orange Order parade had been attacked by Catholics.

Hume knew the lid could blow off in Derry if the annual march of the Apprentice Boys – named after the seventeenth-century heroes of the siege – were to go ahead, so he made direct approaches to both the Dublin and British Governments to head off the catastrophe. The Taoiseach, Jack Lynch, listened politely to this articulate young MP, who was becoming a familiar face on Irish television, but since there already was a Northern 'expert', Agriculture Minister Neil Blaney, from just across the border in Donegal, Hume's views were not given full weight. In London Hume was unable to see James Callaghan, and was fobbed off with a ten-minute meeting with Lord Stonham, his deputy in the Home Office, which extended into a three-hour lunch at the Athenaeum Club. He succeeded in impressing Stonham with his fears about the march, and these were reported up the line to Prime Minister Harold Wilson. But again Hume's opinions were regarded as alarmist, and London was persuaded not to intervene, after meeting strenuous opposition from Belfast.

Similar pleas to the Stormont Government, by Hume and other opposition politicians, fell on deaf ears, against the fear that all Unionist Ministers had of banning Protestant processions, however provocative. In the year of 1969 it would have been seen as abject surrender and, with the police – both the Inspector General and the local chief – registering no objections, the go-ahead was given. A meeting between the Apprentice Boys and representatives of the Bogsiders was seen as a good omen, and there was a promise from the Derry Citizens' Defence Association that its members would do nothing to provoke violence. But even the name of this new Bogside organisation should have alerted the Government to the certainty of the explosion that was to come. The Derry Citizens' Action Committee was in abeyance, with most of its demands met, and its former leaders in Stormont, counselling against street protests. The accent was on politics now, but at street level the fear of another incursion by the police, with loyalists in their wake, was the inspiration for a new organisation, based on defence against the police. Hume had reminded the Northern Ireland Commons a few weeks earlier that, ironically, when the Bogside police station had been closed, years before, there was a petition to keep it open.

This time Derry's old republicans, who had gone underground since the unsuccessful 1959–62 campaign, saw their opportunity to lead and it was at their instigation that community organisations were asked to choose delegates for the founding meeting. Paddy Doherty, now vice-chairman of the CAC, deliberately opted out, but was nominated in his absence and eventually found himself choosing between joining a republican-inspired organisation – and trying to control it – or leaving the protection of the Bogside in potentially dangerous hands. He decided to stay with it and was joined in the leadership by a school administrator who had much more to lose than himself, a building clerk of works. The first mission of the embryo organisation was a visit to Dublin to canvass support for defending the citizens and before the representatives left Derry there was a classic late-night duel in the City Hotel between Hume, the constitutionalist, Daniel O'Connell figure, and Sean Keenan, the old-style militant. The Dublin trip was fruitless and when Derry's political leaders were told, at a subsequent meeting, of the stark alternatives involved in the physical defence of the Bogside they made their excuses and left. They could not take the responsibility as democrats, so they decided to leave it to the Bogside Defence Association to prepare to repel invaders. Hume himself was excluded from the organisation, probably because of his pacifist views, and only later heard about its plan. Pat's mother had just died and his mind was preoccupied.

As the defence plan was finalised, the entrance points barricaded and the petrol-bomb arsenals prepared, an atmosphere was created in which a clash was almost inevitable. The drums struck up on 12 August and the day began with verbal exchanges between the Protestants, high on the seventeenth-century bastion of Derry's walls, and the Bogsiders below. At Waterloo Place, where the march veered dangerously near the Bogside, at the bottom of William Street, the first two-finger gestures rose from the Protestant crowd, and the first stones were hurled in return from behind the rows of barbed wire. Hume, McAteer and Cooper linked arms to keep the two sides apart, but were overwhelmed and when Protestant mobs followed the police into the Bogside, it had 'a profound significance', as Lord Scarman was later to report. The excuse for an uprising was offered and accepted, and for the next two days it raged non-stop.

At first the police had only small metal shields for protection against the stones and petrol bombs that rained down on them, and were reduced to throwing back the stones. But as the situation deteriorated Porter gave the order for CS gas to be used – after getting the British Government's permission. 'Tear smoke' was the official term, but it soon was obvious that this was no ordinary irritant, but a gas that was unsuited to use in a built-up area, where aged or infant non-combatants could be seriously disabled. It added, however, to the sense of siege, and had no effect on the dozen or so teenagers on the rooftop ramparts of Rossville Flats, whose petrol bombs made sure that the Bogside remained impenetrable.

Behind the lines, Dr Raymond McClean, Hume's associate in civil rights days and after, ran a makeshift field hospital, in a sweetshop, treating nearly 1,000 casualties over a two-day period, without running water or proper medical supplies. The authorities insisted that no action would be taken against injured persons reporting to Altnagelvin Hospital, but there was a decided local preference for the Candy Corner or Letterkenny Hospital, across the border in Co. Donegal.

For two days, it was the Bogside versus the Royal Ulster Constabulary, if not the Stormont Government, and the many revolutionaries who crowded into the Bogside from many parts of the North and further afield, to revel in the experience, created a sense of excitement that was intoxicating, even for the most conservative. Bernadette Devlin was on the scene from the start, with a camera crew in tow, playing the part of 'the maid of the barricades' with her inspirational rhetoric, and trying to tell the Bogsiders how to run their own show. As she walked the streets, she was seen grabbing a brush out of the hands of a housewife, posing for a photograph, and giving it back. But she was never allowed to forget that she was an outsider, and on one occasion was warned by a leading member of the Defence Association that if she stepped out of line or caused the death or serious injury of a single person, she would have to answer for it. She reacted emotionally, in her exhausted, depressive state and shortly afterwards left for a fund-raising trip to America. Meanwhile one of her associates had to be smuggled out of Derry, tied up in a bag, having found the mental strain too much.

In the middle of the cheerful communal mayhem, there were ugly tribal forces at work, making sure that foreign bodies were eliminated. A Protestant street was sprayed with petrol, and the inhabitants told that if a policeman was seen a petrol bomb would be tossed in. Other Protestants had to flee for safety over back walls when their streets were barricaded at both ends. Even a Methodist hostel for down-and-outs was petrol-bombed after midnight, and twenty-nine Catholics and five Protestants had to be helped to safety.

Hume knew he had no chance of stopping the rioting, so he took on the role of fireman, walking the streets for two days and nights, almost non-stop, and exercising control where he thought it was possible. As MP for an area that had virtually seceded from the state, he could not dictate to the Defence Association, which was the effective government, but he could use the influence he had acquired during the civil rights period to head off the worst confrontations. His home, a small bungalow in Beechwood Avenue, above the Bogside, became a transit camp for visiting journalists and politicians, some of them attracted from the Republic by alarming news reports. One of these was Frank Cluskey, later to become leader of the Irish Labour Party, who was holidaying in Donegal. During his visit to the Humes, word came about trouble at Rosemount police station, just five minutes away. He and Hume found the station entirely surrounded by a hostile mob, whose aim was to trap the policemen inside and prevent them from relieving their colleagues in the Bogside. Youths in the crowd were throwing stones and, fearing an escalation, Hume climbed a shed to tell them their methods were wrong. Petrol bombs could easily set fire to people's houses, he said, and, at the end of the day, the police would open fire. They could achieve their objectives without any violence, he advised, simply by waiting outside and doing nothing, while the police were inside unable to move. They agreed to join him in negotiations, but when he was halfway to the station door it opened and a gas cartridge was fired straight at his chest. It knocked him flat, winding him, and with the choking gas billowing round him, he was carried half-unconscious to safety, while the crowd seethed. Five minutes later, he was back on his feet and walking the same path to persuade the police not to use any more tear gas. He succeeded, just as they were running out of cartridges, but there was a chilling sequel. Next day, a police sergeant denied that Hume had saved them, pointing to a rack of sub-machine-guns: 'We always had those'. If they had been used, and there had been a massacre on the streets of Derry, the whole of Northern Ireland might have exploded.

Hume's courage was tested several more times in those crucial days, as he strove to minimise the damage that was being done to all his hopes of peaceful reform. The same day as the Rosemount incident, he had enough stamina to take on a crowd that had gathered at the gasworks, below the city walls, intent on setting it on fire. It was a perfect target for the arsonists, and Hume had to argue for two hours to talk them out of it. They were just 'chocolate soldiers', he told them, compared to the youngsters who were in the front line at Rossville Street. There was nothing to setting a gasworks on fire, but they would be claiming the glory, when others had done the real work. Besides, who would suffer, apart from the Bogsiders? It was a subtle approach, drawing on all his powers of persuasion, and it worked. The gasworks lived a charmed life, serving as a paramilitary headquarters at times when no institution was safe. Hume's was the strong still voice of reason, in the background, while the left-wingers who had exploited the latent discontent eighteen months before seized their opportunity to widen the conflict. As Hume saw it, they had no strategy except violence, and more violence, out of which they would gain a position of power. But it was a dangerous game and the genesis not of socialist revolution, but of a new and more violent republican movement. To Hume, it was the very antithesis of the disciplined, peaceful pursuit of legitimate goals that had distinguished the civil rights campaign and he did his best to curb the enthusiasm of the stone-throwers, by asking them why, whenever he could. One of the most active, with whom he failed, was Martin McGuinness, from a well-known Bogside family, later to be a republican activist and Sinn Fein politician.

It was part of the defence to spread the conflict to divert the attention of the miniscule, 3,500-strong RUC, and soon phone calls were summoning contacts into action all over Northern Ireland. Again it was playing with fire, and Hume would have advised against it, if he had been asked. Violence could be confined in Derry to clashes between the Catholic population and the police, but in Belfast and elsewhere the sectarian arithmetic was different and Protestants and Catholics lived too close together to stay neutral.

When the torch was lit in west Belfast, in organised attacks on police stations, the flames spread like wildfire across the sectarian divide, involving whole communities in conflict with their near neighbours. The rioting of August 1969, from which the real start of the troubles is officially dated, had begun, because Derry was unaware or heedless of the risks. Even Austin Currie, who was present at diversions in Tyrone, later admitted that Belfast was a mystery to him, and he had not realised the long history of sectarian conflict, going back to the early nineteenth century. In the rest of Northern Ireland it was possible to sell non-violence at a civil rights meeting, but at a meeting in Andersonstown he was appalled by an assumption that force was inevitable.

The backlash of the campaign to stretch the RUC was unleashed and Currie's wife and family were among the first to take advantage of an evacuation he organised from Dungannon to Gormanstown, north of Dublin. Currie had been in Coalisland when the police station was attacked with a bulldozer and, as the B Specials were called out, he got a tip-off that his house was going to be shot up. Luckily he was home in time to rescue his wife and child before the house was attacked, and the next day he brought them over the border en route for Gormanstown. 'Those were terrible days,' he recalled later. '"B men" were everywhere, and you could have been shot on the side of the road, with no questions asked. For six weeks I was virtually on the run, not sleeping at home and often slipping across the border for safety. It was the same for all in civil rights, who didn't live in ghetto areas. The fear of the Catholic community was such that a lot of people were involved in things they would have run a mile from in the cold light of day.'

Even at this stage, Hume detected no upsurge in nationalist or 'Brits out' feeling, although the Unionist Party, in Belfast, was littering the walls of Protestant areas with posters warning of an imminent republican uprising. But the mood was soon to change, after a radio and TV broadcast by the Taoiseach, Jack Lynch, in response to widespread concern in the Republic. Hume first heard there was to be a broadcast from an RTE journalist, Mike Burns, in the City Hotel and immediately tried to telephone Lynch at his home in Dublin, to advise caution. But the Taoiseach had already left for the TV studio and there was no way of intercepting him, to let him know the state of alarm on the streets of Derry. The Rosemount incident put the matter out of Hume's head, and he was walking home, nursing a painful chest, when people spontaneously spilled out on to the streets shouting 'The Irish army's coming! The Irish army's coming!' What madness, he thought, as he hurried home, where Pat had a different story. Lynch had not announced that he was sending troops over the border; the army was setting up field hospitals in Donegal, for those who did not want to be treated in Northern Ireland, 'and at other points along the border where they may be necessary'.

'It is clear now,' Lynch had said, in sombre tones, 'that the present situation cannot be allowed to continue. It is evident that the Stormont Government is no longer in control of the situation. Indeed the present situation is the inevitable outcome of the policies pursued for decades by successive Stormont Governments. It is clear, also, that the Irish Government can no longer stand by and see innocent people injured and perhaps worse.' (His script actually said 'stand idly by', but whoever transcribed it for the teleprompter made a historic ommission.)

Describing the RUC as 'no longer accepted as an impartial force' and any deployment of British troops as 'unacceptable', he said the Irish Government had asked London to apply imediately to the United Nations for a peace-keeping force. Reunification could provide the only permanent solution, he added, and he intended to ask the British Government to enter into early negotiations to review the present constitutional position of the Six Counties.

If Hume had been able to speak to Lynch he would have asked him, in blunt Derry terms, why he had made no contact before deciding to broadcast. After all, Hume was the local MP and had given a very precise warning about the certainty of violence. Later he was to find out that Blaney, the Dublin Cabinet's authority on the North, had been in the Bogside when the trouble broke out and had persuaded his colleagues to write off Hume, still only four months in politics, as a 'West Brit'.

Later, despite his concern, Hume could see that the speech had given a lift to the Bogsiders at a time when they felt isolated. He realised that in the emotional mood of the Republic, Lynch had done the best he could, mounting a low-key holding operation at the border and providing an outlet for popular feeling. If he had done nothing, Hume believed, there might have been civil disorder in the South, or people might have decided to take action themselves in the North. In Lynch's place, Hume would have addressed his pleas to the British Government, asking them to act over Stormont's head, at a time when the issue was still civil rights, not revolution. James Callaghan, then the Home Secretary, was to regret not taking the bull by the horns and suspending Stormont.

Lynch's broadcast had one effect in Derry, but quite another in Protestant Belfast, where it was seen as proof, after the attacks on police stations, of a new republican onslaught on the beloved province. As a diversionary exercise, a handful of Catholic youths marched a few hundred yards from the Falls Road to the Protestant Shankill, waving a Tricolour. By the time the news spread, the handful had become 'hundreds', and an angry Protestant mob crossed in the opposite direction, to the Falls, burning all the houses in Bombay Street to the ground. The sectarian divide was always much more harshly defined in working-class Belfast than in Derry, and over the next four years an estimated 30,000 to 60,000 people, both Catholic and Protestant, were forced to leave their homes in 'mixed areas' for the safety of their own tribe, in what was considered Europe's largest enforced population movement since 1945.

The police in Belfast were as convinced as the Protestants that they faced an IRA plot, and they responded in their traditional manner, with force. In the built-up Lower Falls, armoured cars careered up and down the main road, loosing off heavy-calibre ammunition in the direction of any threat, real or otherwise. Casualties were inevitable, as the bullets punched through flimsy walls, and between RUC action – they killed four people, according to the Scarman Report – and sectarian gun attacks, the death toll by Saturday 16 August was eight, with thousands injured and hundreds of homes burned out.

By early afternoon of the third day of rioting in Derry, the police were exhausted, and even Bernadette Devlin, who shrugged off the gas like one born to it, was wilting. The B Specials were massing in Bishop Street, where five houses were ablaze, and an extremist mob was with them, apparently ready for an assault. But as Devlin telephoned the authorities in Belfast and London, screaming for troops to be sent in to prevent a slaughter, the process was already under way. Although the Stormont Government had for weeks discussed the introduction of troops, the Army insisted that the last line of civil defence had to be deployed – and Home Affairs Minister Robert Porter believed the reserve police were unarmed, although some 'may have been carrying clubs'. That done, the order to deploy the troops in Derry was given, and the men of the Prince of Wales Regiment moved in smartly, to support the demoralised police.

The Bogside was relieved but there was still a danger of the police regrouping and following the soldiers into the Bogside, which Paddy Doherty knew would be disastrous. Fortunately Stan Orme, a British Labour MP, was visiting Doherty when the news broke and the politician's appeal to the army commander – 'Listen to this man!' –

convinced him that his small force needed no RUC reinforcements. The Defence Association called off its men, allowing the police to be withdrawn, and the Bogside erupted in joy. Free Derry was still intact and anonymous British soldiers had replaced the vanquished enemy.

On the same day, 14 August, the situation was rapidly sliding out of control when Hume left the gas-laden streets of Derry for an emergency sitting of Stormont. The Prime Minister, James Chichester-Clark, set the tone, proposing a Government motion deploring the violence and hooliganism and expressing 'intense admiration for the courage and discipline of the police force'. He defended the decision to permit the Apprentice Boys' march by quoting Hume's support for the right of peaceful demonstration, and lambasted Lynch for importing 'a very serious dimension' into the crisis. The Dublin government was now regarded as 'unfriendly and implacable' and Lynch's suggestion of UN intervention was 'absurd'. But John Taylor, the hardline deputy Minister of Home Affairs, dropped the real bombshell when he said 11,000 members of the armed and exclusively Protestant B Special reserve constabulary had been mobilised – a threat which the Opposition MPs could not ignore.

In a brief speech, simmering with emotion, Hume said he had hoped that the crisis could bring out the best in the Government, but the sterility of Stormont had never been more in evidence. 'I do not wish to engage in any verbal battles with anyone, to add to the bloody mess that already exists, but after listening to Taylor's speech, which was a jackboot speech in the present crisis, I can only say this in reply: we are quite firm, we shall not be moved. My colleagues and I, Mr Speaker, will say goodbye.'

With that, he and six of the opposition MPs walked out, to be told, before they left the buildings, of the latest development. Minutes after Hume had spoken, Robert Porter interrupted a Unionist speaker with a brief statement. The Inspector General of the RUC had asked the General Officer Commanding the Army in Northern Ireland to deploy troops in Derry in aid of the civil power. The step had been taken with the knowledge and approval of both the Stormont and Westminster Governments. Porter failed to mention that the GOC, General Ian Freeland, had already mobilised 152 Squadron of the Territorial Army and had hurriedly withdrawn the order after it was realised the TA could be used only on NATO duties.

The Irish Government, meanwhile, was carefully watching the unprecedented events and preparing its response in co-operation with London. The Irish and British Army commanders in the north west later revealed privately, on separate occasions, that if there had been killing on a major scale and they were ordered to go in and stop it, they had the same instructions. Both were told that if they met soldiers of the other nationality, in Derry, they should stop and hold the line. 'Yes,' said Canavan, when he heard the plan from a British officer, 'We'd be gutting each other and you'd be sitting looking at each other!'

In Belfast, Dr Con McCluskey was granted an interview with Callaghan's deputy, Lord Stoneham. 'Why are you over here now, after ignoring all the statistics on discrimination in jobs and housing that I've been publishing for the last six years?' McCluskey asked angrily. 'Well, there is an emergency now, with all these houses burned and people killed,' he was told. 'All right,' said the doctor. 'The next time I have a case of discrimination I won't send it to you. I'll burn a street of houses.'

During the worst of the violence, Denis Haughey – a future SDLP chairman – met Hume when he travelled to Derry with clothes and groceries gathered by civil rights supporters in mid-Ulster. Sitting on the wall of Paddy Doherty's house, they talked about the re-appearance of guns and the possibility of a revival of IRA violence leading to a shooting match. In the heady atmosphere of the time, no one seemed very dismayed, but Hume saw it differently: 'These fellows don't know what they're talking about. If that starts now it will go on for years and years and will never be stopped.'

8
Free Derry

When a parliamentary constituency is in a state of rebellion, by will of the people, there is little that a responsible MP can usefully do except to be available to smooth the eventual transition to normality. So while the Bogside Defence Association was the effective government of the barricaded area, liaising with the army, providing a law-and-order force and guaranteeing food and fuel supplies, Hume stepped quietly into the background. First, the ground rules of the Free Derry statelet had to be laid down, and Paddy Doherty was joined by Michael Canavan for a crucial meeting with the army commanders in Victoria Barracks, a few hundred yards from the William Street barricades. As forcefully as they could, they explained that if the army and police stayed out, the BDA could restore order without further rioting. There was an awkward moment when the two negotiators were asked to list their demands, for which they were unprepared. Canavan played for time, but eventually produced a list of short and long-term demands, saying the BDA would hold the area until the police were disarmed and the B Specials, the Special Powers Act and Stormont were abolished.

The security chiefs had little choice but to agree to surrender control, provided the defence association could curb the rioters, and for the next nine weeks the Bogside was in the hands of a committee of forty, with Hume left to do his job as MP. Everyone was allotted their task, from policing to refuse collection and the committee met every night of the week to take decisions. As one of them recalled later, 'It was an impossible time for all of us, especially those with a job or a business'.

'Chief of police' was a one-eyed American journalist with an eye-patch, whom Doherty never trusted to have his own direct telephone line. Everyone was on their best behaviour, so there was little lawlessness, and any culprits were effectively dealt with by the American, using thieves to inform on other thieves, like early supergrasses. The judge at the kangaroo courts was a republican

89

idealist, who would lecture young hooligans about the new Ireland of the future, while more practical colleagues set them sweeping the streets with yard brushes.

With his reputation as a tough negotiator, Canavan's responsibility was to liaise with the outside world, especially the army and the police. Often they would meet in his expensive modern villa in Talbot Park, in the north end of the city, and discussions with generals and aides de camp would range late into the night, over well-filled whiskey glasses – Canavan himself did not drink – about how the rebel territory was to be returned to normality. Politicians would appear from time to time, and retire in some amazement, but the real negotiations were with the army, which obviously developed a respect for the Bogside leaders.

A typical problem was presented by the makeshift Bogside barricades, of burned-out cars and scrap metal, which the army said were untidy-looking traffic hazards. They wanted to remove them but Canavan, knowing that the time was not ripe for opening up the Bogside to army traffic, proposed that white lines be painted on the roads instead of the physical barriers. The plan was approved at a public meeting and the army agreed, regarding the removal of the barricades as progress. Canavan himself bought the paint, walking into a shop with a makeshift cloth gas mask round his neck and asking for white paint and straight sticks for marking roads. Later the shopkeeper, Bob Warwick, was telling his wife about the nutcase who wanted to paint roads, and when he turned on the TV, there was his deranged customer down on his hands and knees, painting the no-go lines! True to their word, the soldiers honoured their part of the bargain, and regarded the lines as impassable, in order to wean the Bogside out of its siege mentality. Elsewhere, conditions were equally unreal. Journalists contacted the IRA through the gasworks office, and a hotel porter with IRA connections thoughtfully gave reporters prior notice of bombs planted nearby.

The high point of the nine-week Free Derry period was the visit of Jim Callaghan, when the Home Secretary was for an hour or so the guest of the Bogside 'state within a state', outside the writ of the army or police. Hume set up the visit, knowing how it would strengthen the hand of the moderates, if Callaghan played it right. The two had recognised each other earlier as instinctive politicians and Hume travelled to the Grand Central Hotel in Belfast the night before to brief the elder statesman about how he should handle an unprecedented situation.

As arranged, Hume met Callaghan's car at Littlewood's corner, outside the white-line barricades, and as an added bonus there was an RTE camera crew in tow, filming a documentary on *John Hume's Derry*. But it was the giant Vinny Coyle, one of the Bogside 'policemen', who was first to greet Callaghan at the Guildhall. 'Mr Callaghan,' he said, 'I would like to introduce you to our new MP, Mr Hume.' The way had been prepared, but there were real fears for Callaghan's safety as he left his army escort behind, at the white lines, and headed into the throng, with only an ineffective bodyguard and Hume for protection. Some were chanting complaints about prison conditions, but most were cheering at this open recognition of the Bogside's special status. Shortly before he arrived, there had been an awkward moment when the leftist element, hostile to the visit, had erected a Tricolour at one of the main barricades. The army threatened to seize it, which would have been disastrous, so Doherty knew he had to talk it down. Flags were valuable, he said, and should be honoured and died for, but not used as provocation. A vote was taken and only ten voted to keep it, against hundreds, so the flag was ceremonially removed to Rossville Flats, where it remained for years.

Callaghan had a rough passage into the heart of the Bogside, through the jostling crowds, and Hume noticed that the visitor was looking strained. 'I can't stand this much longer,' he confided. 'I'm fifty-nine.' He was exaggerating a little – at the time he was only fifty-seven – but Hume wasted no time bundling him into Mrs Doherty's tiny two-up-two-down house near Free Derry Corner for a cup of tea and a rest. Callaghan could see that a speech was called for, to the crowds massed outside, and Hume gave the elder states-man an outline of what they needed to hear, before urging him up the narrow stairs to the front bedroom. Megaphone in hand, Callaghan delivered one of the most effective speeches of his career through the tiny bedroom window, reproducing almost word for word Hume's acknowledgment of the wrongs that had been committed in the past and the promise of justice and equality in future. It had been said that the London Government was impartial, he declared, but this was not true: the Government was firmly on the side of justice. It was a huge success, broadcast around the world, and gave Callaghan a perfect exit from the Bogside, on his way to the Protestant Fountain district, which needed somewhat different assurances.

The two politicians had been through the fire together and, as

Callaghan sat down to produce a Government response to the fresh Ulster crisis, Hume's advice during their Belfast meeting was given special weight. Indeed, the so-called Downing Street Declaration, written by Prime Minister Harold Wilson in his own hand – as he told Hume later – and issued after Major Chichester-Clark had been summoned to account for what had gone wrong, underlined many of Hume's favourite themes. It reaffirmed that 'in all legislation and executive decisions of Government every citizen is entitled to the same equality of treatment and freedom from discrimination as obtains in the rest of the United Kingdom, irrespective of political views or religion'. The seeds of Hume's idea for a central housing authority, taking council houses out of politicians' hands, had been firmly planted and Callaghan was persuaded that radical local-government reform was essential.

Where Labour led, the Tories could not be far behind, and just before the Conservative Party conference, their Ulster spokesman, Lord Hailsham, announced his intention to pay a visit, prompting a jocular motion by Canavan that 'there be no Hogg in our Bog'. With reporters milling outside the police barracks, he was driven by jeep from the back door to a rendezvous with Doherty, who took him on a Bogside tour. Later back in Doherty's home, he prefaced his remarks over afternoon tea very carefully: 'I'll tell you some things today and if they're repeated I will refuse to acknowledge them. Other things I will stand over. Is that understood?' Doherty agreed, but for all his punctiliousness, the Englishman gave little away. He warned the Bogsiders not to overstate their case. Northern Ireland was not the worst country in the world. His grandfather had come from Northern Ireland, and he would have been a Unionist. . .

The monologue ranged far and wide for an hour and twenty minutes, but he had nothing to offer and there were no revelations about Conservative policy. Disappointed, Doherty drove him back to his army escort, just as the reporters arrived. But later, listening to the party-conference speech, the Bogside leader appreciated that Hailsham had gone no further than he said he would in criticism of the uprising, and his mention of Mrs Doherty's tea and chicken sandwiches helped cool some of the Tory hotheads. If they had known about the weekend excursions from the Bogside to a Donegal Irish Army camp, for weapons training, they might have been harder to reassure.

As time wore on, the governing of the Bogside became less of a civic duty and more of a chore. The leftists knew the revolution had not arrived and the others that the Republic was not going to annex the left bank of the Foyle. The mixture of communal hysteria and idealism which had launched Free Derry was almost exhausted, and, with the leaders increasingly weary, General Ian Freeland saw his opportunity to move. The army were going in regardless, he said, but would the Defence Association assist in getting the RUC back? Using his remaining bargaining power, Canavan argued for a change in the colour of the RUC uniform, from black to green, to signify a change in attitudes, but Freeland said that was asking too much. The 'defenders' knew the game was up, and that recent political development had tipped the balance for those who wanted to get back to normality. The Hunt Report on the police was issued on 10 October, recommending disbandment of the B Specials, and two nights later a policeman was shot dead, along with two civilians, in Protestant rioting in Belfast. When Callaghan returned to the Bogside, and introduced his new police chief, Arthur Young, he was received ecstatically. Unarmed military police paved the way for the return of the RUC, and the second Free Derry period was over, to everyone's relief. But revolutionary attitudes had been formed, and the gun had been reintroduced, in a way that was to change the political situation radically, for the first time since partition. Hume, watching and negotiating quietly from the sidelines, knew that with the birth of a new IRA, shortly to emerge as the Provisionals in January 1970, time was running out for the democrats, if they wanted to restructure the state.

9

A new party

After 1969 Northern Ireland could never be the same again. The phoney war, which began when the civil rights campaign first threatened majority privilege, was over and violence became endemic. Each community believed it had seen the other in its true light – Catholics as republicans, Protestants as jackboot oppressors – and opinions hardened overnight. The opposition politicians would never again trust the Stormont Government not to put its own interest first, and unionists had seen how impotent the civil rights politicans had been against republican militants in a crunch. Most importantly, relations between Stormont and Westminster had been transformed by the introduction of the troops, as Hume and his colleagues had intended. With British troops on Northern Ireland soil, under the command of a British general, Westminster would be forced to take a direct interest in Stormont's stewardship, as never before since 1921. The first sign of this was the inclusion in the Downing Street Declaration of an order putting the British GOC in Northern Ireland effectively in charge of all security operations. A civil servant who, for comparison purposes, looked up the Stormont Cabinet papers for 1935, when British troops had last been deployed on Belfast streets, was surprised to find only a formal letter from the RUC Inspector General of the time to the army general, thanking him for his assistance during the emergency. The troops from the permanent garrison had been called out temporarily when the police were under pressure, and withdrawn after a few weeks. It was a routine matter and there was no evidence of high-level contact between Stormont and Westminster.

But in 1969 the army's intervention changed the nature of the relationship, yet there was no acknowledgment of it in the political structures, except in the installation of two Foreign Office men at Stormont Castle to represent the Westminster interest. When Currie met the civil servants travelling with Callaghan, he found they accepted the need for minority participation, without which

Stormont was finished. But how to achieve it, and not undermine moderate Unionist leadership? As time went by, this last consideration weighed less heavily with the Northern Ireland opposition.

To counter the polarisation, in the population and at Stormont, bold leadership would have been needed, but Chichester-Clark was having almost as much trouble with the extremists as O'Neill had, and the possibility of a political rapprochement gradually receded. The logic of putting troops on the streets was that Stormont was unfit or unable to govern, but the British Government had no intention of ordering its suspension, until the last possible moment. Hume had seen the ugly face of confrontation in Derry, and was trying to respond positively to the second Callaghan peace package, which included the creation of the central housing authority he had wanted, and a review of local government, the cause of much Catholic discontent. In a statement on 17 October he said civil responsibility must follow the achievement of civil rights. 'If these reforms are speedily implemented, it will be the duty of all who genuinely supported the civil rights movement to play their full part in the life of the community and to involve themselves at every level. The task of building a community of which we can be proud to replace the one of which we have been ashamed is a task which will need the efforts of everyone. Indeed it will require a great communal effort to produce the change of heart and mind that is absolutely necessary to make the equality that the law proposes a reality.'

In this same spirit, he and Currie were determined to keep an open mind on Callaghan's replacement for the hated B Specials – the Ulster Defence Regiment. It was to be a mixed, locally-recruited, part-time auxiliary force, but commanded by army officers, and under the army GOC, like any other British regiment. In the early stages, Catholics were encouraged to join, but assassinations by the IRA and traditional antagonism by the UDR's Protestant members reduced it to a loyalist force, under constant threat. Infiltration by Protestant paramilitaries – members of the Ulster Defence Association were not automatically excluded – led to UDR men's involvement in a few notorious murder cases, which further reduced the force's credibility.

Hume knew that the only way that the opposition MPs at Stormont could apply serious pressure was through a formal party, rather than an informal grouping, and he was caught thinking aloud to a German journalist. He was quoted, before he had prepared the ground, as saying he wanted a social democratic party, and was forced to deny that his thinking was so advanced, in case some of his colleagues were scared off. Although he was always the driving force, he knew they had to make progress together. Meetings were held throughout September of all thirteen opposition MPs – with Vivian Simpson, Labour, and Roddy O'Connor, Nationalist, rarely attending – and by December ten had accepted Hume's arguments for the appointment of shadow 'Ministers' and a temporary Chief Whip, the long-serving Nationalist James O'Reilly. Simpson and O'Connor, who was nominal leader of the Nationalist MPs, still opted out, and Gerry Fitt declined a post because of his Westminster duties. With nine MPs shadowing seven Ministers, Hume and Currie had to double up as shadow Ministers of Development. But at least there was now a structure to bind together the loose alliance which had made its mark in over 100 hours of debating the Public Order Amendment Bill – designed to strengthen Government powers in dealing with demonstrations – and at Question Time, tripping lazy Unionist Ministers.

At last Hume was making some progress towards an organised approach to opposition politics, which had always been lacking. He had long believed that if there had been a democratic party organisation behind the Nationalist politicians, instead of autocratic nomination conventions, there would have been no need for the civil rights movement. The party would have attracted better candidates and its demands could not have been ignored by the Government, as they normally were. Austin Currie had tried his best and the intellectuals' NDP had provided a model, but it was left to Hume to create the instrument that was to weld the disparate elements together. There was backing for his aim of establishing a social democratic party from the British and Irish Labour Parties, but the Northern Ireland Labour Party preferred a proposal to merge the Northern Ireland and British parties, which was doomed from the beginning. Wilson's party was too dependent on the immigrant Irish vote to align itself with a pro-partition faction in Ulster.

While the politicians edged together, the paramilitary forces were regrouping, and the old-fashioned green republican 'Provisional' IRA broke away from the socialist-minded 'Officials', with initial help from Fianna Fáil sources who feared Marxist influence in the South. As the newcomers flexed their muscles, the honeymoon between the army and the Catholic community ended, and pressure grew for a more coherent political alternative. The National Democratic Party set up a unity conference without result, although Hume's speech to the delegates laid foundations for a merger, and the Labour Government dropped several hints through intermediaries that it would prefer dealing with a single entity, representing Catholic nationalist opinion, than with a handful of individuals. Even the formation of the Alliance Party – representing a combination of the O'Neillite wing of the Unionist Party and Catholic liberals, together with the mixed membership of the reforming New Ulster Movement pressure group – added urgency to the necessity for action.

Politicians in the Republic had an obvious interest in seeing a moderate and broadly nationalist party emerging from the collection of political personalities in the North, and it was a Donegal Fine Gael TD, Paddy Harte, who set up the first North–South meeting with the Fine Gael front bench in September 1969 in the Park Hotel, Virginia, Co. Cavan. The civil rights MPs were naturally retiscent about being seen to associate with Southern politicians, but news of the meeting leaked to the media and, when reporters gathered around, one of the Fine Gael members refused to leave his car. Gerry Fitt and Paddy Devlin failed to turn up, but Hume, Currie, Cooper and O'Hanlon had their first useful contacts with members of the Dáil. Harte could see that they also needed to keep in touch with the Government party, Fianna Fáil, and in the early stages he was the contact man between the Northern MPs and the Taoiseach, Jack Lynch.

At Hume's instigation, the ten MPs began a series of weekend meetings at his favourite holiday spot of Bunbeg, on the wild west coast of Donegal, where they got to know each other as people, as well as politicians. Away from the pressure of constituency business, they were able to take a longer look at where they were going, which was Hume's purpose, and to consider the advantages of organising themselves as a party, rather than operating as individuals. Each one was a personality in his own right, with a strong personal following, and not all were convinced they had anything to gain. There was no tradition in nationalist politics in Northern Ireland of party membership or democratic structures, and several like Fitt enjoyed the freedom this informality allowed. But Hume managed the discussions skilfully, allowing all the divergent views to be expressed, and then weighing in with his own strong preference for a new kind of nationalist politics, based on policies rather than personalities.

Hume and the other civil rights MPs, Cooper and O'Hanlon, already had independent constituency organisations and a common political platform, so it was mainly a matter of seeing who would join them from the other parties and what price there would be to pay for unity. Currie was a kindred spirit, and had been preaching a similar doctrine in the Nationalist Party since 1966, but the Belfast pair, Fitt and Devlin, were a problem. They would provide the Belfast working-class element, which was essential for an umbrella party, but the unpredictable Devlin was wary of what he regarded as green tories, and Fitt valued his independence highly, as the titular head of the Republican Labour Party. He did not drive and so was not a regular attender of the caucus meetings. Even at this stage, the personality differences between the two contenders for leadership of the opposition alliance, Hume and Fitt, were glaringly apparent. Both came from working-class backgrounds, but Hume was a product of the post-war scholarship system, with a solidly academic education, while Fitt was a self-taught, street-wise ex-merchant-seaman, accustomed to living off his sharp political wits and ebullient personality. As the Westminster MP, and by far the more experienced politician, both in Belfast Corporation and Stormont, Fitt could have been excused for resenting the central role which Hume assumed in organising the alliance, although it was obvious to everyone else that the serious, intelligent and persuasive Derry man was the natural leader and innovator. Fitt was always to regard Derry as a place apart, where the border was so close, and the Catholic majority so large that the Protestants did not constitute a physical threat. Hume, for his part, realised how important it was to include the Belfast element in the new party, to create the balance which previous anti-Unionist groupings had lacked.

Eventually, force of circumstances brought them together and after a long business session at the Errigal View hotel, Bunbeg, an agreement was hammered out in July 1970. By this time there were only six or seven MPs remaining, plus Senator Paddy Wilson, but the combination of external pressures and a growing sense of cama-raderie, as they argued and drank and sang at Irish nights, had helped to narrow their ideological differences. For a basically shy person, Hume revealed a surprisingly warm, extrovert side to his nature in the late-night sessions, with a full range of party pieces, sung in a steady baritone, featuring 'Plaisir d'Amour' and 'Danny Boy'. The outcome of the talks had to be formalised, so Hume accompanied

Currie to his home at Donaghmore, near Dungannon, and from 9 pm on Sunday evening to 3 am Monday morning they drew up a document, typed by Anita Currie, setting out what had been agreed on the composition of the party. Currie had never made any secret of his desire for a new opposition unity party, and had no problems with fellow-Nationalists, but Devlin, as Northern Ireland Labour chairman, was subjected to some understandable criticism by that British-orientated party.

Immediately after the Bunbeg weekend, the agreed document was taken to Stormont and all seven signed it. A new party was born, and all that remained was to christen it and name its leader, for which another long session was needed. The media were on the trail by this time, so the 'cover' was that they were meeting in Toomebridge to discuss the future of Lough Neagh eel fisheries, and any inquisitive political correspondent was to be told that Gerry Fitt and Paddy Devlin were representing the west Belfast eel fishermen! There was a long debate on the name, with Currie and Hume, who was an admirer of the German socialists, arguing for Social Democratic Party and the Belfast representatives insisting that they would not enter a party without 'Labour', preferably in first place. In the interests of unity, Hume and Currie eventually agreed and the debate moved on to another subject. Suddenly Paddy Devlin, who had taken no part in the discussion and was sitting with closed eyes, half asleep, snapped to attention: 'You can't do that. Think of that, the LSD party, money and drugs.' So it was SDLP.

Everything bar the leadership was signed and sealed, and it was with much relief that Hume drove into Donegal to Roneragh House, on the shores of Lough Swilly, to meet some British and Irish politicans. The Labour MP, Maurice Foley, who had turned his attention from the Nigeria-Biafra conflict to Ireland and was a firm supporter of the new party, was there, as was Frank Cluskey, the deputy leader of the Irish Labour Party and Paddy Harte. But Harte's reaction to the manifesto was unenthusiastic; he told Hume he would have much preferred to have seen him get together with Dick Ferguson, the Liberal Unionist MP – one of them as leader and the other as deputy. Such a combination of strong personalities, Harte argued, would get a warm response from both Catholics and Protestants. But the Donegal TD was being idealistic; it was difficult enough to unite the anti-Unionist MPs, without trying to engage O'Neillite Unionists, whose commitment to staying in politics was questionable.

Other influences from the South were of a very different nature, as attempted gun-running, allegedly with the approval of Government Ministers, led to the sackings of Neil Blaney and Charles Haughey, and the 1970 Arms Trial, which cleared them of involvement but left blots on their reputations. Other Northern politicians were not surprised, but Hume was able to claim no knowledge of what was going on because his opponents in the Dublin Government were determined he should be kept in the dark. If he had known, he would have opposed any reintroduction of the gun, however desperate the situation.

Concern for the plight of Northern Catholics was widespread, and a committee was set up in Dublin to gather money in street collections and transfer it in cash to troubled areas of Belfast and Derry. One of the women involved was surprised at the ease with which premises and equipment were put at their disposal, and one day when a member of the staff who had exclusive use of the telephone was out a call was received from a surprised Government Minister. A doctor on the committee was asked to register a piece of heavy equipment as an electro-encephalograph machine, for transfer to Northern Ireland, but on examination it turned out to be a radio transmitter. It was a time when many laws and rules of behaviour were broken, because of the perception of the dangers which Northerners faced. Hume was later to regard himself as lucky not to have had knowledge of such unauthorised activities. Many Northern politicians helped to channel funds to defence committees in the North, and their names appear in unpublished Dublin documents, but Hume's is not among them.

Before agreement could be reached on a new civil rights party, the June 1970 Westminster election intervened, forcing Hume's independent organisation into a deal with Eddie McAteer's Nationalists, to avoid a damaging split vote, even though the Unionists were certain winners. Negotiations went on literally all night between the two sets of supporters until Hume, who was unacceptable to the Nationalists as the candidate, agreed to act as election agent for McAteer, on the understanding that he would write the manifesto, and that the two party organisations would eventually merge. But even though he persuaded McAteer to fight on a moderate platform identical to his own of 1969, Hume incurred the wrath of Cooper, who had his own candidate, the Protestant Senator Claude Wilton, who had been nominated to the Senate on civil rights votes, and would have made a popular cross-community choice, capable of winning Protestant and Catholic votes and acting as an ice-breaker for the new non-sectarian party. For a time, Cooper and Devlin were not on speaking terms with Hume and undoubtedly the election deal in Derry was a setback to the idea of a countrywide party.

The alliance was hardly a successful combination, for not only did McAteer finish a poor second, with Eamonn McCann capturing 7,565 votes in third place, but the Nationalists continued to steer clear of the emerging party – much to the relief of most of its supporters. In a way, it was a death blow for the Nationalists, having been swamped by the civil rights tide in 1969 and then, having adopted their programme, failing in 1970. It also helped to delay the launch of the new party, after Hume had aligned himself so closely with the old-style Nationalists, and there was more foot-dragging into the summer months. But with the arrival of a Conservative government, more amenable to Unionist pleas for tougher action against 'republicans', a new and dangerous element was added. Orange marches went ahead, with army protection, and the inevitable results were civilian deaths, rioting and a first taste of armed combat for the new Provisional IRA. This was compounded after an arms find led to a three-day Falls curfew, which confirmed Catholic opinion that security policy was no longer impartial.

The leadership issue was still unresolved, though it was clearly between Hume and Fitt, the only Westminister MP and the best-known anti-Unionist figure in Britain. Already a rural/urban split was developing and to avoid the SDLP being compared to the old Nationalist Party, which had no base in Belfast, the rural members were prepared to pay almost any price the city MPs put on their participation. For Fitt, the price was clearly the leadership, but nothing was said, and the whole concept of the new party went into abeyance during the holiday season. Again, Fitt was hanging back, reluctant to commit himself and arguing that he needed time to bring his party around. The others thought he had been consulting regularly with his party colleagues, who were Belfast city councillors, but subsequently it turned out that he had not. In an attempt to accommodate Fitt, Hume added to his own three-point platform – a democratic party organisation, left-of-centre bias and unity by consent – assurances about the new party's desire for trade union links.

Currie, always a close friend of Fitt, tried to convince him that the days of personality politics, as a means of getting results, were over, and that an organisation was necessary to avoid the besetting nationalist sin of splits. But still he delayed until, with power slipping away in the mounting summer violence, Hume decided to strike. While on a visit to Dublin in August, he made his usual contacts with the media, a practice that was becoming second nature, and on Monday the *Irish Times* carried an inspired lead story by its political correspondent, Michael McInerney, on the formation of a new political party in Northern Ireland, suggesting that only the choice of leader was holding it back. That morning Currie got a telephone call from Dungannon journalist Sean Hughes, asking him had he seen the *Irish Times*. He had not, but he soon got hold of a copy and decided to take the bull by the horns.

The local correspondent was asked to ring Mike Burns of RTE and tell him Austin Currie was ready to be interviewed. The call came through from Dublin and all was revealed in the way Currie wanted. No, he said, there was no truth in the report that there was a problem over the leader. The only one with sufficient experience, ability and acceptability was Gerry Fitt. Was it just his opinion? Yes, but he thought it would be shared. Privately, Currie felt that it was essential to have Fitt as leader, to overcome the Belfast/country division. The country members would accept a Belfast person as leader, but there was no way that Gerry Fitt would have accepted Hume. Currie might also have been reluctant to see Hume confirmed as the leading personality west of the Bann, and Cooper would hardly have backed his Derry rival. O'Hanlon, Hume's only backer, was well aware that the voting would have been five-two for Fitt, so the question was never raised. Having done the interview, Currie rang Hume at home and told him what he had said, and why. Hume agreed, as the matter had been dragging on too long, and he was happy to be Fitt's deputy.

Next, Currie rang Hunter's public house in Ballyvoy, which had the nearest phone to Fitt's north Antrim holiday house. He left a message, and when RTE made contact Fitt hitched a lift to Belfast for a studio interview. On air, and without any proper consultation, Fitt coolly accepted the leadership, when he heard that both Currie and Hume had nominated him. It must have been the first time in history that an acceptance of party leadership had been made in response to a radio interviewer's question. Privately, Fitt was less buoyant. 'This won't last,' he told another doubtful participant, Paddy Devlin, 'but it would be unfair not to try it.'

They were in business at last, and a formal press-conference launch was hastily arranged at the Grand Central Hotel. In the end, there were only six MPs – Hume, Fitt, Currie, Devlin, Cooper and O'Hanlon – plus Senator Paddy Wilson, later to be assassinated by a loyalist terror gang. O'Reilly declined, explaining that it was too late in his career to change horses, and his refusal was accepted with mixed regret and relief. (Ineptly, he had been chosen to speak on TV for the opposition, against Faulkner, and had been reduced to incoherence.) Hume's long struggle to establish a credible opposition party, open to Protestants and Catholics, had cleared another obstacle – but still to be tackled were the formulation of a constitution and the setting up of grass-roots organisation in all six counties.

In his opening statement to the Press, amid the tinkling coffee cups, Fitt explained the main reason for the new party: 'We regard this present crisis as being particularly urgent in view of the real possibility that there may be an extreme right-wing takeover of the government of Northern Ireland, with a consequent interference in the reforms which have been recently placed on the statute book. In this situation there is also the possibility that the Westminster Government may be forced to intervene and we have recognised that in such a situation, the Westminster Government would want to hear the voice of the people who have been opposed to Unionism in Northern Ireland.' He continued: 'We are not negatively non-sectarian. We will be forcibly anti-sectarian and wherever sectarianism rears its ugly head we will demand and command the support of all who have faith in the new party to take very stern action against it.'

Fitt then read out the Bunbeg document, bearing the hallmarks of the two Belfast socialists and emphasising the left-of-centre bias of the new party. The second of the four party aims included eleven specific commitments, among them the obtaining of 'a just and adequate distribution of wealth'; upholding 'the rights and principles of organised labour'; promoting the spread of co-operatives; working for a minimum wage and equal pay for men and women; ensuring public ownership of fishing rights and inland waters; and working for the establishment of state industries. Only in the third aim was there a mention of Irish unity: 'To promote co-operation, friendship and understanding between North and South with a view to the eventual reunification of Ireland through the consent of the majority of the people in the North and in the South'. (The last phrase was important, since it insisted on a majority in the North, not just in the thirty-two counties, thus recognising the Northern majority's right to opt out.)

The question-and-answer session with the journalists also gave Fitt the chance to play down the national question. Asked what the party's attitude in Stormont would be towards the border, he said the priority was 'to maintain and apply pressure to the Unionist Party to ensure that there is no backtracking in the reforms. If we are successful, it will bring about a more normal state of political life and at that time we can then decide what we would do if we were elected to government.' He supported the maintenance of Stormont 'at the present time', to bring about reforms, but added, 'We intend to work for the reunification of this country with the consent of the vast majority of its people.' But already there was a warning of a boycott; if there was a right-wing takeover Fitt favoured a withdrawal from Stormont.

Hume had to field some awkward questions about his involvement with Eddie McAteer in the June election, and how this would affect the SDLP's standing, but he quietly asked both Protestants and Catholics to look at the aims and decide for themselves. It was an up-beat conference, Gerry Fitt contributing to the mood with a typical last-minute quip for the Press: 'We ask for your assistance — don't inter or intern us without trial.' Although he was soon to try the patience of his colleagues, Fitt still generated more goodwill among journalists than any of them did.

After the launch, there was the matter of finance to be discussed, and the MPs headed down High Street to the nearest Munster and Leinster Bank branch to talk to the bank manager. With an overdraft of £1,000, the new party was ready to take on the might of Unionism and all its money, on behalf of the poor, the dispossessed and the newly-rich who still identified with the civil rights heroes of Derry and Dungannon. Press reaction to the party was favourable, the *Times* commenting that 'the fragmentary and quarrelsome nature of anti-Unionist politics in Northern Ireland is one of the things that make the province ungovernable. . . an initiative to provide a stronger political organisation and a more united front is worth having'. It felt, however, that the stand on the constitution made it most unlikely it would win much Protestant support. The *Irish Times* asked why it should be assumed that the new party was for

Catholics only – 'If Protestants found in it something worth working for they should drop their stereotype visions of the Catholics and get in.'

The Nationalists were left floundering, just as they were about to discuss their own form of opposition alliance, and their fifty years' domination of anti-Unionist politics vanished overnight. A stagnant party had thrown up unimaginative, sectarian representatives, incapable of meeting the new challenge. Many of its supporters transferred their allegiance, particularly where the civil rights tradition was strong, but this was not the case with Fitt's own party, Republican Labour. Paddy Kennedy, his erratic colleague at Stormont, was furious over the desertion of the party's leader and its only Senator, vowing to expand Republican Labour's activities in Belfast. The promise was never kept, and the party faded into oblivion, but any organisation it had was lost to the SDLP, and the lack of a proper base in Belfast was never tackled until the defection of Fitt and Devlin in the late 1970s. As Fitt was to explain, his constituency workers regarded the SDLP as too much like the Nationalist Party, and deserted him for Official Sinn Fein, the left-wing republicans.

On the plus side, there was a welcome response from the Southern parties who, like the British, preferred dealing with a united non-unionist front. The National Democratic Party, which had been kept in touch with developments was predictably enthusiastic about the formation of the party of its dreams, with the strong personalities it lacked, and an early meeting voted to disband and defect *en masse*. Already the SDLP had acquired rented premises from a well-wisher, in an old Georgian terrace house in College Square North and Paddy Devlin, as the only party activist based in Belfast – apart from Fitt, who had no interest in organisation – was in charge of the office. Members and money were needed and a quarter-page advertisement in the *Belfast Telegraph* invited applications for membership, with a 50p subscription. But the newspaper had to apologise for an unfortunate misprint in the second aim – the party was apparently committing itself to uphold and support the democratic rights of 'wealth', whereas its commitment was to 'the principles of organised labour'.

Although Devlin's leftist hand was to be seen plainly in the aims, he was still wary of attempts to broaden the party's appeal by involving mainly-Catholic business and professional people in discussions about the future. Fearing betrayal, Devlin engaged in a typical pre-emptive strike, going to Dublin, ostensibly to seek affiliation with Irish Labour, but also to present himself as a radical socialist who would turn Catholic Ireland upside down. It had the required effect, he claimed, and the few Nationalists who might have been tempted to join hurriedly backed off. Hume, however, was well aware of the difficulties of reconciling the different ideologies and was not to be deterred in his aim of building a broad-spectrum party. To place it on the left or right, he knew, would limit its potential for growth into the mass party which could provide the political alternative to violence.

Devlin fell into the role of unpaid organiser and fund-raiser, finding more financial support in the South than the North. Fianna Fáil backers, he discovered, were inclined to hold back initially in case the party would not succeed, but subscriptions began to pour in from other Southern sources. Ulick O'Connor, in his Saturday night RTE programme, was particularly helpful, persuading many viewers to send in cheques from £5 to £50. Fellow presenter Gay Byrne, too, threw in a favourable mention. Eventually a support branch was formed, with representatives of all the parties, under a Newry-born academic, Dr John Kelly, holding regular fund-raising functions and generally acting as a sounding board in Dublin for SDLP policy. From the early days, the South has been a good source of funds, probably because of the long tradition – uncommon in the North – of raising finance by public appeals for political parties. Every year a Sunday is set aside for an SDLP church-gate collection in the Dublin area, in the same way as the Southern parties have theirs.

After the launching fanfare, the MPs had to sell the idea in their own constituencies, and months went by before there was any real attempt at providing the promised six-county-wide party organisation to underpin the parliamentary party. But the disbandment of the NDP, in October 1970, provided a core of experienced volunteers, and when a worried Hume put the wheels in motion in January 1971, the only people with the know-how were former NDP members. One of them, Ben Caraher, was disappointed to find, at the first meeting to discuss organisation, that, far from the new party throwing up fresh faces, nearly all those present were his former NDP colleagues. When drafting of a constitution was raised, there was little understanding of what was required and Gerry Fitt interjected 'Haven't we got one already?' But the bare aims had to be fleshed out and the task was deputed to Caraher and Devlin, whose main contribution was to provide copies of the British and Irish Labour Parties' constitutions. When the new programme appeared, it drew heavily on these documents, again relegating the call for Irish unity (by consent) from the foremost role it had in conventional nationalist parties to the fourth of six principles.

In the country, the organisations of Hume, Cooper, O'Hanlon and Currie provided the models on which others were based, but there were decades of political neglect to be overcome in areas which traditionally returned Unionist MPs. Broadly speaking, nationalists had organised, through the autocratic convention system, only where they had a chance of winning a seat and this meant that the SDLP was tilling virgin soil in many of the constituencies which were normally uncontested. It was better off in local government, where the NDP controlled Strabane and Downpatrick and had representation in three of the six counties.

Since the background of Hume and several other leading lights was in the Credit Union, the bias was towards a highly-structured organisation, which provided essential stability as the party was finding its feet. Once again Hume was involved in a missionary enterprise, travelling around Northern Ireland, persuading former civil rights activists and disillusioned nationalists to stop complaining and start organising. Many a phone call was made, reminding civil rights supporters of their obligation to take another stand before the gains they had made were lost in violence or Unionist intransigence. The point was taken, and branches sprang up all over the country, in response to the exciting prospect of fighting the Unionists on a united ticket. An election was needed to provide the finishing touches, in many areas, but for the first time every non-unionist elector had access to a local political party and real policy-making. It was the crowning achievement of years of struggle by Hume and others to get the Catholic population off their knees and fully involved in the political process. Dividends were slow in coming and for long periods appeared non-existent, but hope could survive so long as the local organisation remained.

To Hume, the father figure still in his early thirties, this was the real value of his efforts to produce a coherent political voice for the minority. But first there were problems of professional jealousy to be resolved, and Paddy Devlin used some physical persuasion to show Gerry Fitt that he was leading a party rather than a one-man band. In a Stormont debate on health the SDLP members had adjourned to the bar, after preparing themselves for a long sitting, leaving Fitt in charge. Suddenly the division bells rang, signalling the end of the debate. Devlin ran to his place and angrily asked Fitt what had gone wrong. The leader motioned that he would discuss it outside and when Devlin went one way, he went another. But Devlin sensed what was happening, doubled back along the corridor and struck the party leader with a heavy punch. 'After that,' he said, 'we had a party.'

10
Bloody Sunday

Hume now had a party with which to test the willingness of the
Unionists to count the non-unionist minority into the political
process, but to no one's surprise their response was negative. In a
state with continual one-party rule, the majority had no need of
opposition votes, and the emergence of a new opposition grouping,
bringing together only six of the thirteen MPs – against thirty-nine of
all varieties of Unionist – was not regarded as significant. As Hume
put it: 'The Unionists treated politics as a match between Rangers
and Celtic – a match that Rangers (the Protestant team) always won.
That was their downfall. Politics is not like that – total victory is not
possible.'

Even the gradual implementation of the 1969 reform package,
with its law outlawing incitement to hatred and the establishment of
an Ombudsman, or Commissioner for Complaints, a Community
Relations Commission and what became known as the Housing
Executive, did nothing to increase the Catholics' sense of involvement or strengthen the hand of the politicians. As early as January
1971, the SDLP was arguing against the introduction of internment
and in favour of 'an acceptable police force' for the troubled areas,
but it shared the growing isolation of its supporters as the
Government battened down the hatches against terrorism. Even
Callaghan, an old friend, insulted them by insisting on meeting them
together with the chairman of the Northern Ireland Labour Party, an
offer which they refused.

Increasingly the focus was on the street battles between the two
IRA factions and the British Army, which had become an alien
occupying force, and the first soldier was killed by IRA gunfire on
6 February 1971, on the same night as the first off-duty IRA man was
shot dead. As the offensive was stepped up, with three Scottish
soldiers lured to their deaths near Belfast, Prime Minister Chichester-
Clark came under heavy pressure to go for a military solution, to end
the no-go areas in Belfast. But London's response was half-hearted

and he resigned in March, still opposing the Unionists' ultimate deterrent, internment.

Hume's own thinking was beginning to crystallise, as the Unionists showed they were unable to deliver on meaningful reform, and in an *Irish Press* interview he laid the foundations for the power-sharing concept. Institutions had to be created in which all the people could have confidence, he said, and from which a system of law and order could be devised that people would respect. 'The Northern Ireland problem can only be solved by creating a new constitution which recognises that power and decision-making must be shared between the different sections of the community.' The way forward, he believed, was the creation of an assembly, elected by proportional representation, and in turn electing an executive by PR, on the Swiss model.

On Articles 2 and 3 of the Irish constitution, claiming sovereignty over the whole island, Hume did not think changes would have any effect on unionists – 'in any case it is foolish to imagine that the present constitution of the 26 counties, however amended, would be the constitution of a united Ireland. It is quite obvious there would have to be an entirely new constitution, which would be agreed by the people of the North and which would recognise the rights of all minorities in the country.'

He had moved considerably from the position set down in a personal submission to the Crowther Commission on the United Kingdom constitution in February 1970, in which he had made four basic proposals. He had wanted it accepted that any citizen could advocate constitutional change by peaceful means; that proportional representation should be introduced for Stormont and local-government elections; that a periodic referendum should be held removing the constitutional question from party politics and that a Bill of Rights should be enshrined in the constitution. There was no reference to minority participation in government, although Fine Gael – at the instigation of Garret FitzGerald – had introduced the concept in its policy statement on the North of September 1969. Hume was the first of the opposition MPs to overcome a natural antipathy to any form of collaboration with the Stormont regime, and eventually power-sharing – an idea which he had first sold to Home Secretary Reginald Maudling – was to be taken up by the British Government, the SDLP and some Unionists.

Just as the Conservative victory in the 1970 Westminster election

signalled an end to Labour's softly-softly approach to the IRA –
thereby adding fuel to the flames – Brian Faulkner's succession to the
Northern Ireland premiership in March was a turning point. From
then on Stormont's slow decline in its power to influence events
became terminal. No sooner had Faulkner taken office and announced his strangely-assorted Cabinet than the SDLP, through
Hume, was posing hostile questions. What assurances had Faulkner
given to Agriculture Minister Harry West, who had said the reform
policies 'will be implemented in a different way' and had hinted that
Bill Craig would soon be joining the Cabinet? How could John
Taylor, who had backed Craig's policies, be appointed Minister of
State at Home Affairs? Why was the one Minister who had the
support of non-unionists, the eccentrically aristocratic Phelim
O'Neill, dropped? The SDLP statement went on, 'We find ourselves
totally disgusted by the shameless and nauseating horse-trading
which is typical of the political record of the present Prime Minister'.
Faulkner was 'one of the chief architects of Northern Ireland's sick
society' and his actions had 'completely debased and devalued
accepted standards of public life'.

While the amiable Chichester-Clark could be excused for his
honest ham-fistedness, the businesslike Faulkner had the reputation
of a sly, self-seeking but capable parliamentary performer, who had
helped bring down O'Neill – mostly by offering him no assistance –
and would blow with the wind of Orangeism. In his choice of
Cabinet he had confirmed SDLP suspicions, and a hardline statement against rioters, interpreted as a licence to the army to 'shoot to
kill', sparked fierce controversy.

The SDLP had experience of his devious ways – from a clumsy
attempt in 1970 to gerrymander Fermanagh council by the inclusion
of an unrelated Protestant area in Tyrone – and there was healthy
scepticism, as well as genuine puzzlement, when he proposed to
establish four new parliamentary committees to deal with social
services, industrial development and environmental matters, at least
two of which would have opposition MPs as salaried chairmen.
Earlier, Reginald Maudling had pointed to just such an experiment,
when he suggested that where the majority in government did not
change, 'it is reasonable and desirable to see how it is possible to
broaden the basis of government and certainly to avoid a situation
where a man of talent who can serve his country is debarred from
doing so solely by religious beliefs'. Whether or not he had been

111

pushed, Faulkner had offered something oddly resembling a hand of friendship, and Paddy Devlin described it as the Prime Minister's best hour. A committee system had been mentioned, in fact, in the SDLP's submission to the Macrory Committee on local-government reorganisation.

Even Hume, later to say he was 'appalled' by Devlin's acceptance of the committee deal, was complimentary: 'It should be made clear to all people today who say that no change has taken place that this is simply not true. There have been changes in this community.' On the fiftieth anniversary of its creation, the Northern Ireland Parliament seemed to have been given another lease of life, but on the following day the atmosphere was different. Having sampled party opinion, Austin Currie praised Faulkner for raising the tone of the debate, before reminding him that the idea of committees was the SDLP's, and that institutional changes were necessary where there was no alternative government. Faulkner, always the optimist, regarded the SDLP man's speech as further endorsement. Currie, who three months earlier had called for participation 'in government' by both sections of the community and 'institutional changes', was not to be bought off by the committee offer. Besides, there were hints coming from the SDLP's frequent meetings with the British representatives that much more, amounting to places in government, might be on offer. Any further doubts were dispelled, instantly, when four days later it was revealed that Faulkner and several leading members of the Cabinet had travelled to the Lurgan headquarters of the Royal Black Institution, the senior Orangemen, to explain themselves.

As the Orange marching season built up to its annual climax, the rioting, too, became fiercer until on 8 July 1971, the inevitable happened and the army claimed its first Derry victims – teenagers Seamus Cusack and Desmond Beattie. They had been shot, the army said, because one had been carrying a rifle and the other a nailbomb, but since there was no evidence, the official version was disbelieved. Derry's lucky streak was over, and as crowds of angry teenagers massed at a recruitment rally for the Provisionals the next Sunday, Hume and his party colleagues – except Devlin, who was in Dublin, and Fitt, out of telephone range – drafted an ultimatum to the British Government, over Stormont's head. Either a full inquiry was set up into the deaths, within a week, or the SDLP would pull out of Stormont indefinitely.

Viewed from anywhere but Derry, it seemed like over-reaction.

But the MPs were unanimous that it was time to have done with tinkering solutions, to force the British Government to face up to its responsibility – now that the Faulkner Government was exerting political control over the use of troops – and close down Stormont. A new regime was needed, if opposition politicians were to be allowed true 'participation', and only the British could impose it. Meanwhile, to underline the minority's withdrawal of consent to be governed by Stormont and to provide a political alternative to violence, Hume proposed that an 'Alternative Assembly' should be set up, to give non-Unionists a platform. Though essentially a stunt, it was not a meaningless one.

Devlin and Fitt later voiced opposition to the walk-out threat, but whatever their views at the time – and Devlin, *en route* to Dublin, gave an SDLP member the impression that he was very disillusioned with Stormont – they went along with the majority when, inevitably, the British promised an early inquest, but no inquiry. Once again Hume's ability to draft a pithy press release, which was always one of the secrets of his weighty influence over policy, ensured that his view of events went on the record, as the reason for withdrawal. The inquiry, he said, was a basic test of the 'sincerity and determination of the British Government to proceed in an impartial manner towards a political solution'. The Derry deaths had been the last straw, leading to increasing doubts about the usefulness of the SDLP MPs' role. 'We have now been driven to the point where we have been faced with a clear choice – either to continue to give credibility to the system which in itself is basically unstable, and from which derives the unrest that is destroying our community, or take a stand in order to bring home to those in authority the need for strong political action to solve our problems and to prevent any further tragic loss of life which derives from the instability of our political institutions.'

Since the 1970 election, he said, the actions of both the British Government and army had tended to confirm increasing suspicions about the role of the army in Northern Ireland, dating from the arrival of the present administration. 'Is it any wonder that we feel that the role of the military has changed from being that of impartial keepers of the peace to that of shoring up and supporting a particular individual in the office of Prime Minister? Has the British Government even yet faced the logic of its presence in Northern Ireland? What did that intervention mean other than that the Northern

113

Ireland system itself had failed to produce the basis for peace, justice and stability?' British policy was still governed, as it always had been – except for a few short months in 1969 – by the threat of a right-wing backlash, he said. There could be no solution until the right wing was confronted, nor until account was taken of the voice of non-unionists, as well as unionists.

As if in answer to the SDLP and to Jack Lynch, who on 11 July – fifty years after the Anglo-Irish truce – had called for Britain to declare that it favoured an end to partition, a massive army-police swoop in Belfast on 23 July saw more than 100 houses raided and searched in an apparent dry run for internment. Without an opposition presence at Stormont and with a compliant government at Westminster, the way was clear for Faulkner to overcome previous army objections and look to internment to solve the terrorist problems, as it had in every decade of Northern Ireland's history. Paddy Devlin was in Springfield Road Barracks with Paddy O'Hanlon, trying to probe the mystery death of a man shot by the army when his car backfired, as the news came in – the round-up of 337 republicans and civil rights agitators had begun at dawn on 9 August. Reaction was swift and bloody to the crude, one-sided operation, based on outdated intelligence, and inside two days twenty-three people were dead – one a priest shot while administering the last rites. Hundreds more Catholics and Protestants were burned out of their homes or fled in fear from mixed areas into the ghettoes. By the end of 1971, 172 were dead – 144 of them after the introduction of internment – and 1,576 had been arrested under the controversial Special Powers Act.

Forced to justify the disaster, Faulkner claimed success in his effort to 'flush out the gunmen'. But in doing so, he had put them on the streets to stay, with popular support. In Derry, Hume had returned briefly from holidays in Bunbeg to his three-storey terrace house overlooking the Bogside and was awakened by loud knocking on the door. Relatives of men who had been arrested wanted to know what was happening and where they were being taken. The police were no help but, acting on a tip-off, Hume climbed into his car and headed for Magilligan, a remote sandy peninsula at the head of the Foyle estuary, where a disused World War II army camp was to be used as a prison transit camp.

He arrived before the internees and, as he waited at a roadblock, a requisitioned furniture van came along, with the men inside banging hard on the sides. When it stopped at the barrier, Hume beat the sides with his fist and shouted out 'It's me, John Hume'. He was answered with shouts and more banging, before the barriers swung open. Back in the Bogside, the days of the first and second Free Derry periods were re-enacted, this time with the guns on open display. Hume's home was in the firing line, backing onto a police-army base, and day and night constituents beat a path to his door, telling tales of disaster. Though no longer attending Stormont – now in recess – he was still the only public representative for Catholic Derry. A Development Commission was still running the city, without any elected councillors. In normal times, it would have been onerous enough, but in a time of insurrection, with thirty people arrested every night, it was a nightmare no other MP in the United Kingdom would ever experience.

Later, when the Magilligan prisoners had been transferred to the prison ship *Maidstone* in Belfast harbour, he drove down to check on their conditions. They were no better nor worse than he had expected, in a smelly old ship's tender moored to a jetty. (In wartime years, the *Argenta* prison ship had been anchored in Belfast Lough and proved more secure; in 1972 seven prisoners swam to freedom from the *Maidstone* and hijacked a bus to safety.) But any consideration of the cramped conditions was swiftly eclipsed by the story Hume was told by the prisoner he had come to see – the Bogside's Sean Keenan, a veteran of the *Argenta* and number one on every internee list. Hume listened with mounting concern to the accounts of key prisoners being made to stand spreadeagled at a wall with hoods over their heads and subjected to a constant deafening noise, designed to reduce them to mental wrecks and turn them into informers. With typical efficiency, Keenan had signed statements ready, which he passed over in a final handshake, for Hume to slip into his shoe. Outside, reporters were waiting for his account but, thinking fast, he decided not to relay all that he had heard. Coming from him, an interested party, the allegations might not carry much weight, so he quietly took aside the *Sunday Times* man, whom he already knew, and gave him the statements. They made exciting reading, exactly what an 'Insight' reporter wanted, and when put together with all the other accounts of beatings and rough treatment, provided the basis for the major scandal of 'interrogations in depth', as developed in Aden and Cyprus, and carried out by the police under army instruction.

As the stories leaked out, in the *Sunday Times* and the Irish papers, defenders of civil liberties were outraged. A Government investigation, carried out by Sir Edmund Compton, was later to deny the methods amounted to 'physical brutality', but to assert that they constituted 'ill treatment', and they were abandoned, with thousands of pounds compensation paid out to the victims. The Irish Government took the claims to the European Court of Human Rights, and leading Foreign Affairs officials had their baptism in Northern Ireland's problems, interviewing prisoners for their harrowing statements. Seven years were to elapse before a verdict was found in the Republic's favour, holding that some prisoners had been subjected to 'inhuman and degrading treatment' but not to torture. Some valuable information was obtained, the police claimed, but at the cost of lowering Britain's reputation for scrupulous police methods and associating Stormont and the RUC with brutality. Faulkner was later to claim, apparently sincerely, that he had no idea unusual techniques were being used. He was told of interrogations, but did not inquire further.

Internment had changed the whole nature of anti-government protest, from the opposition boycotting Parliament to the professional agitators on the streets. All were united in the cause not only of ending internment, but in bringing down the regime which had ordered it. Stormont had finally proved itself irreformable, and there was broad agreement, across party and class lines, that it had to go before progress to a just society was possible. Looking back, the SDLP leadership could see that by opting out of Parliament in July, it had removed the last obstacle to Faulkner's internment policy. But few were convinced that if the Unionists had been determined to introduce internment, a threat of withdrawal by the SDLP would have deterred them.

The announcement of the Alternative Assembly had been a safety valve for the nationalist community in July, but internment demanded a new and dramatic response, which a rent and rates strike offered. It was a tactic beloved of the far left, mooted as far back as 1966, but all previous attempts had failed before the SDLP and the remnants of the Civil Rights Association – by now depleted, because of a leftist takeover – rediscovered it. Elected representatives of all the opposition parties met in Dungannon on 9 August, calling for an immediate rent and rates strike and asking Westminster to suspend the Stormont government and initiate talks on new political

116

constitutional arrangements. 'All those who hold public positions, whether elected or appointed' were asked to announce their withdrawals, to prove that the system of government set up by the 1920 Ireland Act had failed – a call which over 100 Catholic councillors obeyed. By 27 August the SDLP and NICRA were placing a joint advertisement, which was to haunt them later, making it clear that the rent strike applied only to tenants of publicly-owned Housing Executive houses and that 'no arrears will ever be paid for the period internment is in operation'. Surplus money could be contributed to a fund for dependants.

Meanwhile there was a flurry of activity on the political scene, with Hume and others winning the backing of Lynch and Harold Wilson, in Dublin and London respectively, for the 'suspend Stormont' demand. At first, Heath was defiantly behind Faulkner, telling Lynch by telegram not to interfere in an internal UK problem, but by the end of September he had convened the first tripartite talks – London-Dublin-Belfast – gravely damaging unionist confidence. By now the British were fully aware of the crisis, and there was a spate of visits by both Government and Labour politicians, desperately seeking a compromise. For Wilson, this meant a dramatic call for a British declaration of intent to leave Ulster, and talks between the three governments, followed by a fifteen-year transitional period before complete withdrawal. For Maudling, who had talked about achieving 'an acceptable level of violence', it meant an 'active permanent and guaranteed' place for Catholics.

But Hume had made up his mind that the one-party system of government, established in 1920, was the root cause of the problem, and he was not to be deflected: 'We are prepared to accept in the short term the charges of creating polarisation in order to remove the real roots of sectarian discord'. No real solution could come until the British Government faced up to the threat of a right-wing unionist backlash – 'when the power of the threat is broken the solution to the Irish question will be remarkably easy'. Quoting Craigavon in 1938, 'We are too small to be apart or for the border to be there for all time', he asked the British Government to declare publicly what was the private conviction of all British parties, that Irish unity was inevitable 'and that it will take all steps necessary to encourage the agreement that will bring it about'.

Again he emphasised the need for a new Irish constitution: 'Most

117

Irishmen today would have little difficulty and indeed would be determined that a constitution of a united Ireland would be a pluralist one.' Such a country could well be dominated by the Northern Protestant, he said, using a 1912 quotation from Churchill: 'No man can measure in words or can tell the blessing that Ulstermen have in their power to bestow on their fellow country-men... if they would lead a united Ireland home.'

Even at this stage Hume was anxious to confront the South with the realities of the situation. The major difficulty, he said, was that the South viewed partition as a purely territorial problem and, until the recent crisis, showed little evidence of wanting to improve know-ledge or understanding. While the British might discount the special pleading of the politicians, they could hardly ignore a reasoned commentary by a group of Northern Catholic public servants – the 'haves' as opposed to the 'have-nots' – which expressed grave reser-vations about the reform programme. They were pointing to changes more radical than could be achieved by the appointment of a non-political Catholic, G.B. Newe, to the Cabinet – another of Faulkner's ploys – and Hume's Alternative Assembly helped to underline this fundamental alienation.

The more formal aspects of the Assembly were pure farce, with attempts to site it at Derry Guildhall and Strabane ending in failure before Ivan Cooper finally secured the castle in Dungiven. Only when they arrived did many of the delegates realise it was a ball-room, in a nineteenth-century folly, and Hume had to adopt his most schoolmasterly approach, as elected president, to inject some dignity into the proceedings. The media were scornful, on the two occasions that it met, but Hume regarded it as a dramatic demonstration by all shades of nationalist opinion of the extent to which the minority had withdrawn its consent to be governed by Stormont. Echoing Edward Carson in 1912, he said he 'did not care tuppence' if the Assembly was regarded as treason or not. Even the participants found dif-ficulty taking it seriously, but not Faulkner. He knew Stormont could not survive an indefinite nationalist boycott, and timed major announcements to distract media attention from Dungiven.

Faulkner showed that in an emergency he was even prepared to have Catholics in government, but he could only go part of the way to meet the SDLP because of the pressure building up from his own right wing. Protestants were alarmed by the strength of the Catholic reaction to internment, and the intervention of Dublin and London convinced them they had to look to their own defences rather than to Stormont. Paramilitary groupings flourished, notably the newly-formed Ulster Defence Association, and by early 1972 Craig had united hard-line unionism behind his new Vanguard organisation. With its Fascist-like mass demonstrations, it represented a challenge to parliamentary government which the authorities could not ignore. The first signs of a harder army line were felt in mid-January, during an anti-internment rally on Magilligan beach. Hume's intention was simply to get as near as possible to the camp, so that the speeches might be heard by the prisoners, and the obvious means was to use the right of way along Magilligan strand, a glorious stretch of pale yellow sand reachable only by tramping for miles over rough terrain. But the soldiers feared an attempt would be made to storm the camp from the beach, and after a famous televised confrontation, in which Hume argued with an officer for the right to march, fighting broke out. The officer was cool enough, but the soldiers panicked, and rubber bullets were fired off at close range after a baton charge. Only a lack of missiles on the bare windswept strand prevented a pitched battle between the soldiers and 2,000 marchers, and Hume had to lead as dignified a retreat as possible. But he had been alarmed by the soldiers' belligerent mood and when approached to speak at another anti-internment march in Derry, eight days after Magilligan, he declined, warning that the army's blood was up. He had a pre-monition of the turning point in Anglo-Irish relations that was to be known as 'Bloody Sunday'.

But before this, Jack Lynch had passed on Hume's concern to Ted Heath in Brussels and Harold Wilson in London, urging the British Premier to form a community government in the North, with a share of power for the minority – the shape of things to come. On Hume's advice that 'someone will be killed', at the Derry rally on 30 January the SDLP members decided not to take part as a group, but to leave it to individual conscience. Currie arrived late and watched events from outside the barricades, but O'Hanlon was in the thick of the action when the illegal parade arrived at Free Derry Corner and the Paratroopers, who were keyed up for confrontation, opened fire. At first he thought they were rubber bullets, because he was certain no shots had been directed at the army, but when a man fell dead six yards away he fled in terror like the rest. Trapped in the built-up area, the Bogsiders were sitting targets for the army marksmen, and a total of thirteen men were shot dead. According to O'Hanlon, who

119

could hardly believe what was happening, all the shooting came from the army. After an hour, he said, a couple of isolated IRA gunmen opened up from the heights above the Bogside, but by then it was all over. Bloody Sunday had taken its place in Ulster's grim calendar, and subsequently the Widgery Tribunal was to confirm that none of the victims had been handling guns or explosives.

Hume had stayed away, not wanting to offer any encouragement to what he regarded as a highly dangerous exercise, organised by the CRA in conjunction with a shadowy National Resistance Movement. But his instincts told him to stay on call and he was sitting in his front room, which doubled as a dining-room and constituency surgery, when the shots rang out. He said to Pat, 'That's it. There it goes. The lid's really off now.' A friend of Pat's, Kathleen Donaghy, came running up the street towards them, screaming, 'They're murdering everyone down there. The army's just opened up. People are being killed left right and centre.' Almost immediately crowds began appearing, bombarding Hume with questions about relatives, for as well as the thirteen dead, another forty-five had been arrested by army snatch squads. Phoning the hospital was impossible, so eventually he drove to Altnagelvin himself, to find the waiting-room crowded with distraught relatives and friends. Breaking the bad news to relatives was a harrowing experience, for he knew nearly all the families of the dead and one of them, Gerry McKinney, had been a next-door neighbour at his previous home and a schoolmate.

Hume's home was like a railway station for days to come, as the world's Press, and the entire Irish establishment, Government and Opposition, beat a path to his door. Interviewed by RTE Radio on the city walls the day after the deaths, he was asked what feelings were like in the Bogside, and he gave an answer which was to haunt him ever after. 'Many people down there,' he said, 'feel now that it's a united Ireland or nothing. Alienation is pretty total and we're all going to have to work very hard to deal with the situation.' Brian Faulkner was the first to seize on the line 'united Ireland or nothing' and make it appear to be Hume's own opinion. Others followed suit, to the point where it is part of Protestant mythology, but Hume, in his dogged way, refused to explain. It would be too long-winded and confusing, he felt, so he said nothing, leaving it to colleagues like Denis Haughey to attempt to clear the matter up, without significant success. It was repeatedly used against him and the party in the

February 1974 election, but Hume never responded – nor did he hold a grudge against Faulkner for picking it up. Bitterness, as more than one surprised politician was to learn, is not a part of his nature, even though his sensitivity to criticism is acute, like many an out-wardly self-assured political figure.

Charles Haughey, Neil Blaney, Brendan Corish and Garret FitzGerald were a few of those who stopped at West End Park for a briefing, and often a plate of stew, from the virtual field kitchen which Pat and a next-door neighbour had set up to cope with the rush. Everything stopped for three days, out of a sense of shock as much as mourning, and Hume came up with his customary safety valve – a mass meeting for the following Saturday in Brandywell football stadium. Some said it was provocative, but he chose the venue carefully, in an enclosed arena, off the streets, and promised a hardline message. Till then, he said, nothing should be done and, in fact, nothing was. Not a stone was thrown in Derry in the week following Bloody Sunday, which was all the more remarkable con-sidering the wave of anger which swept the country and resulted in the burning of the British Embassy in Dublin. Derry held its breath, focusing on the non-violent alternative, and the expected explosion did not occur.

Thousands filled the football ground, just as they had lined the streets for the mass funeral, and again Hume pitched his message astutely. Civil disobedience was the answer, he said, renewing the call to a rent and rates strike and pledging the SDLP to redouble its efforts to bring Stormont down. The crowds went away satisfied that something was being done, but Hume was far from euphoric. He knew it was a race between the SDLP and the IRA to show which had the answer to Stormont's mismanagement. Teenagers were openly flocking to join the paramilitary organisation, as never before, and funds were pouring in from America at unprecedented rates. But Hume had one more weapon to use – his appeal against a £20 fine for obstructing the army, dating back to the previous August, which was to make constitutional history, and help bring Stormont down.

The moderate Alliance Party even made a contribution to the suspension of Stormont, for although they were without an MP until February 1972, they were beginning to be consulted by the British as rational pro-union politicians, in an irrational province. Bloody Sunday had, incidentally, upset their plans for a grand entry into parliamentary politics. The night before, Dr Robert Simpson, a former

Unionist Minister for Community Relations, had agreed to join, along with Millar Cameron, a prominent Unionist Senator, also from Ballymena. Senator Paddy Wilson, who had been one of the founder-members of the SDLP, but was increasingly worried about its rural nationalist base, gave his agreement by phone, and the others were already pledged. All was suspended when the Derry news broke and only the original three – Phelim O'Neill, a former O'Neillite Minister of Agriculture, Bertie McConnell, another Unionist, and Tom Gormley, a liberal ex-Nationalist – crossed over in the end, weeks later. Like everyone else, Alliance could see that Stormont was dying and therefore wanted the maximum number of parliamentarians to join, in order to have a seat at the bargaining table.

But even without any MPs, Alliance had asked for a meeting with the British Prime Minister, and immediately after Bloody Sunday their request was granted. In Downing Street, party leader Oliver Napier advised Heath to take security policy away from the Stormont Government, knowing that this would cause its resignation. The Alliance man's aim was to precipitate the introduction of direct rule from London in a way that would provoke less trouble than its imposition by Westminster. Heath listened intently, asking questions but making little contribution, in contrast to the bored Reggie Maudling, whom Alliance had met on a Northern Ireland visit the previous October. Twice inside twenty minutes he gave them exactly the same advice: 'There are pressmen waiting downstairs, and when you leave you are entitled to tell them what you have told me, but not what I told you.' That confirmed for them that he had little to offer.

Heath's immediate response to Bloody Sunday was to appoint an inquiry under Lord Widgery, but Hume threw it back in his face: 'We cannot accept a British judgment on a British crime,' he said, calling for an international tribunal and for the inquiry to be opened up to discuss the political background to the march. There was never a chance of that, he knew, and the question of whether or not to co-operate became a divisive issue in Derry, as nine priests consented to give evidence although they felt the terms of reference, simply into the shootings, were too restrictive. But two days after the killings, Lord Balniel had given the official verdict in the Commons, largely pre-empting the inquiry. The soldiers had fired aimed shots at gunmen or bombers in self defence, he said. He rejected entirely the suggestion that they had fired indiscriminately, as well as the slurs on the Parachute Regiment. But Bernadette Devlin was prophetic: 'The Government may well have lit a fire in Ireland, the flames of which may not die out until the last vestige of British rule has gone from that country'. Fitt, who followed, said he agreed with every word. 'Suspend Stormont and take the British Army out of Northern Ireland,' he said.

The very next Sunday the marchers were back on the streets again, breaking the Government ban in a mass parade in Newry, which was miraculously peaceful, despite a heavy media and security presence. Thirty, including Hume, were prosecuted, although Hume could not be served with his summons at his home inside Free Derry, and refused to go to the police station. Faulkner lashed the organisers for their 'irresponsible brinkmanship', but Heath had got the message and, although his call for peace talks was firmly rejected by Fitt, he was moving inexorably towards suspension of Stormont.

It was a time when both wings of the IRA were fishing for go-betweens to put their case to the British Government, and an Independent Unionist MP at Stormont, Tom Caldwell, a former Territorial Army colonel and art gallery owner, was their surprising choice. His first contact was with the Provisionals, soon after internment, but on the advice of the Army GOC, General Harry Tuzo, who said 'It will be all over by Christmas,' he turned down their invitation. Next the Official IRA made an approach, at the opening of an art exhibition in London, and this time he agreed, having received a discreet nod from the Foreign Office representative in Ulster, Howard Smith. Copies of his report on the talks were circulated, and Harold Wilson invited him to London. 'Very interesting,' he said. 'But you are speaking to the wrong people. You want the people who are bombing.' When Caldwell told him he had turned down an invitation on the advice of Tuzo, Wilson exploded. 'You bloody fool,' he said. 'You should have known better, as a politician, than to ask a soldier. You've wasted six months.' Caldwell took his point and, after the bombing of the Abercorn Restaurant in Belfast, in March 1972, decided to strike. He had two meetings with the Provisionals, at two levels of seniority and, a fortnight later, Wilson – acting independently, but hoping to succeed where Caldwell had failed – met the lower echelon in Dublin. Both found it impossible to convince the Provisionals that their violence was counter-productive, but Caldwell clarified the IRA's three demands: an end to internment; withdrawal of the British Army to barracks, and later to Britain; and a timetable for reunification. The first two would be easily obtained, he told them, after a ceasefire, but the third was asking too much. Wilson, while in Dublin, reiterated his fifteen-year plan for British withdrawal, encouraging the SDLP, who detected echoes of the conflict in Rhodesia in his demand for 'unimpeded progress towards majority rule' in the whole island, along with quadripartite talks involving London, Dublin and both sides in the North. Although Wilson later admitted his failure to Caldwell, the list of aspiring mediators with the IRA lengthened, despite these initial setbacks. General Sir John Hackett, a retired Northern Ireland GOC, chose his own rendezvous, but had no more success.

By the spring of 1972 Heath had decided to close Stormont, and Faulkner, who had been directly assured three weeks after Bloody Sunday that 'we're in this thing together', was oblivious to all warnings, even leaked lobby stories, that it was all up. He alone was stunned to hear Heath's turnaround in Downing Street, and after returning to Belfast for a gloomy Cabinet meeting, he had no choice but to hand Heath his resignation on Friday 24 March, as had been anticipated. It was a shattering blow, after a nightmare term as PM, but a day later his civil servants found him bouncing back. 'Well it's such a new thing, it might just work,' he said. 'It will either work in a short time or not at all. But it will have been worth it if it does work.' He was talking in security terms, and still felt bitter and betrayed. Earlier, his certainty that Heath would not intervene had been based on his belief that it would be disastrous for the British Government, and would be irreversible. Hume and the SDLP also saw it as a watershed, but one that could be the foundation of a new order in Northern Ireland, leading in its own good time to a new order in Ireland as a whole. All depended on the reaction of the Protestants and the IRA. They were soon to learn how little had changed, even though fifty years of Unionist rule was at an end.

11
Talking to the IRA

When news of the dissolution of Stormont broke, the SDLP MPs were already in conference at the Intercounties Hotel, Lifford, in Co. Donegal, so confident was Hume that Heath would pull down the curtain. He had established good relations with the British representatives – the Foreign Office men who acted as the Westminster Government's eyes and ears – and was convinced that the Press speculation about direct rule was correct. Once again Hume had a lengthy statement mentally prepared, and before it was released the next day, coinciding with the arrival of William Whitelaw to prepare for the 'difficult and awesome' task of Secretary of State, he made a lightning visit to Dublin with Paddy O'Hanlon to consult Jack Lynch. The statement was an SDLP attempt to speak for the entire Catholic community – Nationalist Party leaders were also briefed – by appealing to the Provisional IRA to call off its campaign and to the British Government to end 'military repression' as well as internment. 'We ask those engaged in the campaign of violence to cease immediately, to enable us to bring internment to a speedy end and make a positive response to the British Government's proposals.'

To the Protestants, Hume had this to say: 'We do not regard our political achievements as a victory over you, rather do we regard them as a step forward and as an opportunity for all of us. We ask you to join us as equals on the road to permanent peace and justice and to add your considerable talents to ours so that we can build together, in agreement, a new society in which the sectarianism that has scourged our country will be but an unhappy memory.' But neither the Provisionals nor the Protestants, shattered by the abolition of their parliament, were impressed. The message from the IRA – which Hume regarded as one of the great blunders in Irish history – was simply that 'the war goes on', while Vanguard loyalists called a two-day strike for 27 and 28 March, culminating in a march of thousands to Stormont and defiant speeches by Unionist leaders. The scenes on the balcony were unrehearsed comic opera, with

Faulkner agreeing to appear only when the army GOC pleaded with him to do so. The army feared that if the crowds left in an ugly mood, without a political message, they could wreck east Belfast. Although Faulkner doubted this, since most of the loyalists came from the area, he saw that he would have to speak up to avoid a takeover of his party by Craig, the featured speaker.

At a late stage, the sergeant-at-arms realised that the microphones had been set up in the precincts of Parliament without his approval, and he summoned the police to halt the proceedings. But the entire Cabinet was already on the balcony and when the official tried to stop a civil servant delivering an important message to Faulkner, he discovered that Mr Heath had diminished his high office, too. 'Get out of the way, you stupid bastard,' he was told, as he was elbowed aside. Although the photographs of the event emphasised Unionist unity across the spectrum, Faulkner was simply trying to hang on to his party, in the hope that when the British tried to restore devolution on their terms, he would have less opposition from his backwoods-men and more co-operation from the SDLP. But that was a long way off, and the IRA's decision to keep up the pressure inevitably led to the amalgamation of the various Protestant local defence committees under the umbrella of the Ulster Defence Association, vastly in-creasing the opportunities for confrontation. Hume was frankly appalled at the IRA's attitude, as he genuinely felt that many unionists had a sense of guilt about the way Stormont had operated, and were ready to make a new start.

Meanwhile on 19 April the verdict of Lord Widgery on the Bloody Sunday killings did nothing to ease Whitelaw's task of involving the SDLP in political talks, even though they continued meeting civil servants. Widgery put the blame on the march organisers, ques-tioned the wisdom of the army's arrest operation and held that there had been some near-reckless shooting by soldiers. But generally he exonerated the Paratroopers and found that they had been fired on first. Said Hume, 'In reality this tribunal was a case of the accused holding an inquiry into their own misdemeanours. We reject the findings of Lord Widgery utterly.' In contrast, Derry's coroner, an ex-major, Hubert O'Neill, declared that the army had 'run amok'. 'I say without reservation it was sheer unadulterated murder.'

The dangers were felt personally by all the SDLP members, reaching the stage of gun attacks on Devlin and shots being fired at the homes of Cooper and Currie. Hume himself was alleged to be the target of an assassination gang, but his home in the Bogside was out of bounds to loyalists and he continued to take only the most elementary precautions. He was more concerned then, as later, with the danger to his family. A girl who looked like his daughter Aine was seized on her way home from school, only to be released later, and all his children – three girls and two boys – had to get used to anti-SDLP harrassment.

Hume's weakness, according to his critics, was that he lived and thought like a Catholic in a majority situation – unlike Belfast – and his optimism was still brimming over in an RTE interview in April. Reunification was a lot nearer in time than many people believed, he said. The time for negotiation was quite near, provided there was an immediate cessation of hostilities between the IRA and the army. With an eye to the IRA's problems, he said the preconditions for talks were an end to internment, an amnesty for those on the wanted list and assurances that wanted men would not be arrested if hostilities ceased. In future he saw three possibilities for discussion – total integration with Britain, a restructured North or Irish unity. 'The only viable one is the last and that is what we should be negotiating, as of now.' But there was an acknowledgement that the 'leaderless' unionist community would need time to think, after a ceasefire. If that happened, he was certain that a section would go in favour of creating a united country.

Already he was ruling out the possibility of a restructured North as 'impractical', as was Stormont itself. The SDLP was not suggesting a takeover of the North by the South, he said, but a completely new situation where, by agreement, they could build a completely new country. Once the decision was taken, there would be no point in waiting years and years – implementation should go on immediately. Agreement was possible with 'a significant section of the Northern Protestant community, if there was the right approach now'. He was infected, as were many nationalists at the time, by the euphoria following the downfall of the Unionist government – the finishing touch to the civil rights movement which had begun four years before. His hope of reconciliation within Northern Ireland was fading, in the light of extremist Protestant reaction, but he felt that if all the pieces fell together – and both wings of the IRA could be persuaded to cease fire – radical developments were possible. In some ways, it was a contradiction of his earlier emphasis on unionist consent before unity, but it represented an attempt to take the bull by the horns, at a crucial moment, and to alert the Republic to its responsibilities. Frankly, he said, he did not think the people of the Republic were ready for unity. But he declared it was 'time that blueprints for Irish unity were ready to show what sort of country we are all looking for', anticipating his New Ireland Forum initiative eleven years later. If change was going to come rapidly a new constitution was needed, he said, in which all sections would be involved. As a first step in the overall strategy the SDLP three days later called on all who had withdrawn from public bodies since internment to return 'as a demonstration of their determination to bring about community reconciliation'.

In another RTE interview, he claimed that the muted Protestant reaction to direct rule had vindicated his consistent stand that 'there would be no Protestant backlash against a British political decision, backed up by a British authority'. But it was early days, at a time when Catholic reaction to the killing of Ranger Best, a Derry soldier home on leave, led directly to the Official IRA laying down its arms. Originally the Officials had rejected Hume's criticism, but he had a perfect Derry man's answer, which touched the heart of the growing movement for peace: 'They have a brass neck on them to talk of slobbering moderates, when what the moderates are trying to to is save people's lives.'

Pressure mounted on the Provisionals to follow suit, and with a hunger strike in progress in Belfast's Crumlin Road jail, demanding political status for paramilitary prisoners, three of its leaders, Sean McStiofain, Daithi O'Connell and Belfast man Seamus Twomey, travelled to Derry for a press conference. They wanted to show the reasonableness of the IRA against the intransigence of the British Government, and when Hume heard their terms for a meeting with Whitelaw, he pricked up his ears. It was not the cheek of the IRA offering the Secretary of State free passage to meet them in Free Derry to discuss a seven-day ceasefire – an offer promptly dismissed – but the fact that peace feelers were being extended while internment lasted. Was there any meaning in this, he asked a Provisional contact, in view of the fact that even the SDLP was unable to talk to the British Government because of internment? Yes, came back the answer, so a meeting with McStiofain and O'Connell was arranged and they virtually agreed that if he could get anything out of the Government, they would respond. Hume took it from there, with Paddy Devlin brought in for party reasons, beginning a week's shuttle diplomacy between Whitelaw and the IRA leaders, all conducted in total secrecy, because of the internment question. The IRA had two preconditions before negotiations – firstly that the Government should meet the prisoners' demands for political status and secondly that Gerry Adams, then twenty-five and a leading Provisional in Belfast, should be released from detention to take part in the talks. After that would come the usual short-term and long-term demands, always aimed at British withdrawal.

The first precondition was the real problem and Hume's diplomatic skills were fully tested as he motored between Laneside, the Foreign Office's plush retreat on the Co. Down 'gold coast', Rinmore Drive, in the Creggan, and a pub in Donegal town for rendezvous with the Provisionals. It was an extremely delicate exercise, from everyone's point of view, and Hume's only explanation of his role, when asked, was to say that he was engaging in a 'public dialogue' with the IRA. At the time, he was meeting Whitelaw one day and the IRA the next, but he managed to avoid answering awkward questions directly, without telling lies. 'I am in a public dialogue,' he told one non-plussed BBC interviewer, who wanted to know if there were any face-to-face meetings with the Provisionals. 'They hear what I'm saying.'

What they heard was that the British were gradually being persuaded that political status – or, in their words, 'special category status' – would be a small enough price to pay, in return for an end to the hunger strike and a ceasefire, leading to definitive negotiations for peace. But progress was painfully slow and signals had to be given by Whitelaw, in speeches in the Commons, that he was getting the IRA's message and wanted the dialogue to continue. In the meantime, Hume and O'Connell built up a relationship of relative trust and respect, as the Derry man ferried his fugitive passenger to and fro across the border to meetings with IRA associates. There had to be no danger of him being arrested, so the military commander in Ebrington Barracks drew up a letter of safe conduct which was to be produced in emergencies. No name was mentioned, but Hume was empowered to transport 'one body' wherever he pleased. At the end of the negotiations, he presented it to O'Connell as a souvenir of an unrepeatable episode.

As Hume's wheeling and dealing reached its climax, he and Devlin made their final journey to Laneside to tie up the loose ends. There was agreement with O'Connell and McStiofain, but the prisoners had to give their approval by telephone from Crumlin Road jail. Proinsias McArt was their spokesman, in the absence of the hunger-striking Billy McKee, whose life was already in danger, and Hume found his terms well received. Everything was perfect from the prisoners' point of view, McArt said, and he was extremely grateful to Hume for the part he had played. 'You've saved a lot of lives,' he said. All that remained was to tell O'Connell and, with Whitelaw and his two Foreign Office advisers, Frank Steele and Howard Smith, holding their breaths, Hume dialled the number of a 'safe' house in the Creggan. 'All right,' said O'Connell without hesitation, 'you've got a ceasefire at midnight on 26 June.' Whitelaw literally jumped for joy, embracing Hume in a bear hug. The British were delighted to have the prospect of an end to violence, and to Hume the price was a small one.

Later Whitelaw was bitterly to regret his concession on political status, which led to the 'paramilitary colleges' within prisons, and was dismantled with much difficulty by later Secretaries of State. It could be said to have been the genesis of the 1981 hunger strike, which was basically to restore the old prisoner-of-war status, after the introduction in 1976 of a policy of treating terrorists as common criminals; but in 1972 the trade-off would have been difficult to refuse. Hume genuinely believed the IRA wanted a ceasefire or he would not have gone ahead, but his doubts began with the sickening prelude to the truce. As McStiofain wrote later, the IRA decided to go out with a bang, and in the three weeks prior to the ceasefire, there were twenty killings. Three soldiers were blown up and killed near Derry on the last night, and at five minutes to midnight, a policeman was shot dead in Newry.

The ceasefire terms, hammered out in a secret meeting near Derry between the IRA men, including Gerry Adams, and two of Whitelaw's representatives, Philip Woodfield and Frank Steele, were that the truce must be bilateral; that all harassment would cease; that there would be no arrests or raids, and that within ten days the republican leadership would meet Whitelaw and members of the British Government to discuss conditions for ending operations. The promised meeting took place in the Chelsea flat of a Government Minister on 7 July, with six IRA leaders flown from Belfast by special RAF plane, but it was unproductive. To ensure their safe return from London the IRA insisted on holding two army officers as hostages. Newspapers reported that the Provisionals had kidnapped two unarmed officers in the Bogside – an unlikely story – and the penny didn't drop with journalists until after the London meeting.

The Provisionals simply reiterated their three impossible long-term demands: a public declaration by the British that they recognised the right of the Irish people, North and South, to self-determination; a declaration of their intention to withdraw all troops within three years; and an amnesty for all 'prisoners of war'. Whitelaw demurred, promising that serious consideration would be given. But, according to Provisional IRA sources, agreement was reached on several short-term demands – the IRA and army were to have freedom of movement on the streets; the IRA were allowed to bear arms as long as they limited displays to their own areas; and there would be no more searches of persons, cars or houses. Without movement on a release of internees, repeal of the Special Powers Act or removal of the ban on Provisional Sinn Fein, those who wanted to give peace a chance were in the minority. Two days later, sectarian rioting broke out in Lenadoon on the outskirts of west Belfast, over the allocation of houses to sixteen Catholics in a mixed area, and the army intervened, arresting two IRA volunteers. Whitelaw refused to release them, and the ceasefire was over, after fourteen days, defying an attempt on 17 July to resurrect it with a meeting between the IRA and Wilson in London.

Hume, who had gone on holidays to Bunbeg, happy that the ceasefire was holding, was appalled. He rang O'Connell in Dublin, asking if it could be true. 'Surely they're not so stupid as to throw this whole thing away over the allocation of houses?' he said. O'Connell was very calm: 'We're on a new plane now and we won't need you the next time. It'll be Heath and us the next time.' From that moment on, Hume had no dealings with the Provisionals. Lenadoon was a carefully staged operation, he believed, because the IRA lacked the ability to negotiate effectively. They needed him to set up an opportunity for dialogue, and yet when difficulties arose and they felt they were being duped by the British, they did not even bother to consult him.

He had been prepared to accept that Bloody Sunday had been a crucial factor in driving many republicans into violence, but after his experience of mediating successfully on behalf of the Provisionals and then being cast aside, he developed a professional contempt for their negotiating ability. In a strange way, however, he made a favourable impression on both O'Connell and McStiofain, whose political philosophy was so different from his own. O'Connell was later quoted as saying too often for his own good that Hume was someone worth listening to, and McStiofain praised him for keeping his promise not to claim any political credit from the negotiations. When a British paper speculated that the SDLP was responsible for obtaining political status, Hume immediately issued a statement giving the credit to the prisoners. Afterwards, he had no regrets about his involvement, which had been aimed simply at getting the violence stopped and creating the right atmosphere, rather than attempting a political solution. Nine years were to pass before his next contact with Adams, who was seeking support for the anti-H-Block campaign in 1981. As Adams went to leave the house where they were talking, a door jammed, and Hume had to wrestle it open. 'The only time I meet you is when I'm opening doors for you,' he said, but the joke passed unnoticed.

The IRA's 'politicians' had taken a chance with the ceasefire and could claim to have been undermined by concurrent Government talks with loyalist paramilitaries, so their resumption was all the more brutal. Within three days, eight soldiers and a policeman had been killed, sparking violent loyalist retaliation. Altogether there were thirty-three violent deaths in a week – ninety-five in the month, including twenty-one members of the security forces – and 7,000 refugees fled South in fear of civil war. Finally, any prospect of an IRA political role went up in the smoke of Bloody Friday, 21 July, when twenty-two bombs were exploded in Belfast in seventy-five minutes, killing nine and injuring 130. The TV pictures, of bodily remains being shovelled into plastic bags at a blasted bus station, went round the world, setting the scene for the army to peacefully reoccupy the no-go areas of Derry and Belfast after eleven months. The Government took steps to inform Dublin, whose main concern was a possible refugee problem, about the purpose and the strength of Operation Motorman, and when the tanks rolled in the IRA had already left. Their only response was to choose the quiet village of Claudy, ten miles away, for a car bomb that took eight innocent lives, sinking the paramilitaries' stock still lower.

The IRA had thrown away an opportunity to negotiate something less than total victory and the SDLP were accordingly let off the hook of 'no talks while internment lasts'. Jack Lynch intervened, the day after Motorman, by flying Hume, Cooper and Devlin by helicopter to Dublin to test reaction and to back their natural urge to take part

132

in Whitelaw's preparations for a political initiative. But they could not convince Whitelaw at their first meeting that fixing a date for the end of internment was possible, after Motorman, and they found unacceptable a promised review of the internment procedure – to be renamed 'detention' and made subject to semi-judicial hearings.

On that basis they could not take part in the round-table talks called by Whitelaw in Darlington, Co. Durham in September, but instead issued a definitive document about the way ahead as they saw it, 'Towards a New Ireland', knowing it would be on the agenda. Again it reflected Hume's emphasis on the need for new structures, North and South, to deal with the national identity crisis which was at the heart of the Ulster problem. There were seven proposals, the first calling for an immediate long-term declaration by the United Kingdom that it would positively encourage a united Ireland on terms acceptable to all the people of Ireland and the others dealing with the interim arrangements. Pending unity, the party proposed an interim condominium system of government, under the joint sovereignty of the United Kingdom and the Irish Republic, reserving to London and Dublin all powers on foreign affairs, defence, security, police and financial subventions. The two sovereign governments would be represented by commissioners who would sign all legislation or refer it to a joint constitutional court.

The document also proposed: an executive of fifteen members, elected from an eighty-four member Assembly by proportional representation; a chief executive, to allocate departmental responsibilities subject to the approval of both commissioners; no representation for Northern Ireland in either Westminster or Dublin parliaments; all powers of security to be under the direct control of a department headed by both commissioners; and the creation of a new National Senate for Ireland, with equal representation, by PR, from the Dublin parliament and the Assembly, 'to plan the integration of North and South and agree on an acceptable constitution'. Ironically, Hume purposely avoided the emotive term 'Council of Ireland', in deference to unionist susceptibilities, only to find it appearing in a Unionist document on the way ahead, under the title of 'an Irish inter-governmental council'.

There was, of course, no British precedent for such a radical plan and Ted Heath gave the SDLP little encouragement in a late attempt to persuade them to take part in the Darlington talks, starting on 25 September. His refusal to fix a date for ending internment – insisting that a hard core of fifty were too dangerous to release – was no more acceptable than Whitelaw's so the boycott stood, despite Hume's natural inclination to attend. But a rapport was achieved in special talks at Chequers between Heath and the fellow professionals of the SDLP, which was to pay hefty dividends in the months to come, as the real bargaining began. Part of this is attributable to the unusually disciplined preparations for the Chequers talks, after a quiet night in a London hotel. Normally, the SDLP delegates would have stayed at the Irish Club and spent the night socialising at the bar, but their new English-born secretary, Julian Jacottet, had unknowingly booked into the out-of-the-way Charles Dickens Hotel, where there were few distractions from the important business at hand. Even at Chequers, the Irish were on their guard when the drinks cabinet was opened, and all the favourite spirits of the SDLP were displayed. Clearly the chemistry between Gerry Fitt and Ted Heath was wrong and, since Fitt would never have let Hume lead off the SDLP case, Austin Currie became the compromise candidate, with Fitt winding up. Personality differences between the leader and deputy were an increasing problem, with the self-made Fitt revealing a chip on his shoulder about Hume's educated approach. Currie found himself having to mediate between the two, as Fitt tried to demonstrate his independence of Dublin, and his grassroots socialism. A typical blunder was his attack on Fianna Fáil, describing it as a 'Siamese twin of Unionism' and accusing Fianna Fáil of doing nothing for Northern Ireland. True or false, it overlooked the fact that Hume's lines of communication with Dublin were very close, and that part of the party's funds came from Southern supporters, either in Fianna Fáil or Fine Gael. From 1969 onwards, Hume had a relationship of total trust with Jack Lynch, and any significant initiatives were taken together. Lynch's attitude to the North was accepted as genuinely conciliatory, and even Garret FitzGerald would report to him on his missions to Belfast or London.

While most members of the SDLP regarded the New Ireland document as a neogotiating stance, to be qualified behind closed doors, Hume was deadly serious about the need for Southern involvement in a long-term solution. Writing after the Chequers meeting, he said the lack of representation from the Republic at the Darlington conference was 'a guarantee that it will not produce a lasting solution'. Yet all the parties, including the Unionists, argued for some kind of involvement by nationalists. A month before, Hume was even more revealing about his insistence on proving that politics, rather than violence, could bring change in Ireland. Patriotism in the 1970s involved the spilling of sweat, not blood, he said. Non-violence had succeeded in cracking the Unionist monolith where the IRA had failed, and yet violence had been glorified and magnified.

Eventually only three parties attended the Darlington talks, the Official Unionists, Alliance and the Northern Ireland Labour Party, representing less than 50 per cent of the electorate, but they did focus minds on the future, producing a series of documents which, together with the SDLP's 'Towards a New Ireland', formed the basis of the Government's proposals in the year ahead. Brian Faulkner's Unionists reverted to the June 1971 system, proposing five committees, three of them chaired by opposition members, with power over the police, temporary anti-terrorist laws and a Bill of Rights. The Governments in London, Dublin and Belfast would sign a tripartite declaration affirming the right to self-determination, and discussions would begin on co-operation against terrorism and review of extradition or common law enforcement. If the plan was adopted, an Irish inter-governmental council would be formed to discuss matters of mutual interest, primarily in the economic and social fields.

Hume's reaction to Darlington, in a speech in Enniskillen, again demonstrated his impatience with short-term solutions. No one had asked why Dublin should be involved, he lamented, the most important question of all. Northern Ireland as a political unit was inherently unstable and it was impossible to find within it a basis for stability which would give a lasting peace. The solution must be found in a wider context; any solution based on Northern Ireland alone, dependent on the whim of a British Government, would be a solution on an extremely insecure base. The SDLP's proposals did not impose anything on anybody, but invited the Northern majority, in particular, to reject the defensiveness of the past and to step forward with their fellow countrymen and mould the sort of Ireland they wanted to see. 'We need a new vision that will end the old quarrels,' he said. 'It is either that or return to the old instability with the periodic violence, death and destruction.'

His idealism was still going strong a month later at an Oxford Union debate, although he was ready to admit that, because of the present violence and emotion, there could not be an immediate, permanent settlement. Real reconciliation could be based only on the realities, and on full equality of citizenship, which included 'my right in my own country to say I am an Irishman and to work for the unification of this country'.

Any doubts that the SDLP's ideas had shaped the thinking of the British establishment were dispelled in Whitelaw's Green Paper of October, which was to pave the way for a White Paper in March and for the Sunningdale proposals. The new element was a section intriguingly entitled 'The Irish Dimension' which laid down that 'whatever arrangements are made for the future administration of Northern Ireland must take account of the province's relationships with the Republic'. It was 'clearly desirable' that any new plan 'be, so far as possisble, acceptable to and accepted by the Republic'. Power-sharing was not mentioned, as such, but the role of the minority was repeatedly underlined in the criteria for new institutions. They should 'seek a much wider consensus than has hitherto existed'; an assembly 'must be capable of involving all its members constructively in ways which satisfy them and those they represent'; as a minimum this would involve assuring minority groups of 'an effective voice and a real influence' or 'by giving minority interests a share in the exercise of executive power'; there would have to be 'absolute fairness and equality of opportunity'. Hume had planted the seed of 'participation' at a meeting with Maudling in Westminster two years before, and now it was bearing fruit.

The SDLP could hardly help but welcome such a glowing endorsement of its own well-publicised views, and went straight to the point that while certain unionist options, like total integration with Britain, a unilateral declaration of independence or a revived Stormont, were ruled out by the insistence on an Irish dimension, the way was clearly open to future Irish unity. But there were criticisms too, which were pure Hume. Reconciliation had to precede reunification, and it was necessary to stress the differences in national aspiration in order to find structures and institutions to give them full expression – as in the SDLP's proposal for joint sovereignty. This would meet the 'crucial' need for a law-and-order force with which all could identify, but the Green Paper had failed to face up to it.

Hume's voice was heard, more directly, in support of a motion at the third SDLP party conference in Dungiven, calling for immediate discussions with Whitelaw on the party document. He believed that the party's refusal to talk – though it had technically been breached several times – was counter-productive. 'I think the time has come for us to come out and say frankly that we are prepared to talk to anyone and to talk now.'

Hume had succeeded in establishing himself as the Catholics' man of destiny, for an opinion poll in Northern Ireland put him second in the popularity table behind Faulkner, far ahead of his nearest nationalist rival, Gerry Fitt, who came eighth. But he should have been warned by the ominous polarisation in both communities, showing how little cross-community feeling there was. While Faulkner expressed the views of 44 per cent of Protestants, he appealed to only 2 per cent of Catholics, and Hume's rating was almost the reverse – coming top with 40 per cent of Catholics and 1 per cent of Protestants. Fitt was the choice of only 13 per cent of Catholics and no Protestants, the mirror image of Paisley's position.

Hume's reputation in the Republic was growing steadily, and he received a tempting offer to stand for election to the Dáil seat in Co. Louth of Frank Aiken, the former IRA leader and de Valera's Foreign Minister, when he retired in 1973 after a lifetime in Fianna Fáil. The party would not have contested if Hume had been interested, and a glittering career in Southern politics was dangled before him, with more than a possibility of becoming Taoiseach. But the pull of Derry and the North's problems was much stronger, and even Austin Currie, to whom the offer was passed, turned it down. Aiken had wanted to preserve the dying tradition of having a Northern voice in the Dáil, and Hume had been a natural choice.

Unionist right-wingers could see Ulster locked into some form of power-sharing, with a role for the Republic, and their minds were now turning towards independence for Northern Ireland, with the status of a British dominion, rather than as an integral part of the UK. This interested Hume and Cooper, who were always doubtful of the Government's intentions, and there were contacts with Bill Craig and John Taylor to probe the unlikely possibilities of common ground in a non-British context, until reality dawned in the spring of 1973. An invitation to talks was issued by the SDLP to the United Loyalist Council, in an attempt to get through to Protestant working-class elements in the UDA, but advance publicity frightened them off.

Hume, however, never ceased hoping that if he got the right formula of words, Protestants would look seriously at his condominium proposal. Three days before the 8 March border poll – which Heath had seen as a way of taking the border out of politics, and which the SDLP was boycotting – Hume produced his positive alternative in a full-page advertisement in the Protestant *News Letter* asking the question 'What is the alternative to partnership?'

The Protestants gave their answer, in a 58 per cent poll – ignored by nationalists – which produced a 97.8 per cent vote in favour of the British link. Only two simple questions were asked, for and against an Irish unity which was not defined. Hume advised a boycott on the grounds that the poll would be a foregone conclusion in the absence of a third question, asking whether voters would agree to unity on terms that were acceptable to the people of Northern Ireland. Before the poll he wanted the Government to state in its White Paper its terms for continued support for Northern Ireland, but Whitelaw had his reasons for giving the Protestants a morale booster, without strings attached. Twelve days after the vote the Unionists learned what the Government had in store for them – an eighty-seat Assembly elected by PR for a fixed four-year term, with an executive which could not be based on a single party if it drew its support from one side of the community. In other words, one-party Unionist rule was out, and a coalition was inevitable.

On the Irish dimension, the Government confined itself to stating that it favoured and was prepared to facilitate the establishment of institutional arrangements for consultation and co-operation between Northern Ireland and the Republic. The SDLP's welcome was cautious, regarding the statement as a negotiating position and the Assembly as a conference table. Hume was disappointed that the White Paper did not provide for a 'meaningful Irish dimension' and again sidestepped the police issue, but he was willing to fight the election, in the certain knowledge that the SDLP would have a major say – as well as a veto – on the progress towards an agreement.

But before the Assembly poll, there was an election for the revised structure of twenty-six local authorities, stripped of all the controversial powers over housing, planning and education which had brought the old system into disrepute. Until then the SDLP had largely consisted of former Stormont MPs and their local organisations, with minimal support elsewhere, but the 30 May vote necessitated an instant provincewide organisation, which produced impressive results. From a standing start, the SDLP polled 13.4 per cent of the first-preference vote, capturing eighty-three of 103 anti-partitionist seats – among them that won by Seamus Mallon, a Co. Armagh school principal whose nomination was completed, and £15 deposit borrowed, a minute before the deadline, when another member dropped out. Like many another, he was a natural candidate a month later for the Assembly election, when the SDLP, fighting on the basis that the Assembly provided the only possible way to a solution, increased its share to 22.1 per cent of the vote.

The SDLP had arrived, nearly three years after its formation, as the unchallenged representative of the Catholic community, taking nineteen of the seventy-eight seats and finishing second only to Faulkner's Unionists. But even in victory – and Hume romped home easily with 12,596 votes, against a quota of 8,308 – there was the realisation that the fragmentation of the Unionists was a mixed blessing. The Faulkner Unionists, who were basically pledged to co-operate in the White Paper plan, leaving their attitude to power-sharing uncertain, won only twenty-three seats, against eighteen which went to a right-wing loyalist coalition and nine to 'unpledged' Unionists. On paper the would-be co-operators had a majority of fifty-one to twenty-seven. There was the basis of an agreement, but it would be on shaky loyalist ground.

12
The Sunningdale experiment

The Assembly election on 28 June 1973 was a rushed affair, following hard on the heels of the council elections and before the Bill on which it was based had finally been passed at Westminster. (The Bill came in two parts, one setting up the election and the other finalising the terms for the Assembly.) The effect was to allow the parties to campaign on the basis that they could still alter the White Paper conditions on power-sharing and an Irish dimension, thus letting the Protestants avoid a straight choice between pro and anti-power-sharing parties. Faulkner's line was typically ambiguous, promising not to share power with parties 'whose primary aim is a united Ireland', but refusing to say whether this included the SDLP. After the manifesto was published, he telephoned Peter McLachlan – a talented researcher with the Conservative Party who was returning to join Faulkner's team in South Antrim – asking if it would be wise to request candidates to sign a pledge to support the White Paper proposals. On the spur of the moment McLachlan said 'Yes'. It could split the party – as it eventually did – but, on the other hand, it meant that Faulkner knew where he stood and did not have a clique holding back progress. In the end, twenty-three who signed were elected, as well as ten who refused, including Bill Craig, who told Hume much later that he had been responsible for the inclusion of the low-key 'Council of Ireland' – the term previously avoided by the SDLP – in the Unionist manifesto.

Alliance, who were close to the Whitelaw administration, blamed Merlyn Rees, the Labour spokesman on Northern Ireland, for pressing hard for the hasty election, which they felt would have been held in a more stable atmosphere in the autumn. There was a threat that delay might affect Westminster's bipartisan approach to Ulster, and this was emphasised two days after the election when Rees telephoned Alliance deputy leader Bob Cooper to warn that if the parties did not open talks soon, the British public would get very impatient. As it was, relations were at their frostiest after a bitter

140

campaign in which the SDLP emphasised its commitment to a high-powered Council of Ireland, as a preparation for long-term unity by agreement. The other three main themes, stressed by Hume in another full-page advertisement, were equally abhorrent to Protestants: the ending of internment, an amnesty and a new police service to replace the RUC, 'reflecting the loyalties of both sections of the community'. In a prophetic statement, stressing the need to face such difficult questions, Hume added: 'There is no point in trying to fool the people that if Brian Faulkner and Gerry Fitt sit down in an Executive together the Northern Ireland problem is solved.'

After the election, and a series of talks with Southern leaders, he insisted that a Council of Ireland with only advisory functions would be 'unacceptable'. He was very conscious of the mistrust in his party of any deal with Unionists and saw a meaningful council as an essential selling point. One of the sceptics, Seamus Mallon, later claimed to have told a colleague on the first day at Stormont, 'We're making an awful bloody mistake', and to have found the feeling mutual. For the more nationalist-minded, power-sharing and the Irish dimension – even condominium – was something to be tried as a temporary substitute for unity. The nineteen-member SDLP parliamentary party was going to be much more difficult to hold together than the original six – and an attempt by Hume to broaden the party's Catholic base by recruiting a Protestant candidate, John Robb, had failed. The surgeon, who had spoken up bravely after IRA bombings, accepting his Irish identity but rejecting violence, would have been an ideal choice, but he preferred to attempt to give a moral lead from his own tribal camp. Having just moved from Belfast to Ballymoney, in Paisley country, he had to establish his credentials.

The Republic's new coalition government of Fine Gael and Labour, serviced by the Foreign Affairs officials who had been in constant touch with Hume, was particularly anxious to lend any help to Hume's plans. Foreign Minister Garret FitzGerald wasted no time ensuring that there was a Dublin input to the British Government's White Paper foreshadowing the power-sharing Executive. After receiving the seals of office at 9 pm, and bidding his farewells at the *Irish Times*, the new Minister began work on a document at 2.30 am. He had it cleared in Cabinet at 9.30, and by noon it was being considered by the British Cabinet in Downing Street. Hume was now moving into a negotiating stance with the British, and in a notably tough speech at the Merriman School in Scarriff, Co. Clare,

141

in August, he advised the Dublin Government not to underestimate its strength or to surrender its position 'to the false liberalism of placating the Unionists'. Placation had governed British attitudes for three centuries, he argued, with tragic results. Only when the sovereignty of the island had been settled could there be real generosity and, to bring that about, unionists should 'hold their heads high and ask Britain to stand aside'. It was a theme he was to return to frequently, but it assumed an acceptance by unionists that peace was impossible in a divided island, and that they should see the sense of negotiating from strength, before they were outnumbered by nationalists. Neither of these notions was in the Protestant creed.

While Faulkner's Unionists were trying to prepare themselves for negotiations with such patently awkward SDLP opponents – and there were to be four defections from his ranks – the anti-power-sharing loyalists, including Unionists and Paisleyites, made it clear that obstruction was to be their policy. Said Craig: 'We will use our position to prevent anything being legislated for in the Assembly.' Twice police were called to the chamber to quell violence aimed at preventing agreement being reached before the deadline of March 1974, after which the Act setting up the Assembly would lapse.

Hume was not to be denied, having got so far, and the SDLP preparation for talks was as meticulous as ever, starting with a conference in Donegal to identify subjects for the Council of Ireland and to prepare background papers. Finally Hume and Devlin retired to the Burlington Hotel in Dublin and, after forty-eight hours without sleep, put together a socialist-style economic and social programme which was eventually adopted, with minor modific-ations. It was the key, in fact, to forcing Whitelaw to break the impasse with the Faulkner Unionists, who were still insisting that the SDLP should accept the Constitution Act – and Northern Ireland's status – and that Taoiseach Liam Cosgrave should give *de facto* recognition to it before inter-governmental talks. Just six years after the 5 October Derry march, the negotiations began at Stormont Castle and, as Hume had suspected, the only document presented was the SDLP's. It had long been his practice never to enter a meeting without a clear plan of campaign, with all the counter-arguments covered in his mind. That way, he found, the worst that could happen was that his plan would be slightly modified. The emphasis on the social and economic programme also suited his purposes from a party point of view, showing that his interest was not simply a matter of job-sharing with Unionists, but putting a social democratic stamp on the policies of the putative Executive. Once again the SDLP was using the experience of the Labour Party in the Republic, which insisted on a similar strategy before entering coalition with a fairly right-wing Fine Gael.

Highly speculative targets were produced about the jobs and houses that would be provided, based on massive public spending, and the only problem arose over the right-wing reluctance of leading Unionist thinker Roy Bradford to endorse government intervention in industry. Brian Faulkner, however, rapidly overruled him, on the grounds that Northern Ireland had always relied heavily on government expenditure on industry, and one of the last obstacles was demolished. Earlier Bradford had approached SDLP members, hinting that he would be a more acceptable Chief Executive than Orangeman Faulkner, but without response. Their old adversary was beginning to win them round with his straightforward dealing and his obvious conversion – traced back to Darlington – to the proposition that Northern Ireland's only hope of survival, with him as leader, was through power-sharing. Faulkner and Fitt were birds of a feather, accustomed to fighting their corner, wherever it was, while Hume's relations with the Unionist leader were cooler, yet increasingly respectful. Faulkner was to describe Hume as 'a formidable political thinker with great personal integrity, but a sometimes exasperating dogmatism', which the Stormont Castle talks brought out. He was also a battler, as Whitelaw discovered when a leak from the talks appeared in *The Times*, and Hume accused him of being responsible. Whitelaw rose to his feet in anger. 'How dare you?' he said. But Hume gave as good as he got. 'Don't you start bawling me out. You'll listen to me whether you like it or not.' Instantly, the anger passed and Whitelaw countered by asking, 'Will you have a drink?'

At Hume's suggestion, the Stormont Castle talks were broken into four parts: seeking agreement on a common economic and social programme; the day-to-day workings of the administration, trying to anticipate problems and leaving major difficulties aside; the number of seats in the Executive and who got what; and the Council of Ireland, conditional on the approval of the Dublin Government. The last two were vital, and last-minute arguments over the 'numbers game' threatened the success of the whole enterprise. The Unionists knew that, for survival's sake, they had to have a majority on the Executive, although their numbers were now equal to the SDLP's and they were already claiming the post of chief executive, having named the Assembly's Speaker. Since the Executive was limited to eleven members, the combination of the three parties had, they argued, to be six-four-one, which the SDLP claimed was unfair and based on a crude headcount, rather than 'widespread acceptance'. Hume, however, had a simple answer – enlargement of the administration to fifteen, including four non-voting members from the three parties, made up of two SDLP and one each Unionist and Alliance. Thus the Unionists had their one-seat majority in the Executive, but were outnumbered eight to seven in the final count, and each could claim victory.

Just before the final agreement in November, McLachlan, who was watching from the sidelines, got a telephone call to his home from Devlin, saying the whole thing was falling apart. Faulkner had mentioned the number of seats each party was to have on the Executive and then had denied it. He had lost everyone's trust and only a retraction could save him. As soon as McLachlan put the phone down, it rang again, with Faulkner telling him he should be the first to know the experiment was not going to work. Deadlock had been reached. Without telling Faulkner he already knew the background, McLachlan got him to explain that the SDLP was claiming he said something which he had not. Even if he had been misinterpreted, said Faulkner, or had said something he had not meant to, how could he retreat? McLachlan's advice was simply to make a clean breast of his problem and Faulkner agreed to 'think about it'. Next morning he made a solemn apology – something he had said had been misunderstood – and the atmosphere was instantly transformed. The Executive was formed the same day, and jobs found for all eleven members.

Bradford had been bidding for Commerce, as a former Minister, but Hume, who was offered the key job of Finance, was not going to concede the most conspicuously beneficial role in the Executive, which could help steer industry to parts of the province previously neglected. Devlin, in Health, and Currie, in Housing and Planning, were well pleased, and Fitt, who had been a spectator at the talks, chose not to add to his Westminster duties, and was Deputy Chief Executive without a department. Whitelaw immediately assigned police guards to the Executive members and made arrangements for them to be supplied with guns. Hume was the exception, never carrying a pistol, because of his non-violent principles, and declining a police guard. Indeed, despairing police were to tell him his security would be improved several-fold, if he would only close his front door.

The Council of Ireland was approved in principle and referred to the tripartite conference to follow, despite Unionist objections to its powers and responsibilities. Later, some Unionists expressed surprise that a Council they had seen as a consultative body, with no constitutional implications, was given such an elevated role, but this was simply a reflection of their poor negotiating ability. Apart from Faulkner and the obstructive Bradford, there were no really experienced men on the Unionist team and if they had read the SDLP manifesto they would have recognised the kind of council which Hume envisaged. It was, as he explained, modelled on the institutions of the European Community, with a Council of Ministers representing the Dublin and Belfast Governments, a parliamentary tier and a permanent secretariat, comparable to the European Commission, which would initiate policy. The underlying intention was to reconcile differences, in the European manner, an idea which had been planted by the late Michael Sweetman, an influential Fine Gael member, in a pamphlet Hume had read before the Assembly elections.

Faulkner would have preferred a low-level inter-governmental body, consulting on matters of mutual interest, but eventually accepted the parliamentary tier on the optimistic grounds that it would involve the loyalists and that the Council decisions would have to be unanimous. He was reaching for the supreme prize, for Unionists, of Dublin co-operation against terrorism, based on the political status quo, and in exchange was 'prepared to go along with a limited amount of nonsense from the nationalists'. But it was a gamble, and after the final emotional scenes on the Stormont Castle steps on 21 November, with tears rolling down Willie Whitelaw's cheeks, the reality dawned on 6 December in the cold light of Sunningdale, the civil service staff college in Berkshire which housed the final tripartite conference. As soon as the Unionists, mindful of the hostile reaction to the agreement, attempted to question the principle of the Council, Hume cut them off immediately. 'But you've already agreed that,' he said, and read out the relevant passage from the Stormont agreement, defining a council with executive powers. Faulkner's advisers tried to get him to press the need for a renegotiation, in the light of 'changed circumstances', but he would have none of it, being confident of his ability to mould the Council to Unionist liking. On Hume's insistence, the agreement was seen as a package, from which nothing could be extracted, and the position of both sides was that 'nothing is agreed until everything is agreed'. This enabled the SDLP to attend Sunningdale as members of an Executive designate, with nothing more than a promise from the Government that internment would be phased out, and theoretically it permitted the Unionists to quit the conference if the tide was running too strongly against them.

On the way over to England by RAF plane Roy Bradford dropped a strong hint of Unionist intentions when he remarked to Austin Currie: 'You've screwed us, and now it's our turn to screw you.' Hume, who had been notably conciliatory at Stormont, in the knowledge that Sunningdale was the real test, was put on his guard, but from an early stage it was obvious there was little to worry about with the SDLP in a majority situation. Heath always had a sympathy with the SDLP – dating back to a private meeting with Hume in his Albany flat, when Heath was Opposition leader – and the balance swung mightily against Faulkner, with all the Dublin heavyweights weighing in behind Hume. Whitelaw would have had an understanding of Faulkner's vulnerability, but he had been made Employment Secretary, for British political reasons, and Francis Pym, the brand new Secretary of State, was completely at sea. Both Hume and Heath, as well as most of the Irish Government, took the view that Faulkner was an experienced member of the clique which had ruled Northern Ireland for fifty years, with singularly little concern for the minority, and that it was up to him to defend himself. If he accepted something, they assumed he could sell it.

Others knew better, however, and some of the best judges were in the Alliance Party, who found themselves increasingly worried about the pressures being exerted on the Unionists. They were convinced that Faulkner had done a deal with Whitelaw in return for a majority in the Executive, and remembered Whitelaw telling them at Laneside: 'For goodness sake, go along with Brian. You'll find he is going to be extremely reasonable at Sunningdale.' The other explanation might have been simply that 'look-on-the-bright-side Brian', as his family called him, believed he had only to be installed as Chief Executive to show that power-sharing could work.

For some in the SDLP, like Fitt, the importance of Sunningdale was to copper-fasten power-sharing and therefore they could be generous with the Unionists, and play down the Council of Ireland. But for Hume, looking to the roots of the problem, the key issue was the Council, and how much power it could be given to bring the two parts of Ireland closer together. Days before the tripartite talks he had given the party conference, which backed power-sharing by 235 votes to 22, his view of how the Council could help establish 'adequate policing', without which the first challenge would bring the Executive down about their ears. Hume saw the Council as vital to the establishment of a stable society and he was determined that its headquarters should be in Armagh, the meeting-place of the great Irish traditions. But he had no illusions about the difficulties or the need to bring Protestants with him: 'We must understand that we are asking a lot of the Protestant people of the North. The Anglo-Irish problem can be solved only when the fears of the Protestant community are stilled.' By his own criteria, Sunningdale was to be both a personal triumph and a failure.

Right from the start of the talks Hume wanted to emphasise the role of the Council in the total concept, and he wrote Fitt's opening statement, which came as a sobering douche after contributions by Heath, Cosgrave and Faulkner. A Council with executive powers had been agreed, Fitt pointed out, and the terms of the conference were to implement that decision, by devising a structure for the Council. The SDLP proposed five Ministers from each side, with the necessity for unanimous decisions, and a parliamentary tier, involving the Assembly and the Dáil.

The agreement of the Dublin Government was a formality, despite Conor Cruise O'Brien's attempts in Cabinet to settle for the 'miracle' of power-sharing, so the first decision of the conference was to endorse the SDLP proposition, leaving the functions to be determined by sub-committees. Since the recommendations were to be regarded as a package, there was a perfect defence in case anything leaked to the media, kicking its heels at a distance from the conference building. This alibi was soon called into use, for word filtered back from Dublin that the *Sunday Independent* was carrying banner headlines, 'It's a Council of Ireland'. Faulkner was furious, and was fully supported by the SDLP, who understood his embarrassment at a one-sided story. The leak was easily traced back to the Irish Information Service at Sunningdale, which had used the British delegation's copying machine to issue a press release – because its own was out of order – and had left a damaged copy in the room. Muiris MacConghail, as head of Government Information Services, accepted full responsibility, and made his apology to Ted Heath. He then approached Cosgrave, in the presence of Hume, and said he was willing to take the consequences, if his resignation was required. It was not, and although rumour subsequently had it that O'Brien, as Minister for Posts and Telegraphs, had authorised the leak, he denies it vehemently. Like Hume, he would have known that the *Independent*'s story was extremely damaging for Faulkner, although it might have added to the Irish Government's prestige. Throughout the conference the Irish delegation was very much aware that it was meeting the British exactly fifty-three years after the partition decision of the Anglo-Irish treaty negotiations, which led to the irreparable split in Irish nationalism between the two sides in the Civil War, and that Fianna Fáil were waiting, like Eamon de Valera in his day, to take advantage of any false move. Whenever anything was being discussed which might conflict with the Republic's written constitution, Attorney General Declan Costello would mutter darkly that the Government could face a challenge in the courts, and the name of Sean MacBride, the veteran republican lawyer, was mentioned as a likely opponent.

After Hume's definition of the aims of the conference had been accepted, Heath identified five outstanding questions, each of which was to be examined by a sub-committee. These covered the nature and functions of a Council of Ireland; extradition and law enforcement; recognition by the Republic of the status of Northern Ireland; responsibilities for the police; and finance. Hume was in the committee on status, which largely concerned ways of shading the meaning of Articles 2 and 3 of the 1937 Irish constitution, laying formal claim to the whole island while accepting that, pending unity, the South's laws should apply only to the twenty-six counties. Heath and Faulkner would have preferred a straight deletion, but by an arrangement with Hume, the Irish Government was left to put up the main counter-argument, which was that it would make little difference to the loyalists, and could precipitate a crisis in the South. Cosgrave, however, was unimpressive, and Hume hurriedly stepped into the breach.

'Look, Prime Minister,' he told Heath. 'You would get the impression that everybody is running round Northern Ireland every day of the week saying "I'm threatened by the two Articles". The reality of everyday life in the South is that nobody is saying "We'll get the North". What has happened is that society has moved beyond the constitution. But if you try to change the constitution you are in a different ball game, because you are dragging up the whole past – rather like your own constitution. Nobody would allege that Britain is a sectarian society. But you have a very sectarian constitution. In fact that man sitting beside you' – it was the Attorney General, Sir Peter Rawlinson – 'can't become Lord Chancellor, because he happens to be in the same church as me.' Pausing, to let the words sink in, he went on: 'That's the situation. Nobody would say that Britain is sectarian. If you were having to change the constitution, to drop the stipulation that the Royal Family and the bishops in the Lords must be members of the Church of England, you might start something you mightn't want to deal with.'

It was a telling defence, which Heath took to heart. 'Next business' was his only comment. But there was a sequel, years later, when Hume met Rawlinson's daughter in Dublin, where she was married to an executive. 'My father speaks very warmly of you at Sunningdale,' she said. 'In fact he was tickled pink at the point you raised that he couldn't become Lord Chancellor.' After Sunningdale, Heath had a private meeting with Harold Wilson and an amendment, dropping the ban, was slipped through without opposition. Hume's interest in Britain's unwritten constitution, as compared with the Irish, had paid off handsomely.

He also reminded the British, in the status committee, that their guarantee to maintain Northern Ireland as part of the United Kingdom so long as the majority so wished was as controversial as Articles 2 and 3. He wanted them to say that they would support Irish unity if the majority wanted it, which was a way of saying that they, as opposed to the Unionists, had no vested interest in the status quo, and would go along with any change. This had never been spelled out before, and Hume saw it as an important weapon to use against his republican opponents. If it could be established that the British interest was to ensure that there was peace and stability, it would mean that the solution relied totally on a process of persuasion, undermining the argument for violence. As Hume said: 'The British would be saying we won't be forced out of here, but if you want change you can have it. We're not against Irish unity.' That was the statement he wanted, and essentially he got it. Neither Articles 2 and 3 nor the British guarantee could be dropped, so as a compromise there were statements from the two Governments, setting out their new and more flexible positions on the North. The Irish were secretly astonished by Faulkner's willingness to accept their wording, and FitzGerald felt Dublin could have gone much further in Faulkner's direction. Eventually the Irish Government said there could be no change in Northern Ireland's status until the majority desired it, and the British said that although their guarantee remained, if a majority wanted a united Ireland 'the British Government would support that wish'. The argument, then, was about which formula should take precedence, since the reading of the second could be governed by the first, and Fine Gael broke the deadlock. Acting on a suggestion by Declan Costello, Garret FitzGerald offered his solution at a meeting with British officials in Pym's room. 'Let's print them side by side,' he said, adding with schoolboy glee, 'and bag's the left!' The British gratefully agreed and although a document was later produced, with the British position on the left, prompting claims of 'betrayal' by O'Brien, these were only in jest. Hume's main task was over, but he continued to roam the other committee rooms and corridors, throwing in ideas and stiffening arguments. Acting without a secretarial back-up, he did most of the paperwork himself, in longhand, and was constantly amazed by the unpreparedness of the Unionists, who seemed to make up their policy as they went along and were struggling to make their mark in what was largely an inter-governmental conference.

The atmosphere in the conference centre was relaxed, if rather remote from the outside world, with an ever-open free bar in the lounge and a well-stocked drinks cabinet in each party's room. Hume took charge of the key until the agreement was signed, and Devlin, who had stopped drinking in 1970, was equally vigilant. But Alliance were generous companions in an emergency, and the Unionists, who were an abstemious group, had plenty to spare. Faulkner, a teetotaller, did not recognise the value of alcohol as a lubricant until almost the end of his political career. Fitt, who declined a seat on any of the sub-committees, explaining 'John loves that sort of thing', spent much of the time stretched out before the fire, asking passers-by what was happening. He was largely oblivious of the proceedings, although, like the others, he took part in the jollity of a bus ride to a dinner in 10 Downing Street on Friday night, which Heath had laid on to impress the Irish with the need for historic decisions. Many of the top Tories were present, and an attempt by Devlin to lower the tone, by asking Heath to join him in 'The Sash', an Orange ballad, was frustrated by the Prime Minister calling for another selection from the Winchester Cathedral Choir. 'Where's the radio?' asked Fitt. Heath was the wrong man for such an informal occasion, and it was left to the Irish to make their own music on the bus, where Faulkner broke all precedent by contributing a song, 'Galway Bay'.

Back in Sunningdale, Heath broke off for a meeting with the Italian President on Saturday afternoon, leaving Pym to drop a monumental brick at a plenary session. To everyone's amazement, he introduced a policy document suggesting that the Government would hand back security to a future Northern Ireland Executive, reversing the decision of March 1972. Faulkner jumped at the proposal, for which he had not dared to ask, and Hume was equally determined that any new structures for policing had to be on an all-Ireland basis. Any chance of agreement that day had gone and when Heath returned to find what had happened, he publicly reprimanded his hapless Secretary of State. No British government would agree to restore security powers, he said, bluntly telling Pym that he had no authority to suggest it. But the damage was done, and the Unionists fought to reinstate the proposal, far into the night and until the following afternoon.

The police issue was the crux of the conference for Hume, for if the Council could be linked with control of the RUC and the Garda, there would be much less of a problem for Catholics to identify with the Northern force. He wanted to be able to say 'Join the police', but needed a new structure, and a new North-South link so that it could not be regarded as a unionist force. Faulkner was in equal difficulties, needing his partners in government, the SDLP, to give full support to the RUC, yet not wanting the Southern Government to have a role. Faulkner had tacit support from Dublin, which was wary of setting up an independent police authority to remove the Garda from political control; and more than once Currie had to kick Irish Justice Minister Paddy Cooney under the table. Under pressure, Faulkner returned again and again to the need for a British promise on a return of security powers, and gradually Hume scaled down the Council of Ireland dimension on policing to the point where its only power – again, with a veto operating – was to have all government nominees to the two police authorities vetted by the Ministers of the two governments, with no operational control whatsoever. Still

151

Faulkner felt he had to have more, both on policing and extradition, if any responsibility was being given to the Council, and at a crucial point Paddy Devlin grabbed Oliver Napier, Bob Cooper and Conor Cruise O'Brien, and said, 'Look, we've got to catch ourselves on here. Brian Faulkner is being nailed to a cross. There is no way Faulkner can sell this.' O'Brien, who had been arguing the same case with his colleagues, was glad of the assistance.

A private approach was made to Cosgrave and FitzGerald, pointing out that for Faulkner to swing power-sharing and a Council of Ireland with executive powers, he had to deliver something concrete on SDLP support of the police and extradition, if not on changes in Articles 2 and 3. But both were as dismissive of the dangers as Heath; they thought Faulkner was experienced enough to know what he could take. They were wrong, of course, for fifty years of unbroken rule had not accustomed Unionist leaders to horse-trading on this scale. Even his Unionist colleagues had to deflate him when he would come rushing enthusiastically into their room with some leaky new formula, usually concocted by Frank Cooper, the Permanent Secretary of the Northern Ireland Office, who was the only continuity with the Whitelaw era.

Extradition was equally troublesome, because of the Republic's prohibition on extraditing offenders who claimed a political motive, and Unionist Basil McIvor, a liberal barrister, was adamant that his party either had to get some concession in this area or go home. He was ready to leave when Faulkner took him outside for a walk on the clear, frosty Sunday morning, and they met O'Brien and Cosgrave, similarly depressed. O'Brien agreed that it was not going to work, but Faulkner was still reluctant to quit, and throw away a last chance of power. Eventually, at 3 am, the British came up with an answer, resurrecting the Criminal Justice Act of 1864 to permit a person to be tried for murder in the territory where he was arrested. Although McIvor still opposed it in the plenary session, the combination of this and an agreement on a joint North-South law commission to look into the possibility of a common law-enforcement area was enough to break the deadlock. Even this lifeline, and the Criminal Law Jurisdiction Act which followed in the Republic, owed their origins to Hume, who before Sunningdale had come across a Latin precept on extradition meaning roughly 'hand over or try'. At Sunningdale the SDLP argued the international principle was that either you hand a fugitive over, or try him yourself. This would achieve the same object as extradition, without bringing into question the impartiality of the RUC, who were still unacceptable to nationalists.

But there was still the policing issue to be decided, after a debate that continued, with brief interruptions, from Friday morning until 5 am on Sunday; and, with Basil McIvor putting on his coat and gloves, ready to leave, Heath and Frank Cooper descended on the Unionist room to add another ounce of pressure. For two or three minutes Heath looked round the room in silence, trying to stare them out, before delivering a schoolmasterly lecture: 'What do you people want? You're being absolutely intransigent. What do you want?' The Council of Ireland connection with the police was an unimportant gesture, he declared. He listened as McIvor and others disagreed, and then he silently left the room, shoulders shaking with laughter, as Cooper turned and winked. It was a last defiant gesture by the Unionists, but the prize was too tempting, and resistance was too low.

Out in the grounds, Bradford made a last attempt to persuade Faulkner to use the only weapon he had left, a walkout, in the firm conviction that Heath would not let him go. With memories of the suspension of Stormont, however, Faulkner was not ready to call Heath's bluff, if it was that. Alliance, who held out longer on the police issue, for the same basic reason, got the same treatment from Heath. When he threatened to destroy them by holding them publicly accountable for the failure of the talks, they had no alternative but to give way. Policing was a crunch issue for Heath, Hume and Faulkner, for very different reasons. Bloody Sunday – and the Hume case – had left a deep impression on the British, who wanted to keep security powers firmly in Westminster, and Hume saw it as fundamental that policing had an all-Ireland dimension. Faulkner, on the other hand, regarded a promise of a return of security powers as a trump card to use against his loyalist critics.

At 5 am, however, the final outcome was still uncertain and Heath called one from each delegation to his room. Faulkner was talking about going home, but at 6.15 am Hume interrupted: 'Look, everybody is very tired. Let's all go to bed. There's no point in saying we'll meet at nine in the morning, because it's so late. We'll meet at three in the afternoon and say nothing about it till then.' When Faulkner protested that he would be destroyed by Sabbatarians if he negotiated on a Sunday – much earlier he had warned that he had a pressing hunting appointment on Saturday – Hume countered: 'In

the name of Jesus, what have you been doing for the last six hours?'
At 3 pm, the final trade-off was agreed, representing a modest
climb-down by all parties; there would be a very low-level Council of
Ireland link with the police, requiring the two governments to submit
for approval names of nominees to the police authorities, in return
for a very conditional promise to 'discuss the devolution of responsibility for normal policing' to the Executive. It had held up the
agreement for a vital thirty-six hours, while most of the participants
were unemployed and, ironically, it was never referred to during the
Executive's brief life. Hume, who could recognise huge chunks of his
own drafting in the final communique, was far from elated, and
admitted to feeling physically drained. He had just finished two-and-
a-half months of the most intense negotiations, at the highest level,
interrupted by a brief spell of hospitalisation, before Sunningdale.
(Originally his problem was feared to be angina, when Dr Joe
Hendron had been summoned to examine him at Stormont Castle,
with Willie Whitelaw in some distress, but exhaustion was diagnosed.) He had tried his best to strike a balance between the needs
of both communities to relate to the institutions of law and order,
and was by no means sure he had gone far enough on the Catholic
side. He could only hope that the minority could identify sufficiently
with the Catholics on the Executive and the Council of Ireland to
drop their ambivalence towards violence, but it would take time.
Until the agreement was ratified by the three administrations, he
knew he could not risk giving the police the support of the SDLP.

That was the central weakness of Sunningdale for Hume, though it
can be argued that even as it was, the Council of Ireland was too
strong. To him, it was a structure to give an opportunity for the two
sides to grow together, with the British agreeing to adopt a low-key
role. But he might have guessed, from the attitude of the Unionists at
Sunningdale, that the ability or the willingness to grasp the
opportunity was weak, and that if the Faulknerites were worried
about their supporters back home, how much more hostile would be
the Paisleyites and Craigites.

Fitt signed the final document and stayed on for the radio
interviews but, by chance, Hume, the main architect of the agreement, was the party spokesman on TV. The main hall looked like the
centre of attraction, full of reporters and radio commentators, but
the TV interviewing rooms were far more important for the
supporters back home, glued to their sets, and Hume had a free

run. It was time the Sunningdale politicians had their say, for although the loyalist politicians had unanimously declined a late invitation to the conference they had been able to dominate the television discussions on Friday night, scoring valuable points. Hume was not alone in believing that if the conference had been wrapped up by Friday night, or by lunchtime on Saturday, the fears aroused about the Council of Ireland might have been checked.

As the delegates flew back from Northholt in the unheated RAF plane, there was a mood of gloom on the Unionist side, and well concealed satisfaction among the SDLP. The British and Irish Governments were heavily committed to the progress of power-sharing and the Council, and it was up to all three parties in the Executive to go out and sell the agreement as hard as they could, while proving that Protestants and Catholics could work effectively together. Hume had no doubts about his own party, but he would have been more concerned about unionist reaction if he had shared the experience of McLachlan, trooping round Orange halls vainly trying to win support, long before Sunningdale. McLachlan knew that it would not be so much a case of selling Sunningdale as of finding an audience. The sinking feeling grew as his house was pelted with stones on the night the agreement was announced.

Much of the plan's success depended on a positive reaction by Fianna Fáil, and after the handshakes Hume was surprised when Cosgrave asked him to phone Jack Lynch and tell him everything. Hume said he realised the importance of Opposition support, and that he was confident Lynch would not rock any boats, but that it was Cosgrave's job as Taoiseach to involve him. Cosgrave ageed, but when Hume saw Lynch shortly after the conference and before a major debate in the Dáil, he discovered that he was the first to brief him fully. Until then, Lynch had only newspaper and broadcast reports to rely upon, without knowing the background. In view of the political and constitutional implications, it was a sorry reflection on the state of inter-party relations and a discouraging pointer for the future.

There were plenty more shocks in store, before the Executive was installed. The first was an open letter from Alliance leader Oliver Napier to the Republic, two weeks after Sunningdale, saying essentially that they had got the best deal they could have hoped for, and the opportunity for better relations on the island. But a piece of paper was not going to bring peace in our time. If they were not open about recognition, did not deliver on extradition, and were not seen

155

to be taking on the IRA, the agreement would be wasted. His SDLP colleagues on the Executive-to-be, who had not been consulted, were furious with such a divisive statement – even if it turned out to be uncannily realistic. But Hugh Logue, an ambitious SDLP Assembly member, came out with an even more damaging speech in a debate in Trinity College, Dublin, describing the Council as the vehicle which would 'trundle' the North into a united Ireland. He showed it to Hume in advance and was told to scrap it immediately, as it was against the whole spirit of the agreement. But it had already been circulated to the Press, and all Hume could do was to berate the politician for coining a phrase which was eagerly seized upon by Sunningdale's opponents. Cosgrave, too, struck the wrong note in an interview in December agreeing that the treaty meant a united Ireland was on the way. FitzGerald stressed that the consent of the Northern majority would be essential, but he could not salvage the situation.

Even the signing-on ceremony on 1 January, in the shadow of Craigavon's statue in the Stormont Great Hall, was not uneventful. There were two swearing-in formulae, one for the eleven full members of the Executive and one for the four members of the administration, but the Lord Chief Justice used only the first. After lunch, apologetic civil servants asked the four administration members to go through the signing ceremony a second time. But there was a far more serious hitch two days later, when Brian Faulkner faced a vote on the Council of Ireland proposals by the full Unionist Council. Before the Sunningdale conference he had had a ten-vote victory for power-sharing, a clear sign of his vulnerability, but despite the efforts of McLachlan, poring through party rule and address books for every potential supporter, he lost by eighty votes. Advisers like McLachlan and Leslie Morrell, who had always believed that Faulkner should have been less bullish about Sunningdale, accepting the package as an interesting offer which required party approval, would have advised him to hang on as leader. But Faulkner was too honourable to brazen out a vote of no confidence and, with his resignation on 7 January, cut himself off from the bulk of his supporters.

He thought he could win round the party from outside, by his success in office. Without the party machine, however, and with his Unionist supporters in the Asssembly in disarray, it was a daunting task. Soon there was another major blow to his hopes – the feared constitutional challenge to the Irish Government's recognition of Northern Ireland in Sunningdale's Clause 5, from Kevin Boland, a former Fianna Fáil Minister. Guided by Declan Costello, the Government took no chances, and to Hume's surprise presented a maximum defence in court, arguing that it had not agreed that any part of Ireland belonged to the United Kingdom. It had been a *de facto* rather than a *de jure* arrangement. The defence succeeded eventually, when the Supreme Court agreed that the sovereignty claim in Articles 2 and 3 had no legal standing, but until then the challenge prevented the agreement being ratified in the Dáil and forced the Government into *sub judice* silence. FitzGerald realised later that, although the advice of Costello, regarded by Hume as the most original thinker on the Dublin team at Sunningdale, was legally sound, it was politically disastrous, and should have been ignored. Meanwhile Faulkner's position was being weakened, day after day, to the extent that he flew to Baldonnel military airport to meet Cosgrave on 16 January. For the first time, he admitted that the experiment might not succeed, convincing Dublin that henceforth it was engaged in a rescue operation.

Hume had made a strong personal plea to Faulkner at Sunningdale that the agreement should be put to an immediate referendum in both parts of Ireland, but the Unionist was not as confident of a 'Yes' vote, knowing the doubts even about power-sharing, and the idea was not pursued. While Faulkner's preference was to show by results that the Executive was working, Hume continued to regret that the people had not been given a chance to lead the politicians and provide a popular endorsement which opponents would have had to overthrow. He saw it as a chance to undermine the classic republican claim that the last real democratic election in Ireland was in 1918, when the single electorate voted overwhelmingly, with the strong exception of the Northern counties, for unity. That mandate would have been altered significantly by a Sunningdale vote, forcing opponents to oppose it politically, rather than violently.

But the real challenge was the United Kingdom general election, called by Heath in February to support his tough stand against a miners' strike which was choking British industry. Faulkner, supported by Whitelaw, had pleaded with Heath not to endanger the fledgling Executive when an election was first mooted in January, but national considerations prevailed, although the prospects in Northern Ireland could hardly have been worse. The Executive had nothing to show, in terms of progress either on jobs or security, and Faulkner was an increasingly isolated figure in Unionism. While the three parties in the Executive had to fight on separate and conflicting platforms, the anti-Sunningdale Unionists could unite forces in the United Ulster Unionist Council, forcing wavering Faulknerites into unwelcome decisions.

Only one Unionist Executive member, Roy Bradford, chose to submit himself to the electorate, and his rejection on the middle-class doorsteps of North Down was to colour his opinions in the months to come. Early in January he had made a strong plea for an attempt to broaden the base of the Executive, to involve loyalists, and although he had received support from Fitt, no action was taken. The other Unionists in the Executive opposed the implication in Bradford's candidacy that it was possible to hold down a Northern Ireland Department and be a Westminster MP, but their non-Executive Unionist colleagues were no more successful in an election dominated by the UUUC slogan 'Dublin is just a Sunningdale away'. Even Faulkner had to say that in his own constituency he would abstain, rather than vote for a pro-Sunningdale SDLP candidate against an anti-Sunningdale Unionist.

The SDLP fought all twelve seats, polling a respectable 22 per cent, while helping a split nationalist vote to concede two seats to UUUC candidates. Gerry Fitt was as personally popular as ever, but otherwise the result was an unmitigated disaster, returning eleven anti-Sunningdale Unionists and proving that 52 per cent of the electorate were against the Executive. There was no alternative but to soldier on, in the hope that every day of the Executive's existence in power improved its chances of eventual survival. By April, Faulkner had formed his own Unionist Party of Northern Ireland (UPNI), an admission of defeat rather than an expression of hope of rallying the moderates.

Hume's Department of Commerce was a hive of activity, pumping out statements on a revival of interest in industrial investment and helping him to target likely prospects in America and Europe, where he opened a branch office in Brussels. Here his background in business, his French and his political contacts in America – where the Kennedy connection had already been constructed – were invaluable sales aids, and officials were impressed with his dynamism. In Brussels, British diplomats were initially sceptical about this strange

158

breed of Minister, from a strange coalition government, travelling on an Irish passport, but his sheer presence and ability to communicate with a wide variety of Europeans left them in some awe. The holding of the green Irish passport, which recognises no border on the island, had long been a token gesture by all Northerners who regarded themselves as Irish, and Hume never thought of switching to the British document. There were more problems about his insistence on travelling abroad by Aer Lingus, the Irish airline, but eventually the civil servants accepted that this was his way of saying that Sunningdale had radically changed conventional views of nationality in Ireland.

Hume's first job as Minister was to draw up a list of functions which could be transferred to the Council of Ireland, and his Department was heavily involved in areas like tourism, energy and cross-border trade. A secret blue paper was produced on the Council's proposed responsibilities, but there was an obvious omission in agriculture, where there was so much common ground between North and South. In Belfast the Permanent Secretary of the Department of Agriculture, Jimmy Young, made it clear he would not concede a blade of grass to the Council, and his attitude was mirrored in Dublin, where civil servants deliberately dragged their feet. Indeed, Garret FitzGerald had had to resort to subterfuge to put pressure on them in the run-up to Sunningdale, when suitable subjects for the Council were under discussion. Bursting into a room where senior civil servants were meeting, he feigned surprise and then told them very deliberately that the Taoiseach attached great importance to their task. The SDLP had not been involved in the allocation of Council responsibilities at Sunningdale, Ted Heath leaving it to the Irish Government and the Unionists, but Paddy Devlin had got wind of the long list that had been agreed and was characteristically blunt about his feelings. 'I'm not going to have that,' he had told FitzGerald. 'The Unionists would be hung from lampposts when they got home.' Taking a pen, he had cut the list in half. It was not the only case of the SDLP representing the Unionists' case better than they did themselves.

To review progress on executive functions for the Council and to demonstrate Northern impatience with Dublin, an inter-governmental meeting was held in January in Hillsborough, south of Belfast, at the former Governor's residence, which convinced some doubting Unionists that power-sharing could work. Some SDLP members tended to side with the Unionists, guarding their Departments against the inroads of the Council, and at one stage Cosgrave bluntly told FitzGerald to back off. Hume was still pressing for a major Council role but, to Conor Cruise O'Brien at least, there was something ominous in the fact that the Dublin party had to be spirited in and out by army helicopter. Even back-bench supporters of the Executive were given no advance notice of the meeting, recalling the secrecy surrounding O'Neill's ill-fated invitation to Lemass nine years previously. Much of the discontent, on the SDLP side, was centred on Secretary of State Francis Pym for failing to live up to the expectations of large-scale releases of detainees, on which a call for an end to the rent and rates strike at the end of December had been based. A section of the party registered its protest by forming a Motion Number One group, to keep up the pressure.

Hume, nevertheless, felt that until the Westminster election, there was a slow swing towards the Executive and away from the naked violence and hatred within the Assembly chamber, where the loyalists were increasingly desperate. Always conscious of the need to demonstrate even-handedness, he seized every chance to talk to the business community, noting that it was the British-based banks, rather than the Irish, which were keenest to invite him. He would have liked to get inside Harland & Wolff's shipyard, the greatest recipient of public money, and heartland of Unionism, but did not press it when regretfully advised by management that there could be trouble. He was particularly interested in foreign investment, stressing the new political stability, and made one unpublicised dash to the Nuremburg headquarters of Grundig to assure them that the one-off kidnapping – and, later, murder – of their Belfast plant chief need not deter them from investing in Newry.

By mid-May, there were 4,000 jobs in the pipeline, many in high-unemployment border areas, and the jobless total of 24,900 represented 4.8 per cent of the workforce, a record low. Even Strabane, perennially at the top of the unemployment league, was in line for a factory manufacturing traffic-light components. Then the loyalists struck. An American industrialist happened to hear Hume's sales pitch on TV during his US visit, and made a point of contacting him about locating his new European plant in Northern Ireland. A well-publicised announcement was to be made in Strabane town centre, but by that time the Loyalist Workers' Strike had begun and the employer, who had just arrived in Belfast, hurriedly backed out. Hume could not protest, since his argument had been that the troubles did not reach the factory floor.

Meanwhile the Executive tried to carry on as if the February election had not happened, bolstered by the unequivocal support of the Labour Prime Minister, Harold Wilson, and a rash intervention by Cosgrave after a London visit, pressing for early ratification. But a pro-Sunningdale motion in the Assembly, tabled in January, had not been passed by Easter, because of the election and a blunder by Speaker Nat Minford. A vote was to be taken before the recess, but when Fitt's speech ran on too long, allowing the Unionists insufficient time for reply, the debate was adjourned, much to Faulkner's dismay. Without endorsement of the power-sharing principle, the SDLP felt unable to consider the pressing business of postponing the implementation of the Council, so precious weeks were lost. The IRA, meanwhile, were bombing city and town centres to pieces, and a two-day blitz, ending up with a car bomb at the Grand Central Hotel, then under army occupation, caused over £1 million damage.

A rephasing of the Council was crucial to the Unionists, because Dublin had failed to deliver in two vital areas, recognition and extradition, and Hume was willing to accommodate Faulkner up to a point. Weeks went by, as tensions inside and outside the Executive grew, and when the pro-Sunningdale vote eventually came it was the signal for a final showdown with the loyalists, not for a new beginning.

Despite the rising temperature in the Assembly chamber, Hume was careful to keep on as good terms as possible with his political opponents. After a particularly vehement outburst against the Executive by Johnny McQuade, a Stone-Age Paisleyite from Belfast's Shankill Road, a Dublin journalist was amazed to hear Hume congratulate him warmly in the corridor: 'That was a good speech, Johnny.' 'Did you think so?' came the astonished but pleased reply. 'Yours wasn't bad either, John.' Even as crunch time approached, Hume was still applying the power of his positive thinking. He was never above an act of kindness to his enemies, which helped to explain the grudging respect he commanded, as well as the fear.

13
Loyalists say 'No'

The idea of an indefinite loyalist strike had been hatched as soon as the power-sharing Executive and the Council of Ireland began to take shape, suggesting that Dublin would have a direct say in Northern Ireland affairs. In the eyes of most Protestants, this was an unthinkable price to pay for a devolved government, and it could be claimed with some justification that Faulkner had no mandate for the deal he had done. The terms for devolution were incomplete when the election was held, and the scale and scope of the Council of Ireland, as agreed at Sunningdale, were unknown. The old Loyalist Association of Workers had disbanded and in its place some fairly prominent trade union activists had formed an Ulster Workers' Council to try to co-ordinate opposition to the political developments. The legal loyalist paramilitary organisation, the Ulster Defence Association, had to be a part of any protest movement, and the first meetings were with Andy Tyrie, its leader, in the back garden of his house in Glencairn, a solidly Protestant west Belfast housing estate, and later on the Shankill Road. 'Your way has failed,' the UWC leaders told him. 'The politicians' way has failed. But we as workers can do other things.' The answer was obvious to Tyrie: why shouldn't they try to stop the whole community – stop work, stop everything, not just for a day?

At that stage, before power-sharing was seen in action, the Council of Ireland was a focus of discontent. It had been suggested by Unionists as a way of getting the two separate parts of Ireland to help each other, but Sunningdale's version of the Council was interfering and menacing, they thought. At another level there was deep distrust of the civil rights politicians, who had turned united--Irelanders – but that was a secondary consideration for the strike leadership.

An attempt was made to enlist politicians from the Unionists, the DUP and Vanguard at the Laharna Hotel, Larne, but it soon became obvious that they felt the strike had no chance. Paisley, who chaired

162

the meeting, thought the strike was irrelevant, remembering three previous twenty-four-hour strikes and – like John Taylor, Harold McCusker, Frankie Millar and Douglas Hutchinson – was prepared to rely on parliamentary methods. Only Bill Craig, who was equally pessimistic, was prepared to back the UWC 'to the hilt', lending them his Vanguard party headquarters in a dilapidated mansion in middle-class Hawthornden Road, less than five minutes from Stormont. It was the only help they needed, until the closing stages of the stoppage. Preparations for the strike were being made as early as January and a co-ordinating committee was set up under the chairmanship of Glenn Barr, a personable trade-union representative from Derry, who combined his membership of the UWC with his role as local chairman of the UDA. He was vehemently against enforced power-sharing, which he saw as institutionalised sectarianism, but he decided that the Council of Ireland was a much better target for attack.

Once Tyrie committed the UDA to a strike, he knew it had to succeed, for he reckoned that failure would set back the organisation by at least three years. The UWC would provide the acceptable face, through new spokesmen like Jim Smyth and Harry Murray, but the muscle would be the UDA's, through the many UWC men who were also in the paramilitary organisation. Several dates were rejected by Tyrie as premature, but Barr advised that the Assembly vote on Sunningdale on 14 May provided an ideal springboard, after protesting UWC spokesmen had been snubbed at Stormont. (The loyalists later had a more friendly reception from the British Government, being flown over to London for talks in the Northern Ireland Office with Merlyn Rees and Stan Orme, and being given a chauffeur-driven limousine, with police escort, for a rapid return to Heathrow when they warned that Belfast airport might be closing.) An advertisement in the *News Letter* set the scene for the strike and the BBC's new TV studio at Stormont was used to let Murray announce provincewide that the strike had begun, after the Executive motion was passed by forty-four votes to twenty-eight.

That was when the worries began for Tyrie, who had tried to get across the message that this was to be a strictly non-violent protest, though with threatening overtones. There would be the usual street barriers, to discourage strike-breakers walking to work, but if the police tried to dislodge them the tactic was to move down the road, or around the corner, setting up another barricade. All confrontations were to be avoided, because they helped the authorities to brand the UDA as hooligans and incite the public against them. But clubs would be carried for intimidation purposes and members would be given cameras without film to take non-existent 'snapshots' of would-be strike-breakers. To a large extent it worked, because the pressures were so subtle and unpredictable, but the discipline failed near Ballymena, where two Catholic brothers were murdered for refusing to shut a bar. Headquarters was furious but to its relief there was no reaction.

The first results were far from encouraging, as relatively few answered the call to stop work, and Tyrie telephoned to ask Barr, who had been responsible for much of the strategy, to lend a hand. It was a crucial decision, for the Derry man revealed a flair for organisation and handling people which put him in the centre stage for the next two weeks, chairing the co-ordinating committee and sleeping at Tyrie's home. Sub-committees looked after oil supplies, milk, bread, et cetera but the real executive consisted of six para-militaries, three UWC and the three party leaders. Paisley arrived back from a funeral in Canada about a week after the start and, in Barr's absence, failed in a clumsy attempt to take his chair at a committee meeting. 'That's mine,' said Barr, returning to the room, and when Paisley complained about his sore back, the chair was moved down the table, still leaving Barr in charge.

Later both Paisley and Harry West, who had succeeded Faulkner as leader of what was now the Official Unionist Party, had to be prevented from telephoning their constituents to take credit for UWC decisions on supplies of feeding-stuffs. Both were curtly instructed that the UWC press officer was responsible for statements. When Paisley asked for Aldergrove to be kept open for his trips to Westminster, Tommy Lyttle, one of the UDA representatives, shot back: 'It's not true then. You can't walk on water!' An appeal for special transport for Paisley's Ulster Hall services was turned down with the quip: 'Not unless you let us take the collection!'

Meanwhile, Barr's old Derry adversary, John Hume, was fuming at the failure of the dithering Secretary of State, Merlyn Rees, to order the dismantling of UWC barricades and call what Hume believed to be their bluff. At one stage Executive members lost patience with Rees's denials that barriers were in place and led him to a window where one was plainly visible. Hume would have dearly loved to have taken over the Executive's publicity function, but was

164

forced to leave it in less competent hands, knowing any contribution by him would have been a red rag to the loyalist bull. Like the strikers, he knew the key to their success lay in the control of the power stations, by which the UWC was able to turn down the power available and make it increasingly difficult to keep factories open for those who still wanted to work. Another disincentive to normal business activity was the Government assistance freely available to all who claimed the strike had prevented them from working. There was no way that Paddy Devlin's social security staff could distinguish between willing and unwilling strikers, so all got paid for what, to some, was a two-week summer holiday. The UWC closed the pubs, however, after protests from resentful wives who could not get their hair done at the hairdressers' because of power cuts. Shopkeepers who attempted to profiteer had their shelves cleared by the UDA and goods handed over to pensioners.

As the Minister responsible, Hume tried every possible ruse to beat the shutdowns, suggesting once that Coolkeeragh power station, near Derry, where loyalists were not in charge, could supply the whole grid, but he was frustrated at every turn. The army had no answers, after threats from the UWC to withdraw all power station personnel, and Hume suspected a reluctance on the part of both the generals and the British Government to confront what was an increasingly popular strike on ideological and practical grounds. Another complicating factor was that the English head of the Northern Ireland Electricity Service was suffering from a terminal illness.

After the first three days the strike-leaders regarded the battle as won, as the police were obviously not going to use strong-arm tactics, and the likelihood of armed clashes – which would have been a last resort – receded. In the glorious summer weather people needed little encouragement to participate and the businessmen, including representatives from the CBI and from Shorts aircraft factory, who had trooped up to Stormont to urge tough action on Hume, swung round to accepting the inevitability of the strike's success. The UWC gave farmers free passes for transporting fodder and then told them to complain to Stormont about its inaction, greatly angering the Civil Service.

On the political front, Bradford led the 'wets' who felt the time had come to talk to the strikers, just as Stan Orme, Rees's deputy, had already met Barr and Craig on 17 May. Although Hume was adamantly opposed to talks, he backed an alternative strategy of rephasing the Sunningdale agreement in accordance with an Executive decision. A tense meeting of the SDLP was held at Stormont on 22 May and when the result went against the leadership – eleven to eight opposing any change – one of the hardliners, Seamus Mallon, bet a companion that it would be reversed. Sure enough, the meeting was reconvened by a worried Fitt and – after an impassioned speech by Orme, virtually promising strong Government action against the strikers, and an end to internment – the motion for a two-phase Council, consultative at first, but not to develop on Sunningdale lines until another election, was passed by twelve votes to five.

By now Hume was very pessimistic about the chances of beating the strike, and helped to win the case for revision, in the parliamentary party and afterwards in the Executive, to prove his contention that the real opposition to Sunningdale was to Catholics in the government and not to the Council. Since the strike continued – even though the Council had been postponed for four years at least – and unionist opposition persisted, he concluded that he had been right. Some elements in the SDLP, however, felt a marker had been put down about the party's priorities that would cost it dearly in the future. Mallon thought the Executive already had the smell of death about it and that it was more important to hold the party line than to obtain a temporary reprieve.

Another SDLP problem was the running sore of internment – by then only sixty-five had been released since January – and Austin Currie had an agonising decision to make on a 25p fine for all Housing Executive tenants still failing to pay rent or rates, against the advice of Devlin and Hume. The Unionists demanded the penalty as a sign that the SDLP accepted their responsibilities, although the announcement was followed almost immediately by the strike, and the politicians tried to backtrack. Devlin, whose Department bore the responsibility for collecting the fine, spent most of an Executive meeting with Rees ostentatiously writing on official notepaper. When he threw the note down in front of the Secretary of State and stormed out, amazed colleagues saw he was issuing his resignation, unless all internees were released. Hume and the others followed him up to Stormont to placate him – not an uncommon event – using the argument that he would be blamed for bringing down the Executive, in response to bombs set off in a combined UDA–UVF exercise in Dublin and Monaghan, which killed twenty-five and injured 100 on

17 May. He took the point and 'froze' his resignation, until it was brought out after the strike to prove in retrospect his credentials against internment.

Hume was increasingly worried about confidential information which appeared to be leaking to the UDA, and many people suspected Bradford, the dissident in the Faulkner camp. He denied everything – just as the UWC denied receiving any leaks from him – but Jim Smyth and Ken Gibson made a visit, authorised by Tyrie, to Bradford's home, as concerned constituents. They conveyed back the impression of a split Executive, as any observer could have guessed, but Bradford did not respond to their request to resign and bring it down.

The UWC's main source of information was through a former senior civil servant who retained good contacts at Stormont, and there was a valuable reassurance in an anonymous telephone call midway through the strike. A man with a cultured voice, who seemed to know what was happening inside Stormont, simply told Tyrie to 'keep up the good work' and victory was certain. Hume still thought Bradford was a spy in the camp, however, and after indications that the UWC had early warning of security decisions, talks on the subject were suspended.

Even when Hume tried to have face-to-face talks with Rees on security matters affecting his Department, Bradford insisted he had to be present, as Environment Minister. Tempers were particularly frayed after Bradford's open espousal of talks with the UWC on BBC and RTE, but Faulkner refused to accept the Minister's proffered resignation. He considered him more of a danger outside the Executive than inside and Bradford allowed himself to continue in an Executive which he believed had no future. He later regretted his weakness, but did not want to be the one to bring the Executive down, although he knew he could have been an instant loyalist hero and perhaps might have salvaged his political career. If the troops were put in, he warned, he would join the protest himself.

The pressures on the Executive were mounting, as power cuts brought normal life to a near standstill, and the electricity service's public relations officer, Hugo Patterson, became an hourly 'voice of doom', predicting terminal damage to the power plants. One suggestion, by Agriculture Minister Leslie Morrell, that the BBC should be taken over, to stop the bad news, was ignored and not until the end was near did Hume unsuccessfully ask for Patterson, an employee under his Department, to be taken off the air. Around this time, Hume began to feel that the information he was getting from his civil servants was politically biased and this was confirmed by a signed letter from a senior civil servant, posted from Helen's Bay, telling him he was being fed false information about the power stations.

By now Hume's life was totally disrupted and his normal civilian driver was forced to abandon his duties, because of dangers on the road and possible intimidation at his east Belfast home. The driver, who had previously driven for Roy Bradford, had become a firm friend of the family, after the shock of his first visit to the Bogside. On that occasion, as they neared Derry, Hume had noticed that the man was becoming increasingly nervous and his condition worsened when he was invited into the Humes' for a meal. His face began to swell up and he became so hysterical that a doctor had to be called to give him an injection to calm him. When his sleeve was rolled up, the cause of his problem was obvious – a tattoo with the UVF slogan, 'For God and Ulster', which he said dated from his youth. He recovered overnight and from then on regularly stayed at the Humes' instead of a hotel and drank at a pub across the road. At the height of the strike, however, Ministers were helicoptered to Stormont from all parts of Northern Ireland – even Basil McIvor, from loyalist Lambeg, taking off from Lisburn army barracks and Devlin and Fitt from Victoria Barracks. Executive limousines did not dare stop for petrol, in case the occupants were recognised.

The night before the final curtain, Hume stayed for convenience in Lurgan at the home of party member Brid Rodgers and her husband. He was to be picked up by Seamus Mallon, who was able to get petrol in the Republic, near his home in south Armagh, and there were three other Assembly members as passengers – Tom Daly, Frank Feeley and Paddy O'Hanlon. Outside Portadown, Mallon was refused safe conduct through the town by the army, without explanation, and there was a tense moment at a UDA block as Mallon did a U-turn, with two of his passengers fingering their legally-held guns. After a roundabout trip, they picked Hume up and were on the outskirts of Belfast, at Shaw's Road, when a police car screamed in front of them, forcing them to a stop. The policemen hauled them bodily out of the car, with guns at their heads, before the explanation came out – someone had spotted Hume in the back seat of a Volkswagen and had assumed he was being kidnapped!

Ten days into the strike it was clear that without a major initiative by the army – whose officers regularly appeared at UWC headquarters for friendly chats – the Executive was doomed, and in a final bid the three party leaders flew to Chequers to supply Harold Wilson with Hume's plan of action for oil supplies. It called for a Government takeover of selected petrol stations, which Hume had decided would be manned by neutral civil servants under army protection, rather than by regular staff who might be victimised later. But although Gerry Fitt came back with reports of Wilson's support, he had always been fearful of a Protestant explosion if a clash with soldiers had produced casualties. He knew, too, of the Labour MPs' reluctance to confront the cleverly-named Ulster Workers' strike – in case it would be used by the Conservatives as a precedent for strike-breaking in Britain – and he had no confidence in the willingness of the unionist-minded Defence Minister, Roy Mason, to oppose the Protestants. In any case, the Prime Minister's broadcast on Saturday afternoon was an anticlimax. While he lectured the loyalists for 'sponging on British democracy', outraging their sense of patriotism, he promised no action of any kind. General King's view, that if the army got involved it would have to escort every milk float and bread van, had prevailed. The whole Rhine Army could not do it, he said, nor could it run the power stations. Bluntly the soldier told the politicians they would have to sign the orders for military action themselves.

The day before the broadcast, there was evidence that Wilson had other more aggressive plans when some UDA leaders were picked up for questioning by the army. The UWC retreated to the safer haven of suburban Ballybeen, leaving a 'shadow' committee to be arrested, if that was the Government's intention. But Hume's impression was that Wilson had sized up the ability of the Executive to survive and had decided in the course of the day at Chequers, as the drink flowed liberally, that it was not worth saving. Hume's worst fears were realised as he heard the Prime Minister launch his provocative verbal attack on the Unionists, without any military follow-through. A meeting of the SDLP members was called at Fitt's house the following day to enlist Dublin's help to put pressure on Wilson, and eventually the news came through that he had agreed to use the troops to guarantee petrol supplies. When told by Rees that the Executive would collapse if this were done, he reportedly said 'Go ahead'. But the UWC had already anticipated the move, thanks to their high-level informant, and had their own list of petrol stations. They closed them forthwith, so that the Government action resulted in less petrol, not more. Supplies to the Catholic Falls Road, which the UWC had ensured were adequate, dried up.

The last day of the Executive was predictable. After a doom-laden meeting of the Permanent Secretaries, they felt it their duty to tell the Chief Executive about their fears and Faulkner heard their news with mounting alarm. If the army continued to provide guards for the petrol stations, the strikers would pull the plug on the electricity service – something Hume had quite correctly refused to believe, all along – and in low-lying areas like the lower Falls and Sydenham, sewage would be bubbling through the manhole covers. The telephone system would die and chaos and anarchy would reign. It was unthinkable, so the Unionist Party agreed with Faulkner that there was no alternative to talks. The UWC had warned – and General King told the Cabinet – that if the soldiers took on one public service, they would be left running everything, from bakeries to supermarkets and dairies. Reporting back to the Executive, Faulkner said with emotion that he was not in public life to destroy Northern Ireland and that, rather than that, he would talk to the strikers or resign. Hume, however, was unmoved, saying he refused to talk. 'I'll sit here until there is shit flowing up Royal Avenue and then the people will realise what these people are about and then we'll see who wins.' It was useful, he argued, to show who were the builders and who the destroyers. He would have gambled on the strikers backing down, as they saw the chaos they had helped to create, and there was some evidence for this. The UWC leadership fully expected arrests, after what they saw as a 'dry run' in south Antrim, but hoped that their retreat to the Protestant heartland of Ballybeen would delay the process. Any show of army force, however, had probably been left too late to be effective.

The SDLP refused to resign, so Faulkner left, eyes brimming, to hand in the Unionist resignations to Rees and the five-month experiment had ended, with a whimper rather than a bang. The only moment of light relief, on the last day, was when Austin Currie had to leave the Executive meeting to hear that his wife had had their fourth child, Austin. When Faulkner was told that the birth of their first child had coincided with the first civil rights march, he asked Currie to make him a promise: 'For God's sake, don't have any more children!' Ironically, Currie's last ride in the Ministerial limousine

170

was to the maternity ward. Back in his room, the teetotal Faulkner opened his drinks cabinet for the last time and Hume joined him at a window, looking out over a gathering loyalist crowd. 'Do you know what Carson said once?' asked Hume. 'No,' said Faulkner. 'He said unionism's last fight would be between the forces of the right and the forces of the Crown. That's it all started now. Once a confrontation between the loyalists and the British begins, it's all over for what you would call unionism.' Faulkner hadn't heard of Carson's warning, but said, 'You know, you're right.' To Hume the historian, the British Army had once more avoided the confrontation, just as they had at the Curragh in 1914 when ordered to move against the Ulster Unionists. The Executive's dependence on Westminster for its own preservation was its undoing and even Dublin had done little, in practical terms. Executive members had complained about an IRA caravan near a border bridge at Clady, which was plainly being used to shoot from Donegal into Northern Ireland, but punitive action was painfully slow.

Others appreciated the historic nature of the last day in different ways. Gerry Fitt surprised colleagues by taking out his portable tape recorder and giving a running commentary, for his memoirs, of the scene below. Bob Cooper said he could understand how Marie Antoinette felt at Versailles when the mobs arrived from Paris, and Roy Bradford began to assign parts to all of the Executive Ministers, starting with Leslie Morrell as the 'bluff, hearty Desmoulin'. When someone suggested that Bradford himself could be the renegade priest, Talleyrand, he agreed. He remembered that someone had asked Talleyrand what he had done in the Revolution and his reply had been: 'I survived'. The irony was that, politically, Bradford did not survive.

The Assembly was due to sit as usual at 2.30 pm and, in the absence of an official announcement, the only clues to the dramatic events were the empty places on the front bench, normally occupied by the Unionists. SDLP Ministers answered their questions as usual, in a pretence that there was still a job to be done, but soon their bluff was called and half-hearted, behind-the-scenes attempts by a few Faulknerite back-benchers to nominate Oliver Napier as Chief Executive fizzled out. Like the SDLP, Alliance did not resign, but were dismissed the next day. With no prospect of forming another Executive, Rees closed down the shop – though not before Currie and Fitt, then acting Chief Minister, had rescinded the 25p fine order

171

while they were technically still in office. (Later, Paddy Devlin was to write a book to try to clear himself of any connection with the penalty.) All the Executive drinks cabinets were emptied, drowning sorrows – except one owned by SDLP member Eddie McGrady.

Had the Executive proved anything, in its short span of life? Unionists like Roy Bradford were very dismissive, citing the lack of original ideas or legislation, but Hume thought it had shown potential for growth, if it had had the fair wind it needed. Given a little more time, results might have been achieved to prove that effective even-handed government was possible and that advances could be made in security if the Catholics identified with the authorities. As it was, it was too fragile a plant to survive the storms, and the political will was lacking at Westminster to save what was, after all, a Conservative creation. In the limited time available, however, the SDLP Ministers proved their competence to govern in the interests of all and to argue their cases in Cabinet far more effectively than the Unionists. They also won the respect of their staff, which was mutual, until the final days when Hume concluded that the civil servants had acted politically. The only flaw, from the officials' point of view, was the SDLP Ministers' poor time-keeping – Hume making up at the end of the day what he often lost by failing to reach Stormont before noon – and a tendency to talk, rather than act. Another weakness was their insensitivity to unionist suspicion of their frequent forays to Dublin, sometimes for rest and relaxation but often to prod the Dublin Government into action, and certainly not to take orders.

While trust was still lacking between politicians who differed so much in character, as well as tradition, there was a slow growth of tolerance and understanding which might have developed in time. But Hume knew that it would take ten years to evolve, and the failure of Faulkner, the cleverest of the Unionist leaders, was proof of the size of the obstacles to be overcome.

As for the UWC, Barr and Tyrie heard the news of the collapse of the Executive with mixed emotions. They had wanted fresh elections and the removal of the Sunningdale agreement as a prelude to a new political order, with a new, strong breed of loyalist politicians. Some were prepared to fight on for that goal, but Tyrie could see that the people were satisfied, and warned doubters that the UDA would have to shoot their own supporters to prolong the strike. In fact, at one stage there had been a dramatic break-in to a UUUC meeting by an armed loyalist paramilitary threatening to shoot the lot, Paisley included. They had won, but could do nothing with their victory, and the old political moulds remained unbroken. The outcome might have been very different, if an earlier plan had been put into practice. The UWC politicians were to get the paramilitaries into Stormont, and hold all the Assembly members, unionists and nationalists, in the building by force of arms. In such a case, the British Government could hardly have stood idly by.

14

Into the deep freeze

Disappointment but not despair was the mood of the SDLP after the fall of the Executive and Hume's own attitude was typical of his unemotional approach to politics. 'To be honest,' he told a journalist, 'being a Minister had very little effect on me. When the Executive resigned I didn't miss anything. I didn't lose anything. To me it was a job that had to be done.' The power and the glory of being in charge of a Department meant nothing to him; he was in politics to find solutions to the Irish problem, not to open factories or make speeches. But he still felt the 'great experiment' had been worth a trial. Within ten days of the collapse he had a chance to fulfil a Dublin speaking engagement at the Irish Transport and General Workers' Union conference. The Executive had not been a failure, he said, because there were things in it which would stand the test of time. For the first time in three centuries of bloodshed, Protestants, Catholics and dissenters had worked together to administer part of the island. 'The experiment has for the moment been suspended, and many are asking where do we go from here? It would be easier to wrap the respective flags around us and beat our popular drums, but our difficulties call for a much more sane approach. It is much more difficult to give real leadership and to say that we did not seek victory for our point of view, but that we rather sought a solution to the real problems of this country. We cannot crush the aspirations of our Protestant fellow-countrymen in the North and any solution has to be founded on the basic belief that everyone has the right to their aspirations.'

It was a sign to the British that although the battle to save Sunningdale had been lost, its spirit would survive, and there was an almost immediate follow-up by Cosgrave, emphasising that the South would stand clear. Because of the violence, he said, the people of the Republic were now expressing more and more the idea that unity with an area or close association with a people so deeply imbued with violence and its effects was not what they wanted. No shock was registered by the SDLP and they challenged the loyalists to say whether they would work with the Catholic community in governing the province if its only aspiration was to an 'agreed Ireland', not a Council of Ireland.

The British were more inclined to acknowledge the failure of Sunningdale, and to prevent what Rees saw as the growth of 'a new form of Protestant nationalism' he made an early bid to fill the political vacuum with a White Paper proposing a Constitutional Convention. Unlike the Assembly, which called the parties to a carefully-prepared conference table, presided over by the British Secretary of State, the Convention would simply ask the politicians 'to consider what would be likely to command the most widespread acceptance throughout the community', with a six-month time limit which could be extended for a further six months.

Without a strong commitment to power-sharing or an Irish dimension, the Convention could be seen as a calculated insult to the SDLP and a surrender to Protestant intransigence, factors which Hume was not slow to identify. Speaking in Derry on 8 August 1974, he said the Government faced a clear choice – to confront the loyalists or to withdraw. 'What sovereign government anywhere in the world,' he asked, 'would allow part of its territory to decide for itself how it was to be governed, unless it was prepared to let it go?' Besides weakening the SDLP's position, Rees had destroyed the argument used by all liberal unionists that there was no choice between power-sharing and British withdrawal. The UWC had openly challenged the authority and the sovereignty of the British Parliament, Hume said, yet not one of them had been tried for what a former Lord Chancellor, Lord Gardiner, had described as treason. How then could the present Government talk of the rule of law, or expect any respect for its administration? (If he had gone further back, he could have aired his theory that the British Government's passivity at the time of Protestant gun-running, in defiance of Parliament, during the 1914 Home Rule Crisis, legitimised violence in Irish politics, and was a signal to unionist and republican extremists.)

Although Hume dismissed as 'claptrap' the notion that the loyalist leaders would agree to power-sharing if the SDLP dropped its Irish dimension, the party was still prepared to accept a UDA invitation to talks, more as a gesture by the socialist-minded Assembly members to grass-roots Protestants than with any hope of success. In the event, the talks – without Hume – proved fruitless, partly because of the

175

media attention, pressurising both sides. Travelling around Northern Ireland presented considerable hazards for instantly-recognisable politicians like Hume, and he was involved in a worrying incident in Aldergrove Airport, *en route* for a London meeting with Rees. Two men in blue denim, one with a tartan cap and wearing Protestant badges, tried to seize him as he waited for a plane and, when they were challenged by police guards, took out British Army identity cards, which the police accepted as genuine.

As the IRA campaign continued, after taking a brief respite during the UWC strike in order not to interfere with the loyalists' defeat of the Executive, the SDLP came under increasing pressure to lend active support to the police, rather than withhold it as a political bargaining counter, to be traded for a place in government. But Hume, who had been the architect of the policy, drew a distinction between co-operation with the police in crime detection and co-operation to the extent of advising Catholics to join. 'There is nothing the SDLP would like to see more than effective policing and the removal of troops from the streets. But, to put it bluntly, if the minority are to be asked to police Northern Ireland they will want to know what sort of Northern Ireland they will be policing.' His insistence that nationalists must have a role in government, before giving their full approval to the police, was a policy that was to dog him and the party for the next decade. But he was immoveable, even when the Catholic bishop in Belfast, Dr William Philbin, pointedly said that if the Catholics needed the police, as they did, they should join them. As time would tell, Hume's judgment of the alienation of the nationalist community from the police was correct; unless the SDLP could have some control over the RUC, it had to keep its distance.

A Westminster election intervened in October, and the SDLP gave notice of its hardline approach to the Convention in a manifesto, 'One Strong Voice', which called for a British declaration of intent to withdraw from Northern Ireland, if the loyalists rejected both power-sharing and an Irish dimension. It recognised the new situation, after Sunningdale, and acknowledged that a change in unionism required a change in British policy. Unionists regarded the threat to their guaranteed place in the United Kingdom with horror, but the manifesto helped rally flagging support for the SDLP, and its vote held up well, at 22 per cent, compared to the UUUC's 58 per cent.

176

There was pressure on the SDLP leadership to fight the election as a preparation for the Convention and Hume lost his unbeaten record in an impossible contest for Derry city and county, although he maximised the anti-unionist vote. Poor Brian Faulkner's party, four months after the fall of the Executive, polled a derisory 1.9 per cent.

In view of the size of the anti-power-sharing vote, the Convention lost what little attraction it had for the SDLP and by December Hume was asking the British to spell out their intentions, if the loyalists went for a restoration of Stormont. Fitt was eager to contest the Convention election, as always, but Hume was reluctant to commit himself, in a divided party, before the British showed where they stood. The Government, meanwhile, was subtly trying to ensure that the elections would be held in the best possible conditions and when a mixed party of Protestant church and lay people from Britain and Northern Ireland decided on secret talks with the IRA, senior NIO officials wanted to take advantage of the meeting. They had no part in the organisation, when all negotiations were conducted by word of mouth with Rory O'Brady, code-named 'David', and Daithi O'Connell, alias 'Jim', but became involved after the story leaked and police arrived at the meeting place in Feakle, Co. Clare, four hours after the paramilitary representatives had been tipped off by a source in Dublin Castle. The churchmen only had about six hours with the IRA, but it was enough to convince both sides that it was a worthwhile exercise, if only to encourage the Sinn Fein politicians in their perpetual battle with the militarists.

From Feakle the peace mission flew to London, with a warning of a possible IRA bombing campaign in the London underground which alarmed Rees. The message went back to Dublin, conveyed by the Rev. William Arlow, secretary of the Irish Council of Churches and travelling as Father William James, that if the level of violence fell, the talking could begin. A ceasefire was called for two weeks from 2 January 1975 and the IRA's tough terms were that unless there was an assurance of talks and a release of four or five internees – among them John Joe McGirl of Ballinamore – the campaign would resume. At this early stage, communications were touch and go, and once an IRA Army Council member had to drive for an hour to make a call from a phone box, trying to contact Frank Cooper in a helicopter *en route* to Aldergrove. Arlow protested to Stormont Castle that matters were too serious to be left to chance, so the first face-to-face meeting between the NIO officials and Sinn Fein representatives was held in Laneside, near Holywood. It was to be the first of many.

At that stage the clerical go-between stepped aside and a battle of wits ensued, with the civil servants dropping the strongest hints that if the ceasefire continued, the troops would retire to barracks, first in Northern Ireland and then in Britain. But the Army Council wanted a guarantee in writing and there was a three-week break in the truce before it was resumed indefinitely from 9 February, on the promise of so-called Sinn Fein 'incident centres' in Belfast, with British-supplied telephones and Telex machines, to monitor the ceasefire, and a lower army profile. This thoroughly alarmed both the SDLP and the Dublin Government, since elected politicians were being bypassed, and by the end of February the UDA warned that if normal policing was not restored, it would declare no-go areas. At Westminster Gerry Fitt was a lone voice against the deal, prophesying that it would give Sinn Fein a foothold and respectability in ghetto communities.

The ceasefire was stumbling on, against a background of vicious sectarian killings, when the Rev. William Arlow finally blew the gaff. He had promised Unionist John Taylor, after Feakle, that if the Government did something to sell out Northern Protestants he would disclose it publicly. In the spring he heard from two sources – one a top politician in the British Cabinet and the other the IRA Chief of Staff – that the Government had given the IRA a verbal undertaking that British troops would be withdrawn from Northern Ireland, with no time fixed. He warned the NIO that he was going to go public, and the officials' chief concern was to persuade him to time the issue of his statement close to the Convention election in May. They hoped Arlow's disclosure would encourage Protestants to vote for moderate candidates, not wishing to risk failure in the Convention, and British withdrawal.

Arlow refused to play that game, but released his statement about British intentions during a visit to America after the election, having been persuaded by a US State Department official to do so, on the *Today* TV programme. He thought it was a local Washington programme, but afterwards found he had been speaking coast-to-coast, and had created a diplomatic storm. Strangely, neither the British nor the IRA were greatly upset – the British because they still felt it might concentrate Protestant minds on the need for the Convention to succeed, and Daithi O'Connell because it confirmed what he had been trying to tell his doubting colleagues. Two weeks later Arlow told RTE he was convinced the British had given a firm commitment on withdrawal, and in his opinion it could become effective after the failure of the Convention. His conviction was borne out nine years later when, after Merlyn Rees had disclosed that the Cabinet had seriously considered withdrawal, O'Connell said he was not surprised. The IRA, he confirmed, had negotiated on 'devising measures of British disengagement'. Observers at the time were convinced the IRA had something in writing but were not releasing it because of promises they had given. When the talks broke down, the British, after their earlier encouragement, turned on the full heat of their publicity machine against Arlow and photographs were disclosed to the Press showing him visiting the home of the Drumm family, prominent republicans, when he was well known to be carrying on his intermediary role. Despairing of a fair hearing, Arlow did not try to defend himself.

The SDLP had been gearing up for the May 1975 election, without any confidence in the outcome, even though it now had 105 branches in the North, three times as many as eighteen months before. The rural, conservative voice was coming through more strongly but diehard calls for a nationalist boycott were resisted and the manifesto, 'Speak with Strength', called for a return to Sunningdale essentials with the important addition of referenda North and South. Both the Irish and the British dimensions to the problem were stressed.

In the circumstances, the party was happy enough to lose only two seats from the old Assembly – though ominously they were in the republican strongholds of South Armagh and South Derry. The unionist vote was still fragmenting, with the Official party down to nineteen seats, out of an anti-power-sharing group of forty-seven (58.4 per cent), and the loyalist leadership swinging towards the Rev. Ian Paisley's Democratic Unionist Party. Problems began almost immediately for the SDLP, as Cosgrave was forced to repudiate Conor Cruise O'Brien's statement that loyalists could not be obliged to accept power-sharing against their will. This was despite Cosgrave's own earlier remark, when the results had appeared. 'Doesn't it mean that the Protestants have won?' he had said, and O'Brien had agreed.

In an interview in July, just before the inter-party talks began, Hume admitted he was more hopeful than optimistic. He would be optimistic only if progress were made on power-sharing and an Irish dimension, because the philosophy of partnership was vital to the future and these were the concrete expressions of partnership in action. He warned of the danger of a major campaign of violence leading to repartition – 'Because if violence is pursued to the ultimate in a divided society, one finds, in the end, a line drawn between the warring factions'. Similarly, he had very serious questions and hesitations about an independent North, although all options would be discussed in the event of a breakdown in the Convention.

All the parties had sought strict mandates for and against power-sharing – totally against British wishes – and it was with no illusions that Hume, Devlin and Currie embarked on a series of talks with the UUUC on 8 August. The only possible way forward, as Hume saw it, was to persuade Craig, who had ambitions to follow in the footsteps of unionist idol Edward Carson, that a voluntary coalition would give him a chance to bid for leadership. He took the bait eagerly, and for a few weeks a fierce debate raged around a UUUC proposal that 'where an emergency or crisis situation exists, parties, by agreement, come together in the national interest for the duration of the crisis'. The Rev. William Beattie, representing Paisley, was agreeable – as was the DUP leader, who had asked an adviser, 'Give me another word for power-sharing'. But when the news leaked out, in the wake of a particularly savage IRA atrocity in Tullyvallen Orange Hall, Co. Armagh, killing six, Paisley did a sudden about-turn, prompted by the hostile reception of his church. Threatening withdrawal from the Convention until security was improved, he announced dramatically: 'The end of the road has come. Either Mr Rees acts or the Convention will have to act. We can only give him hours rather than days.' Effectively it was the end of the line for Craig, who resigned from the leadership of his Vanguard party, and from the Convention, causing anxious SDLP observers to heave a sigh of relief. Hume himself had admitted privately that the plan was 'dynamite', and could have split the party, as it would have forced it to become part of the establishment.

If the loyalists had made the offer of seats on an emergency executive, the SDLP would have found it difficult to refuse and maintain their reasonable image, even though they would not have been partners as of right and could hardly have maintained party unity under Prime Minister Craig or Paisley. As it was, Hume was able to argue that the SDLP had agreed to 'explore possibilities', without commitment. 'We do not know if we would have reached

180

agreement but we were prepared to try.' The Convention was duly suspended on 7 November, having agreed to submit the majority UUUC report as its final conclusion, advocating majority rule and only committee chairmanships for the SDLP. The party's caution had been vindicated by unionist intransigence. Fianna Fáil seized the opportunity to adopt a new hardline policy on the North, calling for a British commitment to an 'ordered withdrawal' and agreed unity. It was a reiteration of the SDLP's earlier line, marking an end to Dublin's bipartisan approach to the North.

Hume's only real problem, as the year ended, was increasing pressure for a change in the party's policing policy. One Belfast member of the SDLP executive resigned, recalling William Craig's statement that the SDLP deserved better of the UUUC by asserting that the community deserved better of the SDLP. However, all but twelve delegates to the party conference (about 5 per cent) voted to withhold full support from the RUC, pending SDLP involvement in government. The two communities were backing away from one another, and even the release of the last forty-six internees did nothing to improve the prospects of the Convention when it resumed in February 1976, after the UUUC report had been rejected by Westminster. Various ingenious formulae were put forward, including a referendum on coalition government, but Hume was unreceptive to such suggestions, without the agreement of the loyalist politicians. When the Convention was finally dissolved on 5 March 1976 it had served to demonstrate how little common ground there was on alternatives to most people's second-best solution of direct rule, and few disagreed with Rees's conclusion that there could be 'no major new initiative for some time to come'.

Before the deep freeze began, however, Hume made one last attempt in June to see if the Official Unionists might be persuaded to demonstrate their independence of Paisley in a series of private talks. Austin Ardill took the proposition back to his party and the UUUC, of which he was chairman, and found that Paisley regarded it as a joke. 'If you can get anything out of them, God bless you!' he said, giving the talks his blessing. The BBC got wind of what was happening, but agreed to stay away and about half a dozen meetings were held inside a month at Ardill's home at Greenisland, near Belfast, going through the Convention report. He and party colleague the Rev. Martin Smyth felt they were making some progress, away from the public gaze, but when they reported back to the UUUC on changes which would have to be made to its document, Paisley said he knew nothing about the meetings and other DUP members called them 'traitors'. That marked not only the end, for six years, of attempts to achieve agreed devolution, but the end of the UUUC, a loose assortment of loyalist politicians and paramilitaries. It also brought down the curtain, at least temporarily, on the political career of Hume.

15
Kennedy connections

The collapse of the second British attempt to restore some form of devolution in Northern Ireland was greeted with apathy, rather than the Protestant violence Hume at one time had feared. Neither community, it seemed, retained much faith in political solutions and, with three out of four approving direct rule in opinion polls, it was clear that some time would elapse before a London government would test the water again. The prospects for an unemployed politician of thirty-nine, with a young family to support, were decidedly bleak, so it was hardly surprising that he began to look to America for relief, not only in terms of his career, but as a lever to create political movement in Northern Ireland. If no progress was possible in Ireland itself, perhaps the Americans could provide the catalyst, with their influence on the British Government.

Hume had already established a good relationship with Irish-American political leaders, dating from the earliest days of the Troubles, and his television performances, first as a civil rights activist, then as a politician and briefly as a Government Minister, had won him wide respect. As soon as it became known through his influential contacts that he was on the market for an academic appointment, Harvard University found room for a fellowship in its Centre for International Relations, and his training in global politics began.

The American connection with the Irish question goes back to the mass emigration, following the potato famine, in the mid-nineteenth century, and the anti-British attitudes the settlers carried with them. (Earlier, most Irish emigrants had been Scotch-Irish Presbyterians, escaping discrimination which favoured the established Church of Ireland.) The American Irish had a lot to blame the British for, and violent nationalist movements in Ireland found a ready source of funds and sympathy down the years, from the 1860s onward. Even after independence, the clash between the Irish Government and the militant IRA found echoes in east coast America, where violence, not diplomacy, was seen as the best way of uniting Ireland. Irish-American politicians could not stand aside, and when the civil rights campaign hit the streets of Northern Ireland in 1968 they reacted tribally, equating Stormont repression with another British attempt to deny Irish nationalism. It was far too simple a view, but left-wing activists like Bernadette Devlin, with their gift for communication, found it useful to exploit and their early campaigning on TV laid the foundation for much of what has followed.

Part of their success was due not only to the dramatic nature of their protest and the rapid development of satellite TV broadcasting from Northern Ireland, but to its timing, following on Martin Luther King's freedom marches – from which Hume subconsciously learned lessons – and the Vietnam involvement. Liberal ethnic politicians like Senator Edward Kennedy saw a direct comparison between Bloody Sunday and the deaths at Kent State University, with which he had been closely concerned, and felt a moral and political obligation to speak out – usually in terms that were critical of the British.

In the early stages, there was broad support across the Irish-American community for the opposition to Stormont rule, and old IRA veterans could have no quarrel with Kennedy's telegram to the civil rights chairman in June 1969: 'Today the Irish struggle again, but not alone. Your cause is a just cause. The reforms you seek are basic to all democracies worthy of the name. My hopes and prayers go with you.'

The fact that the Ulster Premier, Major James Chichester-Clark, thought it would only increase bitterness and the Minister of Home Affairs, Robert Porter, found it 'untimely, emotive and ill-informed' only proved its effectiveness. At the same time, Tip O'Neill, the Boston Democrat, joined with Representative Philip Burton, a California Democrat, to obtain 100 signatures for an appeal to President Nixon to complain about 'discrimination against Catholics'. As the street protests turned violent and the IRA was reborn, the politicians did not attempt to analyse the new situation or take Protestant feelings into account and in October 1971, in the wake of the allegations about torture of internees, Kennedy called for withdrawal of British forces from Northern Ireland.

By this time, the American media knew enough about the problem to deliver a sharp rebuke to Kennedy, and the *New York Times* warned that his 'arrogant demands' could precipitate 'a bloodbath of unimaginable dimensions'. Unabashed, Kennedy continued to see

Ulster as 'Britain's Vietnam' and refused to accept that it was an 'internal affair' of the British alone. After the 'whitewash' of the Compton Inquiry into torture, he compared Britain's position to that of America 'pursuing the phantom of military victory in Vietnam' and Bloody Sunday was, of course, 'Britain's My Lai'. Cynics interpreted his interest as a bid for the Presidential nomination but, as he pointed out himself, he had no need to court the Irish vote – and other groups would be unimpressed. The high point of his campaign, which involved frequent letters, articles and interviews with the British media, was a three-day public hearing of the House Foreign Affairs Sub-Committee on Europe a month after Bloody Sunday, at which he called for withdrawal of British troops from Northern Ireland, an end to internment and eventual reunification of Ireland. Witnesses from Northern Ireland, including civil rights leaders, heard Kennedy claim that the British were paralysed by the fear that the Protestants would fight to the death to preserve the British tie. Today it was a myth, he said. 'Unionists are not about to commit suicide when the British troops withdraw.'

Despite his initially superficial approach and the Nixon administration's reluctance to tangle with its closest European ally, Kennedy did succeed in raising American consciousness of the Irish problem and was generous enough to greet the suspension of Stormont on 28 March 1972 with praise for Edward Heath. From Bloody Sunday onwards, the first indirect contacts were made with Hume, and there was a marked change in Kennedy's tone. Hume talked the politics of non-violence, which was something many senior American politicians – especially Kennedy – could relate to. The two men spoke the same language, and from then on no major statement was issued without consultation between Hume and Kennedy's aides.

At every stage, Kennedy used the Ulster-Vietnam analogy – in references to the Widgery Tribunal findings and the IRA ceasefire of June 1972 – 'It could be no more difficult for Britain to reach agreement with the IRA than it is for the US to reach agreement with Hanoi'. But the administration was tiring of Kennedy's constant sniping, and the following month California's Governor, Ronald Reagan, on the last leg of a European trip for the Nixon administration, choose Dublin to deliver a broadside. Kennedy's proposal that America should intervene in the Ulster dispute was 'unwarranted', he said. Although twenty million Irish Americans were interested in the situation, America would not become an honest broker unless asked by all the parties involved.

As the plot thickened in Northern Ireland, and the British Government began the long road to Sunningdale, Kennedy finally realised that he needed on-the-spot political advice. Hume had listened to Kennedy's statements with some concern, feeling that although they were sincerely made, they were simplistic, in the circumstances, and ill-timed. But as an unemployed politician, since the end of Stormont, he had no access to Kennedy circles in America, where his contacts were at a lower level. Each needed the other, but it was not until a November morning in 1972 that they realised it.

Hume was in bed, in his Bogside home, when the phone rang. It was Kennedy, phoning from Bonn, where he was a member of the US delegation at a NATO meeting, and he wanted to see him. Could Hume fly to Germany? 'Yes,' he said, even though he knew he could not afford it. At Cologne airport there was a message to phone Kennedy and the American asked if Hume knew somewhere quiet, since he was being tailed by the Press. It was Hume's first time in Germany, but he remembered that a good friend, Sean Ronan, was the Irish ambassador and soon a dinner party was laid on at the embassy. A quarter of an hour before he was due, Kennedy phoned Hume to say he was just next door at a reception in the US Embassy, but would do a few tours of the block by car to shake off the Press, before arriving. His wife, Joan, was with him, as well as Senator John Tunney of California, a son of Gene Tunney, and the mood was right for a convivial and informative evening. The politicians from the Bogside and Boston recognised each other as fellow professionals, with a concern about the Irish problem that went far beyond their own personal careers.

With typical Hume foresight, and an eye to maintaining good relations with the media, RTE were contacted in Bonn and Kennedy obliged by giving an interview with Gerald Barry. The Kennedy name has a magic in Ireland that can never be tarnished, and although Hume has seldom mentioned their relationship publicly he has a quiet pride that he and the Senator are personal friends, who have much more in common than politics. Even in Derry, which is difficult to impress, Hume gets credit for being important enough to know the Kennedys – although in the next breath he may be criticised for not being seen enough in his constituency. Unlike Jack and Bobby Kennedy, who had little cause in the 1960s to interest themselves in Irish politics, Ted Kennedy assigned his staff to keep in touch with the situation and regularly set aside time to study their reports. His concern did not mean that he promoted the trading interests of Ireland above those of his constituents, as Irish Embassy officials duly noted, but his moral support for the Hume/Dublin line on terrorism and the non-violent alternative was a valuable asset.

Hume's American apprenticeship began in 1969 when, carrying the film *John Hume's Derry* under his arm, he arrived at a hall in south Boston to address the local Donegalmen's Association. According to an observer, it was not a particularly impressive performance, as he assumed too much knowledge on the part of the audience – mostly second or third-generation Irish, with their ideas rooted in the 1920s – and talked over their heads. In small private groups, however, he did make an impact and when he returned a year later he knew exactly how to reach his audiences. Most visitors, in the early years, tended to concentrate on the traditionally Irish cities of Boston, New York and Philadelphia, but Hume soon realised that Washington was the real centre of power, and someone in a hurry had to base himself there. He learnt the true nature of Irish-American politics, and where its heart lay, the hard way. While others gravitated to the Boston mayor's office, for headlines in the local papers, he sought out John McCormack, the ageing Speaker of the House of Representatives, for advice on the best way of getting national publicity for his cause.

Bernadette Devlin, his old rival from Free Derry days, had preceded him, mesmerising the media with such antics as throwing the ceremonial key to New York back in Mayor John Lindsay's face, and much of Hume's time was taken up trying to overcome her erratic image. He had much more serious business to do, trying to raise funds for the Northern Ireland Resurgence Trust, formed after August 1969 to encourage self-help in Belfast – including the rebuilding of burned-out Bombay Street – and provide employment in neglected nationalist areas. The US branch of the Ancient Order of Hibernians, which was in a moderate phase, raised large sums and there was valuable assistance from middle-class Catholics of Irish stock who had acquired great expertise at raising money for the Catholic Church. As the newly-formed support group for militant republicanism, Irish Northern Aid (Noraid), began to spread its wings, Hume's efforts meant that Irish Americans who wanted to help relieve the suffering in Northern Ireland had another outlet for their money. While other personalities came and went from the TV screens, Hume was a constant presence, building a solid reputation with thinking politicians and journalists. His knack of forecasting events was widely recognised, and his concentration on the evils of internment and the injustices in Derry was a sober and ultimately more effective contribution to American understanding than were Devlin's frequent spectaculars.

With the upsurge in support for the Provisional IRA, Hume's next mission in America was to use his considerable influence to discourage fund-raising by Noraid and provide a positive political alternative to the philosophy of violence, through the SDLP's policies. In this he had the backing of the Irish Government, who realised how effective with Irish Americans was the voice of a Northern nationalist. He kept in close touch with the Irish Department of Foreign Affairs, to avoid crossed lines, while the British watched from a distance, wary that he might try to prise the US State Department away from its pro-London, anti-interventionist line. Indeed, it was partly to break the State Department's hold on policy that Hume concentrated on the politicians, who in America wield real power. Soon good lines of communication were set up with the new Speaker, Tip O'Neill, arguably the most influential politician on Capitol Hill, who was to confess that he had been a modest Noraid contributor himself until he learned how the money was being spent. His grandparents had emigrated from Buncrana, only a few miles from Hume's own ancestral home in Burt, and those who watched them together noticed almost a father-and-son relationship developing, which was to cost the IRA dear.

Another idea to divert funds away from the IRA was the Ireland Fund, a development of the Resurgence Trust concept, which was founded by one of Ireland's most brilliant entrepreneurs, Tony O'Reilly, then vice-president of Heinz, in Pittsburgh. The old image of the poor immigrant Irish was dying, as the sons and grandsons rose up the ladder of social and political success, and there was a vast pool of goodwill and money waiting to be tapped by over 600 active Irish groups. From small beginnings, the Ireland Fund grew into what has been described as a money tree, with Irish-American executives vying for the size of their contributions. The story is told of someone who started ringing big businesses for donations, and twenty minutes later had netted 300,000 dollars. The fund was already well established in 1974 when Hume had his chance to put his five years of solid graft to work, during his period as Commerce Minister for the power-sharing Executive, and the Northern Ireland civil servants watched in awe as the Irish dimension went into action. A phone call to O'Reilly set up a meeting with heads of companies who would never have known about Northern Ireland's potential, and the message that Protestants and Catholics were working together at last was rammed home. Interest picked up enormously and although it subsequently fell off, as the violence continued, many of the 11,000 jobs in American companies in Northern Ireland date from that era.

During his visit to the US in April 1974 Hume outlined for the first time the two themes which were picked up by all moderate Irish nationalists, both in America and Ireland, for the rest of the decade. In Boston he lashed the 'so-called patriots' who contributed to the flow of cash across the Atlantic. 'Dollars mean Irish lives,' he told them. 'In 300 years, violence has not solved our problem. It will not do so now.' His speech to influential politicians in Washington concentrated on the political alternatives. 'The conflict is not between unionism and nationalism, between Britain and Ireland or, still less, between Protestant and Catholic. It is a struggle between those who believe in the political process and those who do not.' To sentimental Irish Americans he conveyed this difficult message: 'I am not interested in the removal of lines, however arbitrary, from a map, or in the reunification of square miles of territory. Ireland without her people is nothing. The only unity I cherish is that which has the whole-hearted and freely given consent of my Protestant fellow countrymen. Unless that consent is forthcoming, unless there is a union of heart and mind, there can be no unity.' It was an amplification of his remarks in an interview with political commentator William Buckley a month earlier, which caused a predictable storm among Ulster unionists. Asked if the Sunningdale agreement would lead to a united Ireland, he had replied frankly: 'My answer is that I hope it will. I think it creates the circumstances in which there can be free expression of the aspiration towards a united Ireland and in which it can be achieved by agreement.' But while Barbara Walters, interviewing Hume in April for the *Today* TV show, was impressed with his salesmanship – 'it is the most optimistic report we have heard on this programme about Northern Ireland' – another visitor to the US had a different message. 'We were never so close to victory,' said Seamus Loughran, a leading Belfast Provisional. Such forecasts helped discredit the IRA, which had to contend with Hume's cultivation of the media and his ability to translate the complexities of Northern Ireland into understandable American terms.

The stalemate in Ireland was producing negative effects in Irish America, with Noraid helping to spawn the Washington-based Irish National Caucus in 1974, designed to lobby politicians dependent on the Irish vote. While the Caucus could never hope to make the Irish question a national political issue, it developed considerable skill, under its Fermanagh-born director, Father Sean McManus, at raising awkward political issues for the British and Irish Governments and organising an 'Ad Hoc Congressional Committee' to monitor events from an Irish perspective. From the committee's formation in 1978 under New York Congressman Mario Biaggi, it built up to a membership of 130 mostly nominal supporters in 1979, but had strictly limited success during a period of close US-British relations. Although Father McManus, an unashamed republican, exiled from England, had once spoken out in support of the IRA, his relations with them deteriorated as he began to attack violence from all quarters, concentrating instead on allegations of religious discrimination in Northern Ireland and attacking British rule.

The chief asset of the republican support groups was their permanent presence among the grass roots of Irish America while Hume – the unrivalled American expert in the SDLP – shuttled in and out, about twice a year on average. He was preaching an unpopular line, based on reconciliation rather than liberation, and his effect was limited outside the corridors of power, where national policies could be slowly influenced. Money continued to pour into Noraid coffers – over two million dollars during the 1970s – even though Kennedy's early assistance with visas for fund-raising republicans had ceased. The Noraid money, largely controlled by ageing Irish immigrants who saw the IRA's 1970 campaign as a continuation of the 1919–21 War of Independence, was channelled to the Green Cross, an Irish-based charity set up ostensibly for aiding relatives of republican detainees and prisoners. But American Government officials accepted that there was no way of checking how much cash found its way to Ireland illegally, through couriers. As proven links with gun-runners increased, legal steps were taken in 1977 requiring Noraid to register as an agent of the Provisional IRA, beginning a long-running battle through the courts.

By 1976, the progressive Kennedy-O'Neill campaign – inspired by

Hume – was bearing fruit and Liam Cosgrave, as Taoiseach, lent his assistance in a St Patrick's Day address to Congress, which was followed by a joint communiqué with President Ford. This rapport between Irish-American political leaders and the Dublin Government was something new on the political scene, which Hume did his best to foster. Traditionally, the American Irish had kept Irish Embassy officials at arm's length, regarding them as collaborators in partition, but under Hume's guidance the picture changed dramatically. Neither he nor the SDLP – which he also kept fully informed – gained much credit for what was being done, but the insertion of SDLP philosophy into major statements from Washington and Dublin was satisfaction enough. It also helped counter the British Embassy's recurrent theme that Northern Ireland was Britain's problem alone, and proof of Hume's effectiveness was the succession of British Ministers and civil servants sent to drown his message. His influence failed to breach any barriers in Belfast however, and when the Convention finally folded Hume gladly took up the chance of an extended study of the American scene, during a term at Harvard.

The Kennedys greeted him in style, with a phone call from Ethel – Bobby's widow – inviting him to a reception in his honour in Washington, where a glittering array of politicians and media people welcomed him to America. (From then on, the Kennedy connection grew stronger, and several members of the family, including Bobby junior, the Shriver children and Jean Kennedy Smith, have visited or stayed with the Humes in Derry.) Thanksgiving 1976 was spent with Tip O'Neill at his house on Cape Cod and then it was straight into the election campaign, travelling throughout Massachusetts with Kennedy.

During his Harvard period Hume struck up a close relationship with Carey Parker, Kennedy's closest adviser, and out of this came the first of the so-called 'Four Horsemen' statements on St Patrick's Day 1977. Hume was in New York for the big occasion, and the thought struck him that although separate statements of moderation from Hugh Carey, Tip O'Neill, Edward Kennedy and Daniel Moynihan were important, their impact would be greater if they spoke in unison. He phoned Parker, who agreed it was a great idea, and then Hume read out a statement he had, of course, already drafted. It formed the basis of the most influential declaration yet, calling on Americans to join a quest for peace and 'to renounce any action that promotes the current violence or provides support or encouragement for organisations engaged in violence'. Even the response of militant republicans played into the politicians' hands, labelling them the 'four ignorant horsemen' and ensuring that their subsequent St Patrick's Day statements would be given special prominence. Garret FitzGerald, who had previously enlisted President Ford's support for his anti-IRA campaign, was also in New York at the time and was able to add his voice to the criticism of Noraid. As a direct rule of this publicity barrage, donations fell away by 75 per cent, justifying Hume's claim that the four Americans had saved many lives in Northern Ireland by their brave stand.

Since the Convention, the political scene in Northern Ireland had gone dead and, in an attempt to get things moving again and provide an alternative, the Kennedy-O'Neill axis was working on a plan to involve the US Presidency, for the first time in history. Hume was consulted, and in accordance with his philosophy of going only for the attainable, he knew it was unrealistic to expect President Carter to come out and publicly attack Britain. He suggested that Carter could use a carrot to interest the British, offering American economic assistance in the event of political agreement being reached. That was the genesis of the statement, delivered on 30 August 1977, but it took eight months of hard bargaining, after an Irish civil servant, Michael Lillis, wrote the first draft and it was batted between the British, Irish and US Governments. Hume's role was crucial at this point, advising how far to go and when the timing would be right, but always he knew he had a trump card in Tip O'Neill's support. Carter needed the Speaker's help to get legislation through Congress and, once the statement was agreed between the State Department and Jim Callaghan's Government, with Peter Jay, the British ambassador to the US, in support, the machine went into action. In the end, the wording was a little weaker than intended, but there were no objections from Jack Lynch, who had become Taoiseach only weeks before, and was surprised to find the statement in the works.

Carter was kept informed by several close aides, including Dr Bob Hunter, who had Protestant antecedents from Kilkenny, but the Georgia 'mafia' had little understanding of the subtleties. The day before the official announcement, press officer Jody Powell, in reply to a British journalist, gave a misleading answer which diminished the statement's impact and had to be corrected later. While re-iterating the Nixon-Ford position of impartiality, Carter called for the establishment of a government which would command 'wide spread acceptance' – sidestepping the term 'power-sharing' in deference to Orange sensibilities. Any 'just solution', he said, must have a role for the British and also required Irish Government support – a minimal gesture to Dublin, which had wanted direct involvement in devising a solution. But the new element, at Hume's suggestion, was that the US would join with others to encourage additional job-creating investment in the event of an internal political settlement. No figure was mentioned, because of Irish fears of offending Protestants, but there was US Government support for 100 million dollars, and Kennedy suggested 500 million in talks with Carter. Difficulties arose with the British over the link between a solution and economic inducements, but the wording of the statement made it clear that Carter was offering incentives, not aid. Under US law, grants cannot be made to countries with a per capita income higher than 6,000 dollars, but experts suggested that tax concessions might be offered to imports from Northern Ireland or to American firms based there.

Perhaps because it contained only conditional promises, against heavy odds, the statement failed to break the Ulster deadlock, and Unionists either dismissed it as interference or complained that US investment should not await a settlement and might help towards one. But it still represents a bench-mark of Presidential concern, re-endorsed by President Reagan in 1982, even if Kennedy rather overstated his case with talk in the Senate of a 'mini-Marshall plan'. Hume himself was disappointed with the negative reaction in Northern Ireland, as he had hoped for some pressure within the Protestant community to see what the American contribution might be. Again it showed him that, despite his demonstration of the positive force of the Irish dimension, the Protestants still regarded it as demeaning. Potentially, they had some of the most powerful friends in the world, but they saw such friendship as politically threatening and rejected it.

Another initiative, suggested by Hume, was an open acknowledgement by Kennedy and O'Neill of the part played by Ulster Protestants in the establishment of the American state, and this took the form not only of an academic study sponsored by Kennedy, but of meetings with Unionist politicians. Hume wanted leading Irish-American figures to hear at first hand the unionist viewpoint, to improve understanding on both sides, and one of the first to be received by Kennedy in Washington was the Rev. Martin Smyth, a prominent hardliner, who later became a Westminster MP. Because of his more positive attitude to the Northern Ireland problem, Kennedy was no longer the Protestants' bogeyman and Unionist politicians or leading churchmen had little hesitation in approaching Hume for an introduction to him or other influential politicians, confident that their requests would be secret. Times had changed when Andy Tyrie of the UDA could be quoted in a Boston paper in 1978 saying, 'We believe Senator Kennedy is the one man who would be acceptable in both communities here. Tell him that we need his help.'

Kennedy himself, speaking at an Ireland Fund dinner in 1979 – an invitation he accepted only when he made sure Hume would be a guest speaker – paid his own tribute to his friend. 'John Hume is one of the finest and most creative political leaders of our generation,' he said, 'a man of extraordinary courage and wisdom and under-standing.' Earlier, he had praised Hume's work in America. 'It has made a significant difference in the moderating of the extreme elements in the US. In this way he has been a great service to all the people here and in the North. It is vital that people like him stay in politics.' For someone who had blown his top at the time of Bloody Sunday and had jumped to a lot of wrong conclusions, Kennedy had travelled a long way. In return, Hume regarded Kennedy as America's best Senator, in terms of effectiveness and influence, whose tragic experiences had developed and strengthened him.

After the low-key response to the Carter initiative and the political inertia of the new Northern Ireland Secretary of State, Roy Mason, the Four Horsemen toughened up their St Patrick's Day message in 1978, blaming the British Government and intransigent unionists for the lack of progress, and denouncing the security forces for violations of human rights. They had equally harsh words the following year, urging the British to consider a confederation of the two parts of Ireland, along lines advanced latterly by FitzGerald and earlier by Hume in the seminal 'Towards a New Ireland' document in 1972. Like the SDLP, the US ethnic politicians were having difficulty staying relevant in a time of stagnation, and they had to suffer the praises of the Irish National Caucus for their change of attitude. Outwardly there was no sign of a British response, due mainly to the non-political approach of Roy Mason, and Tip O'Neill drew fire from London when he complained about British politicians' tendency to use the Irish question for party-political purposes. But by the end of 1979 a new Conservative government, under Margaret Thatcher, was trying to get the political process moving again, at least partly because of the mounting pressure from the Americans, primed by Hume and the Irish Embassy, for a political initiative to set against the IRA's violence. If the British were immoveable on the political front, there was little the Four Horsemen could do to turn their people away from the only visible opponents of British rule, the IRA.

After ten years of high-level diplomacy, Hume had little to show, in concrete terms, for his efforts in America. But he had converted a generation of Irish-American politicians, against their inherited instincts, to the politics of non-violent nationalism, and had prevented a united front developing in favour of militant anti-British republicanism. He had also deeply impressed one of Britain's most active ambassadors, Peter Jay, helping him in their long discussions to a better understanding of a problem which the Ambassador estimated occupied more than 10 per cent of his every working day. Within three months of leaving office, Jay was to announce to the world that London should align its policy with that of Jack Lynch, declaring that the long-term future of the thirty-two counties was to come together, by agreement, and not at the point of a gun. By misfortune, his RTE interview was recorded six weeks before the killing of Lord Mountbatten, and transmitted immediately after it, damaging Jay's credibility and his message. But the fact that Her Majesty's former Ambassador should have expressed himself so forcefully, so soon after leaving office, says something for the influence of the Irish Embassy and, primarily, of his mentor on Irish politics, John Hume. The Irish Ambassador to the US, Sean Donlon, who had been two years junior to Hume in Maynooth, was also a friend and confidant of both men, helping to raise the Irish profile in Washington and accurately representing the line agreed by Hume and the Dublin Government. Together, their influence with the Irish-American community and the British ensured that US support for violent republicanism in the 1970s was confined to a tiny, if hard-working, minority, mostly in the east coast cities, and that Fianna Fáil attempts to construct a united anti-partitionist front failed. Without such voices of moderation, constantly arguing for political initiatives, the American involvement in the IRA campaign – painfully evident in arms shipments and a ready supply of cash – would have been very much greater.

Hume's American intervention also acted as a major protection for the minority position in Northern Ireland. It prevented the British from ignoring the problem, or from drifting back to support of the unionists. In the vacuum that was Northern Ireland it kept politics to the forefront, as an alternative to violence, and wide coverage in US newspapers and on TV was picked up in Ireland, keeping hope alive.

16

A healing force?

While Hume opened up the American dimension, after the failure of the Convention in March 1976, the SDLP underwent a long period of reappraising its most basic policies. Every constitutional road was blocked and Britain's refusal to confront the loyalists meant that far more radical solutions than reconciliation were openly debated. A lobby for independence surfaced in the party, under Devlin, arguing that if some unionists, including the UDA, were beginning to question the value of the British link, the idea might be worth supporting as a viable half-way house towards unity. Hume never accepted the argument, seeing independence as a means of re-establishing Protestant dominance, but when he returned from his two months in America to the party conference in December, he found opposition to his policy coming from a more serious 'Brits out' lobby, as well as from independence supporters.

A Paddy Duffy motion, supported by Seamus Mallon, calling for a straight British declaration of intent to withdraw, was only narrowly defeated, by 158 votes to 111, indicating a significant swing back to old-style nationalism, contrary to the advice of the leadership. While Hume prided himself on the collective approach to policy-making, it was obviously going to be more difficult in future to weld together the different elements in the party's make-up – from rural conservatives to moderate professional people and urban socialists. Mallon was slowly emerging as the leader of a 'green' faction which, although it went along with the mainstream, felt the need to stress the Irish dimension at a time when the British had abandoned it. The difference at this stage was one of emphasis and timing, rather than content, but there was a growing feeling that any sign of weakness on the national question would be exploited by the British and could undermine SDLP support in a frustrated Catholic community. The Press commonly described the SDLP as a 'mainly-Catholic' party, but it had no more than a handful of Protestant activists.

Mallon's contention, which he did not express until later, was that if the party challenged the South to support British withdrawal – especially after his friend Charles Haughey had recovered his position in Fianna Fáil – it could not have failed to respond positively. That way, he argued, the SDLP would make sure of holding on to its broad nationalist support and prevent any drift towards republicanism, as well as forcing the South to take a more active interest. In 1976, the enemies were apathy and disillusion among SDLP supporters, but to react by demanding simple British withdrawal would have meant abandoning everything Hume stood for in his effort to prove that London and Dublin had a vital part to play in a solution. Hume himself would have stayed to fight if the withdrawal motion had succeeded, but Fitt would probably have resigned, in a blaze of adverse publicity. Within the party, Hume argued forcefully that baldly demanding British withdrawal was using Provisional IRA language which only a military strategy could hope to make effective. The SDLP had to oppose such a divisive approach and go for a more long-term strategy, trying to persuade the British to back the nationalists, rather than the loyalists, and minimise the risks of conflict. The objective was to unite the Irish people, and that meant showing that the party's plans included the Protestants. Unionists were not going to like what was being done, but the presentation of the case must not be threatening.

The Duffy challenge was beaten off, but the vote was partly an acknowledgment that the politicians were losing control of events, as the British Government stepped up its policy of criminalisation – phasing out the special category status introduced by Whitelaw in 1972 – and the Provisionals hit back with their blanket protest inside the jails (inmates refused prison-issue clothing, wearing only blankets) and more murder and mayhem outside. The Peace People provided some relief, staging mass marches in town and country for the thousands who felt no tribal allegiance and hoped that crying 'stop', without any coherent political programme to deal with the constitutional crisis, might weaken the paramilitaries. It did, while the movement was active on the streets, but it had already lost its momentum by the time its founders, Betty Williams and Mairead Corrigan, won the 1976 Nobel Peace Prize. Inside two years the violence which had driven people together forced them apart, and the rhetoric faded.

In September 1976, the arrival of the new Secretary of State, Roy Mason, was another hammer-blow to the discarded politicians, since he had no intention of involving them in new political initiatives, good or bad. Security was his prime concern, as a former Minister of Defence, followed by economic development and, a poor third, political stability. Following the policy of the Americans in South-East Asia, the British gave orders for the 'Ulsterisation' of security, phasing in greater numbers of local Ulster Defence Regiment volunteers and police, while gradually withdrawing the army from the front lines. With increased undercover activity, the security forces began to put the squeeze on the IRA, while taking advantage of an ill-conceived loyalist strike in May 1977 to discredit the UDA.

Ever since the 1974 strike, the UDA had been under pressure to try again to force the British to take more notice of loyalists' pleas for a government of their own and a harder crackdown on the IRA. The fact that there was little logic in adding to the security problem in order to protest about it did not weigh heavily with Ian Paisley, who was the political figurehead, or with Andy Tyrie, who was again the strike organiser, under an Action Committee title. Neither did they appreciate that the Government had learned its lesson in 1974, nor that Roy Mason was a very different proposition from Merlyn Rees, whose dealings with the IRA were the root of the earlier protest. For every move of the strikers, the Government had a counter-move – suggesting that there were spies in the camp – and, without the support of the power workers, who were taken for granted but refused to be the leaders a second time, the factories and offices stayed open. As Tyrie told the politicians on the third day, it had to be revolution or nothing – and by their expressions they showed they had no stomach for it. They wanted to humiliate the British and put forward Paisley for Prime Minister, but Tyrie's fanciful idea was to seize power and go for a form of independence, which most Catholics, he thought, would go along with. Strikes could destroy, he and Paisley learned, but they could not construct, although several tougher security measures were announced shortly after the ten-day stoppage.

By standing up to the strike, Mason and the police retrieved much of the ground that had been lost in 1974, and the IRA was at its lowest ebb, being forced to reorganise in small 'cells' to avoid wholesale arrests. Strong-arm police interrogation methods, per-fected at the newly-opened Castlereagh holding centre, were eating into the IRA command structures, and a significant speech by Jimmy Drumm at Bodenstown in June 1977 marked an end to the purely

199

military approach, in favour of a 'long war', combined with greater political involvement. But Provisional Sinn Fein was still hooked on a policy of abstention from elections, and the SDLP again proved its right to speak for the minority in the 1977 local council elections, when the virtual demise of the pro-Union Northern Ireland Labour Party helped to raise its total of councillors from eighty-four to 113 with 20.6 per cent of the first-preference votes, almost eliminating independents. Paddy Devlin did particularly well in West Belfast, polling three-and-a-half times as many votes as he needed for election, and his speeches began to reflect his frustration with the party's drift from socialist principles towards old-fashioned nationalism. His personality differences with Hume, who had a subtlety he lacked, also came to a head in a bruising exchange conducted in front of Mason. As Hume was arguing that the British should not accept the loyalists' veto on Government policy, but should take them on, Devlin suddenly exploded, charging Hume with advocating the shooting of Protestants.

The 1976 conference debate on withdrawal was resumed in 1977, despite Mallon's attempts to avoid another confrontation so soon, and this time Hume's gradualist line easily prevailed. The 'green' wing had been defeated, as Mallon had feared, but the arguments rumbled on, weakening Fitt's position as leader and causing Hume to shift slightly to the right, in order – as Paddy O'Hanlon put it – to remain in the centre of the party. The emergence of the Irish Independence Party, calling for British withdrawal as a prelude to negotiations, contributed to a hardening of attitudes, although its threat was short-lived.

Mason's insensitivity to Catholic opinion did nothing to ease the SDLP's problems and his insistence on including Northern Ireland in the Queen's Jubilee Year itinerary drove the two communities further apart. While one celebrated, the other sulked and increasingly doubted whether reconciliation was worth pursuing. In response to this mood, Hume was beginning to think in different contexts, accepting the insolubility of the problem inside Northern Ireland and tossing around different constitutional approaches. 'Until now,' he told an Oxford University debate in February, 'unity has never been more than a slogan. Now is the time for the meaning of unity to be spelled out very clearly.' People who opposed unity saw it only in terms of a victory of the South over the North, but they were attacking a concept no one was advancing. The essence of unity

200

was not about victory to either side, he said.

Expanding on this theme, he produced his first ideas on a federal solution at a seminar in Queen's University, Belfast, in May 1978. The present constitutional position could never provide security and prosperity, he said. The unionist population must realise that real security rested not on the changing winds of British political parties, but in their own numbers and their ability to come to an agreement with the people with whom they shared the island. 'One form of partnership I would suggest for discussion would be a federal Ireland, in which the North ruled itself. It would have enshrined in its constitution a Bill of Rights which would provide the basis for civil and religious liberty in both parts of Ireland.' In other divided societies, federalism had proved to be the method whereby differences had been harmoniously accommodated and diversity allowed to flourish. 'One of the greatest examples of federalism, the United States, owes much to Presbyterian Ulstermen who were among the chief architects of the American constitution. Could it be they left their mistakes behind them in Ireland and used them to their benefit in America?'

But the unionists were not interested, especially now that Labour had promised them extra seats in Westminster, in return for supporting a wafer-thin majority, and the IRA's fortunes had revived, despite the fire-bombing of the La Mon Restaurant, near Belfast, on 17 February – killing twelve civilians – which cost them considerable support. Hume was constantly defending the SDLP against the charge that it was capitalising on the IRA violence, and his reply in May 1978 was definitive: 'What the IRA are saying is that the British have no role in the solution, other than getting out. What we are saying is that the British Government have a very big role to play in solving the problem and they should not leave until they have played their part in bringing us all together. While the sovereign government continued to say "It's not a matter for us, it's a matter for themselves", then the vacuum is very clear and will be exploited by violent men.' One of the effects of the Government's policies could be seen in the hundreds of suspects shuttling through the interrogation centres, and repeated complaints about maltreatment finally resulted in a much tighter regime being imposed by the recommendations of the Bennett Committee. The RUC Special Branch had learned nothing from the row after internment and the adverse findings of the European Court of Human Rights – nor had the Police Authority, nor the Labour Government.

Hume's sights were moving on to Europe, as another means of creating the dynamic which was missing from the Northern Ireland situation, and his well-cultivated contacts in Dublin Government circles led to his appointment as a special adviser to Richard Burke, the Irish EEC Commissioner for transport, trade and administration. The timing was perfect, as it helped to tide Hume over a barren political period, when his wife's teaching provided the only income, apart from earnings from the media, and prepared him for the European elections in June 1979. Without direct elections to the parliament, Northern Ireland had no representation and little interest, outside the farming community, in European affairs. But, as Hume said in Belfast in June 1978, this was not so much the fault of Europe, as of the unwillingness by national governments to give the EEC either the instruments or the means to have an effective regional policy, or a meaningful regional fund. The only way of closing the gap between the richer and poorer parts of Europe was by strengthening the central institutions, so that they could deliver massive regional aid. Hinting at his future policy in Europe, he said the regional fund to date was 'derisory' and had been treated as a subsidy to existing expenditure.

But the SDLP was more concerned with domestic matters, where Mason's inaction, allied to Conservative Shadow Secretary Airey Neave's declaration that 'power-sharing is not practical' forced the party leadership onto the offensive. A carefully-worded motion by Austin Currie describing British disengagement as 'inevitable and desirable', but proposing four-sided talks between London, Dublin and the two Northern Ireland traditions, was passed almost unanimously at the SDLP conference in November 1978, showing how far the party had moved since the question had first been raised in 1976. Almost immediately SDLP leaders embarked on what they described as a 'New Ireland' campaign, not only to convince world opinion that the policies of both Westminster parties were leading nowhere, but to make it clear that the SDLP had not shifted from its aim of unity by consent.

The 1976 conference had marked the beginning of the party's drift away from internal Northern Ireland solutions, and key debates revolved around propositions that talks should be held with the Provisionals – an idea backed by Mallon and Paddy Duffy – and a study instituted on negotiated independence, supported by Duffy and Devlin. All possible models were being considered, in view of the unionists' intransigence, and it was only with difficulty that Hume,

Fitt and Currie succeeded in keeping power-sharing on the agenda.

Meanwhile, Devlin had finally broken with the party in September 1977, claiming that the SDLP had shifted its emphasis from social democracy to old-style nationalism, and that it had ignored signs that support for traditional Unionist politicians was dwindling, offering hope of breaking the old moulds. His party colleagues had long forecast his departure on such grounds, but regarded his ambitions for a seat in the European Parliament, over the head of Hume, as a more important factor. Asked repeatedly to account for his attacks on the deputy leader, Devlin had made no reply and had been duly thrown out of the party. The rural-urban split had opened and, although Devlin had taken no-one with him, a power-base in working-class Catholic Belfast had been lost.

By the end of 1978, ten years into the Troubles, it was clear that there was little fundamental change in the political scene – dominated by the prospect of forthcoming European and Westminster elections – while the IRA were described, in a depressing British Army document intercepted by them, as virtually unbeatable. Faced with Mason's indifference, Hume took his political campaigning to America in a coast-to-coast tour in January, emphasising that the violence concealed a much more deep-seated political question, ignored by the British.

The guarantee to unionists of their constitutional position was not a neutral stance, he argued, but fostered a seige mentality which was a barrier to a real and lasting settlement. Comparing Northern Ireland to Rhodesia, where Ian Smith's regime was on its last legs, Hume asked: 'If Britain were to guarantee Ian Smith that white Rhodesians could remain linked to Britain for as long as they wished, would he even talk to the leader of the black population, other than on his own terms?' Before withdrawing, Britain should declare that her political objective was to promote the coming together of both parts of Ireland in agreement, he said. The unionists should negotiate their future now, rather than leave it to the whims of the British Parliament. As proof of Hume's standing in Irish America, Kennedy, O'Neill, Carey and four state governors were present at a reception in his honour in Boston. 'They are with us all the way,' he said, 'and pressure is being and will continue to be put on Britain to do the right thing in Ireland after half a century of disaster.'

Already the European election campaign had begun, and it rapidly developed into a contest for the leadership of the two Northern Ireland communities, to prove that Paisley was the top Protestant and Hume the top Catholic, and by how much. There were three seats because Garret FitzGerald had insisted, and the other countries agreed – after raising the national quotas all round – that a third seat would virtually guarantee representation for the North's Catholics, without which the elections would be politically disastrous. Another concession by the British was to allow proportional-representation voting for the Northern Ireland seats, unlike the rest of the United Kingdom, to make sure the Unionists could not carry off all three.

But before the European poll in June, Callaghan called a snap Westminster election in May, which provided some embarrassment when Austin Currie defied the party executive to run as an independent in Fermanagh-South Tyrone. He objected to the SDLP dropping out for the second election running – to avoid the possibility of the anti-unionist member, Frank Maguire, losing his seat to a Unionist – and only Gerry Fitt spoke out in his favour. Currie did not get enough votes to block Maguire's election, and he lost considerable prestige, as well as his Chief Whip status, before he was finally rehabilitated in the party, with Hume's help.

The party manifesto repeated the conference demand for quad-rapartite talks and an end to the 'one-sided guarantee' to unionists. 'For the SDLP the question is not whether Britain should disengage from Ireland, but when and in what circumstances,' it said, claiming that the party was the only obstacle to the Government strategy of restoring unionist majority rule. But the rhetoric only served as a reminder of how alienated the SDLP had become from the political process, after years of frustration, for neither Labour nor the Conservatives showed any sympathy for what would have amounted to an enforced Sunningdale. While Labour wanted to extricate themselves by restoring Stormont, the Conservatives sought a return of powers to local government and virtual integration of Northern Ireland into the British system.

Fitt was still the only SDLP MP, with a majority of 8,235 in West Belfast, but a month later the European election confirmed that Hume was popularly regarded as the real leader of nationalist opinion in the North, with 140,622 first-preference votes, adding 14,297 votes to the total SDLP poll in May and pushing the party's share of the vote to a record 24.6 per cent. Catholics had responded to his appeal, reminding them that this was the first election since 1918 in which both parts of Ireland were voting to send representatives to the same parliament, and it was indisputable that some

Protestants had also voted for him. His pro-European stance was in marked contrast to the vast majority of the candidates, describing the EEC as 'a healing force' for Northern Ireland's problems and an extra source of external funds. His old rivals, from civil rights days and later, were relegated to also-rans – Bernadette Devlin McAliskey polling 33,969 votes and Paddy Devlin 6,122.

Paisley's massive 170,688 votes put him firmly on top of the Protestant heap, with John Taylor, another of Hume's old adversaries, taking the third seat, after an undignified wait for transfers. The electorate had had its say and it overwhelmingly endorsed the spokesmen for two incompatible views of Northern Ireland's future. Hume needed all his native optimism, as he took his seat in the new parliament building in Strasbourg in July, especially as Paisley had grabbed the Belfast headlines with a complaint about the British flag being flown upside down and had registered his first noisy protest against the presence of the Irish Taoiseach, Jack Lynch. Paisley, however, was relegated to the back benches, beside maverick Italian independents, while Hume took his place with the largest parliamentary bloc, the Social Democrats, and quickly began to create a whole new circle of influential friends.

He had found himself a political niche, as Fitt had done at Westminster, but there were no prospects for their party colleagues, some of whom had given up good jobs and rendered themselves virtually unemployable by their political associations. They worked on, for no reward except the doubtful privilege, shared by all former Executive Ministers, of having direct access to the Secretary of State. Few dropped out or transferred their allegiances, because there was nowhere for non-violent nationalists to go, but the SDLP's hopes of survival as a party of influence increasingly rested on Hume.

17
Party leader

The problems which Ireland was presenting for the English in the latter half of the twentieth century were only a repetition of what had been going on for 800 years, but for Rome they were something new. While there had been difficulties coping with the conflict between republicanism and Catholicism in the past, they had been of short duration and never seriously threatened the Church's authority, or the loyalties of the clergy. The picture had changed, however, because of the intensity and duration of the IRA's campaign, and when Pope John Paul decided to visit America in the autumn of 1979, he deliberately found time to stop off in Ireland *en route*.

There were plenty of reasons for his visit, ranging from his interest in the Marian shrine at Knock, Co. Mayo, scene of a nineteenth-century apparition, to the desire to express admiration for the faithful in Ireland, among the most devout and conservative in the western world. But he had a special message for the men of violence, who were creating havoc with the lives and beliefs of young people in Northern Ireland, and he wanted to deliver it in person, in St Patrick's own primatial city of Armagh.

The Catholic bishops were agreed from the start that he should visit the archdiocese of Armagh, which spans the Irish border, and Archbishop, later Cardinal Tomás Ó Fiaich – Hume's old tutor – provided alternative sites, one near the Catholic cathedral in Armagh and the other near Drogheda. The Armagh site was perfectly positioned for access by road, in a natural amphitheatre in the sports fields of St Patrick's College, capable of holding about 250,000. With the active encouragement of the police, preliminary arrangements were made for a landing by helicopter near the gates of the cathedral and a drive up the hill past the grave of Cardinal Conway before descending to the site of the Mass. The Pope actually said to someone in Rome, 'Will I be able to visit the grave of my friend?' Inside the cathedral, Ó Fiaich planned to have him meet people from both sides of the community, Protestant and Catholic, who had been injured in the Troubles.

Because of the prospect of adverse reaction by Protestants, and even an assassination attempt, the bishops were wary of pushing too hard for Armagh. But while Paisley was warning that the Pope must not set foot in Northern Ireland, threatening massive opposition, an unusual Protestant deputation was received at the Primate's residence, Ara Coeli – 'the altar of Heaven' in Latin – behind the massive cathedral. John McKeague, leader of the outlawed Red Hand Commando, which had claimed responsibility for several vicious sectarian murders in east Belfast, told Cardinal Ó Fiaich, before several paramilitary colleagues, that there would be no problems over the Pope's visit. Paisley could complain, he said, but he had no 'muscle' without them and they had no objections. Another worry for the Catholic Primate was the matter of protocol if the Pope landed first in Dublin, to be received by the Irish Head of State, and then was shuttled to Armagh. But the local police commander assured him – presumably on higher orders – that the visit could go ahead. The question of protocol could be arranged by the Pope being received by a local dignitary, Ó Fiaich believed.

Pressure was mounting on all sides for the Pope to cross the border and, in response, Ó Fiaich drew up a list of reasons why he should come, totalling an unlucky thirteen. (The Church of Ireland Primate, Archbishop George Simms, also sent a letter of invitation.) A decision on the Pope's programme was to be made in August, so the list was sent out with a priest who was flying to Rome; and Father John Magee, the Newry-born secretary to the Pope, telephoned to say the Armagh visit had been approved in principle. The details had to be worked out, so to make sure that all went smoothly Ó Fiaich flew to Rome himself on 27 August – the blackest day of the Troubles, when the IRA murdered Lord Mountbatten and three others in his holiday boat, off Mullaghmore, Co. Sligo, and followed it up with a devastating ambush near Warrenpoint, Co. Down, which killed eighteen soldiers.

Two days later, the Pope's itinerary had to be finalised, and his own reaction was typical. 'Is this not all the more reason why I should go to the North?' The decision was postponed for a day, while Ó Fiaich contacted as many churchmen as he could, in Rome and the North, to receive the same sad message – for security reasons no one would accept the responsibility for advising the Pope to go to Armagh. So Drogheda it was, although if the Pope's programme had already been announced before the Mountbatten killing, there was no doubt that it would have gone ahead as planned.

All the leading SDLP members were invited to the open-air Mass, on a brilliant Saturday afternoon in early October, but Hume was one of only two politicians – the other was the local member of the Irish Parliament, Padraig Faulkner – to participate in any of the Pope's services, reading a passage from the Bible. He was honoured to be invited by his former professor, Cardinal Ó Fiaich, to be part of a historic occasion, and felt no qualms about identifying himself or his party with one side of the religious divide, despite republican murmurings. There is little piety about the SDLP leadership, and Gerry Fitt joked about his invitation, 'That means I'll have to go to confession in London. If I go in Belfast, I'm only asked about politics.'

The Pope rose to the occasion, before hundreds of thousands of Northern Catholics, with a dramatic address to all engaged in violence: 'I appeal to you, in the language of passionate pleading. On my knees I beg you to turn away from the paths of violence and to return to the ways of peace. You may claim to seek justice. I too believe in justice and seek justice. But violence only delays the day of justice.' Sinn Fein's response was predictable: all violence was the result of British occupation and, unfortunately, the war could not be ended until its prime cause had been removed. They would hardly have been more receptive to the speech – inspired by Bishop Cahal Daly, a Northern-born moderate, who was based in Rome for a month before the visit – if it had been delivered in Armagh itself. But it would have had even more impact in the North, and some of the references to the city of St Patrick, which were retained despite the change of venue, would have been more relevant.

A week before, Hume had taken the opportunity of a conference on American-European relations in Waterville, Co. Kerry, to challenge the Republic, as well as Britain, to accept its responsibility for Northern Ireland's sorry state and try to work out a joint initiative. It was an important speech, foreshadowing the thinking which led to the creation of the New Ireland Forum four years later, but early reports suggested that he had called for a moritorium on Irish unity, which had to be quickly denied. In fact he criticised the South for failing to make its intentions clear. 'Do they accept that the goal is a pluralist Ireland, one that is dominated by no section or tradition?' he asked. 'I believe that they do, but it is long past the time when the meaning of unity should be spelt out. Agreement, yes, coercion, no.' London, he said, exercised 'a frayed and somewhat reluctant sovereignty in Northern Ireland, while Dublin maintained a somewhat reluctant claimed sovereignty'. Events cried out for joint, decisive action, and underlined the Republic's essential role.

As a starting point for an initiative, he wanted both Governments to declare there should be no unconditional guarantees for anyone – only an objective to achieve guarantees for all. Secondly, they should make it clear that there was no solution as such, but only a process that would lead to a solution. Having declared their commitment to such a process – the process of integration of the different traditions – they should invite all parties to participate in building a new Ireland and carry on regardless of boycotts. It was the first time an SDLP leader had been so critical of the South for not stating that it was prepared to accept the sacrifices involved in real unity, and the speech reflected a general impatience with the Fianna Fáil regime. In visits to Dublin, another leading SDLP member said it was impossible to tell what Jack Lynch's Northern policy was. He seemed to have lost interest, prior to resigning in December.

But before the arrival of the rehabilitated Charles Haughey as Taoiseach came the departure of Gerry Fitt from the SDLP leadership. It had been building up for some time, as Fitt became more and more alienated from the anti-British sentiments of his rural colleagues, and felt his position eroded by Hume's massive European vote. He was no longer the sole member of parliament, or even the most popular vote-getter, and his ability to bend SDLP policy to suit his well-cultivated socialist image at Westminster was curtailed. Most of all, he was wearying of the struggle to keep the hardline nationalists in check, and one of the last straws was what he regarded as the reluctance of some, in private, to condemn the IRA unequivocally for the murder of Lord Mountbatten. Like Paddy Devlin, he had prepared his exit, and it was only the way he left – in protest against the SDLP's decision not to take part in inter-party talks – that was surprising. The terms of reference of the so-called Atkins talks, proposed by the new Conservative Secretary of State, Humphrey Atkins, banned any mention of the Irish dimension, and on the day the SDLP were to meet in Dungannon to decide their attitude, Hume phoned Fitt with a warning to be careful. (Hume himself was to be absent in Brussels on European business, reviving claims by Fitt that he often missed difficult meetings.) To accept these terms, Hume said, would be to throw away the Irish dimension, which the party would not wear. They should be rejected and an attempt made to have them broadened. Fitt indicated to him that he was in agreement, and that there would be no problems. But it was an awkward meeting for Fitt, for although no one pointed the finger at him, there was a widespread belief that he had already told the British that the terms were acceptable. It would have been unusual for him not to have been consulted at Westminster and it would not have been the first time that he had misrepresented the party's point of view, without a mandate. In any case, he did not disagree with the mood of the meeting, which was unanimously against participation, though the last person to speak to him noticed he was rather morose. In retrospect, the view was that his bluff at Westminster – which was that he could manipulate the party – had been called. Devlin's defection, and his subsequent attacks on the SDLP's socialist credentials, had made life difficult for Fitt in west Belfast and he could hardly have forgotten that the only election he had ever lost, until that time, was a council election in which Devlin was the victor. As the SDLP's orientation swung towards Dublin, Fitt clung to London, where he was a fully-accepted member of the Labour set and enjoyed a freedom he was denied in his own constituency. His bravery, in the face of Provisional intimidation, was never questioned, but his decision to concentrate all his fire on their violence eventually isolated him from his own community.

He had not intended to resign on the Atkins talks issue, but when he returned home from Dungannon, with the angry voices of the SDLP hardliners ringing in his ears, he found his wife, Anne, in tears, bemoaning criticism of his leadership by Mallon on TV. Something snapped, and he told her: 'Don't worry. They can keep their party.' But for his wife's intervention, he would have contacted Atkins in the morning and tried to find a compromise formula for talks, playing down the Irish dimension which he still believed had wrecked the 1974 Executive. Instead he called a press conference at Westminster to announce his resignation from the leadership and party of which he had never been a fully-subscribing member. He had long regretted not resisting the pressures for a united opposition party and forming a Belfast socialist alliance, with Paddy Devlin and others, which could have hammered out a working arrangement with the out-of-town nationalists. It might have been more successful in keeping non-republican socialism alive in Belfast, but it is doubtful if it would have been nearly as effective as the SDLP. The image of a six-county party, broadly representative of minority opinion, was vital to retain credibility with the British parties and media.

210

The next day, Hume got a call in Brussels from Robin Day of the BBC *World at One* radio programme, asking for an interview. Surprised, Hume asked what it was about, to be told, 'Well, you're now the acting leader of the SDLP'. Fitt had already been interviewed, condemning the SDLP for 'going too green', so after hearing the tape, Hume dived straight in. He dealt with Fitt's remarks more in sorrow than in anger and concentrated most of the interview on explaining the SDLP's position, saying how it would be impossible for them to enter talks without any discussion of the Irish dimension, which the British had introduced six years before. It had the desired effect of rallying the demoralised troops back home, after the media had lavished its usual praises on Fitt and his brave stand against the 'green Tories'. All his political life, Fitt has had a special relationship with the media, because he is such a warm-hearted, wise-cracking, generous person, but only his close colleagues, who saw behind his public relations, could tell the full story. They still liked him as a drinking companion, but recognised that he was a figurehead leader of the party, who had little part in formulating policy – which was Hume's job – and whose primary role was as a populist 'fixer' at constituency level.

His much-attacked home in north Belfast was his only advice centre, where he did all his business, leaving others to try to fill the gap in his west Belfast constituency. When he joined, he brought no organisation with him and when he left, he left alone. But he had a characteristic quip for anyone who asked why he had announced his resignation at Westminster before telling his party colleagues: 'They didn't tell me when they appointed me, so I didn't need to tell them when I left.' His personality won him an immunity from criticism that was available to few others, even when a party full of school-teachers watched the leader mount the rostrum every year and deliver his speech from notes on the back of an envelope. He had instinctive political skills, they admitted, and he did an invaluable job in publicising Catholic grievances in the 1960s, but the party had paid a heavy price for electing him leader, which was the only means of securing his allegiance and his influence as an MP. Although he had always argued in the party that Belfast was different, and that there was no real nationalism in the city, events have proved otherwise.

Part of the explanation for Fitt's resignation could be seen in the agenda for the party conference three weeks earlier, 3 and

4 November. As well as Hume's proposals for an Anglo-Irish initiative – which O'Hanlon described as 'an early letter to Santa Claus' because of the Unionists' non-co-operation – it also contained a rural motion calling for talks with the republican paramilitary organisations, aimed at attempting reconciliation with loyalists. Some fifty delegates voted in favour, which Fitt regarded as fifty votes too many. The gulf between him and what he knew as the 'Provisional' wing had grown too wide.

The Atkins initiative was generally regarded as a Thatcher move to prevent the Northern Ireland question – and the lack of any political progress – becoming an issue in the 1980 US Presidential election. In April, during a visit to Ireland, Tip O'Neill had accused the Westminster parties of using Northern Ireland as 'a political football' – a reference to Labour's 'sale' of five extra Ulster seats, in return for Unionist support – and had later lent tacit backing to a ban on the export of US pistols for the RUC. During his visit he met all the Northern political leaders, in the neutral territory of the Consul-General's home in Belfast, before travelling by helicopter to a civic reception in Derry, where Hume returned his hospitality and escorted him to Buncrana, home of his ancestors. To the extent that the Atkins talks at Stormont showed a sign of willingness to resume the political process, suspended by Mason, they received a guarded welcome, and Hume had little trouble devising a plan to enable the Irish dimension to be raised at parallel talks, if not negotiated upon. The British at first held out a carrot to the SDLP of payment of expenses for participation, but were flatly turned down. It has been a principle, which the party can ill afford, to reject all cash inducements, even the use of headed Stormont notepaper or postage. Atkins was learning, like his predecessors, that Hume's reasonableness should never be mistaken for weakness around a negotiating table.

This time it was the Official Unionists' turn to boycott, trying to out-Paisley Paisley, who was attracted by heavy hints that a moderate Paisley might be an acceptable Prime Minister. Hume held a watching brief, certain that the talks would founder on DUP objections to power-sharing, but anxious for that to emerge clearly. Atkins kept suggesting that Paisley was saying amazing things in private, and would come round, but Hume was unconvinced. Finally, in Hume's absence, the DUP representatives went to war, in a blistering session, and Atkins was quite shattered. 'Maybe you'll believe me now,' said Hume, as the talks stopped. For him, the real significance of the talks was their aftermath, when he had a long face-to-face session with Atkins and his permanent secretary, Ken Stowe, at Hillsborough. Others find stimulation and relaxation from a night at the opera or a good film, but constructive political discussion is Hume's ideal, and he felt in particularly effective form. Stowe was receptive, in view of the failure of the talks, and Hume could see that his ideas of an Anglo-Irish approach to the Northern problem were taking root.

His point was that the only way Britain could get majority rule in Northern Ireland – and thus extract itself – was as part of a federal Ireland. The two Governments, he said, should be taking the initiative on an Anglo-Irish Council and going back to an EEC-type approach, with North and South as part of a larger community of the British Isles. Around the same time, John Biggs-Davidson, the English Tory, had made a speech about a wider association, the Islands of the North Atlantic (IONA), which fitted in with the concept, and Hume drew parallels with other inter-governmental bodies, like Benelux and the Nordic Council. Under such an Anglo-Irish Council, certain functions could be retained, such as citizenship, to protect the Britishness of the North, while majority rule could be acceptable to nationalists in a federal Ireland framework. It was a radical approach to the identity problem, which is at the heart of the Northern conflict, but it was unlikely that the Protestants would ever buy federalism, regardless of how hopeless their position, and how determined the British were to impose it. Hume and Stowe kept in touch, as the Anglo-Irish strategy evolved over the next few years, and from the very first Thatcher-Haughey summit, which emphasised the two nations' 'unique relationship', Hume could see evidence of the plan he had unrolled at Hillsborough. Dublin, of course, was fully aware of what was going on, as Hume had always made a point of bringing the Southern Government with him, wherever possible. His background in Maynooth, which many of the Republic's policy-makers in church and state had also attended, provided him with a wide circle of friends and acquaintances now reaching high office, including Ó Fiaich, Michael O'Kennedy, of Fianna Fáil and Sean Donlon, of Foreign Affairs. From his earliest days in politics he had always been conscious of where the levers of power were and who pulled them, so that he could make the best use of his time and effort. Every head of the Northern Ireland desk

213

in the Republic's Department of Foreign Affairs had been his close confidant, often spending weekends at his home and debating far into the night. As his SDLP colleagues knew, no one was as adept as Hume at picking others' brains and putting their best ideas and his to good use. If he and others sometimes forgot where the ideas originated, it did not really matter.

During the Atkins talks, Hume had one exchange with Paisley, which he felt went to the roots of the loyalist identity crisis. 'Look,' said Hume, 'what exactly is it you want to protect, so that we can go away and come back with proposals? Because you keep shifting from one foot to another. In Sunningdale protection was built into a rock, with the veto in the Council of Ireland and the status of Northern Ireland written in. You threw that away. What is it?' To which Paisley replied: 'It's very simple. I'm loyal to the Crown so long as it remains Protestant.' Hume turned to Atkins and said facetiously: 'You can solve the Irish problem if you can get Prince Charles to marry a Papish!'

To Hume, Paisley's answer described the qualified nature of the Britishness which he found difficult to understand, but which had somehow to be preserved. He knew the English, Welsh and Scottish were proud of their nationality, but the Northern Ireland Protestants were unique in wanting to be 'British'. In reality, it was a pride in being a part of Britain's heritage, as opposed to Ireland's – which was seen as something alien and primitive, even by those whose names revealed that their ancestors had been a part of it, before changing sides. How to reconcile the Irish and British identities – given that converts to a tradition are all the more attached to it – was the essence of the problem. Although Hume had some of his own roots in Scottish Presbyterianism, he was perhaps too far removed from them, in nationalist Derry, to appreciate the depths of inter-community alienation in Belfast.

The two giants of Ulster political life, Hume and Paisley, developed a strange relationship over the years. If they met, away from the public gaze, they would talk quite amicably about anything except politics, because of Paisley's desire to avoid acrimony. Both have a respect for each other as highly intelligent, very political beings, who can not only produce speeches, but are effective 'operators', actually getting things done for people of all persuasions. Their careers have almost moved in parallel since the 1960s, as each community sensed that it needed someone of weight and authority to confront a strong-man opponent. None of the other politicians are in their class as communicators, and it is commonplace for Protestants, even from Derry, to admit to wishing they had someone as effective as Hume, or 'John' as he is called by friend and foe. He has been one of the few politicians to score off Paisley in public, and when he has done so it has been devastating. When the Convention was about to be wound up, Hume decided it was time to let fly, and in his final speech introduced a quotation attacking the police: 'I would rather trust the devil himself than trust the RUC.' The Unionists were howling with anger, but Hume silenced them by asking them, in schoolmasterly fashion, who had said it. 'John Hume,' said Harry West. 'No,' replied Hume, pointing along the Unionist benches to stop at Paisley, looking very sorry for himself. 'Who said it? . . . Mr Paisley.' It was a delicious moment, puncturing Paisley, and helping to ensure a quiet end to the Convention, unlike the Assembly roughhouse.

As the Atkins talks petered out, Hume began to test his ideas about a new Ireland, very far from the conventional notion of Irish unity which still persisted in his own party. Speaking on RTE, he said Britain was part of the problem, and therefore should be part of the solution, by encouraging a dialogue between the two traditions. That would not take place as long as the guarantee was there and was the basis of British policy. 'Agreement between all sides need not necessarily be the emergence of a unitary state. The term "united Ireland" has become loaded. It has come to mean to many people the conquest of the North by the South and the absorption of the Protestant people into a predominantly Catholic state which will not respect their rights.' But any hope of Margaret Thatcher abandoning the thirty-year-old guarantee was dashed the next month, when she told the Commons: 'No democratic country can voluntarily abandon its responsibility in a part of its territory against the will of the majority of the population there. We do not intend to create any precedent of that kind.' The two biggest problems – which Hume identified in an important article in the influential US quarterly *Foreign Policy* as the British guarantee and the unionists' dependence on it – were to remain, regardless of well-intentioned appeals.

Nevertheless, Thatcher did meet the Taoiseach, Charles Haughey, in May 1980, and one of the Prime Minister's Cabinet colleagues told friends he was sure he detected a 'sexual' attraction for the smallish, rather worse-for-wear Irishman. At the time, Haughey was more on Hume's wavelength than was Lynch, who emphasised devolution more than North-South links, and an agreement to hold regular meetings was seen as progress towards a new Anglo-Irish approach, on SDLP lines. There was an acknowledgment of this in a joint government discussion paper on devolution which talked about 'a unique relationship' between the United Kingdom and the Republic and 'a need to further this relationship in the interest of peace and reconciliation'. But otherwise the Atkins initiative had flopped, with no enthusiasm for hints of 'rolling devolution' through a consultative assembly, and Seamus Mallon warning of a certain boycott. Even when Hume offered to operate power-sharing for ten years without an Irish dimension, the Unionists rejected the proposal.

As 1980 drew to a close, the Thatcher-Haughey talks provided the only hope of movement, and if there was any chance of the delegates to the SDLP conference forgetting that a hunger-strike had begun at the Maze Prison they were reminded by chanting demonstrators outside their Newcastle hotel where Hume delivered his first keynote speech as leader. Again a party document, 'Strategy for Peace', had called for a joint Anglo-Irish initiative with a constitutional conference, and a preference was expressed for a federal or confederal Ireland, as a means of the two parts learning to work together. But Hume reserved the most powerful section of his address for the IRA. 'Years ago Thomas Davis asked, in connection with a vicious killing at a time of great deprivation in Ireland, "The people of Munster are in want. Will murder feed them?" He also asked if there was something special about the blood of landlords that would fertilise the land. I would ask is there something special about the blood of an RUC or UDR man, murdered in his own country, that will bring the unity of this country any closer?' The conference accused the British Government of ineptitude in its handling of the prison dispute, calling for prisoners to be allowed to wear their own clothes and a new regime to be introduced, 'based on human dignity', but a tragic twelve months was to pass before such a solution was arrived at.

Even if there had not been the reminder of the hunger-strike, symbolic of the great divide over national identity, Hume would never have yielded to pressure to settle for partnership without an Irish dimension. That might have brought short-term gains, but the long-term problem of finding a framework in which both identities could flourish would have remained unaffected, and Hume was not going down that road. Already he had a clear picture in his mind of the way ahead, telling a reporter before the conference that he wanted 'to launch an open and public debate in Ireland, North and South, on forms that a pluralist Ireland might take and the creation of a genuine partnership between the different Irish traditions'. To those who wondered why the SDLP laid so much emphasis on constitutional problems, to the exasperation of many, he had a significant message, showing a rare glimpse of his social democratic principles: 'The reality is that politics in Ireland, North and South, have been dominated by the constitutional issue, and the division of the working class in the North is incomprehensible to an outsider. There will never be a serious right or left division in Irish politics, North or South, until the problem is settled and until we have created a genuine pluralist Ireland.' He was still looking for solutions, rather than deals, a fact which made him such an unusual Irish politician.

18
Hunger-strikes

Almost all republican campaigns in Ireland have been founded on the grievances of the ex-convicts from previous campaigns and the bitterness stored up within their family circles. The men behind the 1969 violence were veterans of the 1940s and 1950s, but because there was no peace in the 1970s there was no amnesty and the prisons themselves became the source of the rebirth of violence in the 1980s. The problem had been building up since 1971, when the introduction of internment and the rapid increase in the prison population led to an attempt by the Government to buy peace in June 1972 by establishing 'special category status' for prisoners who claimed political motivation for their crimes. Thereafter the prisons became a focus for discontent and subversion, which unfavourable verdicts on the treatment of prisoners, in a series of legal and Government reports – including censure by Amnesty International and the European Court of Human Rights – did nothing to dispel.

With the Government trying desperately to 'criminalise' the violence, the prisoners resisted the label of 'common criminals' and began the first sustained protest in Long Kesh – renamed the Maze – in September 1976 when the first IRA man to be refused special status decided to wear only a blanket instead of the normal prison-issue clothes. This moved on to the so-called 'dirty protest', in which prisoners 'on the blanket' literally lived in their own excrement, and matters came slowly to a head with the publication of a long-awaited report by the European Commission on Human Rights in the summer of 1980. While it found no justification for awarding political status and found the British not guilty of inhuman or degrading treatment – because the conditions were 'self-inflicted' – it expressed concern at the 'inflexible approach of the state authorities which has been more concerned to punish offenders against prison discipline than to explore ways of resolving such a serious deadlock'. Meanwhile the killing of prison officers went on, eighteen up to January 1980.

Cardinal Ó Fiaich and the Catholic Bishop of Derry, Edward Daly, had been negotiating with the Government since February, trying to head off the inevitable escalation to a hunger-strike, but the best the British could do, by October, was to offer civilian-issue clothes, and the clerics realised this was not enough. A statement from the H-Blocks, named after the ground-plan of the single-storey cell blocks, demanded nothing less than political status, so on 27 October seven prisoners began refusing food. Two weeks later, Gerry Fitt intervened to attack the Cardinal and advise the Government on no account to give the prisoners special status – a statement which Mrs Thatcher used in justification for her resistance.

On the same day that Secretary of State Atkins made a statement to the Commons, Hume urged him to accept the European Commission's judgment as the basis for a solution. It was a respected body, especially by Catholics, and when it said that the prison population was unique, there were grounds for unique solutions. Otherwise, Hume warned, the strike could result in an emotional explosion which could do a lot of damage. Atkins, while wary, said he was willing to go some way down that road. The IRA's prison leadership was genuinely worried, it said, about the effect of the dirty strike on seventeen and eighteen-year-olds. It realised that it had to escalate the protest to resolve matters, despite the opposition of Sinn Fein, expressed by Gerry Adams, then SF vice-president, who wrote: 'We are tactically, strategically, physically and morally opposed to a hunger strike'.

Hume deliberately concentrated his appeal to the Government on two crucial issues – freedom of movement for the prisoners, so that they could have association with other wings of the H-block, and freedom to wear their own clothes. These offered the most promise, he thought, and eventually the prisoners had taken the bait, with their leader, Brendan Hughes, contacting him through a prison chaplain. If Hume could deliver on these issues, he was told, the strike would be over. Atkins was very excited by the prospect and asked him to stand by the following day, when there was a Cabinet meeting. Meanwhile Hume sent a message to the prisoners indicating that if he appeared in person with an official their points would be guaranteed. If he did not there would be no guarantee, whatever they were told. The strike was at a crucial stage: Sean McKenna, whose father had been one of the 'hooded' internees and died partly as a result, was going blind and fading fast, fifty-three days into his strike.

Late in the afternoon, when no call had come, Hume rang Atkins at Stormont Castle to find out what was happening, only to be told: 'Well, we weren't able to meet your points'. Angrily, he asked why he had not been told, but obviously the Secretary of State had other things on his mind, for the strike was ended that day, 18 December. In fact, a Northern Ireland Office official had arranged to meet a Redemptorist priest, Father Meagher, at Aldergrove that evening and both travelled to the prison to present a long document to the starving prisoners. Some deal had been done, Hume believed, between Stormont Castle and the Provisionals outside the prison, in order to prevent him taking any political credit – which he had promised not to do. So once again, as at the time of the IRA's 1972 truce, Hume was cut out of the final deal, having been used to set it up. When the small print was read, the agreement was not what it appeared. The prisoners should have known, from Hume's instructions, that there was something wrong, but it sounded to him as if Sinn Fein had insisted on taking charge, leaving the prisoners in ignorance. Some at SF headquarters were by no means convinced that a hunger-strike was in their interests.

The document was simply an expanded version of the thirty-two-page explanation of rules which had already been circulated to the prisoners and it would have taken a skilled negotiator, like Hume, to read between the lines and improve on it. But the prisoners had an agonising decision to make, with McKenna fast losing his sight, and they voted four-to-two to come off. Bobby Sands, an unremarkable, quick-tempered young IRA man who was standing in for the hunger-striking Hughes as the Provisionals' commanding officer, accepted Sinn Fein's word that the British had been just about to capitulate if the strike had lasted another twenty-four hours. Out of his subsequent feeling of betrayal, the next hunger-strike was born.

Part of the deal was that the prisoners would be allowed their own clothes in recreation time, and prison-issue during working time, but the prison management stuck rigidly to the rules, insisting that the protesters should first replace their blankets with prison clothes. Sands, now the CO, with Hughes in hospital, simply looked at the prison clothes, brought in with his own, and snapped, 'You can take those out, they'll never be worn'. Always a confrontationist, described as someone who would run across a soccer pitch to join in a fight, Sands had no time for the subtleties of the negotiating process and from late January the second hunger-strike, to begin on 1 March 1981 was unavoidable. Lessons had been learned, however, and

Sands worked out that, rather than put seven on hunger-strike together so that collective decisions had to be made and weak links could be exploited, he would go first. To break the strike, they had to break Sands, and that, he knew, would be impossible.

Simultaneously with the start of the fast, the prisoners were to end their dirty and blanket protests, to focus attention on Sands and to spite the prison warders, who were making big money in overtime, cleaning up after the prisoners.

Those who came in contact with Sands knew him as a spiky individual, irritable, not very pleasant to talk to, and by no means a natural leader. But he was a totally reliable team-player, who led by example rather than speeches, and had thought out every move in advance. Two weeks before the hunger-strike, he called aside a visiting chaplain, Father Denis Faul, after Mass and arranged a meeting the next Sunday. He wanted to discuss the morality of what he was doing and Faul answered, as a Catholic theologian, that in the circumstances he did not think the hunger-strike was suicide. He believed there were genuine grievances – the alleged beatings and obscene treatment by the warders during searches – which were being ignored. They were not seeking prisoner-of-war status, he thought, and there were good arguments for getting their own clothes. Nevertheless, said Father Faul, the hunger-strike was immoral, not because it was suicide, but because it would cause too much unrest in the community, risking lives, and would stir up hatred. Sands, who had been in prison almost continuously since 1971, was too remote from the outside world to see this argument and ended the talk by saying: 'Greater love hath no man than this, that he lays down his life for his friends.' Said Faul: 'Bobby, there's no answer to that. We'll leave it there.' As he left him, the priest knew Sands intended to die for his fellow prisoners, regardless of what appeals were directed at him, from whatever quarter. As he had said: 'This is between me and the British Government and that is it. Between the two of us.' He was not prepared to talk to anybody but the British Government. Then, five days into the strike, came a stroke of luck for Sinn Fein – Frank Maguire, the old-style independent nationalist MP for Fermanagh-South Tyrone, died suddenly, leaving vacant a seat with a built-in nationalist majority, and Sands, stretched out on his bed in the prison hospital, was eligible to fill it. The SDLP was in an awkward position, wanting to contest but unhappy about splitting the nationalist vote against a man literally fighting for his life. It was left to the party executive to decide, and after voting sixteen-to-three to put up a candidate, its decision was reversed by eleven-to-eight a week later, when Noel Maguire, a brother of Frank, promised to oppose Sands as an independent. Austin Currie sat in his Dungannon office, with his nomination papers complete and his £150 deposit in notes, fully prepared to repeat his 1979 independent challenge if Maguire backed out. He did – after direct Provisional threats – but just ten minutes too late for Currie to make his move.

Sands had a majority of 1,446 votes in a tribal contest, but the British were unmoved, and he was to die four weeks later, on the sixty-sixth day of his fast, 5 May 1981. The SDLP had been out-manoeuvred – and Sinn Fein, which had abandoned its traditional abstention policy, had laid the foundations for a political comeback – but Hume defended his party's decision on the grounds that the SDLP had had nothing to gain. The local party had been split, as was the adjoining branch in Mid-Ulster, and if the voters had concluded that Sands' death was due to SDLP intervention, the effect on the district council elections in June could have been serious. Hume had been asked – chiefly by Unionists – to gamble his party's future in the hope of stopping Sinn Fein taking advantage of a strike he thought the British could have avoided. Maguire's nomination had been a satisfactory compromise, until it fell through. As it was, the SDLP's vote held up well in the local government poll, dropping only 3 per cent to 17.5 per cent, against the anti-H-Block vote of the Irish Independence Party (4 per cent) and the independent republicans (2 per cent). To counter the sympathy vote for Sands, the SDLP fought the council elections on a mandate for the Anglo-Irish summit talks, which were due again in Dublin. In the overheated political climate Paisley's DUP just topped the OUP vote for the first time. The outcome of the Unionists' virility contest changed nothing, argued Hume, except to emphasise that the problem would have to be tackled in a wider context than Northern Ireland.

After his previous experiences, Hume knew he was unacceptable as a mediator for the hunger-strikers but, with feeling building up in the Catholic community, he made a final attempt to convince Mrs Thatcher of the long-term effects if men died. He realised it would be a crucial meeting in Downing Street, and the night before he soaked in a hot bath, with a stiff whiskey, to prepare for the fray. Again he would concentrate on the European Commission report, with its refusal of political status, but its recognition that changes might be possible in the prison regime. If other countries allowed prisoners to wear their own clothes, why shouldn't Northern Ireland? Freer association, between one wing of an H-block and another, would be a further way forward. But although he had his arguments well marshalled for their evening meeting, he found the Prime Minister totally insensitive. While he tried to warn her that the strike could endanger democratic institutions North and South, as well as swelling IRA support in America, she played down its importance, repeating 'A crime is a crime is a crime'.

Even when Hume angrily butted in, describing how, a day before, he had watched a library van being set on fire at the bottom of his street, the penny did not drop. Derry was as British as Derby and Thatcher was not going to bend her principles. Atkins, who had been stuck in a corner, hardly spoke, although he gave the impression of wanting to be reasonable. He lacked the political clout however, as, it had to be admitted, did Hume. Rebuffed, he told her frankly what he thought of her, as an Irishman to an Englishwoman, before, in his own words, 'being thrown out'. On the steps, the BBC *Newsnight* cameras were waiting, and he poured out his resentment to the nation. Back in a friend's house, he repeated in despair, 'She doesn't understand. She doesn't understand.'

At the same time, he tried to get across to Michael Foot, the Labour leader, the importance of a compromise, but was baulked by Gerry Fitt, who entered Foot's room as Hume walked out. Later Fitt issued a statement to say that Foot was following his advice – to say nothing – rather than Hume's. But although he made no headway in London, Hume knew he had to keep the pressure on, if only to show that someone understood the concern of the Catholic community. If he had reacted like Fitt, he reasoned, respect for democratic politicians would have been destroyed, with disastrous consequences. As Hume saw it, Fitt had made the same mistake as Conor Cruise O'Brien, in branding all nationalists as Provisional supporters and ignoring the essential subtleties. It was as if Labour should abandon its social objectives, just because a left-wing element was prepared to use street violence to achieve them. The truth was that if the SDLP had abandoned the hunger-strikers to their fate, it would have left the field open to the Provisionals and spelt the SDLP's political downfall – just as Fitt's attitude had been his undoing.

Earlier, Thatcher got more than she bargained for when she called the heads of the Protestant churches together to win their approval for her policy. After listening to her lecture about the need to stand up to the hunger-strike, the Methodist President, the Rev. Sydney Callaghan, a charming but steely Dubliner with a rare appreciation of Protestant and Catholic attitudes, quietly took her on. 'I would like to make it quite clear,' he said, 'that fundamentally our Methodist people and I personally would agree that the Government must not politicise criminality. But you do not fully understand how a Celt responds to a hunger-strike. If somebody dies in one of your prisons or decides to do it, that is what he wants to do and let him do it. But a Celt does not think that way. Under the old Brehon law, the biggest disgrace is to have someone die on your doorstep. There is something you are doing to the Celtic psyche that you don't understand.' He paused, as Thatcher flushed with anger. 'I have been here on quite a few occasions,' he continued. 'I have always come, but I sometimes have the feeling that it is a public relations exercise, that you speak, and when we respond with our opinions it is quite obvious that you don't listen. I am merely saying what it feels like. I am not here to take issue, I am here to reflect and I am telling you that to a Celt, you are playing with something quite profound.'

Thatcher was equally unmoved by pleas from Cardinal Ó Fiaich and Bishop Lennon, demonstrating a lack of sympathy and awareness which they found incredible. 'We fought the Germans and the French,' she said, 'and now we're on the best of terms with them. Why are we fighting the Irish?' 'But Prime Minister,' replied the Cardinal, 'you're not occupying the Rhine.' When he explained that in his own home parish of Crossmaglen he had to cross the border to say Mass, there was no comprehension. Finally, in an effort to mollify the upset clerics, she offered a drink, only to have to admit that Downing Street had no Irish whiskey.

Northern Ireland Office representatives were dispatched around the North to sound Catholic opinion, and the message was coming back: 'Settle'. The demand for political status had been replaced by five demands, infinitely negotiable on the surface, but Sands had set his face against dealing with anyone other than the Government, and the Government was equally adamantly opposed. One by one the would-be mediators, including Monsignor John Magee, acting on Pope John Paul's instructions, were rebuffed. (The Newry man was later to tell associates that he suspected his prison meetings with Sands had been bugged, because of subsequent remarks by Atkins in a final interview in which the Secretary of State had disclosed a transparent hostility.)

The world's media, expecting an explosion of sectarian violence after Sands' death, was disappointed – and a French TV team had to be asked to leave by the Belfast consul, for staging 'confrontations' – but the 100,000 who joined the funeral procession for an unknown Provisional showed how the campaign had united a community against the British and their unionist supporters. There was a welling up of sectarian hatred among Catholics, which had previously been lacking in the Troubles, and it spurred Father Faul to greater efforts. By now the Dublin-based Irish Commission for Justice and Peace, a little-known Catholic body, had got Sinn Fein to describe the hunger-strikers' demands in more detail and there were signs that progress was being made. Michael Allison, the Northern Ireland Prisons Minister, indicated that certain things had been agreed, but when his own document was finally presented the next day it was watered down and mainly concerned with the 'own clothes' agreement. 'There is a lady behind the veil,' he told newsmen, leaving them to guess that Mrs Thatcher thought he had gone too far.

Faul had left for his holiday in France confident that the strike was as good as settled, until reports of riots at the funeral of hunger-striker Joe McDonnell brought him home two weeks early to another death, that of Martin Hurson, after only forty-six days. He confronted the new CO, Brendan McFarlane, and accused him of changing the nature of the protest by putting one prisoner a week on strike. The fasting had been an instrument of protest, but if it was turned into an instrument of death the whole protest became immoral. Two more died, after seventy-one and seventy-three days – breaking the seventy-two-day fast record of Terence McSwiney, Mayor of Cork, in 1920 – before Faul decided to attack, calling a meeting of strikers' relatives in Toomebridge on 28 July. He put all his cards on the table, explaining how Mrs Thatcher had showed the clerics on 1 July that she neither understood nor cared. The granting of 'own clothes' was all that was to be had, and further deaths would be needless. After three hours of heated debate, all agreed that the strike should be ended, so they piled into cars for a hastily-arranged meeting with Gerry Adams at Sinn Fein headquarters on the Falls Road and spent four hours listening to his eloquent defence.

Adams promised he would try his best to convince the prisoners that the British would let them die; and he did so, in person, with

Atkins' permission. But he saw them singly, where they did not want to seem disloyal to the others, and he failed. Faul himself was not allowed by the authorities to see the protesters, because of his constant criticism of the prison regime. (Fortunately he had just avoided losing the right to say Mass in the Maze, when he was accused of smuggling cigarettes and writing materials in July 1980.) But he obtained a breakthrough when a mother told him of her son's kidney trouble, and she agreed to take him off the strike as soon as he went into a coma. Other families were still wavering, and got little encouragement from Sinn Fein – with the approach of a by-election in Fermanagh-South Tyrone, caused by Sands' death – but a pattern eventually established itself. As soon as the kidneys failed and the striker went into a coma, the relatives had two to three hours to get to the Maze and ask for medical attention.

The tenth and last striker died on 20 August, the day of the by-election, and with men being pulled off the strike one by one, Faul got a strange request from Sinn Fein to address a relatives' meeting. He was being attacked by them in the Press, so he expected a rough ride, but eventually he concluded they needed him to end a strike they knew had run its course. A meeting between the relatives and the new Prisons Minister, Lord Gowrie, was arranged, at which the elegant aristocrat, who had lectured in English at Harvard, turned on his Anglo-Irish charm and won their confidence. Jim Prior, the new Secretary of State, was equally benign when he received the Cardinal and Faul, but was unable to agree to the Dungannon priest's request for 100-per-cent restoration of lost remission as a bold bid for an IRA ceasefire. When the civil servants suggested 20 per cent, Prior agreed that was useless and eventually it was settled at 50 per cent, along with the concession on wearing 'own clothes' at all times, which Faul believed could have been agreed in July. On 3 October, three weeks after Prior's arrival, the hunger-strike was called off, after sixty-one violent deaths in the province – thirty among members of the security forces.

The prisoners publicly continued to blame Faul for ending the strike, accepting Sinn Fein's story, but privately the attitude of many was different. Without his initial credibility in the republican community, built up during many years of confrontation with the authorities over torture and ill treatment, he would not have been able to act as an intermediary. He helped save lives, but the psychological damage which had been done between April and August was to change the political map for years to come.

Just as Mrs Thatcher could not understand the deep significance of her unfeeling attitude towards the dying hunger-strikers, she was impervious to SDLP pleas that the by-election after Sands' death should be postponed until the heat had died down. Most unusually, it took place in the holiday month of August – Parliament having passed an Act banning prisoner candidates – and the SDLP again had to decide whether to fight in the worst possible circumstances or give the anti-H-Block nominee, Owen Carron, a free run. The executive stuck to its promise not to repeat April's debacle, but the weak local organisation again could not produce a candidate, and Hume, who was present, did not intervene. Some whispered that Hume should stand himself, and there was genuine dismay at the second retreat in a row. But he had no intention of possibly throwing away his and his party's future on such a losing cause, in a situation for which he held Britain responsible. Feelers were put out by John Robb that he, as a radical Protestant, might relieve the SDLP's dilemma if he stood as an independent, with the party's backing. But Hume, though tempted, did not bite, and in any case Robb developed a chest illness, after weeks of preparing his campaign, and had to back out. In view of the SDLP's good general-election performance two years later, Robb might have won enough votes to prevent Sinn Fein from taking the seat, and might have set back their policy of fighting elections. Carron won the by-election with an increased majority of 2,230, and although the SDLP's attitude was understandable in the circumstances, its image as a strong, non-violent alternative to Sinn Fein suffered considerably. It was a no-win situation in republican Fermanagh, for the third time in two years, and the only satisfaction was that the SDLP's critics were mostly pro-unionist. Few opponents had noticed that Hume had rejected anti-H-Block supporters' demands for SDLP councillors to withdraw from district councils, but the Fermanagh-South Tyrone by-elections were to be a permanent blemish. Arguably, Hume's 'hands off' attitude in August was short-sighted, as it gave Sinn Fein a second chance, in ideal conditions, to test their strength – leading almost inevitably to a successful reinvolvement in politics, North and South.

Survival was an end in itself in hunger-strike year, with nationalist representatives under constant pressure to back the pseudo-politicians in Sinn Fein who would happily knife them in the back. But the Anglo-Irish initiative provided a lifeline, as Hume had hoped when he helped launch it, suggesting that constitutional politics could still deliver the goods. It was only a small beginning, and Haughey's tendency to oversell its implications for unity was a constant worry, but the potential for growth was there. Sadly for Hume, it lasted only until the 1982 Falklands war, when Ireland's backing for Argentina destroyed what remained of the Thatcher-Haughey entente, and boosted unionist confidence in Britain's guarantee to the Northern Ireland majority. Hume agreed with Dublin opinion that Mrs Thatcher had acted recklessly, and found plenty of politicians in Washington to agree privately. But the way the British people had rallied to the cause of 1,800 islanders, 8,000 miles away, was depressing for politicians like Hume, relying on a radical rethink of British policy in Ireland. There was also food for thought in the Catholics' instinctive support for Argentina, while Protestants cheered 'their' victories. Nationalism went very deep in the North, and the exclusiveness of both identities was Hume's greatest problem.

During the hunger-strike year American politicians with Irish constituents were under increasing pressure to provide positive alternatives to the veiled republicanism of the Ad Hoc Committee, and Hume took the opportunity to promote the Anglo-Irish initiative, as well as to broaden the annual St Patrick's Day appeal of the Four Horsemen. With Ronald Reagan in the White House and more Irish-Americans voting Republican rather than Democrat, as they moved up the social scale, it was necessary to give the moderate Irish nationalist case a more bipartisan image. The idea of a new grouping was floated by Hume in a talk to sympathetic Congress members under the chairmanship of Tom Foley, a Washington State Democrat. It would provide a contact point for their constituents and a source of reliable information on Irish Government and SDLP opinion – unlike the propagandist Ad Hoc Committee, many of whose members were becoming disillusioned. Shortly afterwards, Hume met Foley and Senator Chris Dodd of Connecticut at an Oxford conference and thrashed the subject out – including the name he had suggested, the Friends of Ireland, an unconscious throwback to the United Friends of Ireland, founded in 1840.

From then on, statements which had been confined to the Four Horsemen now went out in the name of a much larger group from both parties, which had a greater impact. By 1983, there were seventy-eight signatories – thirty Senators, including Edward

Kennedy, Daniel Moynihan, Gary Hart, John Glenn, Thomas Eagleton and William Proxmire, and forty Congress members from a broad base, not concentrated on the east coast like the Ad Hoc Committee. The Friends' yearly commentaries were heavily influenced by Hume's advice on the principle of unity by consent and supporting links with the Irish Government and Dáil. The high quality of the membership, as compared with Biaggi's organisation, ensured that it quickly came to represent the voice of responsible Irish Americans. Reagan, whose great-grandfather emigrated from Co. Tipperary in the early nineteenth century, showed a personal interest in Ireland, through regular St Patrick's Day contacts with the Irish Embassy, and it obviously paid any politican with an Irish constituency to keep in touch and avoid being embroiled in controversy. His pre-election 'roots' visit in 1984 demonstrated that Ireland would continue to command his attention, even if he was reluctant to embarrass Mrs Thatcher over the North.

In Europe, Hume's other sphere of influence, the concentration was on economic aid for Northern Ireland, in accordance with his 1979 manifesto. His experience in the Commission showed him that the North was losing out, compared to the Republic, because of Britain's basic lack of interest in Europe, and he could see how an energetic MEP could exploit the opportunities for the common good. The sums involved were not large, beside the £1,500,million subsidy from Britain to Northern Ireland in the early 1980s, but they would demonstrate the practical side of the European ideal, which had enabled the warring countries of Western Europe to settle their differences inside a Common Market context. All Hume's own constitutional designs, dating back to Sunningdale, had been EEC-based, and he hoped to show Europe's relevance to Ireland, both in the economic and political field.

An important asset was the SDLP's long association with the European Socialists, the largest grouping in the parliament, who promptly elected Hume as treasurer in the summer of 1979. They gave him a key role in all matters concerning Northern Ireland, even though he himself sat only on the committee for regional policy and planning, and was a substitute on the agricultural committee.

Within six months of his election to Strasbourg, he had tabled a resolution inside the 124-strong Socialist group, calling for an investigation into ways in which the EEC could help the Northern Ireland economy, and a process was begun that was to result in significant bonuses. After an on-the-spot inquiry, Simone Martin, a French MEP, drew up a report which endorsed Hume's call for financial aid and prompted the EEC Commission – the policy-making body – to open a special line in the European budget, unique to Northern Ireland. Largely as a result of Martin's study, concentrating on bad housing conditions in Belfast, the city was chosen, along with Naples, for a pilot Integrated Operations scheme to co-ordinate the spending of money, from Europe and the national governments, on urban redevelopment. The British were much slower than the Italians to put their plan together, but they moved quickly enough to take advantage of extra EEC aid for Belfast, which Hume steered through.

Originally the special assistance – worth about £63 million over three years – was earmarked for housing, and Prior made a special journey to Brussels to solemnly promise it would be additional to the Government's budget, and not absorbed. But when the plan was put to the Council of Ministers, where representatives of the ten member nations pass or reject Commission proposals, it was blocked by the German and Danish Governments, reluctant to add housing to the strained European budget. Hume immediately began to lobby inside the Socialist group, and after a favourable meeting with Anker Jorgensen, the Danish Prime Minister, he had two meetings in Bonn with German Department of Finance officials, arranged by Willy Brandt, the former German Chancellor. It emerged that the Germans were very sympathetic to Northern Ireland's claims, provided that the money was not designated for housing, and a compromise was arrived at, approved by Regional Commissioner Antonio Giolitti who had asked to be kept informed. The money was paid over for urban redevelopment work in Belfast, releasing funds which the Government then transferred to new housing, meeting the EEC's conditions. In one stroke, Hume had met two of the commitments he had made in his 1979 manifesto – to obtain special regional aid for Northern Ireland and to ensure that the money was additional to normal Government spending. To Sinn Fein, European cash constituted a 'bribe', but that was an unconvincing argument to set against Hume's most lasting monument in Derry, a new £27 million bridge over the Foyle, partly financed by Brussels.

However, Hume's negotiating on behalf of the British Government and Belfast's working class yielded scant results in terms of domestic politics; the British still paid little attention to the SDLP's political demands and tenants of the Belfast houses failed to associate them with either Europe or the SDLP. The EEC was more appreciative, and largely as a result of Hume's efforts, the Commission set up a special sub-committee consisting of the two British Commissioners, the Irish Commissioner, Richard Burke, and the Commissioners for Regional Affairs and Transport.

The aid for Belfast was intended to be only the first instalment of EEC assistance for Northern Ireland, noted in a community-wide survey to be the second poorest of 131 regions, finishing just above Calabria, in Italy. Hume could justifiably claim credit for the housing grant, which was all part of his strategy of using Northern Ireland as a test case for a more effective EEC regional policy, with enough funds to compensate the regions for their distance from Europe's golden triangle. It was a popular cause for the Socialists and for small nations like the Irish Republic, which needed all Hume's expertise, patience and horse-trading skills to deliver. Although he had only one vote and one voice, he was able to combine for maximum effect with the Socialists and the Irish 'mafia', which had a foot in all the European groupings.

At the political level, Hume launched his European initiative when the Thatcher-Haughey talks had broken down. He asked the Republic's MEPs to get their political groups to table resolutions on the North in the EEC's political affairs committee, as he did within the Socialist group; and although they failed to involve their European colleagues, several individual resolutions were submitted. Realising that Britain would oppose him on the grounds that Northern Ireland politics was outside the competence of the European Parliament – according to a resolution of 1981 – Hume was careful to avoid any mention of solutions, in order to get a report plus a debate at Strasbourg.

John Taylor, who frequently clashed with Hume from his base in the mainly-Conservative European Democratic Group, tried to block the political move with a letter to the Socialist group, only to strengthen its resolve. A report was duly commissioned, to be written by Niels Haagerup, a Danish Liberal. Mrs Thatcher was furious, and instructed that no co-operation was to be given, but since she herself was channelling cash rebates from Europe into Northern Ireland and was constantly asking for more, the Europeans gladly forged ahead. Haagerup's report was more pessimistic about Irish unity than nationalists would have wanted – stressing that it was not possible in the forseeable future and essentially backing power-sharing, with a role for Dublin – but Hume was satisfied. Although not a member of the political affairs committee, he had been instrumental in setting up the inquiry, as the Socialists' Northern Ireland representative, and was nominated as the sole Socialist spokesman in the Parliament's debate on the report in March 1984. The important thing for him was the resolution contained in the report – which was simply an individual's assessment of the problem – and the recommendation was that the British and Irish Governments should set up a framework to tackle the question. This was fully in line with the policy of the New Ireland Forum, which Hume had already helped to set up a year before, in March 1983, and when Haagerup's resolution was debated the Unionist objections were overruled. The Conservative members abstained, on instructions, although some were pleasantly surprised by Haagerup's findings, and the only speeches and votes against were those of Paisley and Taylor, with the Republic's Neil Blaney, who opposed British involvement, making an odd trio.

An independent body, looking objectively at the Northern Ireland question, had concluded that both the British and Irish Governments had to be involved in a settlement. It all added to the pressure on Britain which Hume had mounted internationally in favour of his Forum strategy, and there was further backing in May 1984 from the American Congress, which passed its first resolution on Ireland since 1918 when it had urged Irish participation in the Armistice talks. The EEC resolution was not the end of the matter, for MEPs could raise it in the European Parliament, asking Commissioners what response there had been. Once it was on the table of the Council of Ministers, any government could talk about it, including the Irish. The British could veto any proposals for constitutional change, but, according to Hume's strategy, they could not oppose discussion of political change.

Because of Northern Ireland's relative dependence on agriculture, unlike Britain, Ulster farmers often relied on the Irish to argue their case, without any visible sign of gratitude. If anything, a member of the European Parliament had an even more thankless job than his counterpart in the national parliament, though for Hume Europe provided an opportunity to work towards his political and philo- sophical ideals. His experience in Dick Burke's European cabinet had awakened an interest in the small farmers of Northern Ireland, who tended to be neglected by the big wheels of the Ulster Farmers

Union and the Department of Agriculture. He soon realised that their lot could be improved by an extension of the EEC's Less Favoured Areas scheme, qualifying them for better assistance, and by January 1982 the new boundaries, covering seventy per cent of the territory, were in force. For this, and many of the other European projects in which he was involved, Hume worked alone, but was willing to accept the support of Paisley and Taylor when it was offered. In this way, Europe – particularly in agricultural matters – often provided a common platform, unobtainable elsewhere which helped to reduce marginally the tensions of Ulster politics. But while Hume found he could work with Paisley, especially when the latter was in a constructive mood, and could rely on him to deliver the goods, Taylor was constantly seeking political advantage. Both Unionists were elected on an anti-Europe ticket, although they were prepared to use the EEC for what they could get out of it, and Hume's positive approach gave him the edge in dealings with the Brussels bureaucracy which he knew so well.

He even developed his interest in minority languages, in an ad hoc committee on the issue, winning the hearts of MEPs from outlying regions, like Brittany, with his resolution in the parliament on the need to preserve cultural diversity. It argued that there should be no discrimination against those who spoke a language which was not the mother tongue of their nation and that they should have basic rights to education, public administration and the media in their own language. Philosophically, it fitted in perfectly with his theory that Europe would flourish only if it respected diversity, and that unity was about diversity, not the conquering of one culture by another. Irish, in fact, is one of the privileged minority languages in Europe, being formally recognised as the Republic's first language, but there are many others, like Breton, which could benefit from Hume's initiative. With some careful prodding, he managed to have a bureau set up for lesser-spoken languages, with its office, not surprisingly, in Dublin. But he had to admit that his hopes of submerging the Anglo-Irish problem in a European context were unlikely to be realised. Neither the British nor the Northern Ireland British identified with the EEC concept, and they were inclined to discount Hume's efforts.

He was to need all his determination in the years to come, as the hunger-strike proved to be a watershed for the Provisionals, rather than the disaster some had believed it would be. By demonstrating their convictions in the most extreme, non-violent fashion, the hunger-strikers caught the imaginations of a younger generation which was ready to blame the British for all its ills. Recruitment of IRA volunteers increased and Noraid funds from America went up from $75,000 in the first half of 1979 to $250,000 in the same period of 1981. More crucially, the two by-elections in Fermanagh-South Tyrone and two successes in the Dáil election in June encouraged the more politically-minded Belfast Sinn Fein members, under Gerry Adams, to press for a change in the traditional abstentionist policy. With Maggie Thatcher established as a hate figure in republican mythology, for her attitude to the hunger-strikers, it was easy to ask voters to make their mark where it would hurt her most – and that meant a vote for Sinn Fein rather than the seemingly impotent SDLP.

19
Seeking a New Ireland

After a series of lightweight or middleweight Secretaries of State, who proved unequal to the task of reviving hope of devolution, the arrival on 12 September 1981 of James Prior, a front-rank Conservative, gave the SDLP fresh heart. Although he accepted the Ulster post only to keep his place in the Cabinet's economic committee, Prior had a reputation as a conciliator and could be expected to stand up to the bullying which is a part of Stormont Castle life. He obviously wanted to fill the political vacuum in a way that his predecessors had failed to do, and his early consultations confirmed that he was a man of original ideas, in a hurry to carry them out. This suited the SDLP, who had been in the wilderness for six long years and the more they listened to Prior's voluble deputy, Lord Gowrie, the better they liked what they heard.

Prior was an agnostic on Ireland, but Lord Gowrie, who was of Scottish-Irish descent and had spent his youth in Co. Donegal, in private made no secret of the fact that he was emotionally in favour of Irish unity. In unguarded moments he would muse in a donnish way about his hopes for a constitutional system which would tackle the basic question of identity, allowing people in Derry to send representatives to Dublin or London, according to their sense of nationality. 'Grey' Gowrie was a new phenomenon in the Northern Ireland Office – someone who had previously thought, however romantically, about the problem – and the SDLP were encouraged to believe that the Prior initiative, when it came, might be a breakthrough.

At the first meeting in January 1982 Prior had some interesting proposals for a power-sharing administration which he regarded as non-boycottable, because the powers of the executive and the legislature would be separate, on American lines. The Secretary of State, as chief executive, would appoint people to the government, according to party strengths and they could be elected or not, so that if any party refused to take its seats, its places could be filled by representatives from the community at large. The SDLP were intrigued and drew up a detailed response for the next meeting, only to find Prior pushing a new proposal requiring a 70 per cent majority before any powers could be devolved to a Northern Ireland Assembly. 'But what about the other idea?' Hume asked. 'That's gone,' said Prior, to the delegation's obvious dismay. 'It's just not feasible.' Later it emerged that Thatcher had turned it down.

The Unionists had delivered their veto, as they had done so often before, and it gradually emerged that the new plan, for 'rolling devolution' by easy stages, was based on a scheme drawn up more than a year earlier by an *émigré* Ulster GP, Dr Brian Mawhinney, who had a safe Conservative seat in Peterborough. Because of its unwieldy decision-making process, depending on weighted majorities to ensure fair play for the minority, it had been instantly dismissed as unworkable, but clearly some civil servant had dusted it off and sold it to the new incumbent. Disillusioned, Hume decided to probe the only ray of hope in the subsequent White Paper – a paragraph acknowledging that the whole problem was a conflict of identity and that both identities would have to be accommodated. Gowrie, who was obviously the author, expanded at some length, raising expectations, and the SDLP came back with proposals that the Anglo-Irish Inter-Governmental Council – which had already been set up – would have certain responsibilities in matters such as security and nationality.

It was, of course, a throwback to Sunningdale and Hume's attempts to set the most difficult problems in a North-South or Anglo-Irish context. But the British were reluctant to respond and Hume realised that they were stringing the SDLP along, thinking that it had no alternative but to agree to terms that failed to specify either power-sharing or an Irish dimension. Yet another Secretary of State had failed to appreciate that the SDLP never engaged in bargaining on such issues, but stated a position and stuck to it. Even Hume's parting shot to Prior, after their fourth meeting in April, was not believed. 'I just want to tell you,' he said, 'we won't be having anything to do with your Assembly.' 'I regret that,' replied Prior. 'But we have to go ahead.'

Hume's formal statement, after a party meeting, was the clearest possible warning that there would be no turning back by the SDLP. Describing the White Paper as an 'insulting document', he said the 'so-called initiative' had more to do with Mr Prior's political future than with the future of Northern Ireland. By any standards, the plan was unworkable, because even if there was 70 per cent agreement to set up an administration, the minority representatives on it could be outvoted by a straight majority in the Assembly. The identity question had been mentioned in the White Paper, only to be ignored in the legislation and Mr Prior had given the game away by saying it would help to 'tie' Northern Ireland into the United Kingdom.

'So much for an even-handed recognition of both identities,' said Hume, who still believed, unlike some of his colleagues, that an election was avoidable.

Prior had stressed, in meetings with the SDLP, that he was insisting on community support for any devolution of powers, but Hume could see the plan only as a further weakening by the Government. At the start of the 1970s the SDLP had been offered power-sharing as of right, and an Irish dimension. Then the Irish element had been dropped and now the veto over power-sharing had formally been surrendered to the unionist community, who would have more than 70 per cent of the Assembly membership. With the help of Alliance and perhaps one or two SDLP defectors, the Government might even hope to put together a one-sided administration – though the necessity for 70 per cent agreement would make it unworkable. Mrs Thatcher was hostile, having earlier told Prior to 'take the green edges off' his White Paper, ridding it of any Irish content, but Westminster was prepared to give Prior the benefit of its considerable doubts on the Bill itself. His argument was that if the MPs did not accept his plan, a right-wing Conservative Secretary of State might integrate Northern Ireland with Britain, so Labour played along, influenced by Fitt's support for the Assembly and his sniping at the SDLP.

Had Hume been at Westminster to work on Labour, he had little doubt that he could have blocked the Bill, given the lukewarm feelings of the Official Unionists, but Fitt's plausible description of the SDLP as 'green Tories' helped preserve the bipartisanship. Another factor entering into the equation was the Falklands War, driving a wedge between Britain and the Republic, in the persons of Mrs Thatcher and Charles Haughey, at a time when they should have been developing the Anglo-Irish process. Already Mrs Thatcher had been disillusioned by Haughey's exaggeration of the progress that was being made, and his opposition to the Falklands operation in the EEC and United Nations was the last straw. The Anglo-Irish Council virtually went into cold storage for eighteen months and Hume's studied silence concealed a sympathy with the view in Europe and America that Mrs Thatcher had taken an unjustifiable risk of opening up a much wider conflict. In Belfast, the graffiti in nationalist areas soon showed that Catholic sympathies were with the Argentinians, rather than the British. *Viva Argentina* was typical of the slogans facing the army foot patrols.

If the British had let Hume down, so had the Protestants, who had failed to respond to his vision of a new Ireland. In a heartfelt address in St Anne's Church of Ireland Cathedral in Belfast in March 1982 he acknowledged faults on the Catholic side and called for a new initiative from Protestants who cherished their Irishness. He pleaded with them to present proposals for a new Ireland which would be acceptable to Protestantism, as opposed to unionism, and in so doing to 'challenge those of my tradition to spell out in clear and tangible terms what we mean by unity, what we mean by partnership, what we mean by reconciliation'. The central and consistent mistake of Irish Protestantism, he argued, had been to seek, almost as the only means of protecting its distinctiveness, to concentrate all power exclusively in its own hands. 'Exclusivism is an inherently destabilising factor in any society and contains within itself all the seeds of community disintegration and violence,' he said.

At the same time, nationalists had 'failed to define their concept of unity in terms which would be meaningful and truly unthreatening to the other Irish tradition'. Because of this omission, the aspiration had come to mean and be understood to mean conquest, while 'unity and agreement should be synonymous words, meaning the deliberate abjuring of conquest and triumphalism. Those who claim the right to kill and to die in the name of what they conceive to be Irish unity subvert not only the hope and meaning of unity, but the integrity of their own tradition.'

Turning to the role of Britain, Hume said he believed the Irish could understand their situation and grasp their opportunities only if the responsibility of Britain was realised and acknowledged. 'Britain created Northern Ireland. Britain is in charge, and cannot now be regarded as a remote and benign referee whose well-intentioned whistle the participants no longer hear in the din of conflict. Britain is as responsible today for our ills as she was in 1921 and there will be no resolution until she, like us, takes a new view of the interests of all of us.' Northern Ireland, he said, represented unfinished business in the ancient conflict between the two islands. It represented the residual area of failure of the peoples of the two islands to work out their interlocking relationships in a satisfactory way. 'We all need a new and generous vision. We need to abandon the sterile exclusivity of "ourselves alone" and we need the positive encouragement of the third party, the British Government, not by creating structures which underline and advertise our abnormality, but by patient public policy which commits them and us to a new Ireland forged by mutual respect and agreement.'

It was an inspiring speech, delivered to mixed audiences in Belfast and the Catholic priory of Benburb, Co. Tyrone, but, sadly, most of the progressive Protestants to whom he was appealing were present and none was in politics or a position of real leadership. In June, he made another impassioned appeal to them at a special SDLP conference, 'Options for a New Ireland', to commemorate the 200th anniversary of Grattan's Parliament — when Irish Protestants obtained some autonomy for Dublin from Westminster — but a hint of disillusionment was creeping in. 'Civil and religious liberty have always been the declared basis of the Protestant tradition in Ireland. Is it legitimate to ask what has happened to them in today's Ireland? Is it legitimate to ask where are the values of civil and religious liberty in the contemporary leaders of political Protestantism in Ireland? Is there indeed the slightest vestige of the fundamental Protestant values of civil and religious liberty? What has gone wrong?'

But when he reproved nationalists rhetorically — 'where is the blueprint for a pluralist Ireland?' — there was an answer from the leader of Fine Gael, Garret FitzGerald, in a speech to the same conference, acknowledging that the nationalist population held the key to political progress. It could dispel the 'legitimate fears' of Northern unionists and thereby remove the most crucial obstacle to fresh thinking about political structures. Hume's New Ireland proposals fitted in perfectly with FitzGerald's own 'constitutional crusade', launched a year before, calling on the South to accept that elements of their constitution and laws were unacceptable to the whole range of unionist opinion.

The scene was set for the most daring and far-reaching initiative which Hume had yet pioneered — a fundamental reappraisal of where Irish nationalism stood in the 1980s, to be undertaken by the three major parties in the South and the SDLP in the North. He had intended to launch it in the autumn, whether or not there had been an election to Prior's Northern Ireland Assembly, but first the party had to decide its attitude to the October poll.

Before he went on his holidays, to Villiers le Bois, an idyllic French village in Burgundy, with only one public telephone, Hume had a brief meeting with party officials to test the mood. Pressure was building up from the Mallon wing, representing the old-style nationalists, for a boycott of the election in the likelihood that the British would drop it. But Hume was unwilling to commit the party to abstentionism, at a time when it was threatened by Sinn Fein, and a decision was postponed until late August. His first instinct was to go into the Assembly, challenge the Unionists on power-sharing right away and walk out, having exposed their intransigence. Not only would it avoid abstention, but it would make a powerful political point, as well as ensuring an income for several members who had sacrificed their livelihoods for non-paying politics.

When he eventually returned from France, the story had leaked to the Press that the party was almost in a state of civil war, with the boycotters in the ascendant. Hume's view was that if the election took place, and the SDLP opted out, several distortions could occur. Sinn Fein might fight the election anyway, but even if they withdrew and there was a 60 per cent turnout, the Government might argue that it was a representative vote. Alliance candidates and independents like Paddy Devlin might poll well, leaving the Assembly looking credible and the SDLP in the wilderness. Even when you are saying 'no', he told the party executive in Dungannon, you have to show you have support for such a stand. Until he spoke, opinion was swinging strongly towards a boycott, to stop the election, but immediately it fell in behind him. The legendary powers of persuasion had triumphed, as they had so often before, leading respected politicians to despair. 'There's no point in opposing him,' one said. 'He always gets his way.' Others however, felt that if Hume had moved more quickly, returning from his holiday to quell the rebellion, he could have achieved his original objective. He had been feeling sluggish, mentally and physically, all year, and discovered only in December that he had needed medical treatment. Asked if he had not felt depressed, he told doctors that he had thought it was due to the political situation.

A few members of the SDLP executive would have supported the tactic of fighting the Assembly election on the basis of attending, and then walking out, but Hume did not raise it, being convinced the party would not wear it and that the public would not understand. The best hope of avoiding a boycott, he knew, was a compromise: to fight, but not to sit in the Assembly. While Mallon did his best to oppose this course, urging that the two propositions be taken separately – to contest and not to take Assembly seats – he eventually had to admit defeat, by about fourteen votes to seven, having obtained a promise that there would be no second thoughts on attendance after the election. Such a retreat was never contemplated by Hume, who was adamant that the SDLP would not attend any Assembly without another election. Once again Hume had a brand new proposition to win the floating voters, thought out during lazy days in the French sun. It was not enough, he said, for nationalists to reject British proposals, without having any credible alternative of their own. In the South there was no unity about unity, so why not, he asked, try an Irish initiative for a change and set up a body to devise a common nationalist approach, using the election for a Northern mandate?

It was a master stroke, giving the SDLP something positive to put before the nationalist voters, in an otherwise negative and pointless election. But while cynical commentators regarded it as a gimmick, to hold the party together, they overlooked the SDLP's deadly serious approach to manifesto commitments. Everything that had been promised, from the first Assembly to Europe, it had tried to deliver, over a period of years, and the Forum was no exception. As Hume put it in his message to voters, entitled 'Stand Firm', the SDLP found the terms on which the Assembly might acquire power unworkable and, after three unsuccessful attempts to get agreement with Unionists, was not going to pretend it could achieve the impossible. Instead, it sought a mandate to put an alternative New Ireland plan on the table, so that 'the real dialogue' could begin.

Even so, it was a difficult election for the SDLP to fight, on the same semi-abstentionist ticket as Sinn Fein, still benefitting from hunger-strike sympathy. A younger generation of unemployed Catholic voters knew nothing about the SDLP's fight for civil rights and, with only the experience of a decade of violence, turned instinctively to Sinn Fein, as the SDLP had warned. All along, Prior had thought Hume was bluffing about the party's dilemma over the Assembly, but the results proved who was right. From a standing start,

Sinn Fein polled 10 per cent of the vote, capturing five seats and establishing itself as a major threat to the constitutional nationalism of the SDLP, which won fourteen seats and had 18.8 per cent of the vote. The Official Unionists made a comeback against the extremism of Paisley's DUP, by 29.7 per cent to 23 per cent, but otherwise Prior's gamble had only added to the instability.

With both nationalist parties refusing to take their seats, the Assembly had no chance of acquiring devolved powers, so Unionists took out their frustration on Seamus Mallon, who had stood for election knowing that as an Irish Senator he was disqualified as a member of a 'foreign parliament'. His appointment by his old friend Haughey had been a bone of contention among some party members who resented the Fianna Fáil connection, but Mallon, contrary to newspaper reports, had heard about the nomination through Hume and had consulted with another colleague. He had three conditions: that Hume approved, that he would be free to act and speak as he wished and that he did not take any party whip. When all three were met, he accepted the same day and automatically disqualified himself from any Stormont Assembly, unless the British chose to change the law. They did not and the Official Unionist court action to unseat him, followed shortly after by the loss of the controversial Senate seat, set the seal on the Assembly so far as the SDLP was concerned. Although they continued to get Assembly literature – until the Unionists stopped it – and at any time could have walked in and collected up to £20,000 a year each in salary and expenses, they preferred to go without. For men who were still expected to act as contituency representatives it was a major sacrifice and one that few of them could afford.

At the time Mallon had been appointed to the Senate, Haughey surrendered another safe seat – when the Fianna Fáil majority was on a knife-edge – to John Robb, the Ballymoney-based surgeon, who had long been admired in the South. Initially he turned it down, on the grounds that the association with Fianna Fáil might compromise him politically, and Haughey agreed to his suggestion of substituting a like-minded Belfast professional from Robb's newly-formed New Ireland Group, a mainly Protestant organisation hoping to act as a catalyst for reform, North and South. But after accepting, the substitute had second thoughts, and finally Robb agreed to the nomination as an independent on virtually his own terms. Unlike Mallon, he was renominated by FitzGerald after Fianna Fáil was

242

ousted by a Fine Gael-Labour coalition in December 1982, but it was ironic that Haughey, so hated by unionists, had made the first imaginative leap in recent times and nominated Northerners to the national Senate.

As long as the Assembly lasted, in its function of scrutinising departments of government, it was impossible for Prior to take any positive initiative that the Assembly members would not block. For Hume this was proof of the amateurish approach of the British to the Northern Ireland problem; regardless of the lack of experience of successive Ministers in Belfast, the top civil servants were regularly changed just as they were beginning to make a contribution. With no daylight showing inside Northern Ireland, Hume increasingly turned his attention to Brussels, Washington, Dublin and to London, where the challenge of a general election to Westminster could not be long delayed. In view of the rise of Sinn Fein, his old reluctance to get enmeshed in the London scene was breaking down. He felt he was now experienced enough, through Europe, to make the most of the opportunity of influencing British policy at source and, although a number of new seats had been carved out along the border as if they had been designed for the SDLP's benefit, there were no more safe seats anywhere.

But first there was the need to construct a rational nationalist policy, supported by all the democratic parties in favour of Irish unity, and to do that Hume had to sell his idea in Dublin. Haughey had always been the most receptive, since he had begun the Anglo-Irish talks process and had worked closely with the SDLP in rejecting the Prior initiative, which was seen as an unprofitable alternative to the London-Dublin axis. After the Falklands war and Haughey's criticism of Prior's lack of consultation with Britain's inter-governmental partner, London was in no mood for concessions, so instead Fianna Fáil and the SDLP worked together on an all-Ireland initiative, on the lines of a permanent North-South assembly or council. FitzGerald was thinking along similar lines, although he wanted Unionists invited, and kept insisting on this, to make it easier for unofficial spokesmen to attend. When Hume telephoned him in Pittsburgh in October, FitzGerald read out a passage of a speech he was making, expanding on his ideas, and the two agreed to keep in touch. By January 1983, Hume was clear about what he wanted – 'a Council for a New Ireland where all constitutional politicians committed to a new Ireland would together define what we really wish this new Ireland to be'. He asked parties in the Republic to 'join with us in abandoning rhetoric and, by placing their cards on the table, show what sort of role there will be for the Protestant community, what share of power, what safeguards, what sort of economic situation and what would be the relations between Church and State'. With FitzGerald back in power and Haughey reeling from internal party battles, Hume was reasonably optimistic about his chances, but although a New Ireland Council fitted in with FitzGerald's unsuccessful constitutional crusade to make the South more attractive to the North, it was too narrowly based for the new Fine Gael-Labour Coalition Cabinet. Most of them were wary about giving Irish unity such a high priority, at a time when the country was fighting for economic survival – with a foreign debt proportionally greater than Poland's – and insisted on throwing the debate open to pro-unionist parties. The Fine Gael Cabinet members, in particular, still saw power-sharing in the North as feasible, and one of them was in regular contact with the Alliance Party.

By March, Hume had the broad support of only three members of the fifteen-strong Dublin Cabinet – FitzGerald, Foreign Minister Peter Barry and Justice Minister Michael Noonan – and when a story appeared in the *Irish Times* suggesting Government backing for a loose series of consultations between all political parties North and South, far removed from the council concept, Hume decided it was time for a showdown. Coming straight from Europe, he launched into a day of frantic negotiations, shuttling between the offices of the Taoiseach and Haughey, at times pleading and at other times demanding, in an attempt to get agreement. At first, FitzGerald sent Haughey a draft of the announcement he was going to make, which the Fianna Fáil leader thought had glaring defects, and it was only after tough negotiations, leading to extensive alterations, that the text was finally agreed – with Hume effectively getting his way in all matters except the name, 'Forum' for his 'Council'. His trump card, all along, had been his insistence on the need to bolster constitutional nationalism in the North, so that the Sinn Fein threat should not grow to destabilise the South as well. It was a telling argument, as Sinn Fein flexed its political muscles increasingly in the Republic's council elections, and it helped force the archenemies, FitzGerald and Haughey, into their first private encounter for months, taking just two minutes to seal the bargain.

FitzGerald was taking a risk with his own decidedly unenthusiastic

Government, and several agreed in the understanding that the Forum was a political ploy, to upstage Haughey, and would never be convened. Sinn Fein could take part, but only on the same basis as the others, renouncing violence, which it refused to do. The agreed statement, calling for the setting up of 'a forum for consultations on the manner in which lasting peace and stability can be achieved in a new Ireland through the democratic process', represented a personal triumph for Hume. He had obtained a commitment from parties representing four-fifths of the people of the island to define for the first time what they meant by Irish unity, and he had a policy alternative to the Northern Ireland Assembly.

It remained to be seen how important the Catholic voters of the North would deem it, but Hume had proved that the long years of cultivating his image in Dublin, and his good relations with all the main parties had paid off. (Conscious of the shifting sands of Southern politics, he never spoke to one party leader without contacting the other.) He had his detractors – like Conor Cruise O'Brien, who wasted no time calling it the 'make believe' Forum and advised Hume to stay at home – but when the hero of Derry turned to Dublin for help, he could not be denied. He had succeeded in posing the questions about unity by consent which no one really wanted to hear, where Garret FitzGerald had failed on his own.

It was difficult to define his appeal in the South, except that he had represented the embattled, resourceful Northerner throughout the Troubles who, unlike the Alliance leadership or Gerry Fitt, never forgot his nationalist roots. His friends and supporters were everywhere, in the civil service, the church, politics and the media, building his reputation as a good companion in any social situation, as well as a deep political thinker. To the media, he was always available, ready to drive to Dublin or Belfast day or night and guaranteed to fill any spot with good sense and good humour. Wherever he was, there was a plan being hatched, or an inside story to be told, and that was unfailingly attractive to journalists or politicians. Many held that he had 'bumped' the Republic into a reappraisal of its commitment to unity, against its will, but the indisputable fact was that the national question had dominated Southern politics throughout the 1970s. Rightly or wrongly, the South accepted Northern nationalists as part of its tradition, and would have rejected any politician who suggested otherwise.

There was another side to Hume, which few knew about, but

245

which explained how he recharged his batteries in the political off-season. For years his rented cottage in Bunbeg was his home from home in August, and he would hold court for a wide selection of writers, musicians, poets, playwrights, civil servants, journalists, priests and even politicians who would just happen to be passing. The talk would be of anything under the sun except politics, and to whet the appetite there might be a massed climb of Errigal mountain – which he himself would invariably miss – or a stroll down to the harbour to hear the latest fishing news. (From his days with Atlantic Harvest, Hume knew practically every fisherman in Co. Donegal and claimed to be able to distinguish between, say, a Foyle and a Gweedore salmon.) The finale of the holiday would be a dinner party, organised by Hume, after which everyone would be expected to perform a party piece. For someone who had a reputation for never switching off politically, he knew how to enjoy himself, and his storytelling and mimicry of fellow politicians were of professional quality. At party conferences he could be the life and soul, until dawn, and his memory for names and faces was prodigious, as was his patience in suffering fools gladly. Always he had a particular charisma with women, who were the backbone of every election campaign.

While he could be disorganised in his private life, landing in foreign airports without money, forgetting about meals and never wearing a watch, he prepared for meetings with Prime Ministers as meticulously as he researched a topic for the Columcille Debating Society, to the point where he knew the arguments of the other person as well as he knew his own. Like many successful men, he could sleep anywhere, at any time, especially when travelling. Deep inside, he remained a shy, private person, finding it unnatural to approach strangers, even at election times, and tending to keep his thoughts to himself. Even close colleagues, who admired the way he rose to every occasion, apparently paralysing even better minds than his own, would admit, apologetically, that they did not really know him. If he lacked social graces, at times, he had Pat, his ever-present wife and mother of five children – three girls Therese (now 23), Aine (22) and Maureen (12), and two boys, Aidan (20), and John (16) – to prevent feelings being hurt. So many demands were made of him that he could not meet them all, and his life was only possible if he kept strictly to his priorities.

The agreement on the Forum came in the nick of time, for inside six weeks Thatcher called a general election, giving the Dublin

Government just enough time for a public launch before the electioneering began in the North. The opening ceremony in Dublin Castle was a golden opportunity for Hume to spell out, to a television audience that was still unconvinced, the need for change: 'Unless we in common find the necessary commitment – the determination to move mountains – we will all be engulfed in a furious torrent of hatred, violence and despair. . . there is no room, there is no time for opportunism or righteousness or indeed for what is normally understood as "politics". Are we, the nationalists of Ireland, prepared to pay the painful political and economic price that this will involve? Do we have any idea of what that price will be? I fear that many of us either do not or would prefer not to. The work of this Forum will for ever deprive us of the excuse of ignorance or distraction.'

He had this message for the unionists: 'We commit ourselves to take you and your convictions with deep seriousness in our efforts to understand the crisis that confronts us all. Our aim is neither conquest nor coercion; it is primarily to understand each other so that we can solve this crisis with your agreement and your support.' As a symbol of the new Ireland, he chose the now empty throne of King William of Orange in Dublin Castle. 'Let that throne stand today not for a nostalgic order now gone forever, not for its triumphant removal by the new order in this state; let that vacant seat continue unoccupied and become a powerful symbol to both our traditions – that neither will conquer the other, but that both will be preserved and revered and cherished in the new Ireland that we set out to build today.'

The Taoiseach, Garret FitzGerald, made a low key speech, emphasising that the heart of the problem was the two identities, which had failed to accommodate each other in the present structures. 'So far as we are concerned, the agenda excludes nothing. . . The price of failure would be far too high in human terms for any shirking to be permissible in our part.' But Charles Haughey began at his most hawkish, picking up a hardline speech by the Coalition Foreign Minister Peter Barry that the British military and political presence distorted the situation, and insisting that peace and stability could be secured only 'under new all-Ireland structures in the context of which an orderly British withdrawal can take place'. But a new constitution would be needed and he admitted intriguingly that 'we may have to consider some degree of autonomy for Northern

Ireland, be it on the basis of the same area, or a smaller one'. Dick Spring, the new Labour leader, pitched his speech more at the faults in Southern society: 'The Forum affords us the opportunity to analyse and discuss the nature of society that we wish to see evolve on this island and challenges us in the Republic to face up to the reality that our society, just as much as Northern Ireland, will have to change if we are serious in our aspiration of Irish unity. Are we prepared to make these changes? That is a fundamental question for this Forum.'

Ten days later, the Catholic electorate gave its interim verdict in the Westminster election of 9 June 1983 and clearly it was not bowled over by the Forum promises. Out of the seventeen constituencies, six were regarded as marginals and only one of these – John Hume's Foyle – went to the SDLP. Both the Protestant and Catholic votes were split, but the unionists plumped for the candidate who had the best chance of winning – whether OUP or DUP – and the nationalists split too evenly between the SDLP and Sinn Fein to make their votes count. Between them, the Unionists picked up fifteen of the seventeen seats, with 60 per cent of the vote, while the SDLP and Sinn Fein got one each. The combined anti-unionist total of 31.3 per cent, made up of the SDLP's 17.9 per cent and Sinn Fein's 13.4 per cent, represented the highest-ever nationalist vote in a general election, reflecting the changing religious balance, as well as hitherto-untapped republican support.

It was a bitterly disappointing result for Hume, who had hoped to lead a team of three or four to Westminster, and even the knowledge that at least 10 per cent of Sinn Fein's 102,601 votes had been personated was no consolation. The Catholic electorate had been warned, from pulpits and election platforms, that a vote for Sinn Fein would be read as a vote for the IRA, and yet the SDLP's lead, which had been 8.7 per cent in October, had been reduced to 4.5 per cent eight months later. Sinn Fein which had threatened to seize power in Ireland 'with an Armalite and a ballot paper' was acceptable to 42.6 per cent of nationalists, up from 35 per cent, and a man described as a former IRA commander, Gerry Adams, had replaced Gerry Fitt in West Belfast. Fitt blamed the SDLP for splitting the moderate vote, but the same charge might have been levelled at him since he finished third behind Joe Hendron, and this time the party had stuck to its guns by nominating candidates everywhere, even in Fermanagh. Those who watched the West Belfast

248

ballot boxes being opened and who studied the fall in the Unionist vote were certain that many Protestants, perhaps obeying the urging of their paramilitary leaders, had plumped for Fitt as their best bet to keep Adams out.

Hume was still on his own, as the only professional politician in the party, and the burden he had hoped would be lightened weighed on him more heavily than ever. Mallon missed narrowly in Armagh, let down by Newry's stay-at-home voters, and Eddie McGrady was just pipped by Enoch Powell in South Down. The after-effects of the hunger-strike and the experience gained in the October election had raised Sinn Fein to new heights and although they traded Adams' win in West Belfast for Carron's defeat by Unionists in Fermanagh they came within seventy-eight votes of having Danny Morrison elected in Mid-Ulster. British commentators were jumping to conclusions that Sinn Fein were the new force in nationalist politics, ignoring their bully-boy tactics and blatant personation, but Hume, the political operator, was already pacing the Westminster corridors, renewing political contacts and preparing the next stage of his New Ireland strategy. Since Fitt had severed his SDLP connections, the British Commons had not heard the voice of constitutional national-ism or a Catholic critique of their actions in Northern Ireland, so Hume wasted no time swearing the oath – though he privately admitted it stuck in his throat – and making his maiden speech.

To maintain their token independence, the Unionists sat on the Opposition benches, so it was from his place in front of Enoch Powell, and behind the SDP, that Hume rose to his feet on 28 June, in no way overawed by the occasion. He was brief, direct and simple, setting out the terms on which he, a nationalist, approached a British Parliament and although he had notes to remind him of the points he wanted to make, he found he had no need of them. Recalling Margaret Thatcher's customary claim, he asked: 'Does any member believe that Northern Ireland is as British as Finchley? Do any members honestly believe that in their hearts? If so, where is the evidence of their concern? The truth is that if every member spoke his heart, he would say that he has psychologically withdrawn from Northern Ireland. Britain and Northern Ireland would be healthier places if that psychological reality were translated into political reality.'

He looked at the three elements in the situation – the loyalists, who had taken up the violent attitude of demanding the exclusive exercise of power; the nationalists whose argument was 'based substantially on two powerful strands of Irish tradition, the Gaelic and the Catholic, to the exclusion of the Protestants'; the British Government and Parliament which created a majority by a head count and, therefore, had made sectarianism 'the motive force of politics'. In a letter to Michael Collins in 1922, Churchill had written: 'There is nothing we should like better than to see the North and South join hands in an all-Ireland assembly without prejudice to the existing rights of Irishmen'. It was not asking a great deal of the Government, said Hume, to adopt as policy that statement.

He had staked his ground, as an Irish nationalist in the parliamentary tradition of Parnell, but he remained unimpressed and unseduced by the clublike atmosphere. Westminster should be a place for getting things done, he thought, and he compared it unfavourably to the American Congress, where members had staff paid for by the public purse in Washington and the home constituency. The British system was ineffective and impotent, but he was determined to use it as best he could, knowing from experience that the vast majority of MPs were lazy and unprepared to match his prodigious workload. In a not untypical two-week period in September 1983, his itinerary was Boston, Belfast, Dublin, Derry, Donegal, Montpellier, Dublin, Derry, Strasbourg, Oxford, New York, Washington, Baltimore and Dublin. At each stop, he had to be in top form, contending with the demands of Prime Ministers, European Commissioners and Congress members, with TV and radio interviewers tracking him everywhere.

But the debate on hanging, which came early in July, saw the Commons at its best, on a free vote, and Hume's attack on the principle was one of the contributions – along with that of Ken Maginnis, a Unionist and former UDR officer – which helped swing the vote strongly against capital punishment. There was the satisfaction, too, of seeing how an Assembly vote for hanging had no effect whatsoever on the Government, compared with Hume's own single speech at Westminster. Fitt's elevation to the peerage, in appreciation of his stand against the IRA and his endorsement of successive Government policies on Northern Ireland – often in direct contradiction to Hume – assured a continuing hostile presence. But if Fitt had convinced most MPs that Hume was a rabid republican, it did not take long for the Derry man to correct the impression, and fill in the nuances of Irish politics which Fitt had long neglected. After his impassioned disclaimer of the Harrods bombing in December 1983, on behalf of true Irish patriotism, the subtle shades of green were becoming apparent.

Only pressure from outside, Hume now believed, could bring about a change of heart in the British, which in turn could make the unionists see differently. His argument was that a dependent political entity, based on a sectarian head count, was bound to produce sectarian politics, without any impetus for change. Consequently it had to be defused by the sovereign nation which set it up. So, between meetings of the Forum, which remained the number one priority, there were trips to America and Europe, selling the idea of putting the problem in a wider context, which only the British could bring about. On one such trip, partly funded by the Government, he travelled alongside his old enemy Ian Paisley to demonstrate in the clearest way that where jobs promotion for Northern Ireland was concerned, they were united. Some of his American supporters – and virtually all the SDLP's elected representatives – were annoyed that his presence had helped to restore Paisley's US visitor's visa, withdrawn because of his extreme speeches. But Hume was unrepentant, because of the issue involved, and when he extracted a statement of support from Edward Kennedy, Paisley was generous enough to say he could not help but welcome it.

Hume knew the risks he was taking with his own credibility by going on coast-to-coast TV with a man regarded as a hate figure, but he was straight with the viewers. 'I'm not here to pretend that I'm in agreement with this man,' he said. 'There are profound differences between us, but we are agreed that anyone who invests to create jobs in Northern Ireland will be welcomed by both sections of the community.'

His job-hunting efforts were not confined to the TV studios, for Prior had asked him to do what he could to help the Government-owned Belfast planemaker, Shorts, to obtain a valuable US Air Force contract for its small Sherpa freighter planes, against stiff Spanish/US competition. The Irish National Caucus, under Father Sean McManus, had been campaigning strongly against Shorts, on the grounds that it discriminated against Catholic workers, but Hume had no hesitation in advising Tip O'Neill and Kennedy that the order should go to Belfast. Again, his line was clear: 'Of course, Shorts discriminate against Catholics and always have done, but it would be no solution to stop jobs for Protestants. That is the road to the desert. Politically it is important to show that the power of the

Irish dimension in American politics is positive and can help everyone.' The order was landed, in March 1984, worth an initial £115 million, with a prospect of £460 million in total, and was followed by a rush of orders for Shorts' planes and missiles, many attributable to the US Government's endorsement. Any politician anywhere else in the world would have shouted from the rooftops about his connection with the deal, but although he had letters from Shorts and Jim Prior, offering to thank him for his efforts, Hume did nothing. Politically, his support for Shorts could lose him more votes than it could win, and he decided to do without the plaudits – at least until the aircraft factory opened up a plant in a Catholic area. In Irish America, it would be a decidely mixed blessing to be seen to be helping the east Belfast firm, which adopted an 'affirmative action' programme to obtain balanced recruitment only in August 1983, shortly before Hume's brief economic mission to the east coast.

In Baltimore, under attack by Noraid supporters, he suddenly spotted a familiar Derry face in the shouting crowd, so he went over to him. 'Hold on a minute,' he said. 'What I'm trying to do is prevent young people from doing what you had to do – get up and leave your home town and come here for work. I'm trying to prevent that happening and you're telling me I'm wrong. Now just say how I'm wrong.' Against that kind of rational argument, which has been John Hume's primary contribution to the long debate on Northern Ireland, there is no answer. The man turned and walked away.

20
Inside the Forum

After the inaugural meeting in the gilded splendour of St Patrick's Hall, Dublin Castle, the Forum waited for the written submissions to come in before holding the first public question-and-answer session on 21 September 1983 in the subdued brown and grey surroundings of the castle's St George's Hall. From the start if was recognised that one of the greatest difficulties facing the Forum was to show how a small, relatively impoverished Republic could possibly absorb six strife-torn and economically-depressed counties, and Hume was clear that the Forum's credibility was at stake. Rather than begin with the easier aspects of unity, it was decided to jump in at the deep end by asking two distinguished economists, with formidable qualifications for comparing North and South, to look at the economic implications and face the questions of Forum members. There was some surprise among observers not only that Sir Charles Carter, chairman of the Northern Ireland Economic Council, under British Government auspices, was asked to contribute, but that he accepted – lending special weight to the investigation. He and Portadown-born Professor Loudan Ryan, of University College Dublin, presented a fairly gloomy assessment of the prospects for a self-sufficient Ireland. Carter was dismissive of politicians' expectations that Britain would maintain a Northern subsidy long after her departure, and unfavourably compared the straight transfers of money from London to Belfast with Dublin's need to borrow to survive. It was a sobering start to the Forum's proceedings, setting the pattern of witnesses being questioned on their written submissions by spokesmen for the four parties in turn, and Charles Haughey seized the opportunity to show his contempt for economists. Rejecting suggestions that emigration might be a solution, or that Britain, the EEC or the US would refuse to give financial assistance for a reasonable period, he deliberately switched the emphasis from economics to politics: 'If economics is the dismal science, politics must be the profession of hope, and I find it hard to accept that two eminent economists could not formulate for us a prospect of an all-Ireland economic entity capable of developing its own inherent dynamic for progress, provided the political structures are right.' Outside the chamber, his comments were blunter, suggesting that the experts' analysis had been so much manure.

For some, the learning process in the Forum was more difficult than for others, but, as the members gathered at regular intervals to quiz the spokesmen for different points of view, they were forced to confront facts and figures about their political aspirations from which they had always run away. The North, they were learning, was different, and to say that partition had failed was not enough. Two separate states had grown up, over sixty years, with relatively little in common except language and geography, and to bring them closer together would obviously entail sacrifices on both sides, with no guarantee of success. It was clear why the South's politicians had preferred rhetoric to action, but as the leaders delved deeper into the issues, and concentrated on the Northern question for longer than any Irish politicians had done since 1920, their understanding of the subtleties increased. Even the media, inclined to dismiss the whole exercise as a lifeline for the SDLP, were forced to pay increasing attention to a Forum which was occupying so much of the time of the country's leading politicians. Hume would fly in from the four corners of Europe or America to attend, and it became almost a contest for the three Southern leaders to maintain their attendance record regardless of alternative commitments. To maintain secrecy, most of the work was done in Leinster House by the big four themselves, over a conference or a luncheon table, with only the secretariat present, or chairman Dr Colm O'hEocha. Their agreed conclusions were reported back to their party delegations and finally to the plenary sessions, giving an opportunity for discussion, but at the end of the day the leaders had to bear the responsibility for agreement or disagreement.

The first public sessions helped to establish the Forum's credentials, and to underline this professional approach a number of reports were commissioned from independent experts to provide the statistical and informational base that had been lacking from so much discussion of unity. 'The Cost of Violence' helped set the scene, attempting the near impossible task of estimating what the Irish and British economies had lost, as a result of the Troubles. The direct cost, in extra security and compensation was plotted at £5,255 million in the North and £1,019 million in the South, making a total of £6,274 million.

The figures for indirect costs, in terms of lost output and damage to tourism, were £3,680 million in the North and £1,110 million in the South, putting the grand total of exchequer and economic costs at £11,064 million, on 1982 values. In 1982 alone, the cost of violence was estimated at £1,054 million in the North and £268 million in the South – showing how the picture was deteriorating, despite a decrease in terrorist incidents. More hopeful was a subsequent study on 'The Economic Effects of the Division of Ireland since 1920' which countered some of the pessimism of the earlier accounts by finding that standards of living, based on purchasing power, were broadly similar North and South, as were standards of health and education. Although rates of social security benefits were generally higher in the South, fewer people were eligible. Northern Ireland's financial dependence was underlined by the fact that the British subvention in 1981–2 represented 31.5 per cent of the North's gross domestic product and over 70 per cent of the province's annual income was generated by the Government, in the public sector.

For their 1983 summer break, the Humes had retired again, with the two youngest members of the family, to the same Burgundy village. Before leaving, the SDLP leader had circulated a confidential document, 'The Fundamental Problems' – intending to focus the minds of Forum members on the difficult adjustments that had to be made in an accommodation with Northern unionists – and he returned to find it had been leaked to the Press. The publicity was unintentional, but the response was good, and Hume's analysis was to form the basis of the future work of the Forum, being carried over into the final report. He had asked the question: 'Why is it that the constitutional nationalist politicians have hitherto not succeeded in persuading Britain to reassess its own position adequately?' His answer was that 'the problems posed by the loyalist section of the community have been, and remain, the major pretext for the inadequate responsiveness of the British attitude'. Mindful of Southern feelings, he queried whether Irish nationalists adequately understood the mentality of loyalism, and if they had demonstrated their capacity to accommodate the loyalist tradition. The Forum, he said, had to face both these questions.

There were other key issues to be addressed: 'How could we

demonstrate that by unity we simply mean comprehensive agreement – freely arrived at on the structures of a new Ireland, no more, no less? How could we demonstrate with the maximum credibility that we are, with the support of our people, ready to face some of the more expensive or otherwise uncongenial adjustments this would involve for the Irish State as at present structured and administered? For example, in the difficult area of church-state relations as they affect family law, education and the administration of the health services?'

Having identified the principles at stake, Hume had then suggested three ways of accommodating them, which eventually turned out to be the three models examined by the Forum – the unitary state, the federal/confederal system and joint sovereignty/authority. He had also asked for studies on the cost of the violence, and the effect on the two economies, in line with his general thesis that the eventual Forum report should be low-key and analytical rather than declaiming traditional solutions that could not be put to work. His approach was that once the involvement of Britain and the unionists had been accepted, the main objective was to create a process through which there could be discussions and negotiations in a new framework. If the strongest proposition was to be the main subject for discussion, the report would be inviting instant rejection, and the whole case would be lost. But if the bargaining started at a low level, Hume thought, the chances of delivery would be maximised. His strategy was to concentrate on an analysis of the Troubles, never done before in formal documents, accompanied by independent professional studies of the economics and the legal implications. The documentation of the Forum was intended to be the most comprehensive review of Irish partition which had ever been done, with a value for the future of Anglo-Irish relations which would long outlast the deliberations.

The leaking of the 'Fundamental Problems' document had helped to inject a sense of reality, at a time when the Republic was agonising over a referendum effectively banning any future consideration of abortion legislation. But later, when the *Irish Press* revealed the contents of the Forum report's first three chapters of historical analysis, the leaders decided it was time to pull down the shutters. From then on the steering committee of the four party leaders retained all the draft documents, and Forum members had a sight of them only during their meetings, before handing them back. This naturally enhanced the importance of the steering committee and reduced the role of the ordinary members, who claimed that the Forum had been 'hijacked', turning them into proof-readers. The leakages provided an excuse, but some believed that the party leaders' takeover was inevitable to make progress with difficult sections of the report, on which all twenty-seven members might have a say. Even the introduction had been fought over, line by line, and progress was laboured.

Considering the overwhelming influence of the Roman Catholic Church in the institutional and political life of the Republic, and the perception of it in Northern Ireland, initial contacts between the Forum and the Hierarchy were surprisingly casual. At first the church representing 97 per cent of the population in the South and 40 per cent in the North was left out of the original invitation list for written submissions, by a bureaucratic mix-up, and it was only after the Protestant churches had replied that the Hierarchy met in November to organise a response. They chose to make a written submission, confirming Forum suspicions that the church wanted to avoid an open inquisition. But when a condensed version of the document, concentrating on its negative aspects, was leaked to the Press, followed by the entire text, the Northern politicians saw red. It was feared that the document, unless it were explained, could justify Protestant hostility to unity, and when Forum chairman Dr O'hEocha contacted Cardinal Ó Fiaich in Armagh, he found a willing response.

As published, the document was an orthodox exposition of the Irish Catholic Church's conservative stance on all the major social issues of the day, without attempting to address the changed circumstances in a new Ireland, and, hardly surprisingly, it had a poor reception North and South. Hume was prepared to rely on the oral submission to give a different slant, arguing that on paper the church could hardly depart from its traditional teaching. But even within the church there was concern at the document's blunt reiteration of Vatican doctrine, without emphasising the need for reconciliation of the two traditions on the island, or acceptance of minority rights.

A section which particularly aroused SDLP anger was a long philosophical dissertation on the meaning of pluralism, containing three sentences which could confirm the innermost fears of Protestants: 'A Catholic country or its government, where there is a very substantial Catholic ethos and consensus, should not feel it necessary to apologise that its legal system, constitutional and statute, reflects Catholic values. Such a legal system may sometimes be represented as offensive to minorities. But the rights of a minority are not more sacred than the rights of the majority.' Pluralism was a value only through the contribution it could make to the good, and was a subordinate, not the ultimate value. 'Divorced from its relation to the common good, it tends towards division and disintegration,' the document said. Elsewhere, it was even more lukewarm: 'Where the offence to the moral principles of the majority of the citizens would be disproportionately serious, it is not unreasonable to require sacrifice of minorities in the interests of the common good'.

Liberal commentators were disappointed or outraged by the submission's defensive, divisive tone, and Protestant politicians gladly seized on it as proof of the unchanging nature of the Irish Catholic Church, with its clear commitment to majority rule. But it came as no surprise to those who knew the Hierarchy's position in the past. In 1969, Cardinal Conway had told Tom Caldwell, the Independent Unionist MP, who was the first politician he had received at Armagh, that the church sought a united Ireland only 'in the fullness of time', after there was a sizeable majority of Catholics in the North. The church, in fact, was not opposed to the Union and did not want a new constitution in Ireland to cater for a million Protestants. Cardinal Conway had also agreed that at that time over 80 per cent of Catholics did not want a united Ireland in the short term. Although Cardinal Ó Fiaich had never concealed his own nationalist opinions, the Forum submission suggested that the church's attitude had not greatly changed. Neither the Catholic Church nor, therefore, the Republic itself, was the threat that Ulster unionists imagined.

The television cameras of RTE provided a sense of occasion as the bishops and lay representatives took their places for the Forum's last oral submission in February 1984, but there was no need to stress the importance of the first public questioning of spokesmen in the long history of the Irish Catholic Church. The nation watched in rapt attention as the bishops were brought, however respectfully, to account for their attitudes and actions, past and present, and this time there were no slip-ups. Bishop Cahal Daly, an eminently wise, courageous old Northern cleric who had the advantage of several years as an academic at Queen's University to teach him about Protestant sensitivities, trod warily over the ground that had been ploughed up so crudely in the written submission, and conveyed a generosity that had previously been lacking. 'The Catholic Church in Ireland,' he said, 'totally rejects the concept of a confessional state. We have not sought and we do not seek a Catholic State for a Catholic people. We believe that the alliance of Church and State is harmful for the Church and harmful for the State.' Bishop Daly said he was conscious of Protestant fears for their heritage, but it was not for the church to formulate proposals for constitutional change or to draft blueprints for a future Ireland. 'What we here and now declare is that we would raise our voices to resist any constitutional proposals which might infringe or might imperil the civil and religious rights and liberties cherished by Northern Protestants.'

All round, it was an impressive performance by the church panel of four clerics and two lay people, putting the Forum back on course. Only churlish Northern listeners were left to wonder why, if the church was so concerned about Protestant rights in the thirty-two counties, it could not be equally concerned about the rights of the 3 per cent of Protestants in the twenty-six counties. At one stage Dr Dermot O'Mahony, the auxiliary Bishop of Dublin, agreed that minority rights were important, and that there could be many situations where the rights of the minority were far more compelling than the rights of the majority. But his examples of such minorities were the 'travelling people' (gypsies), the unemployed and the homeless – not the Protestants in the South.

Only the Church of Ireland, among the Protestant churches, made a formal submission, complaining bitterly about the heavily Catholic bias in the Republic's family laws, but individual ministers represented the Presbyterian and Methodist traditions, making similar points in a way that was seldom heard publicly. Two unusually open-minded Official Unionists from Newtownards, the brothers Christopher and Michael McGimpsey, bravely ignored party policy and made written and oral submissions, arguing that the Irish identity of nationalists could be accommodated within Northern Ireland. The Alliance Party voice was also heard, although the party had risked a split by refusing to reply formally. Spokesmen representing the Protestant or unionist traditions were accorded special treatment, and even the UDA, through its political wing, had planned to make a formal submission until it changed its mind after the republican massacre of three Protestants at Darkley, south Armagh. Based on independence for Ulster, the submission was later published by the UDA, without explanation.

St Patrick's Day 1984 was looming, with its opportunity for a blaze of publicity in America, but the Forum timetable was slipping — Fianna Fáil were hoping, as usual, for FitzGerald's Government to fall — and the participants felt that the politics of a March launching would have been wrong. The Forum report was aimed at the British and the Northern unionists, and to time it so that the major thrust was in America would have annoyed London and encouraged Protestants to see the exercise as a foreign-based attack on their territorial integrity. FitzGerald, nevertheless, had a series of high-level meetings and speeches planned in the US, in which he strongly pushed the Forum strategy for long-term peace and stability, criticising Britain for its inactivity. In an address to Congress, and at a White House lunch on 17 March, the necessity for a British change of heart was urged, without more than a polite response. Hume, too, had a whirlwind ten-day tour of east and west-coast America, returning straight into a Forum steering committee meeting.

Hume was always closer in temperament to the conciliatory FitzGerald, but his relations with Haughey improved noticeably. Both had carved out their own success unaided, and had a mental toughness and political agility that made them respect each other, even when Haughey's leadership problems in 1982–3 and the unsavoury revelations of his means of clinging to office threatened to discredit the whole Forum concept in Protestant eyes. While others regarded Haughey as a pure opportunist, without any real conviction about unity, except for the political advantage he got from playing the green card, Hume would defend him. The unashamed nationalists in the SDLP always regarded Hume as a fellow nationalist at heart, and the experience of working in a Dublin context for eleven months had sharpened his sense of nationalism. Haughey and Hume were the key figures in the steering committee, as Haughey had a strong grip on his party in the Forum and Hume could deliver any agreement with FitzGerald and Spring. Both the meetings and the working lunches were businesslike affairs, and Spring's main, and, at times, vital contribution was to release the tension with his dry sense of humour. He was absent in America for a time, but otherwise the main Southern protagonists had almost a 100 per cent attendance record, devoting hours of precious time, in fifty-six meetings over eleven months, to a long-term project, while the short term was filled up with the Republic's fight for economic survival. When Hume, in the final ceremony, thanked all three for their devotion to duty, the catch in his throat and tears in his eyes showed that he meant it. In the plenary sessions, where the input from the Southern parties, especially Fianna Fáil, was often un-impressive, Hume played an astutely low-key role, mindful of the frustrations of his party colleagues, cut off from the summit negotiations. No attempt was made to stop them blowing off steam, whether or not they were complying with party policy. Mallon was a constant critic in the latter stages, siding with Haughey on the crunch questions, but, as usual, acting as the keeper of the SDLP's nationalist soul in a way that Hume could understand. The two had a curiously combative relationship, mixed with a fair measure of respect. Relations were particularly strained when Mallon revealed that a crude bugging device had been found in a house where he had been staying, and vehemently attacked FitzGerald's handling of the incident. But the work of the Forum went on undisturbed by this or by sharp Dáil exchanges between Government and Opposition, and when Hume needed help in the last days of the Forum, it was to Mallon that he turned.

Agreement had been obtained relatively easily on the chapters dealing with the 'Origins of the Problem' and 'Assessment of the Present Problem' – although FitzGerald had some difficulties with his party, and his own conscience, over the decidedly greenish colour of the analysis, which he knew would antagonise the British. He allowed it to pass, confident that in the crucial final chapters the wording would be that of the SDLP, Labour and Fine Gael, rather than Fianna Fáil. Whatever fudging there was in interpretation, Haughey was accepting the validity of the unionist tradition – implying a continuing British involvement. He was also forced into accepting that a new and sovereign Ireland must come about with the consent of 'the people of the South and the North', acknowledging separate referenda or elections, although he had wanted to lump the two together as 'the North and South'.

For weeks a potential split had been building up on the question of what the report's recommendations should be on the framework of a new Ireland, and Hume's position was that it should be left open, after investigation of the three basic options. He wanted a statement in favour of the principle of Irish unity, without specifying the form, except to say that there were 'different ways to unity'. Haughey, however, backed and at times pressurised by the hardline Ray

MacSharry, was equally adamant that the unitary state model should be proposed as the only means of achieving long-term peace and stability. To no one's surprise, Mallon supported Haughey rather than Hume, and this encouraged Fianna Fáil to dig in their heels, arguing that if the Forum declined to give a clear lead it would be handing over the nationalist aspiration to the IRA. On Friday 13 April, before Holy Week, the deadlock was complete, and with the media trumpeting an imminent breakdown, Hume allowed domestic considerations to come first and announced that he would not be available for the weekend. In fact he and Pat were flying to Manchester for the wedding of their second daughter, Aine, a medical student at Manchester University, to an English fellow student. Anywhere in Ireland, as the Humes had found at Therese's graduation in Dublin the previous year, attention was focused on John, but in Lancashire he was just the father of the bride. For a day he left Forum worries behind, to join in the celebrations in an ordinary housing estate where Aine and her husband did spare-time social work, in the Hume tradition.

Before he left, Hume detailed Mallon to make a last attempt to patch up the differences and avoid the unthinkable prospect of the Forum delivering two reports. Already the SDLP members had been told that a majority-minority report was to be the subject of a special meeting on Tuesday night, and Mallon appreciated the seriousness of the situation when the contentious chapters, which he had not previously seen, were handed to him. Nothing was said, but he suspected – wrongly as it turned out – that he had been called in with the knowledge of the other steering committee members.

Mallon took the documents home to Markethill, just over the border in Co. Armagh, and spent all day Saturday working through them in readiness for a visit by Wally Kirwan, the master draftsman on the Forum team, as well as a member of the Taioseach's Department and, ten years before, of the Sunningdale team. On Sunday they discussed at length the problem wording in the vital Chapter Five and then prepared three drafts each of the final three paragraphs. The crucial one was paragraph seven, stating a preference for one of the frameworks, because it dictated the form of the remaining two paragraphs. Haughey wanted a clear statement of support for a unitary Irish state, saying that it was the 'only structure' the Forum could recommend, while Hume and the other leaders were holding out for a broad endorsement of unity, leaving aside its

form. Mallon had gone out of his way at the January party conference to condemn such a 'dolly mixtures' approach, which, he
argued, allowed everyone to choose what colour of report they
wished, and when the drafting session broke off at ten o'clock that
night, the line was clearer.

The first meeting, at 10 am on Monday, was with Haughey, who
did not accept or reject the draft, but gave the impression that it was
along the right lines. Next Mallon tried it out on Hume, who reacted
similarly and said he would contact the others. FitzGerald was still
unhappy with the emphasis on the unitary state, rejecting the notion
that it 'alone would provide stability', and preferring his own highly
conditional approach. Changes were made and, after one more
meeting with each, Mallon knew there would be agreement.
Mallon's role as an intermediary was psychologically important, as
it involved him in finding solutions acceptable to all sides, rather
than criticising from the sidelines. He assumed the members of the
steering committee had become so weary of debating among themselves that they were glad of any assistance, especially from someone
who had Haughey's trust, and could deliver. But although
FitzGerald first learned of the Markethill meeting from newspaper
reports, he was not upset.

For Hume, there was some surprise that Haughey had not produced his own draft, and, despite being forced to accept a reasonably
strong endorsement of the unitary state, he regarded the final form of
words – proposed by FitzGerald – as the best possible. Faced with
the alternatives, Haughey wearily said to FitzGerald: 'You're the
clever one. You pick one.' The choice was that the Forum 'would
wish' to see a unitary state established, which meant that Haughey
had dropped his insistence that the unitary state was the 'only'
structure for political unity and had rejected the alternative 'best' in
favour of what Hume regarded as a weaker statement. In saying that
the Forum 'would wish' for a unitary state, the report was reducing
the recommendation to little more than an aspiration and accepting
that the agenda for negotiations would be the report as a whole,
particularly the eleven major 'realities'. Hume had had to concede
something on the SDLP position, but felt it would be understood that
nationalist parties had to see a unitary state as 'the ideal framework',
while the preceding paragraph pointed to 'many varying constitutional and other structures of political unity' such as those of
Australia, France, Italy, Spain, Switzerland and the USA. That

paragraph, together with the last one in the section, saying that the parties in the Forum 'also remain open to discuss other views which may contribute to political development', was Hume's signal that there could be unity and diversity.

One of the few clashes between Hume and FitzGerald involved a reference in the 'realities' section to the British guarantee to the Northern majority, over which the SDLP delegates were relieved at last to be on the same side as Haughey. FitzGerald put up a long struggle, arguing the Fine Gael case that the guarantee was irrelevant, but the report described it as 'inhibiting' to dialogue and 'removing the incentive' to find a solution. Only FitzGerald's long friendship with Hume prevented lasting damage to their relationship.

The next day, the parties had their say in the plenary session and, not surprisingly, the Labour delegates protested about the stridency of the nationalist case, eventually winning some concessions to keep options more open. The ultimate disaster of the Forum ending up with two reports, making conflicting demands of the British and negativing eleven months of hard political labour, had been narrowly averted, at a cost which Hume regarded as manageable. Haughey and Mallon, who worked in tandem as defenders of the nationalist faith, had achieved their objective of setting down a strong statement of principle – conceding little to Sinn Fein – before any negotiating process began. A unitary state was not a practical proposition when there was no possibility of the necessary unionist consent, but to them the report had the virtue of honestly declaring their ideal solution.

Mallon had developed this 'one nation' theme as chairman of a Forum sub-committee investigating the model of a unitary state – while other committees dealt with federation/confederation and joint authority. The Fianna Fáil members wanted Scottish-type autonomy for the North in social legislation, covering divorce and contraception, but Mallon argued strongly for the classic unitary state, with one set of laws and one judiciary for the whole country. A battle royal was fought, to preserve the South's prohibitions, and two reports were issued by the sub-committee. At steering committee level, however, Haughey rejected his party's dissenting line, and two paragraphs in the final report gave effect to Mallon's proposal. (This was just one example of Northern influence on Southern attitudes. Fine Gael members came to understand the SDLP's boycott of the

264

Assembly, which they had opposed; and for the first time FitzGerald fully appreciated the SDLP's reliance on the Republic's constitutional claim on Northern Ireland, which legitimised the aspiration of non-violent nationalists and enabled them to stand up to the IRA.)

Hume's inclination all along had been for federalism, with the North having a separate legislature inside a federal structure. But FitzGerald had introduced the concept of joint authority, as distinct from joint sovereignty, and Hume thought its value was that it was difficult for the British to reject on rational grounds. As stated in the Forum report, it could consist of the London and Dublin Governments having equal responsibility for all aspects of the government of Northern Ireland, and ruling either directly or through a locally-elected Assembly. It would give 'political, symbolic and administrative expression of their identity to Northern nationalists without infringing the parallel wish of unionists to maintain and to have full operational expression of their identity'. Both politicians appreciated that there were many ways of approaching this state – dramatically, or by easy stages – which they were willing to discuss. Another virtue of joint authority, as Hume saw it, was that it offered the best chance of creating a security force for the North with which both Catholics and Protestants could identify and which they could both join. He would not rule out any evolution, but joint authority could be a permanent arrangement, under which a British link with Northern Ireland would be retained, even if – as seemed likely – nationalist-minded Catholics eventually outnumbered unionists. Hume knew that while the British continued to give the Protestant majority a veto on constitutional change there would be no inclination to consider joint authority. But the proposal would remain on the table, in case Britain could be tempted to change the rules of Northern Ireland's membership of the United Kingdom.

Before the SDLP could effectively argue the case for inclusion of the joint authority model in the report, it had to overcome the opposition of Mallon, who shared Haughey's preference for a single proposal. Eventually the party representatives gave their unanimous backing, and Hume, Currie and Hendron weighed in with moving speeches in the Forum, expressing sympathy for the unionist position, but until then Fine Gael had carried the torch. FitzGerald himself would not have participated in the Forum if he had not been sure that it would produce more than one constitutional model, and Hume had refused to sign the report until Haughey agreed, under great pressure, to the inclusion of the sentence saying they were 'open to discuss other views'.

FitzGerald's preference, going back to his 1979 Fine Gael document, 'Ireland – Our Future Together', was for the federal or confederal structure, with virtual autonomy for both parts of the island and a greater or lesser role for the all-Ireland institutions at the centre. (He had even proposed in 1979 the preservation of a role for the British monarch, until his party deleted it.) But, like Hume, he was aware of the enormous difficulties in getting agreement to any new structures, and was willing to enter into any talks based on the 'realities' identified in the Forum's analysis of the problem – including acceptance of the 'unionist identity and ethos' – and on the ten 'necessary elements' of a new-Ireland framework. These incorporated a guarantee that unionists would have 'secure and durable, political, administrative and symbolic expression and protection' of their identity; new structures in which 'no tradition will be allowed to dominate the other'; new security structures 'with which both nationalists and unionists can identify'; and new arrangements to ensure 'the maintenance of economic and social standards', i.e. continuing financial support.

Hume and FitzGerald regarded the 'realities' chapter as the hard core of the report, on which agreement was essential. But there was a fundamental difference in Haughey's attitude to the frameworks outlined, and to the status of the unitary state proposal. To him this was still the only solution, even if the wording had been softened, and he made it clear to the other party leaders that he would stick to this interpretation. The choice for them, even after the Mallon intervention, was between a formal decision to accept openly that there was no agreement on this one point of principle, or merely printing what had been agreed, and leaving Haughey the latitude he needed to interpret it differently. The effect of a formal disagreement, it was felt, would be to label the whole Forum exercise a failure, losing all the common ground that had been obtained and ensuring rejection by the media. On the other hand, accepting the two interpretations of the importance of the unitary state model would be damaging to the Forum's credibility – particularly in the North – but it would not be fatal. So, although Haughey warned the steering committee of his intentions the day before the signing ceremony on 2 May, producing notes from which he would work in subsequent media interviews, it was agreed to proceed as planned.

Hume would have preferred no press conference at all, but when this proved impossible it was decided to have four, one for each leader, rather than to risk exposing their differences more obviously, and damagingly, in a single conference.

Inside the steering committee, FitzGerald and Haughey had established a reasonable working relationship, aided by the healing balm of Hume, but almost as soon as the ink on the report was dry, the party politics began. FitzGerald was first to face the Press, who were still puzzling over the subtleties of the report, and his interpretation was clear. The unitary state was merely the preferred option, but the Forum parties were willing to discuss the other two options, or indeed any others. Listening in, Haughey bristled at what he regarded as the Taoiseach's 'running away from the report' and especially his use of the word 'option', which Haughey understood to have been taboo. From the same seat as FitzGerald, he described the unitary state proposal as 'not an option but a conclusion', declaring that the other models would not lead to peace and stability. According to Haughey, the consent of unionists was necessary for the constitution of a new Ireland, but they had no right to impede Irish unity, which should be the subject of a wide-ranging conference. (This was a line he had tried to pursue in the Forum, with no success; he had wanted nationalists' 'right' to a united Ireland to be acknowledged, but 'desire' has been substituted.)

The historic split over means towards unity, which the Forum had been designed to repair, was publicly re-opened, even if the report still represented a high-watermark of agreement. But Hume was unaware of the controversy, as he gave TV interviews in the castle yard, and the only warning on his way to the rostrum was a whispered comment from a radio reporter: 'Charlie's blown it on you.' He put on a brave face, but for the rest of the day had to answer questions on the significance of Haughey's interpretation, rather than on the positive recognition by nationalists of the Britishness of the Northern majority. He was disappointed, and in retrospect wished the four had faced the media together – with all the constraints for unanimity that would have imposed. But his natural optimism and combativeness carried him through a testing night, from interview to interview, and the next day he dined in a Dublin restaurant with Haughey. Regardless of interpretations, the words in the report were what mattered, and these were a sound basis for negotiations.

As Haughey explained later, somewhat apologetically, he felt FitzGerald had put too much emphasis on the report's openness to discuss a range of constitutional models and was stung by hostile Press questioning into appearing to include the other leaders in his interpretation of the unitary state recommendation. He did his best to backtrack, dissociating the others from his opinions, but he could hardly have been dismayed by the Press reaction, summed up in the exaggerated claim in *Magill* magazine, 'How Charlie Swung the Forum'.

The Unionists had already damned the report in advance as yet another attempt to force or cajole them into a united Ireland and Paisley made a midnight visit to Dublin to stick a poster with a Union Jack and the slogan 'Ulster is British' on the General Post Office building in O'Connell Street, where the 1916 Easter Rising against the British had begun. Haughey received a poster and hung it up, amid laughter, at the last lunch of the steering committee in the Senate anteroom in Leinster House. The poster campaign was a crude publicity stunt, but it typified the traditional unionist rejection of Dublin's role in Northern Ireland's future. As British unionists, they were simply not interested in any plan that could be seen as a halfway house to Irish unity, and the Official Unionist Party cleverly anticipated the all-Ireland solution with its own generalised blueprint for administrative devolution inside Northern Ireland – 'The Way Forward' – proposing limited powers over local government matters, without an Executive. Harking back to the 1976 Convention report, it guaranteed the minority an influential role in committees, a Bill of Rights and explicit recognition of an 'Irish identity'. It came years too late to entice the SDLP, but impressed British observers – as well as FitzGerald – by its conciliatory tone, and provided unionism with a human face that had been lacking.

It was a shrewd move, since the unspoken purpose of the Forum was to persuade the British Government that the time had come – because of the state of Catholic alienation in Northern Ireland – to begin to exert real pressure on Protestants to accept a new relationship between North and South. Without pressure, there would be no prospect of Protestants considering such a plan, let alone giving it the consent upon which the Forum insisted. The British Government had to take the problem seriously enough to accept the risks which went with such a policy, and the Forum report's strategy was to stress that the consequences of doing nothing

– and letting Sinn Fein grow at the SDLP's expense – would be worse than awakening the sleeping paramilitary giant on the Protestant side. Unfortunately for the Forum, the publication of the report almost coincided with the tenth anniversary of the Ulster Workers' Council strike, with potent reminders – reinforced by contemporary warnings from Andy Tyrie, still the UDA commander – of the Protestants' capacity for waging a bloody civil war.

In keeping with the Forum's attempt to provide as much authoritative analysis of the problem as possible, an independent economic study, published simultaneously with the main report, looked at the options for each of the three constitutional models. None of the alternatives offered much improvement, except in the long term, but the message was clear that without change the future of the North was exceptionally bleak. Total unemployment, which was then 120,000 or 21 per cent of the working population, could rise to 150,000 (30 per cent) by the end of the decade. Jobs in manufacturing industry, which had fallen by 30 per cent from 1979 to 1982, would continue to disappear, and the life-saving subsidy from Britain, which was conservatively estimated at £1,420 million in 1983–4, would rise to nearly £2,000 million in ten years' time.

Considering that, on this calculation, these transfers from the British Exchequer amounted to 27 per cent of the North's gross domestic product – at a rate of nearly £1,000 per head per year – the economists had to assume that, to avoid disaster, there would be continuing inflows, from Britain or other sources. London would still have to pay a price to disengage from Northern Ireland, or there would be no prospect of consent. On the basis of the depressing figures, combining a struggling Southern economy with a terminal Northern condition, it was hard to see a majority of electors in either part of the island voting voluntarily for such a shaky economic future. Nevertheless, Prior undertook to study the report carefully and, while describing its account of the British position as 'one-sided and unacceptable', he was positive enough about its opposition to violence and support for consent to suggest that his welcome of its 'open approach to discussion' would be followed up. A fuller response was delayed until after the election to the European Parliament on 18 June – in case it would increase the extremist vote – but generally favourable Press comment in Britain, America and Europe lifted SDLP spirits.

The Forum had been a gamble either way, since it could have failed to reach agreement or could have been ignored by the British, emphasising the impotence of constitutional politicians. Disunity had been avoided, at a price Hume thought could be afforded, and it seemed there was no intention in London of letting the initiative die. Just as Hume and FitzGerald had intended, the 'realities' offered the basis of an agenda for inter-governmental talks, from which new opportunities for consensus might emerge. At the same time, they had to admit that Haughey's continuing attempts to narrow the discussion to the unitary state proposal had weakened the Forum strategy, and that the SDLP had moved still further away from dialogue with unionists. Hume was left wondering what the outcome would have been if his original proposal for an interim report to be sent to the British had succeeded. His idea was to call for a response to the 'realities' – without any conclusions – so that the British might have been encouraged to engage in negotiations. That was the main purpose of the Forum, as Hume saw it, but others, like Haughey, wanted a declaration of the nationalist case, and rejected the interim scheme as a cop-out. Hume's interest was in an early solution, and he would have preferred to demonstrate the Forum's flexibility, in order to get to the conference table.

A month after the Forum reported, Hume faced the European Parliament election. He enjoyed working in Europe, where he was on first-name terms with the most influential people and could operate as an Irish social democrat, but he knew his place was increasingly at Westminster, where he felt he was typed as an Ulster Catholic. There was no escape, however, from an election in which the SDLP had to roll back the Sinn Fein advances or face growing indifference in London and Dublin. Newspaper pundits, especially in the South, were full of grim forebodings, but Hume achieved what he wanted, capturing 151,399 votes, or 22.1 per cent – four per cent more than his party's vote a year earlier – and holding Sinn Fein to 91,476 votes (13.3 per cent), which was 11,125 less than before, despite a higher turnout by nationalists. North and South, Sinn Fein picked up only 7 per cent, significantly damaging their claim to be the inheritors of the republican majority in 1918.

Hume fought solely on his European record, much to the disgust of the media – and some of his own supporters – who wanted more of a tribal tussle with Sinn Fein. But he calculated rightly that a low-key campaign, in which he ignored the Forum's divisive issues and said little to offend supporters of the British link, could only add to his vote and depress Sinn Fein's. He still had moderate Catholics behind him, and as long as Sinn Fein was a support group for the IRA, there would be strict limits to its appeal. But on the unionist side, a staggering 230,251 votes (33.6 per cent) for Ian Paisley, still trading on the underlying Protestant fear and hatred of Irish nationalism and Catholicism, was a setback to the faint hopes of a meaningful British initiative.

21
Future options

As Hume rose to speak on the New Ireland Forum at a British-Irish Association conference in the Oxford Union in September 1983 one Irish delegate said to another, looking around the room: 'I wonder how many people here realise that every new idea about Ireland has come out of that man's head?' Few did, even among the well-informed politicians, journalists and diplomats who were present, but all were aware of Hume's crucial role in the continuing search for solutions. Although Sinn Fein was barking at his heels, and causing problems for his party in hardline areas, he remained easily the most influential Northern politician in the nationalist tradition. He had kept hope alive in the North, when every minority cause seemed lost, and he had constantly reminded the South of its obligation to its 'fourth green field' – Ulster – even when there was scarcely any political or practical advantage to be gained by doing so. Indeed, it occasionally rankled with the Republic's politicians and media people that this man from far-off Derry, with his serious Northern ways, should be able to keep the insoluble problems of the North so much to the fore, for so long, when there were so many other vital concerns to be faced.

His method is simply to think more, to talk to more people, and to put more ideas down on paper than any other Irish politician of his generation. In any gathering, at any time of day or night, he may be spotted staring into the far distance, eyes glazed over, in a world of his own. Some can be offended, but his colleagues recognise that John is turning an idea, or a tactic, around in his head, and is unreachable. When he has come to a conclusion, he will rejoin the company, and, having thought out all the counter-arguments, is ready to test his theory. Politics is more than his job; it is a way of life, lived every waking minute and, in Ireland's current condition, it contains all the challenge for which any man of intelligence could wish. The contrast between Hume and his colleagues and competitors is partly in his intellectual capability for problem-solving, but also in his workrate. Early on in his parliamentary career, he learned that most politicians were basically lazy, and that when faced with a reasonable, well thought-out case, at a meeting for which they were ill-prepared, would usually accept it in one form or another. Hume tries to ensure that it is his ideas they adopt.

To help him, he has a charisma rare in Northern politicians, particularly on the nationalist side, where leaders had no prospect of power or patronage. From his emergence as a public figure in Derry in the early 1960s, he has been looked to as a man of ideas, who can articulate people's feelings in a way that lifts them out of the ordinary. His hearers may not have understood everything he said, but he was obviously a man of learning who was prepared to take their part, and they followed him. The timing of his arrival was important, just as the emerging middle class of the minority community was looking for an alternative to the mindless violence of the IRA and the sterile complaining of the Nationalist Party. He was greeted as a kind of Messiah, born to lead his people to the political power which had eluded them, and even those who thought they could sometimes detect feet of clay chose not to challenge him, because of the need he filled. Colleagues can recall petty incidents where he upstaged them unnecessarily, or took personal credit for a team effort, but they say nothing to besmirch the image. They also calculate that if he can be guilty of ungenerosity, it is evidence of an insecurity hardly surprising in one from his Bogside upbringing. He never conceals his ambition to make his mark on the world, and those who have helped him have done so in the knowledge that there might be little thanks, and that what was good for Hume would also be good for nationalist Ireland. Throughout his career, colleagues have broken away from him, and such is his single-mindedness and lack of sentimentality that the losses barely seem to have been felt. He has regrets, but he is driven on to the next political crisis, and cannot afford to stop. He has never harboured grudges, because such feelings can be a political hindrance, and he and Gerry (now Lord) Fitt still tend to gravitate towards one another in Westminster – where Hume is much less at home than at the Dáil. When friends express surprise, both explain that they have been through too much together to end their relationship.

Most of Hume's supporters are slightly in awe of him, for he has played such a central part in the history of their times, but he has a politician's knack of making them feel their contribution is

273

important and of inspiring loyalty. In company, he is usually the focus of attention, but when the pace slackens, he has a ready ear for the colourful characters who inhabit every Irish bar. It is never far from his mind that he had the luck to be born in time for free education: a year earlier and he believes that, with his head for figures, he might have ended up running a supermarket chain.

At home in Derry, most of Hume's thinking and reading is done in a small back room, about 14 ft by 12 ft, dominated by an oil-fired cooker and an overhead washing line. The floor has a plastic covering, the worn furniture is comfortable rather than stylish, and there is an uplifting religious message on the wall. Family life goes on – daughter Maureen having her hair dried in front of the warm stove, as Hume jots down notes for his next speech. Creature comforts mean little to someone who always prefers to bed down in the house of a friend – often a journalist when in Dublin – rather than stay in a hotel. The rumpled appearance and unfashionable dress are never affected: outward show means nothing in Derry. It would be natural for someone with so many international connections to move from the trouble zone of the Bogside, or to have a country home in Donegal for entertaining guests, but by remaining in West End Park Hume is making a political statement. Whatever the pressures, and the Provisionals are increasingly breathing down his neck, he is not leaving his roots. Only once, after a particularly harrowing attack by petrol-bombers during the 1981 hunger-strike was he tempted to move, because of his youngest daughter's hysteria. Hume had protested when young rioters tried to burn a neighbour's lorry and they then turned their attentions on his house. As the bottles of burning petrol bounced off the armoured-glass windows, nine-year-old Maureen wanted to get away from these 'bad people'. But the Provisional leadership heard of the commotion and, in a uniquely Derry solution, called off the rioters and assured the Humes there would be no repetition.

Given the time, Hume would write more about politics – as he did in the early 1970s – and if he had to turn his back on the political life altogether, would gladly retreat to the libraries of Ireland, rediscovering the satisfaction of historical research. Most of the books he reads are about history. In music, he knows what he likes, mostly Irish, without knowing why. Television is rarely watched, except at weekends, or to catch up on a documentary programme he has missed, and Pat bemoans the fact that they have not been to a cinema for twenty years. Relaxation is a dinner party with non-political, artistic or literary friends, either at their homes or across the border in Donegal, with an accompaniment of good French wines.

Always Hume is sensitive to criticism, telephoning round a selection of respected party faithful to get a sample of reaction to whatever he is doing or saying. The danger is that, with Hume having so pre-eminent a position in the party, the stronger personalities may tire of competing and leave behind only camp-followers who would be unwilling or unable to check his occasional flights of fancy. (In 1984, for instance, he declared in his party conference speech that the Irish Tricolour, with its orange, white and green, was a more appropriate flag to fly on Belfast City Hall than the Union Jack. Theoretically he had a point, but he was speaking as a native of Derry, where the border is regarded as a temporary expedient, rather than as a leader knowing how outrageous such a notion would be in Protestant Belfast.) Fitt and Devlin functioned usefully as critics in their day. Now Hume's confidants are few as, of the founder-members, only Currie remains active in the party. Derry is almost a state of mind, and many who grow up in its overheated atmosphere are so certain of the inevitability of a united Ireland that they discount the opposition to it. Even Hume, with his acute political antennae, was caught out by nationalist pressure for the change of 'Londonderry' Council to 'Derry' Council in 1983; he did not want to force the issue, against Protestant resistance, but popular opinion insisted.

In the early days, he had the advantage of being able to present himself and his party as the intelligent alternative to unionism, a stance which went down well with the media. Gerry Fitt and Paddy Devlin were too erratic and emotional to be universally acceptable as spokesmen, but Hume had an ability to impress any listener, at almost any level. He was an articulate man of the people, who took their aspirations and built them into a credible political strategy, so different from the negative, repetitive laments of the old National-ists. His only obvious lack as a politician – and sometimes it is a grave one – is the guile to lighten his heavy political message with the occasional anecdote, or the kind of witty aside or chuckle that punctuates his private conversation. But politics for him is too serious a business to be manipulated for laughter, and his speeches often read better than they sound; his only concession to colourful oratory is to use quotations from poets who have written tellingly about the problem – Ulsterman Louis MacNeice and W.B. Yeats are favourites — to add fresh insights. His appeal is to the intellect, encouraging people in both communities not to think in terms of 'winning' and 'losing', which have no meaning for him, but to find ways of living together. On one occasion, when members of a delegation from the Forum were attacked with sticks by DUP supporters in Derry, his pacifism took practical form. Some of the politicians were ready for a pitched battle, but Hume's first instincts were to think of the damage that would be done to the Forum's image. Non-violence triumphed.

Some politicians revel in the glad-handing and doorstepping at election times, but Hume goes through the motions with evident discomfort, even though aides say the experience is invaluable, and never as traumatic as he expects. He still admits to being unhappy about thrusting himself at voters, preferring the smoke-filled rooms and the relative calm of his advice centre in Derry, where his talent for putting to work high-level contacts in Dublin, London, Brussels or Washington comes into play. While his Sinn Fein rivals trumpet their concern for the problems the IRA have brought upon the Catholic people, Hume wheels and deals in the upper atmosphere of politics. 'If getting drains fixed is what politics is about, then 90 per cent of people are qualified to be politicians,' he has said, in defence of his globe-trotting, which always has a political purpose for Ireland. At the same time, there is a favourite Derry story of the woman who came to Hume's door, with the city in flames, complaining about mice in her kitchen. Everything stopped while the authorities were contacted.

Sinn Fein, by contrast, focus their efforts in the mean streets of the Catholic ghettoes and housing estates, demonstrating how to get the maximum cash benefit from the British welfare state, while playing down their revolutionary socialist aims for Ireland North and South. It is a new kind of politics, backed by the guns and money of the IRA, and it would create problems for any constitutional leader. Not only is it occasionally seen to be effective, as officialdom responds to unseen threats, but it can operate on a wider scale than the SDLP, which has to raise its money in conventional ways. While Sinn Fein can run almost thirty advice centres, which would cost up to £150,000 a year if they were more than just a presence, the SDLP has to make do with two, on an annual budget of £30,000. All Northern Ireland political parties have had the same money worries, with eleven elections to fight in the eleven years up to 1984, and a middle class which has largely opted out of politics, but the SDLP has suffered most. After fourteen years, Hume is still its only paid politician, and although envious eyes are cast on his salary and allowances for Westminster and Europe of nearly £60,000 this income has to support an office with five staff. Hume's interest in money, unlike that of some leading Irish politicians, has always been marginal; it is a means to the end of getting political things done, and he ignores lucrative 'insider' tip-offs. He and Enoch Powell are the only MPs at Westminster to refuse to disclose their financial interests; Hume has none, but resents, on principle, the assumption in the question.

If at any time he chose to quit politics and leave a life of constant harassment, travel and disappointment, he could be assured of a future in the academic world, journalism or the EEC. A 1983 poll of MEPs named him as one of the most influential politicians in Europe, despite his geographical remoteness. Any of the big jobs in Brussels or any Irish Commissionership could be open to him, and he has briefly envied his friends in the Brussels bureaucracy, who retreat for the summer to country homes in France, instead of a terrace house in the Bogside. But such thoughts are fleeting; his commitment to the Northern Ireland problem is total, and if ever he throws his hat in the ring for, say, the Presidency of Ireland, wide-ranging conclusions about the political future will be drawn. Personal ambition, he insists, has nothing to do with his motivation – although one, other-wise sympathetic, commentator has described him as 'the most self-absorbed politician I have met'. He works for constitutional solutions, but if they were obtained, he would stand aside and let others get on with the business of government. He has no wish to be Prime Minister of anything, or even to run a department. That would require different skills, he says, and he would not have the desire or the energy to take it on. He sees himself as someone who is in politics by accident rather than design, and he could leave without regret. However, the reality, in an Ireland trying to come to terms with a new Anglo-Irish relationship, and under attack by extremists on both sides, might be very different. Having started the political process, he would find it extremely difficult to bow out.

But, for all his achievements on behalf of the Catholic community, helping to transform their housing conditions, if not their job prospects, what has he to show in the field which matters most to him, the reconciliation of the two traditions in Ireland? Very little, it has seemed, as 30-ft brick walls have been erected in Belfast to keep warring communities apart and as Sinn Fein's support has grown in the course of two years to a position only 5 per cent short of his own SDLP, founded in 1970. There has not been agreement even on the nature of the problem. To nationalists like Hume the violence is only a symbol of the underlying political problem, and has to be tackled in a political way; to unionists the violence is the problem, and has to be eliminated before any reconciliation is possible. The very existence of Northern Ireland, Hume believes, is proof of the breakdown in relationships which is at the root of the conflict. Partition has prevented the healing process, and therefore any solution has to be in a British-Irish, rather than a United Kingdom context. It is a subtle, evolutionary strategy, which, in the absence of a British response, began to be compared unfavourably with the elemental simplicity of the IRA/Sinn Fein message. The shadow of the gunman is increasingly acceptable in nationalist Ireland, especially among the children of the Troubles, and loyalist Ulster can more than match the threat, weapon for weapon.

Hume did not create these conditions, but by asking the fundamental question from civil rights platforms – 'Is Northern Ireland reformable?'– he lit a fuse under the British province which has never been extinguished. His challenge was to the unionists to prove that they were willing to accept reform and equal citizenship for nationalists inside Northern Ireland, but it was finally answered, as he had expected, in the overthrow of power-sharing in 1974. Earlier he had believed that if the civil rights reforms, bringing substantial improvements in living standards and expectations for Catholics, had been allowed to take their course, the next phase in his solution – reconciliation – would have taken place naturally, leaving the way open for future reunification. But the IRA demanded a blood sacrifice for its version of unity, and the reciprocal violence of Protestants led to the conclusion that only in a new British-Irish context, providing the maximum consensus within the divided community, could reconciliation take place. It has been a consistent principle, from which he has not budged, even under pressure from all the 'moderate' voices in the pro-unionist community, because he knew the old order, under exclusively British guarantees, would never again win nationalist consent.

Opponents have learned that, in dealing with such matters around a negotiating table, Hume is resourceful, but essentially immoveable. As one responsible for launching his political career has said: 'Anyone regarding John as a soft negotiator, because he expresses himself so reasonably, is making a fundamental mistake.' Hume's refusal to give full support to the police until the SDLP has a part in government has been widely misunderstood in unionist circles, but it merely reflects his commitment to long-term rather than short-term goals. He knows that the only way the police can possibly be made acceptable to Catholics is to introduce a second guarantor of their good behaviour – Dublin. Law and order is central to any political solution, as Hume sees it, and unless a large measure of consensus on policing can be achieved, no political structures can survive.

Such fundamentalism, which some see as a mirror image of the Rev. Ian Paisley's intransigence on the Protestant side, has won Hume much criticism from pragmatists seeking halfway-house solutions. James Prior, the Northern Ireland Secretary from 1981–4, had a warm relationship with Hume, but regarded him as an 'academic' in politics. They have all overlooked the fact that, while Sinn Fein and even the Unionists have their paramilitary wings to back up their politics, the SDLP has only the strength of its ideas, and the leverage it can get from powerful allies, to use as weapons of persuasion. It could have chosen to do a deal at any time, while the British guarantee to the majority was unchanged, but Hume knew the consequence would be to destroy the only nationalist bulwark against Sinn Fein, for a very temporary and limited reward. Although the refusal to fully support the police has strengthened loyalist justification for refusing to share power with the SDLP, and risks increasing short-term polarisation, it is seen as a price that has to be paid, if reconciliation in a wider context is to become possible. Lack of political movement has created a vacuum, which Sinn Fein has partly filled, but Hume has toiled unceasingly to raise Northern Ireland in the list of government priorities in London and Dublin. It is hardly an exaggeration to say that without Hume's advice, Dublin would have no policy for progress in the North, or that, without the SDLP, London might easily have slipped into an acceptance of majority-rule devolution. Throughout the Troubles Hume has been only a telephone call away from the leading Irish-American politicians, but they could easily revert to traditional Irish republicanism if his restraining hand was absent.

As he battles to achieve a fundamental reappraisal of British policy – back to the spirit, since abandoned, of Sunningdale – Hume has had to concede that his insistence on involving the Republic has won him the undying opposition of traditional unionists. When he talks of accommodating the two national identities, the British and Irish, in new structures overseen by London and Dublin, they hear a demand for surrender. As many Protestants see it, the SDLP and the IRA have the same basic objective – a united Ireland – and indeed Hume may be the more dangerous, since he could conceivably argue the British into submission, while the IRA could not. Even Sinn Fein, with its violent associations is easier to oppose. Achieving any kind of reconciliation with such loyalist opponents would be difficult, in the aftermath of a British-imposed settlement, but equally troublesome would be the younger generation of pro-IRA Catholics. So much bitterness has been built up on both sides, as a result of the 2,400 deaths of the Troubles, that even with the new Anglo-Irish treaty which Hume would wish to see, and positive moves to implement it, the chances of avoiding a minor bloodbath would not be high. One possibility is that loyalists would react to withdrawal of the constitutional guarantee – or even the introduction of conditional British support – by attempting independence. That would get them into a negotiating position with Britain and the Republic, which might achieve much the same result, in the end, as an Anglo-Irish treaty. Whatever happens, Hume has few illusions that the process can take place completely peacefully. The longer the conflict continues, and the greater the suffering, the more the options narrow.

To Hume, these truths are self-evident, but despite his efforts to convince the unionists, and the British, that the only way to counter the progressive alienation of Catholics from a British Ulster is to recognise their Irish identity and give them some share of political power, he has met with blank refusals or shrugs of hopelessness. The SDLP's veto against majority rule is matched by the loyalists' veto against the slightest constitutional change, and both sides doubt if the British have the commitment to challenge either community. The brutal fact is that the political divisions which helped split Ireland in 1921 are essentially the same today, except for a demographic erosion of the unionist position, slipping from a two-thirds majority to sixty-forty, mainly concentrated in the east of the province. Fewer Catholics, and relatively more Protestants, have been emigrating, and since 1978 the majority of births have been Catholic. In time, Catholics are likely to outnumber Protestants in the population and, later, on the voting register. But it is to avoid the so-called 'rabbit' solution – which could take place only when enough Catholics were convinced their interests would be served in a united Ireland – that Hume wants the sovereign Governments in London and Dublin to prepare the way for an orderly and honorable transition, just as quickly or slowly as the unionists want it. But although Jim Prior eventually agreed that the danger of doing nothing, and letting the disease spread, was greater than the danger of doing something that might not work, the British Government shared the ordinary people's pessimism in political initiatives, preferring to react to potential disasters, like a Sinn Fein electoral success, rather than attempt to intercept them. The passivity of the British establishment, when the alternative is to confront the unionist majority, has been Hume's biggest single political obstacle.

As a leader, Hume could be, and often has been, accused of failing to stand up for his non-sectarian principles in times of crisis, even when his personal reputation was high enough to weather the harshest criticism. The decision not to contest the second Fermanagh-South Tyrone by-election has continued to haunt him, but he knows his Irish history too well, and understands what has happened to leaders who strode too far ahead of the electorate, or who could be accused of betraying their nationalist roots for the sake of maintaining a moderate image. Gerry Fitt is only the latest example, and it can be demonstrated that the Belfast man's uncompromising denunciation of the Provisionals achieved results which were the opposite of those intended. To strike a moral pose and irreparably damage the hard-won coalition of interests in the SDLP is not an option for Hume, who can understand, without beginning to condone, the IRA. The paramilitaries attack the symptoms of the basic problem, and make it worse, instead of working politically. He regrets the weakness of his party's base in Belfast, where the young Catholic working class has largely transferred its support from socialism to republicanism in the course of little over a decade, and he has been forced to accept that the SDLP's main strength is elsewhere, among those old enough to remember its civil rights origins. The continuing violence, and the heavy security presence in Belfast, have sharpened feelings and made constitutional politics less saleable.

Most of all Hume regrets the failure to attract and keep more than a handful of Protestant activists to remind the SDLP of its roots, but, again, the sectarian nature of the state of Northern Ireland is his explanation. Ordinary left-right politics will not be possible until the context, North and South, is changed to bring about a religious mix. Meanwhile, it is a matter of keeping the SDLP's moderation relevant, in a situation where the whole social fabric of an alienated and jobless community is beginning to unravel. This would be hard enough without trying to reach out to the Protestant community, and here Hume's Derry background has been a handicap. He can understand why unionists will remain intransigent so long as Britain's guarantee lasts, but he has always doubted their willingness to oppose with violence an alternative solution involving Dublin. He believes that if Protestants can be convinced that their future lies in Ireland rather than with Britain, they will be liberated from their self-destructive siege mentality. Just as Charles Stewart Parnell in the nineteenth century worked to eliminate the conflict between land-lord and peasant, in order to encourage landlords to become leaders of the Home Rule movement, Hume hopes that ending the unionists' veto on constitutional change will cause them to accept their role in reforming Ireland. This attitude is a reflection of his optimism, but hardly accords with the political realities.

His problem, however, is not only with the Protestants and the British, but with Dublin, where there is a rival for the leadership of Irish nationalism in Charles Haughey. Sincerely, or for his own political gain – and Hume is more generous to him than most – Haughey is determined to be the man who refuses to compromise with the British, waiting for what he thinks will be the inevitable day when London pulls out. This stance gives the impression he wants, of being a strong man, beside the shilly-shallying of his more accom-modating opponents, but in so doing it strengthens the will of the loyalists, and the British, to oppose any tinkering with sovereignty. It is all highly counterproductive to Hume's strategy, which is to show that the Southern Irish are trustworthy allies, but so long as there is a relatively even balance between Fianna Fáil and the two coalition parties, Fine Gael and Labour, it is difficult to see a leader in Haughey's mould discarding the symbolic 'green card'. While Hume seeks solutions, trying to mobilise the vast majority of the nationalist vote in Ireland to achieve them, Haughey is fighting for power, manipulating the well-known Southern ambivalence about unity in order to keep the problem at arm's length.

Convincing the British of the need for compromise in Ireland is difficult, considering that Thatcher's Government has made a virtue out of patriotism and black-and-white thinking. But Hume has a long history of producing new policies out of thin air, and has no intention of splitting his party over a return to participation in Northern Ireland politics in an exclusively British context. His own innate nationalism would not allow a climb-down from the Forum position, nor would his desire to preserve a mass party as the only effective counter to Sinn Fein republicanism. Though he is always inclined to look south to Dublin, rather than east to London, he is uncomfortable with the political label of 'nationalist', with its imperialistic, master-race overtones. He would prefer to be known as a 'self-determinationist', in a Europe of the regions, but again the narrow confines of Irish politics inhibit his natural instincts. Colleagues on the left wing of the SDLP have no doubt about Hume's leanings toward socialist solutions in a more normal situation. But he works within the system rather than against it, and this tendency has been noticeable in his attitude to issues where the interests of church and state conflict. His Maynooth upbringing showed in his initially unsympathetic approach to the 'shared schools' campaign – an attempt to bring together willing Protestant and Catholic children in an alternative to the state and church school systems – which he felt was artificially contrived. He was also careful not to get involved in FitzGerald's constitutional crusade in the South – which, if it had succeeded, would have made Irish unity less frightening to Protestants – nor to warn strongly of the divisiveness of the 1983 abortion referendum in the Republic. (Protestants were equally opposed to abortion, but were treated to an object lesson in the power of the Catholic Church over Southern politicians.)

A tendency to 'play safe', where there is support to be lost, has been a recurring theme, although it is not unusual in Irish parties which need, against all the odds, to survive. Hume himself has survived politically, because of his ability to create new openings, and the SDLP party organisation has been proof against years of battering by Sinn Fein. While the young, the hopeless and the fanatical may support, until it fails, a policy based on a combination of guns and votes, the majority of Catholics stick to conventional democratic politics, even if it produces little result. But at a time when Hume might have been thinking of slackening the pace of his life, and finding lieutenants to relieve him, he is becoming more, not less, important to the cohesion of the party. Men of ability tend to put politics aside, and concentrate on their professional careers when the pickings are thin and the flak heavy. If he can hold on long enough for the South to realise the implications of the Forum report, and begin to unloose the ties between church doctrine and state laws – thus lessening the threat to Protestant liberties – a new climate in Ireland may be created. But essentially Hume's job is to prove that constitutional politics can get results in a situation where neither the unionist majority nor the British Government – for all the wavering of the British media, public and opposition parties – seems prepared to move. To him, the violence of the IRA proves his case for political movement, and yet its continuation ensures that his approach will not get a fair hearing from the unionists, because they see him riding the same bandwagon. In such an impasse, it is hardly surprising that Hume has to contend with a dissident minority within the SDLP, which believes that the party needs a more cutting edge. Unless it can prove to the British and the unionists that it has the overwhelming support of nationalists, the argument goes, it will not be taken seriously enough to warrant Government endorsement. The dissidents want a more tribal approach, which runs counter to Hume's whole philosophy. In any other party, against any other leader, they might have forced a split, but they know they would be hopelessly isolated, and bide their time. They are a reminder of how easily the SDLP would slip back into conventional nationalism, if Hume's influence waned. The siege mentality which has stunted the unionists' political development and inhibited their natural talents could be just as dangerous on the nationalist side.

There will always be a temptation for Hume to leave politics, as the Irish question keeps changing and defying solutions. But while there are still unexplored political avenues, defeat is inconceivable for someone who sees his destiny in showing the Irish, North and South, how much they could achieve together once their political ambitions were reconciled. The realities identified by the Forum will eventually have to be faced by some governments of the future, before or after greater civil conflict, and when they are, a process could begin that might end Ireland's agony. While constitutional nationalism may be regarded by the British as too idealistic to be worth backing in the elemental struggle taking place in Northern Ireland, it retains the only clear vision of a peacefully reconciled Ireland. Keeping that aim in view will continue to be John Hume's life work.

INDEX

Abercorn Restaurant, Belfast, bombing 123
abortion referendum, Republic of Ireland 283
Adams, Gerry 129, 130, 132, 225, 226, 248
advice centres, Derry
  Hume's 75, 276
  Sinn Fein 276
Aer Lingus 33, 159
Aiken, Frank 137
Alliance Party 44, 97, 121, 122, 135, 140, 144,
  146, 150, 153, 155, 171, 237, 240, 245, 259
Allison, Michael 225
Alternative Assembly 113, 116, 118
America: Bernadette Devlin's image in 187;
  Friends of Ireland 228, 229; fund raising
  in 81, 121, 183, 187, 188, 189, 193, 194, 195;
  Hume's contacts in 183, 186, 187, 188, 190,
  191, 192, 193, 194, 195, 196, 197, 203, 251, 252,
  279; hunger strike, reaction in 228; industrial
  development in Northern Ireland 189, 192,
  193, 251; Ireland Fund 188; Irish National
  Caucus 190, 194, 251; jobs promotion for
  Northern Ireland, in 251, 252, 253; New
  Ireland Forum and 260; Noraid 187, 188,
  190, 192, 233, 253; political reactions to
  Northern Ireland in 184, 185, 186, 187, 189,
  190, 191, 192, 195, 203, 228; Provisional IRA
  and 189, 190, 195; Waterville Co Kerry,
  conference 1979 208
amnesty
  1969 78
  1972, proposed 127, 131
  1973, proposed 141
Amnesty International 218
Ancient Order of Hibernians 187
Anderson, Albert 39
Anglo-Irish Council 213, 236, 238
Anglo-Irish initiative 212, 213, 216, 222, 227,
  236, 278, 280
anti-H-Block campaign, 1981 132
anti-internment marches see internment; marches
appeal by Hume against fine for obstruction 3,
  121
Apprentice Boys of Derry 79, 87
Ardill, Austin 181
Argenta prison ship 115
Arlow, Rev. William 177, 178, 179
Armagh Co: Armagh city 78, 147; Caledon 59,
  62; Craigavon 48, 57; Maghery 53; South
  Armagh constituency 179, 249
Arms Trial 1970 100
arts festivals, Derry 40
Arts Council, Northern Ireland 42
Ashdown, Paddy 4
Assembly, Northern Ireland 1973: anti-power-
  sharing loyalists 142, 161, 162. 163; British
  Government proposals 138; Council of Ireland
  see Council of Ireland; elections, June 28
  1973 138, 139, 140, 141; Executive 143, 144,
  145 – 155, 163, 164, 165, 166, 167, 169;
  Faulkner, resignation 156; police protection,
  Executive 144, 145; power-sharing
  concept 143 – 156; Speaker 144, 161; SDLP
  proposals 133, 138; UWC plan to
  imprison 173, 174; violence in Chamber 142,
  160, 161; vote on Sunningdale, May 1974 163

Assembly, Northern Ireland 1981:
  abstentionism 240, 241, 242; disqualification,
  Seamus Mallon 242; elections 240, 241, 242;
  Fitt, support 237; Hume, election
  manifesto 241; limitations 243; Sinn Fein
  policy 241, 242; SDLP policy 236, 237, 240,
  241; vote on capital punishment 250; White
  Paper, proposals 236
Atkins, Humphrey 209, 210, 212, 213, 214, 215,
  216, 219, 220, 223, 224, 226
Atlantic Harvest Ltd 58, 246
Austin, Campbell 64, 65

B-Special auxiliary police force 69, 84, 86, 87, 89,
  93, 95
Balneil, Lord 122
bans on parades 62, 64, 66, 67, 68, 79
banks, Munster and Leinster 104
Barr, Glenn 163, 164, 165, 172
Barry, Peter 244, 247
baton charges 76, 119
Beattie, Desmond 112
Beattie, Rev. William 180
Belfast: Andersonstown 84; Argenta prison
  ship 115; army-police swoop, July 11,
  1971 114; August 9, 1971 114;
  Ballybeen 169, 170; Bombay Street 86, 187;
  Celtic football team 23; City Hall 275;
  College Square North 105; Corporation 98;
  Crumlin Road jail 128, 130; EEC aid for 230;
  Falls Road 86, 101; Glencairn 162; Grand
  Central Hotel 90, 103, 161; Hawthornden
  Road 163; Lenadoon 131; Maidstone prison
  ship 115; no-go areas 109; riots 83, 85, 86,
  93; sectarian conflict 83, 84, 86; Shankill
  Road 86, 162; Shaws Road 168; Springfield
  Road Barracks 114; West Belfast
  constituency 210, 211
Belfast Telegraph 105
Bennett Committee 201
Best, Ranger, shooting of 128
Biggs-Davidson, John 213
Bill of Rights, Northern Ireland 110, 135, 201,
  268
birthplace, Hume's 5
birth rate, Northern Ireland 48, 280, 281
Blaney, Neil 79, 85, 100, 121, 232
blanket protest, prison 198, 218
Bloody Friday, July 21, 1972 132
Bloody Sunday, January 30, 1972: aftermath 120,
  121, 122, 123, 153, 184, 185, 194; arrests 120;
  Brandywell mass meeting 121; deaths 119,
  120, 122; Free Derry Corner, see also Free
  Derry 119; Hume and 3, 119, 120, 122, 131;
  Paratroop Regiment 119, 120, 122, 123; SDLP
  and 119; Widgery Inquiry 120, 122, 126
Bogside, Derry 1, 2, 5, 8, 13, 14, 18, 28, 35, 48, 54,
  64, 70, 76, 77, 78, 79, 80, 81, 82, 83, 85, 86, 87,
  89, 90, 92, 93, 114, 115, 119, 120, 127, 130, 168,
  186, 273, 277.
Bogside Defence Association 80, 81, 82, 87, 89, 93
Boland, Kevin 157
bomb attacks 72, 123, 132, 161, 166, 177, 200,
  250
border poll, March 1973 137, 138

Bradford, Roy 143, 144, 146, 153, 158, 165, 167, 168, 171, 172
Brandywell mass meeting 121
British Army 1, 2, 3, 6, 42, 84, 86, 87, 88, 89, 90, 91, 92, 93, 95, 96, 101, 109, 112, 113, 114, 115, 119–123, 124, 126, 130, 131, 132, 133, 165, 168, 169, 170, 171, 176, 178, 199, 203, 207
BBC 40, 41, 42, 61, 163, 167, 169, 181, 211, 223
British Embassy, Dublin, burning 121
British Government 3, 4, 7, 18, 45, 49, 52, 53, 67, 68, 69, 70, 79, 81, 85, 87, 91, 92, 94, 95, 105, 109, 112, 113, 114, 116, 117, 122, 124, 125, 128, 129, 130, 131, 133–136, 138, 139, 140, 141, 145–155, 157, 163, 164, 165, 169, 170, 173, 175, 176, 177, 191, 192, 194, 195, 215, 216, 218–227, 236, 243, 249, 268, 278, 279, 282, 283
British identity, loyalist 214, 265, 266, 280
British–Irish Association 272
British withdrawal from Northern Ireland 175, 176, 177, 178, 179, 181, 184, 185, 197, 198, 200
Brookeborough, Lord 37
Bunbeg, Co. Donegal 97, 98, 99, 103, 114
Burke, Richard 202, 232
Burns, Mike 84, 102
Burntollet, marchers at 70, 75
Burton, Philip 184
Byrne, Gay 106

Caledon, Co. Armagh 59, 62
Caldwell, Tom 123, 124, 258
Callaghan, James 79, 85, 90, 91, 92, 93, 94, 95, 109, 192, 204
Callaghan, Rev. Sydney 224
Cameron, Lord 63, 61, 76, 77
Cameron, Senator Millar 122
Campaign for Democracy in Ulster 53
Campaign for Social Justice 52, 53
Campbell, J. J. 42, 44
Canavan, Michael 31, 54, 57, 58, 59, 62, 64, 68, 70, 88, 89, 90, 93
Caraher, Ben 106, 107
Carey, Hugh 191, 203
Carron, Owen 227
Carson, Edward 118, 171, 180
Carter, Sir Charles 253
Carter, President James 192, 193, 194
Casey, Bishop Eamonn 49
Castlereagh holding centre 199
Catholic Church 17, 18, 19, 32, 44, 46, 54, 257, 258, 259
Catholic Registration Office, Derry 54
ceasefire, IRA, 1972 129, 130, 131, 132
census, Northern Ireland 48
Chequers talks 134, 169
Chichester-Clark, James 73, 78, 87, 92, 95, 109, 110, 184
Chichester-Clark, Robin 58
Church of Ireland 40, 66, 207, 259
Churchill, Winston 118
Citizens' Action Committee 64, 68, 69, 70, 72, 77, 79, 80
civil disobedience 116, 117, 121, 160, 166
Civil Rights Association, Northern Ireland 59, 60, 62, 63, 64, 65, 67, 116
civil rights marches see marches
civil rights movement 1, 3, 13, 49, 53, 59, 60, 61, 62, 63, 64, 65, 66, 67, 68, 69, 71, 72, 74, 75, 78, 81, 83, 84, 85, 88, 94, 95, 96, 97, 101, 104, 105, 107, 114, 116, 120, 127, 162, 183, 184, 241, 278, 281
Claudy 132

Cluskey, Frank 82, 99
Coalisland 59, 62, 84
Coleraine 38, 39
Columcille Debating Society 35
committee system in government 111, 112, 135
Community Relations Commission 109
Compton, Sir Edmund, investigation 116, 185
condominium government, proposal 133, 137, 141
confederation in Ireland 194, 264, 266
Conservative Party, British 92, 101, 110, 140, 150, 169, 172, 195, 202, 204, 209, 213, 235, 236
constitution, proposals 110, 117, 118, 128, 133, 145, 148, 149, 152, 157, 175, 176, 177, 178, 179, 180, 181, 182, 191, 192, 196, 197, 200, 201, 217, 228, 229, 243, 244, 247, 249, 255, 258, 259, 262, 263, 265, 268, 269
Convention, Constitutional 175, 176, 177, 178, 179, 180, 181, 182, 191, 192, 196, 215, 268
Conway, Archbishop William 25
Cooney, Paddy 151
Cooper, Bob 140, 152, 171
Cooper, Frank 152, 153, 177
Cooper, Ivan 64, 70, 74, 80, 97, 98, 100, 102, 103, 126, 132, 137
Corish, Brendan 121
Cosgrave, Liam 142, 147, 148, 152, 155, 156, 160, 161, 174, 179, 191
Cosgrove, Dr Jim 54
Cost of Violence, Forum report 254
Costello, Declan 148, 150, 157
Council for a New Ireland 243
Council of Ireland 133, 140, 142, 145–163, 166, 175, 214
Coyle, Vinny 91
Craig, Bill 63, 64, 69, 111, 119, 126, 137, 140, 142, 163, 165, 180, 181
Craigavon, Co. Armagh 48, 57
Craigavon, Lord 48, 117, 156
Credit Union Movement 13, 14, 30, 31, 32, 33, 39, 48, 49, 54, 56, 58, 59, 62, 107
Crowther Commission on UK Constitution 110
CS gas, use in Northern Ireland 81, 86, 87
curfew 101
Currie, Austin 56, 59, 62, 71, 75, 83, 84, 94, 95, 96, 97, 98, 99, 101, 102, 103, 107, 112, 119, 126, 134, 137, 143, 144, 151, 166, 170, 171, 180, 202, 203, 204, 275
Cusack, Seamus 112

Daly, Bishop Cahal 208, 258
Daly, Bishop Edward 219
Daly, Tom 168
Darkley massacre 259
Darlington conference 133, 134, 135, 143
Democratic Unionist Party 162, 179, 180, 182, 212, 222, 242, 248, 276
demographic trends, Northern Ireland 280
Derry: Altnagelvin Hospital 81; Beechwood Ave 35, 82; birth rate 48; Bishop Street 86; Bogside see Bogside; Brandywell 5, 121; Butchers' Gate 76, 77; Christian Brothers' Technical School 27; Citizens' Defence Association 79; city centre 62, 63, 65; City football team 22; City Hotel 64; city walls 12, 62, 65, 76, 83, 120; Craigavon Bridge 59, 63, 65, 68; Creggan 8, 42, 49, 76, 130; Council, name change 275; Dancing Club 33; Development Organisation 57; Duke Street 63, 65; Duncreggan Road 50;

286

Eastway 76; Ebrington Barracks 2, 129; EEC aid for 230; Fahan Street 76; Farren Park 50, 51; Fountain district 91; Foyle Bridge 230; Free Derry see Free Derry; gasworks 83; Glen, The 5, 8, 10; Glen Road 10; Glenbrook Terrace 6; Guildhall 36, 38, 41, 51, 61, 63, 91; Guildhall Square 65, 76; Housing Action Committee 61; Housing Association 49, 50, 51, 56, 59, 61; Lone Moor Road 1; Lower Nassau Street 5; Methodist hostel 82; Pennyburn 58; public buildings, siting of 39; Rinmore Drive 129; Rosemount 5, 8, 82, 83, 84; Rossville Flats 48, 81, 91; Rossville Street 83; Shantallow 50; Shipquay Street 65; South ward 48, 49; Southend Park 5; Talbot Park 90; transport links 38; Victoria Barracks 89; Waterloo Place 80; Waterside 31, 33, 35; West End Park 1, 35, 121, 274, 277; Westland Road 30; William Street 76, 80, 89; *Derry Journal*, 8, 10

detention, Northern Ireland, in 133, 160
Development Commission 68, 115
Devenney, Samuel 76, 78
Devlin, Bernadette 71, 72, 81, 86, 123, 184, 187, 205
Devlin, Paddy 75, 84, 97, 98, 99, 102, 103, 104, 105, 106, 107, 108, 112, 113, 114, 126, 128, 129, 132, 142, 144, 151, 152, 159, 165, 166, 167, 168, 172, 180, 197, 200, 202, 203, 205, 209, 210, 240, 275
devolution, proposals, see also Sunningdale 162, 182, 216, 237
direct rule 122, 125, 128, 181, 183
'dirty protest' 218
discrimination 10, 11, 36, 37, 39, 42, 43, 45, 46, 49, 52, 59, 60, 68, 69, 184, 190, 251
Doherty, Annie 5, 7, 27, 28, 32
Doherty, James 35, 36, 37, 62, 64, 65, 69
Doherty, 'Nana' 34
Doherty, Paddy 29, 30, 31, 48, 54, 72, 80, 86, 88, 89, 91, 92
Donegal Co: Bunbeg 97, 98, 99, 103, 114, 131, 246; generally 5, 6, 10, 76, 78, 79, 81, 84, 92, 188, 212
Donlan Sean 213
Douglas, Paddy 63
Downing Street Declaration 92, 94
Dublin 26, 80, 84, 89, 91, 92, 100, 102, 106, 121, 125, 142, 166, 213, 268
Duffy, Paddy 197, 198, 202
Drumm family 179, 199
Dungannon, meetings etc. 49, 52, 56, 60, 62, 116, 117, 210, 240
Dungiven, meetings etc. 79, 118, 136

Easter Rising, Dublin 1916 47, 268
Ebrington Barracks 2, 129
economy, Northern Ireland 38, 41, 43, 251, 253, 254, 255, 269
ecumenism 66
education: Hume's 8, 9, 10, 11, 16–27, 32, 33, 195, 213, 283; policy 38, 283
EEC and Northern Ireland 202, 213, 229, 230, 231, 232
election agent to McAteer, Hume as 100
elections: Assembly 1973 138, 139, 140, 141; Assembly 1981 240, 241, 242; European Parliament 202, 203, 204, 205, 269, 270, 271; local government 138, 139, 200; Stormont Parliament 53, 54, 55, 71, 72, 74;

Westminster 56, 71, 100, 101, 120, 138, 139, 246, 247, 248, 249
emigration 42, 43, 49
employment: discrimination 36, 37, 39, 49, 69; patterns in rural Ulster 62
European Commission 145, 230
European Commission on Human Rights 218, 219, 222
European Community 145
European Court of Human Rights 116, 201, 218
European MP, Hume as 204, 205, 209, 229, 230, 231, 232, 233, 243, 270, 277
Executive, power-sharing 153, 154, 155, 156, 157, 158, 160, 161, 162, 165, 166, 167, 169, 170, 171, 172, 173, 174, 189, 205, 210
extradition 135, 148, 152, 153, 155

family background, Hume's 5–7
Farren, Bishop Neil 8, 50, 66
Faul, Fr Denis 25, 221, 225, 226
Faulkner, Brian 4, 42, 71, 73, 103, 111, 112, 113, 114, 116, 117, 118, 120, 121, 123, 124, 126, 135, 137, 139, 141, 142, 143, 144, 145, 146, 147, 148, 150, 151, 152, 153, 156, 157, 158, 161, 167, 170, 171, 172, 177
Faulkner, Padraig 208
Feakle meeting 177, 178
federal Ireland 201, 213, 264, 265, 266
Feeley, Frank 168
Ferguson, Dick 99
Fermanagh, gerrymander in 111
Fermanagh-South Tyrone constituency 204, 221, 222, 226, 227, 248, 281
Fianna Fáil 96, 97, 106, 134, 137, 148, 155, 157, 181, 198, 209, 213, 242, 243, 260, 261, 262, 264, 282
film-maker, Hume as: *A City Solitary* 40; *The Open Door* 41; *Target Derry* 40; *Two Hours from London* 41
Fine Gael 97, 110, 134, 141, 143, 150, 239, 243, 244, 264, 266, 282
Fitt, Gerry 96, 101, 102, 103, 104, 105, 106, 107, 108, 112, 113, 123, 134, 137, 141, 143, 144, 147, 150, 154, 158, 161, 166, 168, 169, 171, 177, 178, 200, 203, 204, 205, 208, 209, 210, 211, 219, 223, 237, 245, 248, 249, 250, 273, 275, 281
FitzGerald, Garret 110, 121, 134, 141, 150, 152, 156, 157, 159, 160, 192, 194, 204, 239, 242, 243, 244, 245, 247, 260, 263, 264, 265, 266, 267, 268, 283
flags: Derry 67; Irish Tricolour 63, 86, 91, 275
Flynn, Bishop Tom 22
Foley, Maurice 99
Foot, Michael 223
football, Hume's interest in 9, 23
Ford, President Gerald 192
Forum, New Ireland see New Ireland Forum
'Four Horsemen' statements 191, 192, 194, 195, 228
franchise, local government 52, 68, 69, 73, 78, 110, 222
Free Derry: British Army negotiations with 89, 90, 81; Callaghan's visit 90, 91, 92; committee 89; Corner 14, 70, 77, 91, 119; government of 89–93; Hume and 120, 123, 187; 1971, August 115
Freeland, General Ian 87, 93, 94
Friel, Brian 27
Friends of Ireland 228, 229

Gaelic Athletic Association 18

Gaelic football 13, 23
Gallagher, Jack 'Rusty' 13, 15
Gardiner, Lord 175
gerrymander: Derry 10, 24, 37; Fermanagh 111
Gibson, Ken 167
Gillespie, Neil 5
Glover, Gerald 38
Gormley, Paddy 42
Gormley, Tom 122
Government of Ireland Act 1920 3, 117
Governor of Northern Ireland 59
Gowrie, Lord 226, 235, 236
Griffin, Rev. Victor 36
Grundig factory 160
guarantee, British Government, Northern Ireland, to 149, 150, 215, 278, 279
Guildhall, Derry 36, 38, 41, 51, 61, 63, 70, 91, 118
gun-running 100, 175, 190

Hackett, Gen. Sir John 124
Hailsham, Lord 4, 92
Hannon, Rev. Brian 40
Harland and Wolff 6, 33, 160
Harte, Paddy 97, 99
Harvard Centre for International Relations 183, 191
Haughey, Denis 88, 120
Haughey, Charles 100, 121, 198, 209, 213, 215, 216, 228, 237, 238, 242, 243, 244, 247, 253, 260, 262, 263, 264, 265, 266, 267, 268, 282
Heaney, Seamus 13
Heath, Edward 117, 119, 122, 123, 124, 125, 126, 131, 133, 134, 137, 146, 147, 148, 149, 150, 151, 153, 159
Hegarty, Joe 3
Hendron, Dr Joe 154, 248
Hillsborough meetings 159, 160, 213
Home, Sir Alec Douglas 49
Home Rule in Irish Politics 175, 282
Hone, Pat (Mrs Hume) 33, 34, 63, 78, 84, 120, 246, 262
Housing Action Committee, Derry 61
Housing Association, Derry 49, 50, 51, 56, 59, 61
Housing Executive, establishment 109
housing problems, Northern Ireland: allocation 7, 43, 49, 52, 59, 60, 62, 65, 68, 69; generally 24, 49, 52, 59, 62, 75, 92, 95, 277; shortage 5, 43, 48, 49, 50, 51, 61
Housing Trust, Northern Ireland 49
Hughes, Sean 102
Hume family: Agnes 6; Annie (mother) 5, 7, 27, 28; Annie (sister) 6; children, of John Hume 127, 246, 262, 274; Harry 6; Jim 6; Pat (wife) 33, 34, 63, 78, 84, 120, 246, 262; Patsy 6, 8; Sam (father) 5, 6, 7, 11, 26, 27, 28, 33; threats to 127, 274
hunger strike, 1980, Maze Prison: Adams, Gerry, and 225, 226; background 216, 218, 219; British Government policy 222, 223, 224; deaths 225, 226; demands of strikers 219, 223, 224, 225; effect 225, 226, 227, 232, 233, 249; ending 226; Faul, Fr Denis 221, 225, 226; free association of prisoners 219, 223; Hughes, Brendan 219, 220; Hume, as negotiator 219, 220, 222, 223, 227; McFarlane, Brendan 225; McKenna, Sean 219, 220; Magee, Monsignor John 224; Meagher, Father 220; negotiations 220, 221, 222, 223, 224, 226; Sands, Bobby 220, 221, 222, 224, 225; Sinn Fein 220, 221, 225, 226; threats to Hume's family during 274; Toomebridge relatives' meeting 225

Hunt Report on RUC 93
Hutchinson, Douglas 163

illness, Hume's, 154, 240
incitement to hatred, law governing 109
industrial development, Northern Ireland 43, 50, 56, 143, 144, 158, 159, 160, 161, 189, 192, 193, 251, 269
internment 109, 110, 114, 115, 116, 118, 119, 123, 124, 125, 127, 128, 129, 130, 131, 132, 133, 134, 141, 177, 181, 184, 188, 199, 201
Ireland Fund, The 188, 194
Irish American Caucus 190, 194, 251
Irish Club, The, London 134
Irish Commission for Justice and Peace 225
Irish Council of Churches 177
Irish Dimension, The 136, 138, 140, 141, 175, 176, 179, 180, 193, 197, 209, 210, 211, 212, 216, 217, 236, 252, 280
Irish Free State 6, 18
Irish Independence Party 200
Irish inter-governmental council, proposed, see also Council of Ireland 133, 135
Irish Labour Party 96, 99, 106, 107, 141, 143, 243, 244, 282
Irish nationalism see Nationalists; Nationalist Party
Irish National Caucus 190, 194, 251
Irish Press, The 110, 256
Irish Republic see Republic of Ireland
IRA: American contacts 183, 184, 189, 190, 195, 233; Army Council 177, 178; blanket protest, prison 198; Bloody Friday, 1972 132; Bloody Sunday, 1971 120, 121; bombing campaign 132, 161, 177, 201, 250; British Government and 123, 124, 127, 128, 129, 130, 131, 132; campaign, 1959–1962 52, 80; ceasefire 1972 129, 130, 131, 132, 185; ceasefire 1975 177, 178, 179; Feakle meeting 177; Fermanagh-South Tyrone by-election 222, 227, 248; funding from America 121, 187, 188, 190; generally 69, 72, 86, 88, 90, 95, 109, 111, 123, 124, 125, 137, 156, 171, 184, 206, 273, 276, 278, 280; Hume's 'public dialogue' with 129, 130; hunger strike see hunger strike; Lenadoon arrests 1972 131; NIO officials' meeting with 177, 178, 179; Official 96, 123, 128; old 33; Protestant paramilitary response to 126; Provisional 33, 42, 93, 96, 101, 112, 120, 121, 123, 125, 128, 129, 130, 131, 188, 189, 190, 198, 210, 216, 274; recruitment 121, 233; reorganisation, 1976 199, 200; resumption of campaign after UWC strike 176; SDLP and Provisionals 126, 127, 128, 129, 130, 132, 201, 202, 216, 222; Tullyvallen Orange Hall killing 180; US political reactions to 190, 192, 195; Westminster elections, Sinn Fein vote 248
Irish Times, The 42, 43, 52, 102, 104, 141, 244
Irish TV (RTE) 42, 63, 79, 84, 91, 102, 106, 167, 186, 195, 215, 258
Islands of the North Atlantic (IONA) 213

Jacottet, Julian 134
Jay, Peter 195
job promotion tour of America, Hume's 251, 252, 253
John Hume's Derry, TV documentary 91, 187
joint authority, Britain and Irish Republic 265
joint sovereignty, Britain and Irish Republic 133, 136, 265

Jones, Teddy 55
journalists 66, 81, 82, 85, 89, 90, 92, 95, 97, 102, 103, 104, 113, 115, 116, 120, 122, 123, 125, 126, 128, 130, 147, 148, 156, 161, 174, 176, 184, 186, 210, 211, 245, 267, 268, 272, 274

Keenan, Sean 80, 115
Kelly, Dr John 106
Kennedy, Paddy 105
Kennedy, Senator Edward 184, 185, 186, 187, 190, 191, 193, 194, 203, 229, 251
Knights of Columbanus 30

Labour Party: British 49, 53, 63, 86, 96, 97, 99, 107, 111, 117, 140, 169, 201, 202, 204, 210, 212, 237; Irish 96, 99, 106, 107, 141, 143, 243, 244, 282; Northern Ireland 96, 99, 109, 135, 200, 264
Laneside, Co Down 129, 146, 178
Larne, Laharna Hotel 162
law commission, joint North and South 152
left-wing activists 59, 62, 67, 68, 72, 83, 91, 93, 105, 116, 184
Legion of Mary 33
Lemass, Sean 47, 54, 160
Lenadoon 1972, IRA arrests 131
Lennon, Bishop 224
Liberals: Alliance Party see Alliance Party; Catholic 97; Nationalist 99, 152, 175; reaction to New Ireland Forum 258; Unionist 99, 152, 175
local government: elections 138, 139, 200; franchise 52, 68, 69, 78, 110, 222; housing policies 7, 43, 49, 52, 59, 60, 62, 75, 92, 95; reform 68, 78, 92, 95, 112; SDLP in 107, 200, 222
Logue, Hugh 2, 56
Londonderry: City Education Board 36; Council, name change 275; Light Opera Society 42; name, significance 10, 40, 41
Londonderry and Lough Swilly Railway 6
Lord Chief Justice, Northern Ireland 156
Loughran, Seamus 189
Louth, Co, Dáil seat 137
Loyalist Association of Workers 162
Loyalist Workers' Strike 160, 161, 162, 163, 164, 165, 166, 167, 168, 169, 170, 171, 176, 199, 269
loyalists: generally 69, 72, 75, 79, 95, 103, 113, 127, 132; march to Stormont, March 1972 126; paramilitaries 95, 119, 126, 130, 132; political position 132, 139, 158, 160, 161, 179, 180, 214, 255, 278
Lynch, Jack 79, 84, 85, 87, 114, 117, 119, 125, 132, 134, 155, 192, 195, 205, 209, 216
Lyttle, Tommy 164

McArt, Proinsias 130
McAteer, Eddie 38, 52, 53, 54, 55, 72, 80, 100, 101, 104
McBride, Sean 148
McCann, Eamonn 35, 59, 61, 62, 64, 65, 72, 101
McClean, Dr and Mrs Raymond 64, 67, 81
McClure, Noni and Garth 41
McCluskey, Dr Con 49, 52, 53, 59
McConghail, Muiris 148
McConnell, Bertie 122
McCormack, John 187
McCrory Committee on local government 112;
McDonald, Dr Daniel 50
McDonald, Terence 41

McFeeley, Fr Anthony 15
McGirl, John Joe 177
McGonagle, Stephen 55
McGrady, Eddie 172, 249
McGuigan, Brian 42, 44
McGuinness, Martin 83
McInerney, Michael 102
McIvor, Basil 152, 153, 168
McKeague, John 207
McKee, Billy 130
McKinney, Gerry 120
McLachlan, Peter 140, 144, 155, 156
McManaway, Rev. James 8
McManus, Fr Sean 190, 251
McQuade, Johnny 161
McStiofain, Sean 128, 129, 130, 131
Magee College 36, 38
Magilligan: prison 114, 115; Strand, rally 119
Maginnis, Ken 250
Maguire, Frank 204, 221
Maidstone, prison ship 115
Mallon, Seamus 138, 139, 141, 166, 168, 197, 198, 200, 202, 210, 216, 240, 242, 264, 265
marches: Armagh, 1968 69; Belfast to Derry, 1969 70; Burntollet to Derry, 1969 75; Derry, 1968, 1972 62, 64, 66, 67, 68, 69, 79, 119, 120, see also Bloody Sunday; Magilligan Strand, 1972 119; Newry, 1969, 1972 70, 123; Stormont 125, 126
Mason, Roy 169, 194, 198, 199, 200, 202, 203, 212
M.A. thesis, Hume's 29
Matthew, Sir Robert 47
Maudling, Reginald 4, 110, 111, 117, 122, 136
Mawhinney, Brian 236
Maynooth, St Patrick's College 16–27, 32, 33, 195, 213, 283
Meagher, Fr 220
Member of Parliament, Hume as: European Parliament 204, 205, 209, 229, 230, 231, 232, 233, 243, 270, 277; Stormont 1, 31, 83, 112, 113, 115; Westminster 248, 249, 250, 251, 270, 273, 277
Merriman School, Scarriff 141
Mid-Ulster constituency 56
military solution in Northern Ireland, pressure for 109, 111
Millar, Frank 163
Minford, Nat 161
Minister of Commerce, Hume as 158, 159, 160, 161
Morgan, Billy 71
Morrell, Leslie 156, 167, 171
Motion Number One Group 160
Mountbatten, Lord 195, 207, 209
Mountpottinger Hall, Hume's speech 32
Moynihan, Daniel 191, 229
Mullan, Fr Desmond 9
Mulvey, Fr Anthony 30, 49, 76, 77
Murray, Harry 163

Napier, Oliver 122, 152, 155, 171
National Anthem, British 41, 42
National Council for Civil Liberties 62
National Democratic Party 47, 53, 55, 56, 71, 96, 97, 105, 106, 107
National Political Front 53
National Resistance Movement 120
National Senate for Ireland, proposed 133
National Unity group 42, 52

Nationalist Party 43, 44, 45, 47, 50, 52, 53, 54, 55, 59, 65, 69, 71, 72, 96, 98, 99, 100, 101, 102, 105, 106, 107, 125
Nationalist Political Front 45
Neave, Airey 202
'New Ireland' campaign 202, 239, 240, 242, 243, 244, 249
New Ireland Council 244
New Ireland Forum 128, 208, 232, 244, 245, 246, 247, 248, 251, 253–271
New Ireland Society, Queen's University, Belfast 47, 56
New Ulster Movement 97
New York Times 184
Newe, G. B. 42, 44, 118
News Letter, Belfast 139, 163
Newry 70, 123, 130, 160, 249
Nixon, President 184, 185, 192
no-go areas 109, 132, 178
non-violence, principle 64, 67, 76, 77, 82, 135, 163, 187, 195, 205, 276
Noonan, Michael 244
Noraid 187, 188, 190, 192, 233, 253
North Derry Civil Rights Association 75
Northern Ireland Act 1972 3
Northern Ireland Civil Rights Association 59, 61, 62, 63, 64, 65, 66, 67, 68, 69, 70, 116, 117, 119, 120
Northern Ireland Court of Appeal 3
Northern Ireland Economic Council 253
Northern Ireland Labour Party 96, 99, 109, 135, 200, 264
Northern Ireland Office, meetings with IRA 177, 178
Northern Ireland Parliament see Stormont
Northern Ireland Resurgence Trust 187, 188

O'Brady, Rory 177
O'Brien, Conor Cruise 147, 148, 150, 152, 160, 179, 223, 245
O'Brien, Gay 63
O'Connell, Daithi 128, 129, 130, 131, 132, 177, 178, 179
O'Connor, Roddy 96
O'Connor, Ulick 106
O'Donoghue, Professor Dermot 22
Official Unionist Party 135, 163, 179, 181, 212, 222, 237, 242, 248, 259, 268
Ó Fiaich, Cardinal Tomás 21, 29, 206, 207, 208, 213, 219, 224, 226, 257, 258
O'Hanlon, Paddy 68, 71, 74, 97, 98, 102, 103, 107, 114, 119, 125, 200, 212
O'Kennedy, Michael 213
Ombudsman, Northern Ireland 68, 109
'One Strong Voice' SDLP manifesto 176
O'Neill, Hubert 126
O'Neill, Phelim 111, 122
O'Neill, Terence 37, 42, 47, 49, 53, 56, 68, 69, 70, 71, 72, 73, 75, 78, 95 ,111, 160
O'Neill, Tip 184, 188, 191, 192, 193, 194, 203, 212, 251
Operation Motorman 132, 133
Options for a New Ireland, SDLP conference 239
Orange Order 79, 101, 111, 112, 143, 155
O'Reilly, James 96, 103
O'Reilly, Tony 188, 189
Orme, Stan 86, 163, 165, 166

'Paddy Bogside' 29, 30 and see Doherty, Paddy
Paisley, Rev. Ian 8, 61, 66, 69, 70, 72, 78, 137, 141, 162, 163, 164, 173, 179, 181, 182, 199, 203, 205, 207, 212, 214, 215, 232, 251, 268, 271, 279

Paisleyites 142, 154, 161
Papal visit to Ireland 1979 206, 207, 208
paramilitaries 83, 95, 96, 119, 121, 126, 130, 132, 162, 163, 164, 173, 182, 198, 207, 212, 249, 269, 279, 281
Paratroop Regiment, British Army 119, 120, 122, 123
Peace People 198
People's Democracy 67, 70, 72
personality of Hume 98, 121, 127, 134, 135, 143, 161, 172, 174, 213, 245, 246, 272, 273, 274, 275, 276, 277, 283
personation at elections 55, 249
petrol bombs 81, 82, 274
petrol supplies, UWC strike 1974 169, 170
Philbin, Dr William 176
Plantation of Ulster 47, 48
police: 'acceptable police force' 109, 147, 148, 151, 152, 153, 154, 176; B-Specials see B-Special auxiliary police force; Garda see Republic of Ireland; inquiry, internal 78; Royal Ulster Constabulary see Royal Ulster Constabulary; SDLP policy 154, 176, 181; Police Authority 201
political platform, Hume's 54, 71, 72, 74, 77, 78, 85, 91, 92, 96, 97, 107, 110, 112, 113, 116, 117, 120, 121, 125, 127, 132, 133, 134, 135, 136, 200, 201, 202, 255, 256
political status, paramilitary prisoners 128, 129, 130, 132
popularity of Hume, opinion poll 1972 137
Porter, Robert 76, 81, 86, 87, 184
Powell, Enoch 249, 277
power-sharing concept 110, 119, 136, 137, 139, 140, 141, 142, 143, 144, 146, 147–151, 152, 154, 155, 156, 157, 160, 161, 162, 169, 175, 179, 189, 192, 202, 203, 212, 216, 232, 235, 237, 279
power stations, UWC strike 1974 165, 167
Prior, Jim 226, 235, 236, 237, 243, 251, 252, 269, 279
prisons 128, 130, 198, 216, 218–227
proportional representation (PR) 110, 133, 138
Provisional IRA see IRA
Provisional Sinn Fein, see Sinn Fein
Public Order Bill 1969 78, 96
public speaker, Hume as 22, 23, 47, 66, 119, 135, 141, 174, 175, 189, 200, 201, 214, 215, 238, 239, 246, 247, 249, 272, 273, 275
Pym, Francis 146, 150, 151, 160

Queen's University, Belfast 16, 47, 56, 59, 67, 258

Radio Free Derry 70
railways, Northern Ireland 38, 48
Rawlinson, Sir Peter 149
Reagan, Ronald 185, 193, 228, 229
Red Hand Commandos 207
Rees, Merlyn 140, 163, 164, 166, 167, 171, 175, 176, 179, 180, 199
referendum, proposed after Sunningdale 157, 179, 181
regional planning, Northern Ireland 38
rent and rates strike 116, 117, 121, 160, 166
RTE (Irish TV and radio) 102, 106, 120, 127, 128, 167, 179, 186, 195, 215, 258, 267
Republic of Ireland: American contacts of SDLP and 188, 194; Army 88, 92; attitude to political developments in Northern Ireland 97, 100, 105, 118, 127, 128, 132, 134, 137, 141, 142, 146, 147, 148, 150, 155, 157, 171, 228, 243, 244, 245, 258–71, 272, 279, 282; Constitution 110, 117, 118, 148, 152, 157, 265; economy 254,

290

255, 269; European Court of Human Rights, claims against UK government 116; EEC and 229, 230, 231, 232; Garda 151; political parties see Fianna Fáil, Fine Gael, Labour Party, Irish; Protestant population 259; response to riots, 1969 84, 85, 88, 92, 93; Thatcher-Haughey entente 213, 215, 216, 228, 231, 238

Republican Labour MP, Gerry Fitt 53, 75, 98, 105, see also Fitt, Gerry

republican movement 15, 18, 35, 47, 52, 56, 58, 59, 67, 72, 80, 83, 85, 94, 157, 175, 179, 187, 190, 206, 208, 212, 281

riots, Northern Ireland 48, 64, 70, 76, 87, 88, 101, 112, 114, 119, 120, 121, 122, 123, 225

Robb, John 141, 227, 242

Rogers, Brid 168

Ronan, Sean 186

Rossville Flats see Derry

rolling devolution, proposal 216, 236

Royal Black Institution 112

Royal Irish Rifles 6

Royal Ulster Constabulary 63, 65, 67, 68, 69, 70, 75, 76, 77, 78, 79, 80, 81, 82, 83, 84, 85, 86, 87, 98, 89, 90, 92, 93, 94, 114, 115, 116, 132, 141, 151, 153, 163, 165, 176, 181, 199, 201, 207, 212, 215, 216, 279

rubber bullets, use 2, 119

St Colman's School, Strabane 28, 29

St Columb's Cathedral 66

St Columb's College, Derry 5, 11, 12, 13, 14, 15, 17, 34, 35, 36, 38, 56, 58

St Eugene's Boys' School, Derry 8, 9

St Eugene's Cathedral, Derry 8, 12

St Mary's Teacher Training College, Belfast 33

salmon marketing, Hume's business venture 57, 58

Sands, Bobby 220, 221, 222, 224, 225

Scarman, Lord, report 80, 86

sectarianism 7, 42, 43, 46, 103, 117, 125, 149, 163, 178, 225, 250, 251, 281

security powers, control 145–155, 198

'shared schools' campaign 283

shirtmaking industry 6, 7, 56, 64

Shorts, Belfast planemaker 251, 252

Siege of Derry 12, 78, 79

Simpson, Robert 121

Simpson, Vivian 96

Sinn Fein 44, 83, 105, 131, 177, 178, 200, 220, 221, 222, 225, 226, 227, 230, 240, 241, 242, 243, 244, 245, 248, 249, 264, 269, 270, 271, 272, 276, 277, 278, 279, 280, 283

sit-in, Stormont House of Commons 78

Smith, Howard 123, 130

Smyth, Jim 163, 167

Smyth, Rev. Martin 181, 194

SDLP: abstentionist policy 240, 241, 242; advice centres 276; Alliance Party and 156; American contacts 183, 186, 187, 188, 190, 191, 194, 195, 196, 197; Assembly 1973 133, 138, 139, 140; Assembly 1981 236, 237, 240, 241, 264; attacks on members 126; background to foundation 41, 54, 55, 88; Bloody Sunday and 119, 121; border poll, boycott 137; British Government, negotiations 112, 113, 133–6; Chequers talks 134; civil disobedience campaign 117, 121; civil rights movement and 117; cohesion 1984 283, 284; conferences 202, 216, 275; constitution 103, 106, 107; Constitutional Convention, reaction 175, 176, 177, 179, 180; Council of Ireland, reaction 141, 142, 143, 144, 145, 147,

148; Darlington conference 133, 134, 135; dissident minority within 284; Dungiven conference 136; European elections, 1979 204, 205; European Socialists and 229, 231; Executive, power-sharing 143, 144, 146, 147, 151, 152, 153, 155, 156, 160, 170, 171, 172; finance 104, 106, 134, 276, 277; Fermanagh-South Tyrone constituency 221, 222, 227; foundation 96–9, 103, 104; hunger strike 1981 and 222, 223; internment, policy 128, 132, 133, 141, 166; IRA and NIO talks, 1975 178, 179; Irish Dimension, policy 138, 140, 141; leadership 98, 99, 101, 102, 209, 210, 211; local government elections, policy 138, 139, 200, 222; Loyalist strike 1974, reaction 166, 169, 170; membership 105, 122, 197, 281; Nationalist Party attitudes 100, 101, 106; 'New Ireland' campaign 202; 'One Strong Voice', manifesto 176; Options for a New Ireland, conference 239, 240; organisation 103, 106, 107, 108, 138, 283; Papal visit and 208; personality differences 134; police, policy 154, 176, 181, 279; political status, prisoners, policy 128, 129, 130, 132; power-sharing Executive, policy 152, 153, 155, 156, 160, 170, 171, 172, 174; premises for headquarters 105; press reaction to 102, 103, 104; Provisional IRA and 128, 129, 130, 132, 201, 202, 216, 280, 281; Republic of Ireland political parties and 134, 137, 141, 142, 174, 209, 210, 213, 214; 'Speak with Strength', manifesto 179; Stormont, in 108, 109, 111, 112, 113, 116, 118; subscriptions 105; Sunningdale conference 145–55, 156; suspension of Stormont 124, 125; 'Towards a New Ireland', 133, 134, 135; trade union links 101; UDA, policy towards 175; UUUC talks with 180; ultimatum to British Government, July 1971 112, 113; United Loyalist Council and 137; veto against majority rule 280; Westminster elections, 1970 100, 101; 1974 158, 176, 177; 1979 204, 205; 1983 248

social democratic principles 44, 72, 95, 96, 216

social security payments to strikers, 1974 165

socialist principles 55, 56, 61, 62, 63, 64, 72, 83, 96, 103, 106, 134, 142, 175, 200, 203, 209, 210, 281

sovereignty claim, Republic of Ireland Constitution 110, 117, 118, 148, 152, 157, 175, 209, 282

'Speak with Strength', SDLP manifesto, 1975 179

special category status, prisoners 128, 129, 130, 132, 198, 218

Special Powers Act (Northern Ireland) 1920 2, 68, 69, 89, 114, 131

Spring, Dick 248, 260

Steele, Frank 130;

Stonham, Lord 79

Stormont government 1, 3, 4, 31, 35, 37, 39, 41, 42, 47, 48, 49, 53, 54, 55, 56, 57, 61, 63, 67, 68, 69, 71, 72, 74, 75, 78, 79, 81, 85, 86, 89, 94, 95, 100, 105, 107, 108, 110, 111, 112, 113, 114, 115, 116, 118, 119, 122, 123, 124, 126, 127, 153, 163, 167, 177

Strabane 28, 29, 107, 118, 160

Strategy for Peace 216

strikes: hunger see hunger strike; Loyalist Workers' Strike 1974 see Loyalist Workers' Strike; loyalist strike 1977 199; rent and rates strike see rent and rates strike

students, involvement, civil rights movement   60
Sunday Independent, The   70, 147, 148
Sunday Press, The   74
Sunday Times, The   61, 115, 116
Sunningdale conference   136, 145, 155, 156, 157,
    158, 159, 161, 162, 163, 166, 174, 175, 176, 179,
    186, 189, 214, 229, 236, 262
Sweetman, Michael   145

Taylor, John   87, 111, 137, 163, 178, 205, 231,
    232
teaching career, Hume's   27, 28, 29, 33, 34, 36, 37,
    54, 56, 58
Territorial Army   87, 123
Thatcher, Margaret   195, 212, 213, 215, 216, 219,
    222, 224, 227, 228, 229, 236, 237, 246, 249
Times, The   104, 143
'Towards a New Ireland'   133, 134, 135, 194
trade unions   101, 162, 163, 174
Tricolour, Irish   63, 86, 91
tripartite solutions: Council of Ireland see Council
    of Ireland; generally   117, 118, 135, 145, 198;
    Sunningdale conference see Sunningdale
    conference
Tullyvallen Orange Hall atrocity   180
TV: American interviews with Hume   184, 188,
    189, 190; influence on Hume's political
    development   184; see also BBC, Irish TV (RTE)
Twomey, Seamus   128
Tyndall, Rev. Charles   66, 67
Tyrie, Andy   162, 163, 164, 167, 172, 194, 199,
    269

Ulster Defence Association   95, 119, 126, 137,
    162, 163, 164, 165, 166, 168, 169, 172, 175, 178,
    194, 197, 199, 259, 269
Ulster Defence Regiment   95, 198, 216, 250
Ulster Special Constabulary   69, 84, 86, 87, 89, 93,
    95
Ulster Volunteer Force   166, 168
Ulster Workers' Council   162, 163, 164, 165, 166,
    167, 169, 170, 172, 173, 175, 199
unemployment in Northern Ireland   43, 48, 56, 78,
    160, 187, 269, 277

united Ireland, concept   43, 44, 45, 53, 72, 85, 103,
    104, 107, 117, 118, 120, 121, 124, 127, 128, 133,
    136, 138, 140, 149, 156, 162, 189, 202, 215, 228,
    229, 231, 235, 238, 243, 244, 245, 256, 258, 261,
    262, 263, 267, 268, 269, 275, 278, 280, 281, 283
United Loyalist Council   137
United Nations Organisation   85, 87
United Ulster Unionist Council   158, 172, 176,
    180, 181, 182
University for Derry campaign   38, 39, 48, 64, 73
Uris, Leon   29

Vanguard organisation   119, 125, 162, 163, 180
Viney, Michael   42, 43
Virginia, Co Cavan, Park Hotel meeting   97

Warwick, Bob   90
water cannon   2, 63
Watson, Bertie   19, 22
'The Way Forward,' document   268
West, Harry   111, 163, 215
Western Education Board   37
Westminster elections: 1966   56; by-election
    Armagh 1969   71; by-election Mid-Ulster   71;
    June 1970   100, 101; February 1974   158;
    October 1974   176, 177; May 1979   204; June
    1983   246, 247, 248, 249
Westminster MP, Hume as   248, 249, 250, 251,
    270, 273, 277
White Paper proposals 1973   136, 138, 139, 140
Whitelaw, William   125, 126, 128, 129, 130, 133,
    134, 136, 138, 140, 143, 144, 145, 146, 154, 157,
    198
Widgery, Lord, inquiry   120, 122, 126, 185
Wilson, Harold, PM   53, 79, 92, 96, 117, 119, 123,
    124, 131, 133, 149, 161, 169
Wilson, Senator Paddy   98, 103, 122
Wilton, Senator Claude   55, 100
Wolfe Tone Society   59
Woodfield, Phillip   130
writer, Hume as   40, 41, 42, 44, 45, 46, 47, 52

Young, Arthur   93